The Treasury of Knowledge

Book Seven and Book Eight, Parts One and Two

Foundations of Buddhist Study and Practice

The Higher Trainings in Sublime Intelligence and Meditative Absorption

The translation and publication of this work have been made possible through the generous support of the Tsadra Foundation.

The Treasury of Knowledge

Book Seven and Book Eight, Parts One and Two

Foundations of Buddhist Study and Practice

The Higher Trainings in Sublime Intelligence and Meditative Absorption

Jamgön Kongtrul Lodrö Tayé

KALU RINPOCHÉ TRANSLATION GROUP
under the direction of Khenpo Lodrö Dönyö Rinpoché

This volume translated, introduced, and annotated
by Richard Barron (Chökyi Nyima)

SNOW LION
BOSTON & LONDON
2012

Snow Lion
An imprint of Shambhala Publications, Inc.
Horticultural Hall
300 Massachusetts Avenue
Boston, Massachusetts 02115
www.shambhala.com

9 8 7 6 5 4 3 2 1

First Edition
Printed in the United States of America

♾ This edition is printed on acid-free paper that meets the American National Standards Institute z39.48 Standard.
♻ Shambhala makes every attempt to print on recycled paper.
For more information please visit www.shambhala.com.

Distributed in the United States by Random House, Inc., and in Canada by Random House of Canada Ltd

Designed and typeset by Gopa & Ted2, Inc.

Library of Congress Cataloging-in-Publication Data

Koṅ-sprul Blo-gros-mtha'-yas, 1813–1899.
[Śes bya mtha' yas pa'i rgya mtsho. English. Selections]
The treasury of knowledge. Book seven and book eight, parts one and two, Foundations of Buddhist study and practice: The higher trainings in sublime intelligence and meditative absorption / Jamgön Kongtrul Lodrö Tayé; Kalu Rinpoché Translation Group under the direction of Khenpo Lodrö Dönyö Rinpoché; this volume translated, introduced, and annotated by Richard Barron (Chökyi Nyima).
pages cm
Includes translation from Tibetan.
Includes bibliographical references and index.
ISBN 978-1-55939-399-7 (alk. paper)
1. Spiritual life—Buddhism. 2. Meditation—Buddhism. I. Barron, Richard, 1952–
II. Kalu Rinpoché Translation Group. III. Title. IV. Title: Foundations of Buddhist study and practice. V. Title: Higher trainings in sublime intelligence and meditative absorption.
BQ7815.K6713 2012
294.3'420423—dc23
2012010470

Contents

Foreword

by the Venerable Ringu Tulku

A few years back a respected Tibetan lama told me, "If you have the *Treasury of Knowledge* in English, then you have the whole of Buddhism in English." At that time, it seemed a distant hope that all ten books of the *Treasury* would ever be translated. Even the commentary to the source verses is very compact and difficult to translate. Thanks to the ceaseless efforts of dedicated translators such as Richard Barron and the generous support of the Tsadra Foundation, we are now extremely fortunate in that the entire work has been translated in a series of volumes.

Jamgön Kongtrul the Great incorporates the whole of Tibetan Buddhism and its complete system of education and practice into the *Treasury of Knowledge*. He shows us how all the works of the "ten pillars of study" and the "eight chariots of practice lineages" are genuine and complete paths with unbroken lineages transmitted by realized beings.[1]

Tibetan Buddhism stands apart from other Buddhist traditions in two main respects. In the first place, it follows the tradition of great Indian Buddhist universities like Nālandā and Vikramaśīla and encourages the acceptance, study, and practice of all aspects of the Buddhist teachings, whether those of the śrāvakayāna, bodhisattvayāna, or Vajrayāna. All schools of Tibetan Buddhism follow the practice of each practitioner's observing all three levels of ordination—those of the vinaya, the bodhisattva vow, and Vajrayāna. Different stages of view and path are seen as a building of many stories. One may have a better view from the upper floors, but one must get there by way of the lower floors; the building may exist without an upper floor, but it cannot stand without the ground floor. That is why it is seen as very important for one to study all schools and the views of different traditions.

The other feature of the Tibetan Buddhist tradition is the emphasis on the Buddhist system of logic. Śāntarakṣita and Kamalaśīla were great masters of logic and reasoning who were instrumental in bringing Buddhism to Tibet, where the use of logical analysis and debate (deriving from the teachings of Dignāga and Dharmakīrti) became an important part of Buddhist studies. Provisional truth and definitive truth are defined through analytical investigation; a clear way of reasoning and a reliable method of analysis became very important.

This volume of the *Treasury of Knowledge* is especially important in that it provides a basis for looking at the whole body of the Buddhist teachings and coming to a deeper understanding, free from fragmented ideas. I would like to congratulate Richard Barron for his excellent translation of this challengingly compact work. This is certainly one of the most important texts to study for a deep and complete understanding of the profound Buddhist path.

Ringu Tulku
Gangtok
January 1, 2011

Translator's Introduction

This book is a translation of all of Book 7 and the first two parts of Book 8 from Jamgön Kongtrul Lodrö Tayé's *Treasury of Knowledge* (*Shes bya mdzod*). As such, it deals with two of the three overarching themes of the *Treasury*. For Kongtrul, the project had begun as a treatment of a theme much discussed throughout the history of the Tibetan tradition, that of the "three levels of ordination" and how these are interrelated. As he began work on the book, however, Kongtrul found his inspiration lay elsewhere:

> Lama Karma Ngédön had urged me to write a treatise on the three levels of ordination, ... [b]ut my feeling was that there were already any number of treatises on this subject, and that if I were to write a treatise it should be more comprehensive in scope, something that would be of use to people who had not studied much. So in the periods between my meditation sessions I had been composing the source verses to my treatise [the *Treasury of Knowledge*], a treatise dealing with the three higher trainings.[2]

As Kongtrul noted, the subject of the relationship between the three levels of ordination—the vows of Individual Liberation (Skt. *pratimokṣa*; Tib. *so sor thar pa*) of the Hīnayāna approach of the Buddhist path, the bodhisattva vow of the Mahāyāna approach, and the tantric samaya of the Vajrayāna approach—had already been extensively discussed in a great number of works by masters of all schools of the Tibetan tradition. Indeed, it had been a pivotal issue since at least the eleventh century CE, when the Bengali master Atīśa came to Tibet. According to accounts in the more recent (Sarma) schools founded in the centuries following his coming, Atīśa found the situation of Buddhism in Tibet to have degenerated since the teachings had first been introduced, beginning in the eighth century, and that his activities were part of a "new wave" of Buddhist teachings that were reintroduced from India. It was Atīśa who was credited with establishing the model of the "threefold vajra holder" (Tib. *gsum ldan rdo rje 'dzin pa*)—the ideal of a fully ordained monk (the model was also a male-oriented one) who also upheld the bodhisattva vow and tantric samaya.

To be fair, the more ancient tradition of the Nyingma (which came under criticism from this Sarma perspective for having allowed such "degeneration" to occur) has maintained that it was due only to lay practitioners, who upheld the pure teachings, having "gone underground" during the persecutions of the king Langdarma (in the mid-tenth century CE) that the original Buddhist teachings introduced during the "earlier spread" (Tib. *snga dar*) were able to survive and flourish, revitalized but not replaced by the "later spread" (Tib. *phyi dar*) from the eleventh century onward. The historical circumstances help to explain the important role played by lay masters as holders of Nyingma lineages, as compared to the predominantly monastic presence in the lineages of the Sarma schools. This is not to suggest that the Nyingmapas placed no emphasis on the Buddhist monastic tradition; indeed, the major Nyingma monasteries historically have been centers noted for the purity of the discipline upheld there, and many of the greatest Nyingma teachers, including Longchen Rabjam (1308–1364) and Mipam Rinpoché (1846–1912), were fully ordained monks. But the fact that Langdarma focused his oppressive efforts on monastic institutions and their inhabitants would have made it easier for a lay community of practitioners to escape notice and avoid persecution, and the need to rely on this tactic would have developed over time into an integral model for the tradition.

In any event, although Kongtrul did treat this theme of the interrelationship between the three levels of ordination in Book 5 of the *Treasury of Knowledge*, he expanded the structure of the work to encompass the three "higher trainings"—those of ethical discipline (Skt. *śīla*; Tib. *tshul khrims*), meditative stability (Skt. *dhyāna*; Tib. *bsam gtan*), and sublime intelligence (Skt. *prajñā*; Tib. *shes rab*)—as well as ancillary topics, resulting in a monumental work that covers virtually the entire range of learning available in the Tibetan religious tradition during Kongtrul's lifetime.

In the parts of Books 7 and 8 translated in this volume, Kongtrul presents a number of models that can be used as tools to come to a precise and accurate understanding of the meaning and value of the Buddhist teachings. What emerges from these discussions is a sense of the teachings as a body of knowledge to be evaluated and examined in light of one's personal experience rather than a static list of facts to be memorized or accepted without question.

It might be useful to reiterate the overall structure of the *Treasury of Knowledge* at this point. To cite from Kongtrul's autobiography:

> The first of the Five Treasuries is *The Encompassing of the Knowable*.[3] This begins with an introductory section—the part that is "positive at the outset." It discusses the title of the work, as well as the formal verses of homage and my statement of intent as the author.[4]
>
> The main body of the work—the part that is "positive in the interim"—comprises ten major sections. These discuss the following topics:
>
> - the universe as the field in which beings are guided spiritually[5]
> - the Buddha as the teacher who guided them
> - the cycles of the Buddhist teachings that are the means of guidance
> - the ways in which these teachings spread in India and Tibet[6]
> - the three levels of ethical discipline that serve as the foundation of spiritual practice[7]
> - a detailed analysis of the study undertaken at the outset of the spiritual path[8]
> - a detailed analysis of contemplation as the intermediate phase
> - a detailed analysis of meditation as the final outcome[9]
> - the paths and levels that are traversed through these last three processes, and
> - the eventual way in which the fruition is gained.[10]
>
> Each of these ten sections has four subsections. Through these discussions, one can also come indirectly to understand the Hinayana, the Mahayana, and the special enlightened intent underlying the Early Translation School's approach of the vajra pinnacle of utter lucidity. To summarize these sections, the fifth deals with the higher training of ethical discipline, the sixth and seventh with that of wisdom, and the eighth with that of

> meditative stability; thus they constitute the core of the work, while the rest of the sections deal with secondary topics that are the causes or results of these higher trainings.
>
> The conclusion—the part that is "positive in the outcome"—brings the work to its completion by discussing the nature and value of the treatise and the way it was composed; as well, this part contains prayers of aspiration and benediction.
>
> The source verses, the summary and overview, and the line-by-line commentary comprise three volumes.[11]

Thus, Book 5 of the *Treasury of Knowledge* is Kongtrul's primary treatment of the first training. It is in Books 6 and 7 that Kongtrul turns his attention to the higher training in sublime intelligence, which, in the Buddhist context, is developed in three successive steps. The first of these is that of studying the teachings—literally, "hearing" them because of the emphasis on receiving the teachings from a living teacher (who can clarify difficult points and correct one's misunderstandings) rather than merely reading texts on one's own. The next step is that of contemplation, which consists of reflecting over and over on the points one has already understood with certainty in the previous step. The point here is to deepen one's appreciation of what has been initially understood, so that it begins to affect one's lived experience and does not remain merely intellectual knowledge. There is a saying in the Tibetan tradition that the first level of understanding is like a patch applied over a hole in one's garment, which will fall off eventually, for just as the patch remains an overlay on the cloth, this kind of understanding remains "on the surface" and does not penetrate into one. However valuable it is at the outset to provide one with a framework, intellectual understanding alone will not significantly affect one's direct experience or deal with one's suffering in the final analysis. That final step occurs when one applies what one has become completely certain about through contemplation in the process of meditation, in which the understanding merges completely with one's experience and edifies it to the level of realization; this is the main focus of Book 8.

Whereas in Book 6 Kongtrul presented his summation of the fields of knowledge to be "heard,"[12] in Book 7 he takes the theme of higher training in sublime intelligence to the next level, including that of contemplation as well as hearing. In his own verse summary to the *Treasury of Knowledge*, Kongtrul describes Book 7 in the following words:

> The seventh book discusses how sublime intelligence develops through hearing the teachings:
> the four keys of understanding for evaluating the teachings;
> the topics to be evaluated (the two levels of provisional and definitive truth and the phenomena of interdependent origination);
> the view of the lack of identity in things, which is crucial to all approaches in general;
> and the four contemplations that turn the mind, providing the foundation for meditative discipline.[13]

And in his introduction to the commentary to the source verses of Book 7 (included in the present volume), he notes:

> Whatever teachings you have heard concerning general objects of knowledge, and profound and extensive topics in particular, it is necessary for you to come to a complete certainty about the significance of all this through conceptualization and investigation; hence, Book 7 concerns the stages of contemplation.

The first part of Book 7 is devoted to a discussion of what Kongtrul literally refers to as "keys" (Tib. *lde mig*), in that they help one to unlock the deeper significance of the knowledge one has gained through initially hearing the teachings. These keys are to be used in contemplation, in order to evaluate further what one has learned. It is clear from this presentation that what is meant by "contemplation" is an introspective process of working with understanding that is gained intellectually in a personally meaningful way rather than mere rote repetition of a set of facts for the purposes of memorizing them. As Kongtrul himself puts it in his commentary to Book 7, Part 1:

> It is when you examine each and every word and its meaning, bringing numerous scriptural citations and kinds of reasoning to bear on these, that you authentically arouse in yourself an awareness that entails certainty on a very fundamental level.

These keys that one uses as tools to understand the teachings are of two kinds, the more ordinary and the extraordinary. Kongtrul discusses the more ordinary tools under four headings: provisional vis-à-vis definitive meaning; direct vis-à-vis indirect intention; the "four reliances"; and the four logical principles.

The question of which of the Buddha's teachings can be taken as provisional and which are to be understood as definitive statements has been and continues to be a controversial topic that historically has placed entire schools of thought at loggerheads. What is at issue is the fact that the Buddha, who encouraged serious critical thought in his followers, did not intend that every statement he made simply be accepted blindly. But decisions concerning which of those statements are provisional and which definitive are not individual decisions based on personal prejudice or on a concern to render the teachings "politically correct" with respect to current fashion. The term that is rendered here as "provisional" (Skt. *neyārtha*; Tib. *drang don*) refers to a meaning that, while not to be taken literally, nevertheless leads or guides one to a more complete understanding. It consists of teachings that concern things that are, in Kongtrul's words, "well known in one's ordinary perception." While such teachings are not descriptions of what is ultimately true, they are useful

> as means to gain access to the fundamentally unconditioned nature of reality [and] are evaluated in categories that can be described, imagined, and expressed, and are presented through the use of some conceptual overlay. (Kongtrul's commentary to Book 7, Part 1)

In contrast to this is what is definitive in meaning (Skt. *nītārtha*; Tib. *nges don*), which consists of teachings

> that discuss the significance of the fundamentally unconditioned way in which things abide (which is utterly lucid by nature, beyond all describing, imagining, or expressing). (Kongtrul's commentary to Book 7, Part 1)

The next key is that of the principle of "intention," which is used in this work to translate the term that Professor D. Seyfort Ruegg has described as follows:

> The Tibetan word *dgoṅs pa* is an honorific and is used to translate Skt. *abhiprāya* when the "intention" of an honoured, recognized and authoritative speaker or author such as the Buddha is

> being referred to. *Abhiprāya* may be translated into Tibetan also by the (non-honorific) word *bsam pa*, which also renders *bhāva* "meaning," as well as *āśaya* "proclivity, disposition."[14]

Intention is a factor that allows for certain of the Buddha's teachings (and those of the commentators thereon) to be interpreted rather than taken literally. As in the case of provisional vis-à-vis definitive meaning, however, there are precise criteria for when such interpretation is required. An understanding of the role of intention in the teachings permits one to view them from a larger perspective rather than assigning the same weight to every statement. If taken exclusively at face value, the Buddhist teachings can seem filled with internal contradictions or "magical thinking," but an understanding of the intentions underlying various teachings serves to resolve such problems. Kongtrul cites the example of the statement, "By simply recalling the name of the tathāgata Vimalacandraprabha, you will attain buddhahood." Taken at face value, this pronouncement seems simplistic in the extreme, unless one understands that the intention here is one that is "concerned with eventualities," and that while the attainment of buddhahood will not come solely or immediately from one's recalling the name of a given buddha, that act of recollection can be seen as setting in motion a process of spiritual development that will, in fact, eventually lead to one's attainment of buddhahood. Seen in this light, the statement is not robbed of its inspiring and evocative power but is nevertheless put into a more meaningful context.

Kongtrul highlights the traditional distinction between "direct intention" (Skt. *abhiprāya*; Tib. *dgongs pa*) and indirect intention (Skt. *abhisaṃdhi*; Tib. *ldem por dgongs pa*). He cites from an Indian work by Asvabhāva (see note 75, this volume), which gives the following explanation:

> Direct intention simply plants the idea in the mind; [3.115a] it is not asserted to depend on the other person's absorbing it;[15] indirect intention depends on the other person's absorbing it.

He also cites from the writings of the fourteenth-century Nyingma master Longchen Rabjam, who notes that while a statement of indirect intention is especially not to be taken literally and is geared to the level of understanding on the listener's part, it is nevertheless a valid statement, "falling shy of being a falsehood" (as Longchenpa puts it).

Kongtrul then turns his attention to a well-known theme in the Buddhist teachings, the "four reliances." These can be summarized as follows:

(1) to rely on the meaning of a teaching as conveyed by the words, not the words themselves;
(2) to rely on the teachings, not the individual who teaches them;
(3) to rely on timeless awareness, not the ordinary state of dualistic consciousness; and
(4) to rely on the definitive meaning found in the teachings, not the merely provisional one.

In each case, however, the issue is one of emphasis. While the meaning is of more importance than the words used to convey it, Kongtrul is not advocating a lack of concern for accuracy in the language and terminology used to frame the teachings, only that being overly concerned with these is a distraction from the more crucial factor, that of the message itself.

In a similar vein, in relying on the teachings rather than the individual, the following quote (attributed to the Buddha) is often cited by Buddhist authors:

> Like someone smelting, cutting, and polishing gold,
> my monks and wise people
> should accept my words once they have examined them well,
> and not simply out of respect for me.

Early indications of this spirit of free inquiry are found in the Pāli canon of the Theravada school; for example, in the *Kalama Sutta* we read the following:

> Do not go upon what has been acquired by repeated hearing; nor upon tradition; nor upon rumour; nor upon what is in a scripture; nor upon surmise; nor upon an axiom; nor upon specious reasoning; nor upon a bias towards a notion that has been pondered over; nor upon another's seeming ability; nor upon the consideration, "The monk is our teacher."
>
> Kalamas, when you yourselves know: "These things are bad; these things are blamable; these things are censured by the wise; undertaken and observed, these things lead to harm and ill," abandon them.

> Come, Kalamas. Do not go upon what has been acquired by repeated hearing; nor upon tradition; nor upon rumor; nor upon what is in a scripture; nor upon surmise; nor upon an axiom; nor upon specious reasoning; nor upon a bias towards a notion that has been pondered over; nor upon another's seeming ability; nor upon the consideration, "The monk is our teacher." Kalamas, when you yourselves know: "These things are good; these things are not blamable; these things are praised by the wise; undertaken and observed, these things lead to benefit and happiness," enter on and abide in them.[16]

Granted, the sūtra just cited purports to be a record of the Buddha's advice to a tribe of people who had apparently been exposed to other religious teachers who were somewhat fanatical and intolerant in their attempts to convert the Kalamas. But such quotations are often mistakenly supposed to be encouragements for one to simply take what appeals to one from the Buddha's teachings and ignore or edit out what does not.

In relying on the teachings rather than the individual, the point is not that one should discount the indispensable role of living teachers, for to take this instruction too literally would be to relegate the study and practice of Buddhism to an intellectual exercise derived from the mere reading of books. Particularly in the Vajrayāna tradition in which Kongtrul was steeped, devotion to one's gurus is crucial to one's spiritual progress and accounts in part for the efficacy of this approach. Rather, the cautionary note offered here is to guard against a healthy and necessary respect for teachers devolving into some form of personality cult. When too much emphasis is placed on the individual personality of the teacher, what masquerades as devotion can in fact be more of an emotionally biased attachment on the part of the student for the teacher, something that could actually interfere with spiritual progress if it is an expression of the student's unresolved personal issues. The function of the teacher is not to replace the sources of refuge or the teachings but to serve as the conduit through which the student can gain access to these and become liberated thereby. As well, too much reliance on the individual teacher as an individual can leave the student feeling bereft and without any further support when the teacher (inevitably) dies.

The emphasis on timeless awareness, as distinct from more ordinary states of consciousness, is again one of keeping the ultimate goal in perspective. There can be a tendency for this point to be misunderstood and interpreted to mean that conceptual thought per se is suspect, if not downright harmful to an individual's spiritual development. As important as it is to transcend the limitations of dualistic and conceptual thinking, it is that very thinking process that serves as one's most useful tool in overcoming confusion and developing the precision and clarity of thought that in the final analysis allows one's mind to make that leap. If for no other reason, the fact that the vast majority of the material covered in the *Treasury of Knowledge* could be considered within the scope of "ordinary consciousness" should argue for the vital role played by our rational thought processes. What really comes under Kongtrul's scrutiny as "ordinary consciousness" is thinking that reinforces the limiting effect of one's intellectual and emotional biases.

Finally, Kongtrul revisits the theme of definitive and provisional meaning as the fourth of these reliances. The latter he defines as pertaining to

> those teachings that arouse a sense of disenchantment with saṃsāra; that deal with the will to be free as defined in the various spiritual approaches; that present things in terms of substantial versus nominal existence, or as "mind only," or as an empty state of nothingness—these are provisional teachings that are presented as temporary expedients, and so one should not rely on them. (Kongtrul's commentary to Book 7, Part 1)

But again, to "not rely" on such teachings means not to hold them to be concerned with what is ultimately meaningful—that is, not to lose sight of the perspective of what is useful in the shorter term vis-à-vis what is truly the case in the most authentic sense:

> The definitive meaning is found in those teachings that go far beyond one's immediate perceptions, or intellectual speculation, or the scope of śrāvakas and pratyekabuddhas; and that deal with profound and vast topics that fall within the scope of those of the very highest acumen, which is inconceivable to our ordinary way of thinking. It is this meaning that one should rely on. (Kongtrul's commentary to Book 7, Part 1)

Kongtrul next turns his attention to four principles that provide a logical consistency to our experience of phenomena on the relative level. I have chosen to translate the Tibetan term *rigs pa* here as "logical principle" rather than "reason(ing)" (which is another quite valid translation) because of Kongtrul's own gloss that the term in this context refers not so much to the sense of a human process of thought as to what underlies our experience and proves to be logically the case when we investigate how things manifest in our perceptions.[17] An understanding of these principles is an integral component in one's being able to interpret one's conventional experiences in ways that contribute to one's spiritual development and ultimate liberation rather than merely reinforcing one's confusion and erroneous thinking.

The model of two levels of truth is found throughout Buddhist teachings on the Mahāyāna level and higher, and while it is true enough to say that "the ultimate level of truth is that of emptiness, while the relative level is that of interdependent connection," both of these levels can be explored and understood with great detail and accuracy through the application of such principles as the four discussed at this point.

Thus, things as we ordinarily experience them exhibit a predictability and a logical consistency that are borne out in several ways: their occurrence in relationships in which they are dependent on one another; the functions they perform in our experience of the phenomenal world; the relationships between them that we can infer, perceive directly, or rely on scripture to validate; and the natures they exhibit. The Tibetan term *chos nyid* (here translated as "the nature of things") in this context does not refer, as it does elsewhere, to the true nature of all phenomena as emptiness, but to what things individually exhibit as their respective natures—"for water to be wet, for fire to be hot," as Kongtrul says.

In addition to the more "ordinary" keys to understanding the Buddhist teachings, Kongtrul discusses tools that are crucial to a correct interpretation of the tantric teachings of the Vajrayāna approach, referred to as the "six parameters" (Tib. *mtha' drug*) and "four modes" (Tib. *tshul bzhi*). The parameters concerning provisional vis-à-vis definitive meaning were discussed previously but are here presented in light of their role in promoting an understanding of the more esoteric teachings of Buddhism. Similarly, the category of interpretation (which is to say, those explanations of the teachings that require interpretation versus those that do not) is a recasting of the theme of "intention" that was discussed earlier in Part 1 of Book 7. In addition, words and phrases found in the tantras can be seen in the light of what can be taken literally and what needs to be interpreted, lest too literal a reading actually bring one to a totally erroneous conclusion.

Hand in hand with these parameters come the four modes, which are multiple levels of meaning that pertain to any significant term in a Vajrayāna context. The literal meaning is defined by Kongtrul as the mere reading of a passage word-by-word, using the "dictionary meaning" of the words and treating the language as one would ordinary grammatical sentences. While there are tantric teachings that can be understood literally as given, to treat all such texts in this way can and does give rise to potentially enormous misunderstandings as to their actual intended meaning.

In addition to their literal meaning, words and terms used in the tantric context can have "shared" (or "universal") meaning, which Kongtrul defines as the meaning that "alleviates misgivings." Such misgivings can arise when one does not have the correct perspective on the various approaches within the Buddhist framework and how these approaches support and integrate with one another. Kongtrul notes that one might feel that the approach one was following was not advanced enough and that one was selling oneself short in not following a higher approach. But the efficacy of any approach is dependent on the acumen with which practitioners apply themselves to it rather than it necessarily being the case that "higher is always better." Alternatively, someone following a so-called higher approach might feel resistance to accepting its principles due to a shortcoming in his or her understanding of the underlying purpose and perspective of that approach and its methods. Yet another aspect of shared meaning lies in that fact that in the particular case of the two stages of tantric meditation—that of development (Skt. *utpattikrama*; Tib. *bskyed rim*) and that of completion (Skt. *sampannakrama*; Tib. *rdzogs rim*)—there are themes that are common to (that is, "shared by") both stages and that form the bridge from the former to the latter.

The mode of hidden meaning refers to topics discussed in the tantric teachings that are not appropriate for too public a revelation. Such topics are those that relate to the roles that sex and power play in Vajrayāna practice (which is for the most part far less than many people's imaginations would have it), and the problem lies not in there being any "dirty little secret" to be kept hidden but in the enormous potential for an unreceptive mind to misinterpret and distort the intended message. The late Herbert V. Guenther, one of the foremost Western interpreters of the Vajrayāna teachings, noted the following:

> The term *tantra*, from the time of its first appearance in the West up to the present day, has been subject to serious misunderstand-

> ings. The term was introduced into the English language in 1799 when tantric works were discovered by missionaries in India. These were not Buddhist works. In fact at that time it was hardly known in the West that such a thing as Buddhism existed. The term tantra was then known only as the title of these works, the contents of which were quite different from what people expected in books dealing with philosophy and religion. The missionaries were for the most part quite shocked that other people had religious and philosophical ideas so different from their own. To them the word tantra meant no more than these expanded treatises; but since the subject matter dealt with in these treatises was so unusual from their point of view, the term began to acquire quite a peculiar connotation, a connotation which proper study of the texts has not borne out. Unfortunately, in this case as in so many others, once a false conception has been formed, a nearly superhuman effort is required to root out and set right all the wrong ideas and odd connotations that have grown up around it.[18]

The problem that can arise when what is couched in hidden meaning is made too public can be either one of rejection (as in the case of the missionaries mentioned above) or of a misconception that these issues are far more central to Vajrayāna than is the case. Elsewhere in his writings, Guenther notes that because the subject matter of the tantras does deal with sex and power, these teachings can become a source of counterproductive fascination for people who are obsessed with either of these, and especially those who are obsessed with both.

Finally, there is the mode of consummate meaning, in which the implications of the words and terms used refer directly to the ultimate nature of reality and to the fruition state of enlightenment that constitutes the direct realization of that nature.

Kongtrul notes that any or all of these modes can apply to even a single "vajra word" and that they are geared to the various levels of acumen in the minds of those reading or hearing such words; hence the need for the appropriate meaning or meanings to be understood in every context. An appreciation of these multiple levels of meaning clearly demonstrates that any translation of a tantric source will of necessity be severely limited and will require extensive commentary to bring out the actual intent of the text.

At the conclusion of Part 1 of Book 7, Kongtrul summarizes the importance of the foregoing keys to understanding as follows:

> Lacking these foregoing keynote instructions, no matter how meticulous one's thinking and mental investigation, one will not be capable of developing an authentic state of sublime intelligence; whereas in having access to them, if one applies them to the techniques employed in the sūtras and tantras, this will arouse in one the flawless sublime intelligence that derives from contemplation.

Part 2 of Book 7 covers several crucial themes, the first being that of provisional vis-à-vis definitive meaning as these apply to the three cycles of the Buddha's teachings (the three "turnings of the wheel of the dharma"). The standard Mahāyāna model for categorizing the Buddha's teachings divides them according to three periods in his career as a teacher. Elsewhere in the *Treasury of Knowledge*, Kongtrul refers to this model:

> When scriptural transmissions are classified, the wheel of Dharma has three cycles: this is widely known and accepted among followers of the great way.
>
> The first doctrine the Buddha taught is the scriptural transmission of the four truths; the middle one, the scriptural transmission concerning the absence of characteristics; and the final one, the scriptural transmission of accurate discernment. *The Discourse Requested by Powerful King of Dharanis* states:
>
>> Aware of the dispositions of thoroughly impure sentient beings, the Transcendent Buddha's speeches on impermanence, suffering, absence of self, and undesirability [of the wheel of life] provoked disillusionment in sentient beings enthralled with the wheel of life—those beings entered exalted beings' spiritual discipline.
>>
>> The Transcendent Buddha's diligence did not end with merely that; his later accounts of emptiness, absence of inherent characteristics, and lack of aspiration allowed sentient beings to comprehend the nature of transcendent buddhas.
>>
>> The Transcendent Buddha's diligence did not end with

> merely that; his later accounts of the irreversible wheel of Dharma and of complete threefold purity [of act, agent, and object] placed beings within the transcendent buddhas' domain.
>
> As stated, the Buddha's initial talks of disillusionment given to those attached to the wheel of life compelled them to enter the path of peace. Then, talks on emptiness brought them to spiritual maturity in the great way. Then, talks on the irreversible wheel had them enter the transcendent buddhas' domain and receive outstanding prophecies [of awakening].[19]

The writings of the fourteenth-century Nyingma master Longchen Rabjam were important sources for Kongtrul in composing the *Treasury of Knowledge*. In his *Precious Treasury of Philosophical Systems*, Longchenpa gives the following treatment of the three turnings of the wheel of dharma:

> According to the well-known interpretation of the ordinary Mahayana, in the excellent place of Varanasi, on excellent occasions, the excellent teacher Shakyamuni spoke to an excellent retinue made up of the five noble ones and eighty thousand gods, teaching the excellent dharma—the first cycle of the Buddha's words, the various teachings pertaining to the four truths; this he did between the ages of thirty-six and forty-two. He began by teaching principally the training in discipline, what came to be known as the compilation of Vinaya. The ethical codes of Vinaya contain extensive overviews that classify actions according to their nature or their relation to formal precepts. The discourses of Vinaya concern the stages of meditative absorption and the celibate way of life undertaken in yogic practice. The further teachings of Vinaya give extensive, detailed explanations and analyses of these topics.
>
> Then, at the excellent place of Vulture Peak, the excellent teacher Shakyamuni spoke to several excellent retinues. Among the four relatively ordinary retinues were about five thousand arhats, including Shariputra and Maudgalyayana; about five hundred nuns, including Shakyamuni's stepmother, Prajapati; and groups of laypeople, including the householder Anathapindika

and the laywoman Sagama. As well, there were enormous numbers of gods, nagas, demigods, and gandharvas. The extraordinary retinue was made up of an enormous number of bodhisattvas—including Bhadrapala, Ratnasambhava, and Jaladatta—who had truly attained great levels of realization. On excellent occasions, he taught these retinues the excellent dharma—the intermediate cycle of the Buddha's words, the various teachings pertaining to the characterization of phenomena as nonexistent; this he did between the ages of forty-three and seventy-two. He taught principally the training in mind, what came to be known as the compilation of Sutra. The ethical codes of Sutra classify the precepts of the bodhisattva vow. The discourses of Sutra discuss meditative absorption in profound and extensive ways. The further teachings of Sutra analyze related topics—spiritual levels and paths, powers of recall, and meditative absorption—in great detail.

Then, in excellent places—not any one place—such as the human world and the abodes of gods and nagas, on excellent occasions, the excellent teacher Shakyamuni spoke to an excellent retinue of innumerable monks, nuns, gods, nagas, bodhisattvas, and others, teaching the excellent dharma—the final cycle of the Buddha's words, the various teachings pertaining to definitive truth; this he did between the ages of seventy-three and eighty-two. He taught principally the training in sublime knowing, what came to be known as the compilation of Abhidharma. The ethical codes of Abhidharma have to do with taming the afflictive states in ways that are easy to implement and involve little hardship. The discourses of Abhidharma discuss the vast range of techniques for engaging in the experience of suchness. The further teachings of Abhidharma analyze in great detail the mind-body aggregates, the fields of experience, the components of perception, the controlling factors, consciousness, and tathagatagarbha (the innately, totally pure "buddha nature") and discuss related topics.[20]

Of great importance is the issue of which among these teachings may be considered provisional in meaning (and hence open to interpretation, albeit according to a judicious process and not mere personal whims or preferences) and which should be taken as definitive statements that were not intended to be subjected to any interpretation at all. This classification of teachings into what is provisional and what is ultimate is based on statements found in such sūtras as the *Definitive Commentary on Enlightened Intent* and the *Discourse Requested by Dhāraṇīśvararāja*. Here Kongtrul presents several alternative models of the three cycles of the Buddha's teachings and offers his definition of a sūtra whose content is that of provisional meaning:

> [It is] a sūtra that principally teaches on the relative level of truth, which serves as a means to ensure that the path to the definitive state of excellence can arise in the experience of those who are to be guided along any of the three spiritual approaches. (Kongtrul's commentary to Book 7, Part 2)

By contrast, a sūtra whose content is one of definitive meaning is

> [one] that principally teaches on the ultimate level of truth, so that the few to be guided who can patiently accept its profound meaning can attain nirvāṇa that is not defined by extremes, by meditating on the path to definitive excellence. (Kongtrul's commentary to Book 7, Part 2)

While this may seem at first to be a relatively straightforward set of criteria, an ongoing controversy throughout the history of the Tibetan Buddhist tradition has focused on this very issue. Although (as Kongtrul notes) all schools of Mahāyāna thought consider the first cycle of the Buddha's teachings to be provisional in meaning ("primarily concerned with what is relatively valid"), when it comes to making distinctions between the intermediate and the final cycles, he notes that there is less consensus, at one point stating quite bluntly that

> it would seem that—due to a failure to examine accurately the meaning of the underlying intent of this source [the *Discourse Requested by Dhāraṇīshvararāja*]—there have occurred cases of Tibetan teachers indulging in a lot of nonsense concerning two cycles (that is, the intermediate and the final), as to which is provisional and which definitive, and which is "higher" or

> "lower" than the other. (Kongtrul's commentary to Book 7, Part 2)

Kongtrul presents alternative opinions concerning the intermediate and final cycles: that of the "proponents of things having no finite essence" (that is, the proponents of unqualified emptiness [*rang stong*], a reference in part to the majority of those in the Gelukpa school of Tibetan Buddhism); that of the "yogic practitioners" (that is, the proponents of what became the basis for the view of qualified emptiness [*gzhan stong*]); and that of Nāgārjuna and his followers. He then argues in favor of his own conclusion that

> the intermediate and final cycles of teaching are equally definitive in meaning, with the distinction that the former concerns the definitive meaning that puts an end to conceptual elaborations in the shorter term, while the latter concerns that which reveals the true way of abiding in the far-reaching sense. (Kongtrul's commentary to Book 7, Part 2)

He finishes this discussion by noting that no aspect of the Buddha's teachings, however provisional in nature, should be considered false, for all such aspects partake of a single underlying intent, being simply more obvious or more subtle means to eliminate erroneous concepts and realize the ultimate nature of things. He urges his readers not to fall prey to sectarian biases, an issue that deeply concerned Kongtrul throughout his entire life:

> This being the case, to boast, "I am a follower of the Middle Way!" could be a case of one's implicitly denigrating other aspects of the Buddha's sublime words; and to claim, "I am a tantric practitioner!" could be a case of one's dismissing the repositories of teachings in the śrāvaka approach and so forth as though these were useless straw. . . . Therefore, one should examine and investigate the possibility of one's rejecting the Buddhadharma and exercise caution! (Kongtrul's commentary to Book 7, Part 2)

Kongtrul concludes this section on a touching note of concern: his wish that people not become embroiled in the sectarian controversies that have plagued Tibetan Buddhism throughout its history:

> It is for this reason that the venerable Maitreya emphatically advises one not to misinterpret the tradition of the Sage, which was established by the Buddha himself. With folded hands, I beseech all to respect this. (Kongtrul's commentary to Book 7, Part 2)

The next section of part 2 is concerned with the two levels of truth, relative and ultimate. This Mahāyāna model is found in the source sūtras (the *Reunion of Father and Son*, for example) and is based on the experiential criteria that distinguish what is nominally valid from the perspective of an ordinary being (one who, by definition, is perceiving within a state of confusion) from what a spiritually advanced being perceives while engaged in meditative equipoise. After a comprehensive discussion of the terms used to refer to these levels of truth, Kongtrul analyzes them in detail, outlining the stances taken by the various schools of Buddhist philosophy, including that of the tantras. He then concludes with some remarks on the value of one's understanding these two levels of truth, reminding us that none of what he is presenting in this book is meant to remain theoretical but is to be applied to our own experience in ways that contribute to spiritual liberation and enlightenment.

The final topic of the second part of Book 7 is that of the process of interdependent connection (Skt. *pratītyasamutpāda*; Tib. *rten cing 'brel bar 'byung ba*), a principle that is held to lie at the very core of the Buddha's teachings. This process is usually described from the point of view of how it is involved in the perpetuation of saṃsāra ("the usual progression," as Kongtrul notes), but in addition to discussing it as such on both the external and internal levels, Kongtrul here explores more profound aspects of interdependent connection, seen in light of the true nature of phenomena and the state of nirvāṇa ("the reversal of the usual progression").

In Part 3 of Book 7, Kongtrul provides an exhaustive inquiry into what he terms "authentic view," which he describes as the "principal factor" in the individual's search for liberation and enlightenment. Having established the necessity of cultivating such a view, he discusses the development of a sublime degree of intelligence (Skt. *prajñā*; Tib. *shes rab*), specifically that which brings one realization of the lack of any real identity in any phenomenon or in the individual sense of selfhood, the nonrealization of which, from the Mahāyāna Buddhist point of view, constitutes the fundamental distortion of reality and one's major stumbling block on the path to liberation and enlightenment.

Kongtrul then turns his attention to the four axioms of the Buddhist teachings. These are not seen as some form of dogmatic creed that one must believe in order to be a Buddhist but more as basic truths about the nature of reality that one can convince oneself of through contemplating their meaning. A certainty concerning these axiomatic truths constitutes the foundation on which one can begin to develop authentic view by following what Kongtrul refers to as "the path that avoids dualistic extremes." These extremes are those of naïve realism, in which one assumes that things exist as they seem to from one's limited and confused perspective, and nihilistic denial, in which one denies the validity or meaning of anything and everything. These extremes are also referred to as overstatement (assuming that what is not the case is, in fact, the case) and understatement (assuming that what is the case is, in fact, not the case). In this section Kongtrul is intent on defining more precisely the famous "middle way" of Buddhism:

> In general, proponents of all philosophical systems, both Buddhist and non-Buddhist, presume that they are espousing a "middle way," refuting dualistic extremes in light of their own understanding of what this means. This is because they hold that they profess, according to their own systems, a middle way that avoids two extremes—although lower approaches, in exaggerating what does not exist as existing, incur the extreme of naïve affirmation, while relatively higher approaches, in denying what exists as not existing, incur the extreme of nihilistic denial. (Kongtrul's commentary to Book 7, Part 3)

He discusses the lower schools of Buddhist philosophy to point out the limitations in their approach and then focuses on the Middle Way tradition (Skt. *madhyamaka*; Tib. *dbu ma*) in particular. Kongtrul begins by identifying what is implied by the crucial term "emptiness"—so often misunderstood both in historically Buddhist cultures and the modern West that some translators feel that more interpretive translations of the Sanskrit term *śūnyatā* (Tib. *stong pa nyid*) are called for. He then delineates the understanding of this from the perspectives of both unqualified emptiness (Tib. *rang stong*, "self-empty") and qualified emptiness (Tib. *gzhan stong*, "other-empty"), a distinction that did not exist as such in India but that became highly controversial in Tibet, especially after the Jonang master

Dolpopa Sherab Gyaltsen codified the interpretation of qualified emptiness in the fourteenth century.

However, Kongtrul's purpose—in the present discussion, at any rate—is neither to engage in that controversy nor to decide it but to expose his readers to the fact that distinct interpretations exist. He quickly moves on to a trenchant treatment of the two aspects of identity, that of phenomena and that of the individual, as the primary targets on which to direct the weapon of one's intelligence. He discusses each aspect in turn, presenting the points of view of various philosophical schools, and then concludes with advice on integrating the two mainstream traditions of the Middle Way from India—those of Nāgārjuna and Asaṅga—which were the precursors of the interpretations in Tibet of unqualified and qualified emptiness, respectively. Rather than see the situation as one of a correct interpretation versus an incorrect one, Kongtrul states the following:

> Although there is no question of any hierarchy of higher or lower between [Nāgārjuna's and Asaṅga's] enlightened intentions, the fact that there may *seem* to be one is due solely to one's lack of good fortune and to one's highly restricted intelligence.
>
> That being the case, once one has understood the distinct approaches found in the sources of the two masters who codified these mainstream traditions, if one can integrate these through realizing that the enlightened intent of both is, in the final analysis, one and the same—the meaning of the Middle Way—one is freed from the many flaws of misinterpreted suppositions or denials. (Kongtrul's commentary to Book 7, Part 3)

In his discussion of view, Kongtrul also examines how these interpretations of emptiness from the sūtra tradition are cast from the perspective of the mantra approach, or Vajrayāna. His general discussion of these points is followed by a reference to the writings of the sixth Zhamar incarnation of the Kagyü school, Gargyi Wangpo Chökyi Wangchuk, who lived from 1584 to 1630. I have been able to locate only two short works by this master, neither of which concern the topic discussed here; given the special mention Kongtrul makes of the sixth Zhamar's interpretation of tantra in this context, it is to be hoped that more of his writings will become available in the future.

Finally, Kongtrul concludes Part 3 of Book 7 with a brief summation of the view of "unborn primordial unity" (Tib. *skye med zung 'jug*), in which he succinctly sets forth the view that integrates the approaches of unqualified and qualified emptiness discussed previously and forges the bridge between the approaches of sūtra and tantra.

The fourth and final part of Book 7 begins with Kongtrul's comments on the impact that studying (that is, hearing) teachings and contemplating their meaning is meant to have on one. This impact includes the arousal of a sense of faith and confidence in the validity of those teachings, as well as the instilling of a moral sense of how to conduct oneself as a good human being and a truly spiritual practitioner. This segues into Kongtrul's remaining discussion, for as he notes:

> This being the case, one will not be able to hear and contemplate teachings properly without relying on a deliberate and precise contemplation of such topics as one's hard-won state of opportunities and endowments. Even if one is able to do so, one's experience will not be affected in an ongoing way. So one should carefully contemplate the four contemplations that reorient the mind, which are methods found in the tradition of pith instructions that dramatically reorient an ordinary individual's mind. (Kongtrul's commentary to Book 7, Part 4)

He then lays out his definitive treatment of a series of exercises known collectively as the "four contemplations that reorient the mind" (Tib. *blo ldog rnam bzhi*), which will be very familiar to anyone with any exposure to the Tibetan tradition of Buddhism. While the themes of these contemplations are found in all Buddhist traditions, their particular formulation as a standard group of four seems to be unique to the Tibetan schools.

In fact, Kongtrul's presentation of these four contemplative themes is an expanded version. The idiom usually refers to the four topics that Kongtrul treats in the first two sections of his discussion—that is, (1) the contemplation of the human state of rebirth (or rather, a certain set of circumstances within the human realm) as a hard-won state of opportunities and endowments; (2) the contemplation of one's mortality and the impermanence of everything within the scope of our ordinary experience; (3) the contemplation of karma, that is, one's actions and their consequences; and (4) the contemplation of the shortcomings of saṃsāra. In treating these four topics in two sections, Kongtrul then adds a third section, concerning the cultivation of an altruistic and compassionate resolve; and a fourth, focusing on the development of sublime intelligence that culminates in the experience of a nondual state of timeless awareness.

The progression of these contemplations is that of reorienting one's mental focus in increasingly profound ways. The first section, comprising the two topics of contemplation of the human rebirth and impermanence, deals with reorienting one away from being overly preoccupied with things of this life, while the second section, consisting of the contemplations of karma and the shortcomings of saṃsāra, ensures that one is further reoriented away from perpetuating a continued entanglement with the cycle of conditioned and limited existence in general. The third section is presented to guard against the spiritual complacency of a self-oriented desire for mere personal salvation and introduces the theme of altruism. The fourth section addresses the development of a sublime degree of intelligence that culminates in the nondual experience of timeless awareness that takes one beyond the confines of ordinary dualistic consciousness.

Given the lofty nature of the preceding discussion of view in part 3, it might appear odd for Kongtrul then to treat such seemingly elementary topics as those found in the first two sections, which are generally considered "entry level" teachings. But the practice of Buddhism as a vehicle for spiritual liberation is grounded in a conviction that our present state of being is limiting and confused, coupled with a sincere desire to rise above those limitations and discover our true potential as beings in general and human beings in particular. This certainty—the will to become free of saṃsāra's constraints—is often (perhaps somewhat misleadingly) translated as "renunciation," but it is not meant to be understood as a puritanical mistrust of the world. The four contemplative exercises contained in the first two sections of part 4 are designed to instill in one this will toward real freedom, which lies at the core of the discipline that is the very foundation of all Buddhist practice and is termed "Hīnayāna." I have spoken elsewhere of my reasons for using this term,[21] despite the negative connotations it can be interpreted to convey, as indicative of an individual attitude rather than of any historical group or geographic region.

During the three-year retreat in which I participated from 1976 to 1980, under the auspices of Kalu Rinpoché, in the final year we were introduced to the practices known collectively as the "six doctrines" (Tib. *chos drug*), which are considered advanced Vajrayāna practices. In the context of these practices, the instruction manuals we were studying encouraged us to return to such old familiar themes as the contemplation of impermanence and our mortality. Plainly, as much as such contemplations constitute "beginner's practice," they are not left behind but rather serve like the foundation of a house, important at the outset and never losing their important role as supports, just as the fact that one must begin learning one's alphabet in kindergarten does not mean one can forget or discard it when one moves on to higher levels of education.

The third section introduces the element of altruism and compassion that is the foundation of the Mahāyāna approach—again using this term to refer to the individual's outlook and motivation—while the fourth section focuses on the other fundamental principle of the Mahāyāna, that of wisdom and intelligence and its role in bringing realization of the ultimate nature of mind and the phenomena it perceives.

Kongtrul's presentation of these four contemplations that reorient the mind parallels another model formulated by the great Tsongkhapa, founder of the Gelukpa school—that is, the "three foremost principles" of the path (Tib. *lam gyi gtso bo rnam gsum*), which are (1) the will to become free of saṃsāra, (2) the awakening attitude of bodhicitta, and (3) the authentic view of the nature of reality.[22]

In the case of each of these topics for contemplation, Kongtrul lays out methodical guidelines for addressing it as a topic of contemplation, so that the exercise is not one of merely musing on a subject but coming to a thoroughgoing comprehension of its significance in light of one's personal experience.

In Book 8 Kongtrul discusses the last of the higher trainings, that of meditative stability and absorption. In his verse summary, he describes the contents of this book as follows:

> The eighth book discusses how higher states of absorption develop through meditation:
> calm abiding and deeper insight, the two common foundations of meditative absorption;
> the stages of meditation in the greater and lesser cause-based approaches;
> the tradition that emphasizes the Anuttara tantras of the secret mantra approach;
> and the traditions of the eight lineages of spiritual accomplishment, with emphasis on their esoteric instructions.[23]

A translation of Book 8, Part 3 by Elio Guarisco and Ingrid McLeod has been published as *The Treasury of Knowledge: Book Eight, Part Three: The Elements of Tantric Practice*; a translation of Book 8, Part 4 by Sarah Harding has been published as *The Treasury of Knowledge: Book Eight, Part Four: Esoteric Instructions*. The present volume contains a translation of the first two parts of Book 8.

Once one has gained certainty about the teachings through hearing and contemplating them, the logical next step is that of integrating them into one's experience through the process known as "meditation." It is telling that the Tibetan word for "meditation" (*sgom pa*) is cognate to that for "becoming familiar with" (*goms pa*), resulting in a well-known case of word play: *sgom pa ma yin goms pa yin* ("It is not so much meditation as it is getting 'used-to'").

Part 1 of Book 8 then presents the practice of meditation in the Buddhist context as a twofold process comprising elements of mental calmness and a deeper awareness of the nature of reality. The first element is termed "calm abiding" (Skt. *śamatha*; Tib. *zhi gnas*), the latter "profound insight" (Skt. *vipaśyanā*; Tib. *lhag mthong*). In one way or another, these two factors play a role in meditation as it is carried out on every level of every approach in Buddhist practice. Here Kongtrul is discussing them in light of the general sūtra tradition common to the Hīnayāna and Mahāyāna approaches.

The three-step process of hearing teachings, contemplating their meaning, and putting one's understanding into practice through meditation is entirely logical in light of Kongtrul's analogy of a fine harvest (the understanding) being useful only when it is eaten, as it is intended to be, rather than being left on the level of mere intellectual understanding. It is in meditation that the real purpose of study and contemplation finds expression.

Meditation, then, consists of the two factors of calm abiding (which Kongtrul defines as "a one-pointed state of attention") and profound insight ("the discernment that thoroughly analyzes phenomena"). Kongtrul gives us the traditional analogy of meditation as being comparable to the flame of a lamp burning both steadily and brightly in order to illuminate effectively. Since the relationship between the two factors is that calm abiding supports the development of profound insight, Kongtrul begins by discussing calm abiding. Having examined such preliminary concerns as the supportive circumstances for the cultivation of calm abiding and correct meditation posture, he draws on both mainstream sources (Tib. *gzhung*)—in particular the works of Asaṅga—and personal advice (Tib. *gdams ngag*) to delineate pitfalls in the development of the calm abiding of mind and remedies to address them. He concludes by reminding us that calm abiding, though of crucial importance in the pursuit of liberation and enlightenment, is not in itself sufficient; for while it serves as the necessary basis for all further cultivation of meditative stability in both the sūtra and tantra traditions, the function of calm abiding is simply to suppress the afflictive mental states and their attendant suffering, which interfere with the development of profound insight and obscure the true nature of things, which is the object of that insight.

Kongtrul then speaks to the issue of profound insight in its various expressions according to several approaches, including that of the Vajrayāna, and concludes with a discussion of the integration of calm abiding and profound insight and the results this brings.

In Part 2 of Book 8 we find a treatment of the stages of meditation as these are described in the cause-based, or dialectical, approach—which is to say, the sūtra tradition comprising the three paths of the śrāvaka, the pratyekabuddha, and the bodhisattva. In many respects, this part parallels Kongtrul's discussion of the stages and levels of this approach in Book 9 of the *Treasury of Knowledge*.[24] However, the treatment in Book 9 deals more with the overall theoretical models of the five paths (and only distinguishes the aforementioned three paths incidentally within that general framework), while here the focus is more on the specific process of meditative discipline as a crucial (perhaps *the* crucial) factor in all of those paths, and the distinctness of the different approaches is emphasized. Kongtrul pays a great deal of attention to the appropriate preliminaries to meditative discipline (including practical factors such as attitude and lifestyle) as well as the actual stages through which one progresses in meditation. His discussions of the śrāvaka, pratyekabuddha, and bodhisattva paths here focus more on the actual way in which meditation is practiced. Taken together, the discussion in Books 8 and 9 complement one another and provide a very clear and complete picture of the cause-based approach as a path to liberation and enlightenment.

Sanskrit terms and names have been rendered with diacritics, and the Wylie system of transcription has been used for Tibetan words provided (with place and personal names phoneticized in the text for ease of pronunciation but fully transcribed in the endnotes). I have tried to translate the titles of the texts that Kongtrul cites for the general reader, but these are not in any sense standardized translations, and so I have provided the Sanskrit and Tibetan titles in the bibliography of works cited. Folio numbers embedded in the text refer to the four-volume edition of *The Treasury of Knowledge* published in 1997 by Shechen Publications.

I have received a great deal of help, directly and indirectly, from many people during the course of translating this book. I am grateful for the support and inspiration provided by my colleagues in the Tsadra Foundation community and particularly benefited from the work of Karl Brunnhölzl and Elizabeth Callahan. My thanks go to Dr. Robert J. Taylor, Assistant Director for the Asian Classics Input Project, for his generosity in providing me access to Wylie files of texts in the Kangyur and Tengyur collections, a resource that made verifying citations from source texts infinitely easier.

As always, my thanks and deeply felt gratitude go to the Tsadra Foundation, and especially to Eric Colombel and Anthony S. Chapman (Lama Drupgyu Tendzin) for the support that made this translation possible. Their dedication to support the task of translation is an inspiration to me far above and beyond the personal benefits the foundation affords me. My thanks as well go to Michael Wakoff, my editor at Snow Lion, and to L. S. Summer, who created the index. In preparing this translation, I have also received invaluable help and guidance from Acharya Lama Tenpa Gyaltsen, currently of Boulder, Colorado. There are undoubtedly places where I have failed to grasp the intent of his insightful comments, and where I must accept responsibility for any errors. Nevertheless, my hope is that this translation will aid in the ongoing task of bringing the tradition of the Buddha's teachings in their entirety into the English language.

Richard Barron
May 2011

Book Seven

The Higher Training in Sublime Intelligence

. . . .

The Source Verses

Part 1. Keys to Understanding

Sublime Intelligence Deriving from Contemplation [I]

You come to complete certainty by contemplating the significance
of what has been heard.
This consists of an internal dialogue that involves conceptual thinking
and investigation.

Mundane conceptual thought is associated with ordinary mental
functioning,
while transcendent thought is associated with sublime intelligence;
a discerning mind engages in precise investigation.

Specific Keys to Evaluating the Teachings [II]

Brief Enumeration by Way of Introduction [A]

This involves two factors: the keys that are crucial in order to evaluate
the teachings
and the treasure chamber of the sacred teachings that are to be evaluated.
The standard processes of evaluation are primarily those of provisional
vis-à-vis definitive meaning, direct vis-à-vis indirect intention,
the four reliances, and the four logical principles.

Extensive Explanation of the Significance of These Keys [B]

Ordinary Keys to Understanding [1]

Provisional and Definitive Meaning [a]

Individuality, the state of an ordinary being, origination and cessation,
the mind-body aggregates and sense fields, and so forth—these are means

to gain access to the fundamentally unconditioned nature of reality.
These topics, together with the discussions of them, constitute the relative level of provisional meaning.

Those texts that present the totally pure avenue to the true nature of phenomena, free of elaboration—
that is, the way in which things actually abide—are definitive in meaning.
Those that simply discuss the purposes for such teachings
are held to be provisional in meaning, but this is not necessarily the case.

Direct and Indirect Intention [b]

Four Cases of Direct Intention [i]

Words can have different implications, but the method for interpreting them reveals that there is no contradiction.
Because those to be guided are guided by relying on these methods,
[one considers] the underlying motive, the function, and the seeming incompatibility.
The four cases of direct intention are those concerned with equalness, implied issues,
eventualities, and the attitudes of individuals.

Four Cases of Indirect Intention [ii]

The means to educate others that are not definitive yet capable of leading them
are with respect to śrāvakas, the three aspects of the very essence of things, the overcoming of flaws,
and the profundity of what is expressed. There are four cases of indirect intention,
because they are concerned, respectively, with edification, characteristics, remedies, and transformation.

Differences between Direct and Indirect Intention [iii]

Direct intention simply plants the idea in the mind; it does not depend
on the other person; it is explained that indirect intention does depend.

Four Reliances [c]
Relying on the Meaning, Not the Words [i]

Rely on the meaning, which makes evident the omniscient state of timeless awareness;
do not rely on the words and letters that are conventional terms and designations.

Relying on the Teachings, Not the Individual [ii]

Rely on the teachings concerning unmistaken view and conduct;
do not rely on an individual's family, ancestry, fame, or wealth.

Relying on Timeless Awareness, Not Ordinary Consciousness [iii]

Rely on timeless awareness, which is free of elaboration, without identity, and the very essence of being;
do not rely on ordinary consciousness, which is a mind fixated on characteristics and concepts.

Relying on the Definitive Meaning, Not the Provisional One [iv]

Rely on the definitive meaning, with its profound and vast implications;
do not rely on the provisional meaning that is temporarily expedient.

Four Logical Principles [d]

In mundane contexts, things are established through dependent relationships; the sense faculties, objects, avenues of consciousness, and so forth,
perform functions with respect to specific objects but do not perform these with respect to other aspects of experience;
there is valid cognition based on inference, on direct experience, or on scriptural authority;
and all phenomena can be found always to have their common and individual characteristics:
These are known, respectively, as the logical principle of dependent relationships, that of the performance of functions,

that of establishing what is reasonable, and that of the nature of things.

Extraordinary Keys to Understanding [2]

Brief Discussion [a]

The extraordinary approach of secret mantra is evaluated through six parameters and four modes.

Extensive Explanation [b]

Six Parameters [i]

Given the presence or absence of a fortunate capacity regarding reality,
a single vajra word conveys distinct meanings.
Therefore, the provisional meaning is found in the stage of development and its ancillaries;
the definitive meaning lies in both the causal aspect of tantra and the stage of completion.

A single meaning treated by different and seemingly contradictory statements
is a case of explanation requiring interpretation, in which the meaning being expressed depends on the underlying intent.
Where it does not depend on this, one understands the presentation directly; this is explanation that does not require interpretation. These are two more parameters.

Descriptions of maṇḍalas and other topics in well-known language are to be taken literally;
those that use uncommon language and are bound up in symbolism are not to be taken literally.
Since the words and meanings do not fall outside the foregoing, they are the six parameters.

Four Modes [ii]

The mere reading word by word is the literal meaning.

The shared meaning concerns the alleviating of misgivings concerning the
sūtra tradition and others, and the stage of development.

The teachings on desire are hidden, relative truth is hidden,
and the higher, middling, and lesser degrees with respect to what lies at
the core are hidden meaning.

The path of utter lucidity and the fruition state of primordial unity
constitute the consummate meaning. These four modes can be
differentiated
from a single vajra word, in accord with progressive levels of acumen.

The foregoing constitutes the first part,
concerning a definitive treatment of the keys
for evaluating the teachings.

Part 2. Understanding Truth and Meaning

Provisional and Definitive Meaning in the Three Cycles of Teachings [I]

General Discussion [A]

The principal topics for evaluation are the three cycles of the sacred dharma.

Specific and Detailed Analysis [B]

Common Tradition [1]

All agree that the first cycle is provisional in meaning.

Tradition of Proponents of Things Having No Finite Essence [2]

Proponents of things having no finite essence opine,
"The intermediate cycle is primarily definitive in meaning, the final one largely provisional."
They have no actual scriptural authority for this, only proving their rationale through reasoning.

Tradition of Yogic Practitioners [3]

"The intermediate cycle, putting an end to elaborations, is definitively meaningful in the shorter term;
the final cycle, bringing a definitive conclusion concerning what is ultimate, is definitively meaningful
in the far-reaching sense." So says the tradition of Yogic Practitioners.
Their scriptural authority is found in the distinctions made by the Victorious One himself,
and the further distinctions made by the tradition of the prophesied exalted one, who attained the third level of realization.
The reasoning is found by applying the example of refining a gem and so forth.
Rangjung, Dolpo, Drimé Özer, and others
primarily accept this latter interpretation, others the former.

Explanation of the Exalted One [4]

In particular, it is explained that the three successive cycles of the dharma—

initial, intermediate, and final—undermine, respectively,
nonvirtue, the belief in identity, and all bases for dogmatic opinions.

Incorrect Opinions and Single Intent [5]

Some think of what is provisionally meaningful as untrue, as false,
but this is an incorrect opinion, for the Buddha's word entails no falsehoods.

Because it eliminates elaborations concerning the manner in which things appear while actually demonstrating the way things actually abide,
the great spiritual guide and others accept that the entire Buddhadharma has a single intent.

Two Levels of Truth [II]
Introductory Comments [A]

The sacred Buddhadharma was taught on the basis of two levels of truth.

Actual Classification [B]
Essence [1]

Generally speaking, these are in essence contrived and uncontrived, respectively—
that which is imputed by the minds of ordinary beings and the state of spiritually advanced beings in meditative equipoise.

Derivation of Terms [2]

As for the derivation of the terms, what is conditioned is true on the relative level itself,
while one fact is true on the ultimate level.

Characteristics and Synonyms [3]

The characteristics are those of the object's being either that of a confused consciousness that does not investigate it

or that of the unconfused mind of a spiritually advanced being—that is, deceptive or not deceptive.
The way in which the subjective perceiver apprehends is either one of confusion or its absence.
These levels are presented with many synonymous terms.

Precise Analysis [4]
The Actual Analysis [a]
General Analysis [i]

Without investigating any foundation for analysis, on the basis of what simply can be known,
one can distinguish the way in which things appear from the way they abide—that is, the relative from the ultimate.

Specific Analysis [ii]

The way in which things appear is a state of confusion—the perceptions in the minds of ordinary beings;
the unconfused state is accepted by most to consist of the path and its fruition.
The relative is that of ordinary mortals and the spiritually advanced, or that of mundane people and advanced spiritual practitioners.
The ultimate is in essence indivisible but can be analyzed as having three characteristics, or,
from the perspective of topics under discussion, sixteen aspects, and so forth.

Reasons Underlying the Analysis [b]

Due to the difference in the way that the minds of the spiritually advanced and the spiritually immature perceive,
and the classification based on mutual dependence, . . .

Certainty of Two Levels [c]

. . . truth is certainly twofold.

Two Levels of Truth: Identical or Separate? [d]

Conventionally, this is one nature with separate facets;
ultimately, there can be no discussion of being identical or separate.

Positions Held by Philosophical Systems [e]

If something is destroyed or broken down, the concept of it
can be either discarded or not. More obvious things and streams of consciousness are relative,
while what is indivisible is ultimately true. This is the tradition of the Particularist school.

Things that are ultimately able to perform functions or not,
which are characterized as specifics or generalities—this is the tradition of the Followers of the Sūtras.

Dualistic experiences of perceived and perceiver, of objects and their perceiving subject,
are considered as actually being nondual consciousness. This is the tradition of the Mind Only school.
Sensory appearances, which are proven to be relative, are similar to illusions,
while what is ultimate, like space, cannot be found to exist. This is the tradition of the Autonomist school.

What is imputed by ordinary consciousness is relative (accepted in accord with what is commonly understood in the world),
while freedom from conceptual elaboration is beyond imagination or expression. This is the tradition of the Consequentialist school.

The imputed and the dependent are relative; the ultimate
is the absolute—self-knowing timeless awareness. This is the tradition of qualified emptiness.

In the mantra approach, there is further embellishment due to its special features.
In particular, the relative consists of the appearances that manifest to dualistic consciousness,

which are described as being apparent yet without true existence, like the reflection of the moon on water.
The ultimate is the essence of things, emptiness in its eighteen aspects;
the truth of this is nondual timeless awareness.

Value of Understanding These Truths [5]

Knowing the foregoing, one is undeluded concerning the words of the Sage,
puts the skillful means of moral choices—what to accept or reject—into practice,
and beholds the significance of what derives from those means, reaching the far shore of saṃsāra.

Investigating the Process of Interdependent Connection [III]

Interdependent Connection: The Fundamentally Unconditioned Nature [A]

The totally pure nature of the foregoing
is the way in which things are fundamentally unconditioned—interdependent connection free of limiting extremes.

Interdependent Connection: Saṃsāra [B]

What occurs dependently, externally and internally, constitutes the interdependent connection of saṃsāra.

Interdependent Connection: Nirvāṇa [C]

Whoever beholds the interdependent connection of nirvāṇa—the reversal of the usual progression—
has access to the key points of the Buddha's speech;
therefore realize the significance of these through dedicated contemplation.

The foregoing constitutes the second part,
concerning a definitive treatment of provisional and definitive meaning
according to the three approaches, the two levels of truth,
and interdependent connection.

Part 3. Authentic View

The Need for Authentic View [I]

Given that nirvāṇa—the deathless state—is what to strive for,
sublime intelligence is the remedy to eliminate ignorance, the source of obscuration.
Without it this will not take place, for it ensures that one's view is pure.
Conduct through skillful means brings purification,
and one swiftly gains freedom in the integration of totally pure view and conduct.

In particular, because all the teachings spoken by the Victorious One
are directed toward, and come down to, the basic space of phenomena,
initially one should come to a definitive understanding of the view.
Having properly understood the flawed attitudes of erroneous opinions, one eliminates these
while seeking out and accepting what is definitively meaningful as one's authentic view.

The Way to Develop Sublime Intelligence [II]

With ignorance serving as the cause, the belief in the reality of the perishable aggregates
is the false perception of identity, which is the root of four mistaken ideas.
The remedy to this is to develop sublime intelligence that realizes the lack of identity.

Preliminaries: The Four Axioms [III]

Conditioned phenomena are momentary and impermanent;
all that is corruptible is of the nature of the three kinds of suffering;
both the deeply ingrained afflictive state and the totally refined state are empty and lack identity;
nirvāṇa alone is liberation, the state of peace.
These are the four axioms that denote the general teachings of the Buddha's words.
Contemplating them thoroughly, one arouses a sense of certainty at the outset.

The Path That Avoids Dualistic Extremes [IV]
General Way to Avoid Dualistic Extremes [A]

Next, one follows the path that avoids dualistic extremes.
One uses the sublime intelligence that understands ultimate reality as the perceiving agent
to pare away conceptual elaborations concerning the object that is to be known. This is the tradition of each individual's own school.
Be that as it may, materialists may eliminate naïve affirmation and nihilistic denial
according to their own interpretations, but they still fall into extremes of overstatement and understatement.

Therefore, these interpretations are partly truth but with much untruth.
Because the way of abiding is realized to be free of conceptual elaborations and the way in which things manifest
to be a process of interdependent connection, the Middle Way tradition is entirely true.

Specific Explanation of the Middle Way Tradition [B]
Identifying Emptiness [1]

The scope of its view is emptiness—
the actuality of negating the two kinds of identity, and an aspect of unqualified negation.

Unqualified Emptiness (*rang stong*) [2]

The basis for emptiness is objects in the phenomenal world, which are also what is to be negated and the basis for such negation.
The way in which these are empty, according to the unqualified interpretation of emptiness, is that they cannot be proven to exist in essence.
If this is analyzed, there are sixteen aspects—of outer, inner, both, emptiness, and so forth—
but these can be subsumed within the four aspects of what is substantial, insubstantial, true nature, and alternate reality.

Qualified Emptiness (*gzhan stong*) [3]

The basis for negation is what is absolute, while the factors to be negated are what is imputed and what is dependent.
The Yogic Practitioners profess that it is "empty of these."
They explain that this can be analyzed into fourteen aspects, which can be subsumed within two.

Main Explanation: Two Aspects of the Lack of Identity [V]

Purpose [A]

The hindrances to perception are the ten distracting concepts;
the remedies that dispel these are the two aspects of lack of identity.

Analysis [B]

Lack of Identity in Phenomena [1]

Key Topic [a]

The more obvious aspect of the lack of identity in phenomena is an issue common to Buddhists
and non-Buddhists alike, and so one should come to a definitive conclusion about it at the outset.

Factor to Be Negated [b]

This is, in essence, similar to a rope being taken for a snake;
there is just the fixation in the ordinary mind that this is something self-justifying that is truly existent.

Purpose of Negating Identity [c]

This is negated because it is the cause for misconstruing things to have identity, which lies at the root of the two obscuring factors.

Philosophical Interpretations [d]

Although the Particularists and Followers of the Sūtras do not have a completely perfect understanding of suchness,

they come to their definitive conclusion on the basis of temporary objects in the phenomenal world.
The rationale is that nothing whatsoever is found through investigation;
for to consider this to mean a lack of true existence is their general tradition.

The Mind Only school's own tradition holds that they realize both aspects of the lack of identity;
but if a follower of the Middle Way evaluates this, because nondual consciousness is held
to be ultimate, there still remains a rudimentary sense of identity in phenomena.

Definitive Understanding through Middle Way Reasoning [e]

Although there are many lines of reasoning in the Middle Way, the tradition of the Exalted One uses five
to usher in certainty concerning the integration of emptiness and interdependent connection.
Candra speaks of two models: once perceived objects are negated,
the proof that they do not exist negates the perceiving subject;
and the logic that a single relative thing is empty means that all phenomena are empty.

Lack of Identity in the Individual [2]
Key Topic [a]

The issue that distinguishes non-Buddhists from Buddhists is that of identity in the individual.

Factor to Be Negated [b]

In essence, this is the instinctual fixation on "I" and "mine."

Purpose of Negating Identity [c]

It is negated because from it comes the sense of "other," from which all opinionated views derive.

Philosophical Interpretations [d]

While there are differences in the way in which realization takes place,
all four philosophical systems bring realization.

Definitive Understanding through Middle Way Reasoning [e]

The five aggregates are not the self, the self does not possess them,
nor do they act as supports one for the other. Some twenty alternatives
are negated by lines of proof such as the reasoning based on the chariot.

In *Distinguishing Center and Limit*, there are ten ways of being wise,
as remedies
to ten ways of believing in identity in the individual. There are many
other such ways of reasoning.

Relevant Issues [3]
Identicalness or Separateness [a]

Because all phenomena lack identity, in essence
these aspects are inseparable. The factors to be negated being true
existence and the "I," or self,
the aspects are assigned as this vis-à-vis that from distinct points of view.

Purpose [b]

The purpose of this is in order to care for two types of people.

Factors to Be Negated [c]

Although the actual factors to be negated cannot possibly be known,
due to confusion on the part of the subjective perceiver, they are imputed
as being perceived as the one and the other.

Valid Cognition [d]

The special attitude that derives from inferential knowledge based
on reasoning

is the primary kind of valid cognition that ascertains what is ultimately the case.
If one summarizes the categories of reasoning that rely on logical arguments,
these are proofs of negation, due to a failure to observe something supportive or an observation of something contradictory.

Authentic Reasoning [e]

The key point of all reasoning that investigates what is ultimately so
is investigation that identifies a basis for attributes and then seeks out
that which does not contradict its essential quality and that which contradicts its particular attributes.
Therefore, the freedom from being unitary or manifold negates any finite essence,
while the negation of production in any of four ways negates particular attributes.
These two models are foremost; the rest are simply secondary.
The root of all of these is found in the homage to the Middle Way.

Specific Middle Way Interpretations [4]
Unqualified Emptiness [a]

In the Autonomist tradition, all substantial things are proven not to truly exist;
emptiness is proven so as to eliminate concepts of fixating on them.
The Consequentialists negate conceptual elaborations but do not try to prove a freedom from elaboration.

Qualified Emptiness [b]

In particular, in the extraordinary tradition of Yogic Practitioners,
it is realized that there is nothing other than mind and that mind does not exist.
The nondual basic space of phenomena is endowed with seven vajra properties.

The heart essence of all ordinary beings and buddhas
is free of elaboration, in no way resembling any identity of an individual.

This is the inseparability of saṃsāra and nirvāṇa, free of the mere lack of identity in the individual,
transcending being manifest or nonmanifest, and even interdependent connection.

Empty of adventitious flaws, it is not empty of unsurpassable qualities.
There is nothing to be removed or added, for it is realized through naturally occurring pure awareness.

It is said that ordinary mortals, śrāvakas, pratyekabuddhas, and beginning bodhisattvas
do not have mastery of the view concerning the buddha nature.
This is not an object of inference, because it is beyond language and concepts.
Since this mode is difficult for any mind other than that of a spiritually advanced being to comprehend,
it has become a topic of controversy, but I will not elaborate here.

Advice Integrating Both Traditions [5]

Having realized the individual methods of the two mainstream traditions,
one integrates them as a single underlying intent, free of the flaws of exaggeration or denigration.
One is endowed with flawless vision concerning the sūtras and tantras.

Mantra Approach [VI]
General Position [A]

In the mantra approach, the interpretation of unqualified emptiness is that the subjective aspect is distinguished as the skillful factor of bliss,
but that there is no difference in the objective aspect as freedom from elaboration.
For the interpretation of qualified emptiness, even the objective aspect is not merely freedom from elaboration;
rather, it is posited to be endowed with the most sublime of manifestations, comparable to divination with a mirror.
Some say that other than the mere freedom from elaboration, because of the skillful methods involved,

the difference is like that between an ordinary fire and one of
sandalwood.

Specific Position: Gargyi Wangpo [B]

In the Middle Way of the mantra approach, the profound unity of bliss and emptiness,
the position of the vajra of enlightened speech, who bears the mark of light,
is that there are four special attributes—the function of the central channel, the skillful means to experience emptiness,
the influence exerted with respect to the ground of being, and the attainment of the kāya of primordial unity.

Summation: The View of Unborn Primordial Unity [VII]

If this were not present as the fundamentally unconditioned nature, viewing it as such would not make it so,
and when emptiness is realized, cause and effect are spontaneously ensured.
Whatever is the ceaseless process of interdependent connection
is itself the supreme seal of unborn primordial unity.

The foregoing constitutes the third part,
concerning a definitive treatment of the view that is the principal factor.

Part 4. Foundations of Spiritual Practice
Impact of Study and Contemplation [I]

The impact of study and contemplation is that of arousing an uncontrived faith
in the teachings and the upholders of the teachings without sectarian bias.
Without falling into any extreme, one conducts oneself with precision[25] concerning the effects of karma.
The excellent speech of the buddhas serves as one's advisor, so that one feels a growing sense of freedom in one's ongoing experience.
Nonetheless, there are the four contemplations that reorient the mind, which are methods from the tradition of pith instructions
that dramatically reorient an ordinary person's mind.

Four Contemplations [II]
Reorienting the Mind Away from This Lifetime [A]
Foundation for Reorientation [1]

The precious support, endowed with eight opportunities and ten endowments,
has great purpose and is difficult to obtain (as determined by cause, result, and analogy).

Identifying Opportunities and Endowments [a]
Great Purpose [b]
Difficulty of Obtaining the Support [c]
Contemplation of Impermanence [2]
Recollection of Death [a]

There are three primary topics: death is certain; when one will die is unknown;
and when death occurs, anything that is not spiritual will be of no avail.
There are secondary considerations: death cannot be prevented, life cannot be extended, and there is never enough time;
the time of death is unpredictable, it happens under many circumstances, and life is fragile;
and death does not allow us to take our companions, body, or wealth.
One recalls death by applying these nine rationales.

Rebirth in Other States [b]

Once one has died, one will be reborn in either of two destinies;
having contemplated the foregoing, one reorients one's mind away from this lifetime.

Reorienting the Mind Away from Saṃsāra [B]
Karma [1]
General Contemplation [a]

Such is the process of karma: it is ineluctable; its results are greatly magnified;
actions not committed have no effect; and the effects of actions committed never expire on their own.

Specific Issues [b]

The degree of gravity is greatly influenced by the focus, intention, underlying support, and actual content of an action—
these bring about results due to complete maturation, results consistent with causes, and governing results.

Saṃsāra [2]
Eight Kinds of Suffering [a]

Birth, aging, illness, death, being separated from what is appealing,
encountering what is unappealing, striving for what one desires and not finding it,
and the suffering of the aggregates that perpetuate saṃsāra: . . .

Three Kinds of Universal Suffering [b]

. . . For everyone, moreover,
there is nothing reliable, nothing satisfying, and this has been going on forever.
Contemplating the three kinds of suffering, the mind reorients itself away from saṃsāra.

Reorienting the Mind Away from Quiescence and Naïve Happiness [C]

Through seven practical instructions concerning cause and effect, the basis for arousing an attitude
of concern for the welfare of others is established by an even-minded attitude and a sense of empathy.
Seeking enlightenment as one's goal, with loving-kindness, great compassion,
and altruistic motivation, one reorients one's mind away from quiescence and naïve happiness.

Reorienting the Mind Away from Dualistic Consciousness [D]

Investigating the significance of the unborn nature of all phenomena
with discernment, one reorients one's mind away from dualistic consciousness.

The foregoing constitutes the fourth part,
concerning a definitive treatment of the four contemplations
that reorient the mind.

This concludes the seventh book,
an analysis of the paths and levels to be traversed,
from The Encompassing of All Knowledge,
also entitled The Precious Treasury of Sublime Teachings:
The Compendium of the Methods of All Spiritual Approaches
and A Treatise That Thoroughly Presents the Three Higher Trainings.

The Higher Training in Sublime Intelligence

Whatever teachings you have heard [3.110b] concerning general objects of knowledge, and profound and extensive topics in particular, it is necessary for you to come to a complete certainty about the significance of all this through conceptualization and investigation; hence, Book 7 concerns the stages of contemplation. This book has four parts, which present: (1) a definitive treatment of the keys for evaluating the teachings; (2) a definitive treatment of provisional and definitive meaning in the three cycles of teachings, the two levels of truth, and interdependent connection; (3) a definitive treatment of the view that is the principal factor; and (4) a definitive treatment of the four contemplations that reorient the mind.

Part 1. Keys to Understanding

I. Sublime Intelligence Deriving from Contemplation
II. Specific Keys to Evaluating the Teachings
  A. Brief Enumeration by Way of Introduction
  B. Extensive Explanation of the Significance of These Keys
    1. Ordinary Keys to Understanding
      a. Provisional and Definitive Meaning
      b. Direct and Indirect Intention
        i. Four Cases of Direct Intention
        ii. Four Cases of Indirect Intention
        iii. Differences between Direct and Indirect Intention
      c. Four Reliances
        i. Relying on the Meaning, Not the Words
        ii. Relying on the Teachings, Not the Individual
        iii. Relying on Timeless Awareness, Not Ordinary Consciousness
        iv. Relying on the Definitive Meaning, Not the Provisional One
      d. Four Logical Principles
    2. Extraordinary Keys to Understanding
      a. Brief Discussion
      b. Extensive Explanation
        i. Six Parameters
        ii. Four Modes

The first part involves two discussions: a general discussion of the way in which one develops the sublime intelligence that derives from contemplation, and a specific explanation of the keys for evaluating the teachings.

Sublime Intelligence Deriving from Contemplation [I]

The source verses state:

> **You come to complete certainty by contemplating the significance of what has been heard.**
> **This consists of an internal dialogue that involves conceptual thinking and investigation.**

That is to say, by using the sublime intelligence that derives from contemplation, you come to complete certainty concerning the significance of the teachings you have heard. This means that, under the circumstances, you reflect thoroughly on the conventional words used and their meanings, eliminating any superfluous indecision through a precise process of examination and investigation. For even though you might understand something in a rough way after having heard it once, this does not bring you the certainty that comes with a definitive conclusion concerning what exactly is meant. It is when you examine each and every word and its meaning, bringing numerous scriptural citations and kinds of reasoning to bear on these, that you authentically arouse in yourself an awareness that entails certainty on a very fundamental level.

As to how this process of contemplation is carried out, it involves what can be called an "internal dialogue," involving both conceptual thinking on a more obvious level and mental investigation on a more subtle level. These are used to evaluate the topics concerning what one needs to know.

The source verses state:

> **Mundane conceptual thought is associated with ordinary mental functioning,**
> **while transcendent thought is associated with sublime intelligence;** [3.111a]
> **a discerning mind engages in precise investigation.**

In this regard, the first stage, termed "internal dialogue as an all-absorbing state of sensation,"[26] consists of conceptual thinking that may be either an ordinary process of thinking about some topic to be understood or a function of sublime intelligence. It is a more obvious state of mind that is simply aware of things in general[27] ("this is a vase," "this is a blanket").[28] If we analyze it further, it may constitute either a more ordinary conceptual process (that is, a mundane process of conceptual thought that entails what is merely ordinary mind), or a transcendent thought process (which entails a sublime intelligence, that of one's reasoning mind engaging with the meaningful experience of the way in which things actually abide).[29]

The second stage, called "discerning internal dialogue," consists of mental investigation that, again, may involve either ordinary thinking about some topic to be understood, or a function of sublime intelligence. It is a more precise state of mind that comes to a definitive conclusion by discerning the state of things more accurately ("this is a well-made vase," "this is a badly made vase," "the color of this blanket is a good one [or a bad one]"). If we analyze it further, the same categories apply as in the preceding case.[30]

Thus, the sublime intelligence that derives from contemplation is aroused by conceptual thinking and mental investigation being applied to the topics of the teachings you have heard.

Specific Keys to Evaluating the Teachings [II]

This more specific explanation has two parts: a brief enumeration by way of introduction, and a more extensive explanation of the significance of these keys.

Brief Enumeration by Way of Introduction [A]

The source verses state:

> **This involves two factors: the keys that are crucial in order to evaluate the teachings**
> **and the treasure chamber of the sacred teachings that are to be evaluated.**
> **The standard processes of evaluation are primarily those of provisional vis-à-vis definitive meaning, direct vis-à-vis indirect intention,**
> **the four reliances, and the four logical principles.** [3.111b]

In terms of the way in which the process of contemplation is carried out, this can be concisely defined to consist of two factors: the tools that are crucial in order to evaluate the teachings (which can be likened to keys) and the sacred teachings that are to be so evaluated (which can be likened to a treasure chamber of precious gems).

As for the first factor, there are tools for evaluation that are ordinary and extraordinary. The ordinary tools are primarily the following: the four aspects of provisional vis-à-vis definitive meaning and direct vis-à-vis indirect intention; the four reliances; and the four logical principles.

Extensive Explanation of the Significance of These Keys [B]

The extensive explanation focuses on two points: the ordinary keys to understanding and the extraordinary ones.

Ordinary Keys to Understanding [1]

There are four topics: provisional vis-à-vis definitive meaning, direct vis-à-vis indirect intention, the four reliances, and the four logical principles.

Provisional and Definitive Meaning [a]

The source verses state:

> **Individuality, the state of an ordinary being, origination and cessation,**
> **the mind-body aggregates and sense fields, and so forth—these are means to gain access to the fundamentally unconditioned nature of reality.**
> **These topics, together with the discussions of them, constitute the relative level of provisional meaning.**

When the things under consideration fall principally within the range of sensory appearances that are well known in one's ordinary perception (for example, one's sense of individuality; the state of ordinary beings; the mind-body aggregates, sense fields, and other components of ordinary experience; and the origin and cessation and the coming and going of these), as means to gain access to the fundamentally unconditioned nature of reality, they are evaluated in categories that can be described, imagined, and expressed, and are presented through the use of some conceptual overlay. Such presentations, along with the scriptures[31] and commentaries that discuss them, are referred to as "the relative level of provisional meaning." According to the *Most Majestic State of Meditative Absorption*:

> Just as when emptiness was spoken of by the Sugata,
> so one understands the specific topics in the discourses on definitive meaning. [3.112a]
> Whichever texts discuss things in terms of an ordinary being, an individual, a person—all these teachings are understood to be provisional in meaning.[32]

And the *Discourse Taught by Akṣayamati*:

> One might ask, "Which discourses are those of definitive meaning, and which are those of provisional meaning?" Whichever discourses present discussions for the purpose of one's engaging in the spiritual path are said to be of "provisional meaning." . . . Whatever discourses explain things in terms of identity, the state of an ordinary being, life force, the "surface level" of perception,[33] a person, an individual, a member of the human race,[34] a human being,[35] the agent of actions, the experiencer of feelings; or use myriad technical terms; or speak of what does not exist as some agent as constituting such an agent—these are called provisional in meaning."[36]

And *In Praise of the Inconceivable Middle Way*:

> Whatever discusses origination and cessation,
> the state of ordinary beings, life force, and so forth,
> that is provisional in meaning—that is on the relative level.[37]

The source verses state:

> **Those texts that present the totally pure avenue to the true nature of phenomena, free of elaboration—**
> **that is, the way in which things actually abide—are definitive in meaning.**
> **Those that simply discuss the purposes for such teachings[38]**
> **are held to be provisional in meaning, but this is not necessarily the case.**

The profound significance of the true nature of all phenomena, free of such elaborations as origination and cessation, can be subsumed within the framework of the three avenues to complete liberation (emptiness, the absence of subtle traits, and the absence of naïve speculation)[39]; or, alternatively, four avenues (the fourth being that of the absence of any overt states of ordinary mind).[40] All such presentations, and those that discuss the significance of the fundamentally unconditioned way in which things abide (which is utterly lucid by nature, beyond all describing, imagining, or expressing), [3.112b] as well as the scriptures and commentaries that discuss these topics, are considered to be what is referred to as "the ultimate level of definitive meaning." According to the *Discourse Taught by Akṣayamati*:

> Whichever discourses present discussions for the purpose of one's engaging with the fruition state are termed those of "definitive meaning." . . . Whichever discourses explain things in terms of emptiness, the absence of subtle traits, the absence of naïve speculation, the absence of any overt states of ordinary mind, nonorigination, nonoccurrence, the absence of any substantiality in things, the lack of identity, the nonexistence of ordinary beings, the nonexistence of life force, the nonexistence of an individual, the nonexistence of any agent, up to and including the nonexistence of any avenue to complete liberation—these are called "definitive in meaning."[41]

And *In Praise of the Inconceivable Middle Way*:

> The emptiness of phenomena
> is presented as "the definitive meaning."[42]

Some cite such passages as the following from the *Highest Continuum*:

> Faintheartedness, belittling lesser beings,
> fixating on what is inauthentic, disparaging what is authentic,
> and egocentric attachment: the Buddha spoke of these five specific faults
> so that those who had them could eliminate them.[43]

Such citations are indeed used to claim that the texts that are provisional in meaning are those that present a purpose for the teachings they contain.

But this is not definitive, for the fact that all teachings are entirely for the purpose of guiding those to be guided would then mean that *all* teachings were provisional in meaning,[44] and all those that anyone holds to be definitive in meaning were nevertheless taught for a purpose.[45]

Generally speaking, the *Discourse Taught by Akṣayamati* states that those discourses are definitive in meaning that speak of seven topics (engagement with the fruition state, ultimate reality, the totally pure state of total enlightenment, the exhaustion of karma and afflictive states, the nonduality of saṃsāra and nirvāṇa, the direct perception of profundity that is difficult to assimilate thoroughly, and mind functioning with certainty[46]), [3.113a] and an eighth set of topics (that is, such topics as the three avenues to complete liberation, the absence of ordinary mental states, nonorigination, nonoccurrence, the absence of any substance, and the lack of identity). The sūtra speaks of discussions dealing with anything else being taken to be provisional in meaning. A parallel discussion of the foregoing eight topics is also found in the *Most Majestic State of Meditative Absorption*.[47]

The authentic way of distinguishing provisional from definitive meaning can also be found in the tantras. Vajrapāṇi, the Lord of Secrets, makes such statements as the following:

> Provisional discussions speak of the *bhaga* of the *karmamudrā*; those that are definitive discuss the transcendent perfection of sublime intelligence—emptiness, . . . On the mundane relative level, there is the "bringing together of the circle of ḍākinīs"; with the definitive meaning, there is also the "bringing together of the circle of ḍākinīs." In the latter case, however, the term "ḍākinīs" is a reference to the thirty-seven factors that contribute to enlightenment;[48] the consolidation of these is called the "circle." These factors are expressions of the emptiness that characterizes dharmakāya.[49]

These methods will be dealt with in the next section.[50]

Direct and Indirect Intention [b]

The four cases each of direct and indirect intention are explained in three ways:[51] the four cases of direct intention, the four cases of indirect intention, and the distinction between these two groups.

Four Cases of Direct Intention [i]

The source verses state:

> **Words can have different implications,[52] but the method for interpreting them reveals that there is no contradiction.**
> **Because those to be guided are guided by relying on these methods,**
> **[one considers] the underlying motive, the function, and the seeming incompatibility.**
> **The four cases of direct intention are those concerned with equalness, implied issues,**
> **eventualities, and the attitudes of individuals.**

There are cases in which some inference can be made that is different from a more obvious explanation—from how one understands the words and their meanings. These two aspects, the actual wording and its hidden meaning, can be revealed, through a single method of interpreting them, not to be in contradiction. Because many who are to be guided are guided by the actual wording on which they rely, a teaching is said to be "intentionally interpretable" when it meets three criteria:

1) the underlying motive involves some other meaning;[53]

2) the function is that of those to be guided being guided by such a method; [3.113b] and

3) it seems to involve scripture and reasoning incompatible with the actual wording per se, and so undermine it.

There are four cases:

1) Direct intention concerned with equalness includes such statements as, "At that point I became the tathāgata Vipaśyin, . . ."[54] which takes into consideration equalness with respect to dharmakāya.[55]

2) Direct intention concerned with implied issues includes such statements as, "All phenomena are such that they have no finite essence per se," which takes into consideration the three ways in which things have no finite essence.[56] That is to say:

(a) Things that are imputed[57] have no finite essence with respect to their characteristics, because they definitely cannot be found to exist in actual fact.[58]

(b) Things that are dependent[59] have no finite essence with respect to origination,[60] because they cannot be found to originate through any of four alternative processes:[61]

- things are not produced from themselves, because there is a substantial contradiction in the product and the producer being simultaneous;
- things are not produced from other things, because nothing "other," if examined critically, can be found to exist in and of itself;
- things cannot be found to be produced from both themselves and other things, for this also involves a substantial contradiction;[62] and
- things being produced without cause is an impossibility.[63]

However, the *seeming* origination and so forth of all that manifests as it does is a process of interdependent connection, simply as is an illusion or a dream, and so things are apparent yet nonexistent. The sūtra *Manifest Adornment of Timeless Awareness* states:

> O Mañjuśrī, a dream manifests without being something that exists; similarly, all phenomena manifest without being things that exist. . . .[64]

It continues in the same vein, using the analogies of an illusion, a mirage, a fata morgana, a reflection of the moon in water, a reflection in a mirror, and a phantom.

(c) As for the absolute,[65] this has no finite essence in any ultimate sense,[66] for given that this constitutes ultimate reality, what it epitomizes has no finite essence defined by such conceptual elaborations as "pure" or "impure." As the sūtra *Definitive Commentary on Enlightened Intent* states:

> Taking into consideration that things are nonexistent in their very essence with respect to their characteristics, that things are nonexistent in their very essence with respect to origination, and that there is nothing that ultimately exists in its very essence, I have taught, "All phenomena do not exist in their very essence."[67]

3) Direct intention concerned with eventualities [3.114a] includes such statements as, "By simply recalling the name of the tathāgata Vimalacandraprabha, you will attain buddhahood." While the attainment will not come from that alone, one will awaken to buddhahood at some point after pursuing spiritual development initiated by that act of recall.

4) Direct intention concerned with the attitudes of individuals includes such statements as those that disparage discipline while extolling generosity, spoken to those who are obsessed with the opinion that discipline is an absolute principle in its own right.

Four Cases of Indirect Intention [ii]

The source verses state:

> **The means to educate others that are not definitive yet capable of leading them**
> **are with respect to śrāvakas, the three aspects of the very essence of things, the overcoming of flaws,**
> **and the profundity of what is expressed. There are four cases of indirect intention,**
> **because they are concerned, respectively, with edification, characteristics, remedies, and transformation.**

The words that express ideas may not be definitive but may nevertheless be used in consideration of their simply being capable of providing guidance. As a means of educating those to be guided, teachings may be spoken using words with a certain connotation. This is known as "indirect intention." In this regard, there are four cases of such intention—that which is concerned with edification and so forth—because they are concerned, respectively, with those who belong to the śrāvaka type, with the three aspects of the very essence of things, with the overcoming of flaws, and with the profundity of what is expressed.

1) As for indirect intention concerned with edification, some who are of the śrāvaka type are daunted by emptiness and so do not follow the Mahāyāna approach. In order for them to embark on it, the Buddha said "Forms exist"; while those listening understood by this that these can actually be proven to exist and so embarked on the approach, the intention of the one explaining this was that these "exist" in the way that dream images do.

2) As for indirect intention concerned with characteristics, in order that people come to understand the way in which things actually abide, without any finite essence per se, the Buddha said, for example, "All phenomena are such that they have no finite essence per se." For those who held that phenomena do not exist, he spoke of nonexistence in consideration of what is

imputed, while for those who held that they do exist, he spoke of existence in consideration of what is absolute.

3) As an example of indirect intention concerned with remedies, in consideration of some who felt, "Śākyamuni has such a small stature and short life span that he is inferior to other teachers," [3.114b] the Buddha said, "At that point I became the tathāgata Vairocana." Those hearing this understood the form manifestations of these two to be equal, while the intention of the one explaining this was of three considerations—equality in the perfection of spiritual development, equality in the attainment of dharmakāya, and equality in the ensuring of benefit for beings. As the *Treasury of Abhidharma* states:

> All buddhas are equal in their spiritual development,
> in dharmakāya, and in their conduct to benefit beings,
> but not on account of their life spans,
> their family background, or their physical stature.[68]

4) Indirect intention concerning transformation refers to cases in which something very difficult to fathom was taught in order to remove the flaw of thinking, "This dharma is so easy to understand that it must be inferior to other systems." To give an example, in *Didactic Aphorisms* we read the following:

> Having slain the father and mother,
> and vanquished the ruler and the two ritually pure ones,
> as well as the kingdom and subjects,
> that person who has done so becomes purity itself.[69]

In this passage, the two factors of compulsion and perpetuation[70]—because they contribute to the patterning that sustains saṃsāra—are the "father" and "mother." The basis of all ordinary experience,[71] serving as the support or basis for myriad habitual patterns, is the "ruler." The "two ritually pure ones" are the brahmin who believes in the reality of the perishable mind-body aggregates and the spiritual practitioner who believes that personal rules of discipline and deportment are absolute principles in their own right. The eight avenues of consciousness[72]—the inner aspects of the sense fields[73] and the dualistic consciousness of subject and object they entail—are what is meant by "as well as the kingdom and subjects."

To "vanquish" them—that is, to become purified of them—is to awaken to buddhahood.

Differences between Direct and Indirect Intention [iii]

The source verses state:

> **Direct intention simply plants the idea in the mind; it does not depend**
> **on the other person; it is explained that indirect intention does depend.**

These two—direct and indirect intention—are essentially identical, with certain differences, so that occasionally they are in accord. But if we make a distinction, we may cite from *Explanatory Essays Commenting on the "Compendium of the Supreme Spiritual Approach,"* which gives the following explanation:

> Direct intention simply plants the idea in the mind; [3.115a] it is not asserted to depend on the other person's absorbing what has been said;[74] indirect intention depends on the other person's absorbing what has been said.[75]

In this regard, the omniscient Drimé Özer says:[76]

> "Direct intention" refers to cases that depend on some circumstance or another, so that the explanations follow suit, although they do not depend on whether the other person is influenced or not. The term "intention" is used because when, for example, others ask about the issue at hand, whatever meanings are not fully understood are left within the underlying basis of that intention.
>
> "Indirect intention" refers to cases in which , in order to benefit others, teachings take place in accord with someone's perceptions, using a somewhat oblique approach. This is because the speaker speaks, the other person's understanding is awakened, and this message serves as a basis for understanding of other topics to be further perfected, while nevertheless falling shy of being a falsehood.[77]

Four Reliances [c]

The term "reliance" means that one can place one's complete trust and confidence in the object in question.[78] In this regard, we read such passages as the following from the *Discourse on the Supreme Passing Beyond Sorrow*:

> O monks, you should focus on four things. What are these four? To focus on the teachings and not focus on the individual; to focus on the meaning and not focus on the words; to focus on timeless awareness and not focus on ordinary consciousness; and to focus on the definitive meaning and not focus on the meaning that guides.[79] These four things are things to be realized; they are not four kinds of spiritual individuals.[80]

This theme is developed very extensively in the *Discourse Taught by Akṣayamati*.

Relying on the Meaning, Not the Words [i]

Of these four, the source verses refer to the first as follows:

> **Rely on the meaning, which makes evident the omniscient state of timeless awareness;**
> **do not rely on the words and letters that are conventional terms and designations.**

The "meaning" refers in general to the presentations of factors that contribute to the transcendent state of enlightenment and more particularly to the path of the complete purity of the three focal points (and the fruition it entails) [3.115b]—in brief, the extraordinary methods that make fully evident the completely omniscient state of timeless awareness. It is on this meaning that one should rely.

Mundane terms and conventional designations, ordinary fields of knowledge, and so forth, up to and including the eighty-four thousand collections of the dharma—to follow after the mere terms and words and letters is of little consequence, and so one should not rely on these.

Relying on the Teachings, Not the Individual [ii]

The source verses state:

> **Rely on the teachings concerning unmistaken view and conduct;**
> **do not rely on an individual's family, ancestry, fame, or wealth.**

There are individuals who embody unmistaken view and conduct with respect to the causes and effects of the completely refined state of enlightenment and the unenlightened state of all-consuming afflictive states and who in particular have thoroughly assimilated the methods of the Middle Way, or Madhyamaka, school in the Mahāyāna approach. It is on the fact that they are not in conflict with the mainstream tradition of the Buddhadharma that one should rely.

These individuals may be from great families of aristocracy; they may be descended from great lineages of noble ancestry; they may enjoy great fame as recognized incarnate teachers, or erudite scholars, or accomplished masters; they may be very wealthy, with retinue and students and material possessions. However, while any of these may be the case, if these individuals contradict the dharma in general in their view and conduct, or if in particular they are not in accord with the Mahāyāna tradition, one should not rely on an individual's more superficial appeal.

Relying on Timeless Awareness, Not Ordinary Consciousness [iii]

The source verses state:

> **Rely on timeless awareness, which is free of elaboration, without identity, and the very essence of being;**
> **do not rely on ordinary consciousness, which is a mind fixated on characteristics and concepts.**

Timeless awareness entails (a) understanding that the way in which phenomena actually abide is, from the ultimate perspective, free of all limitations imposed by elaborations of origination, cessation, and so forth; (b) realization of the nonexistence of the two kinds of identity;[81] and (c) unerring knowledge of *sugatagarbha*[82] as utter lucidity, the way in which things actually abide, beyond any context of speculative value judgments.[83] It is on this awareness that one should rely.

Ordinary consciousness entails (a) belief that what one immediately perceives constitutes something truly existent; (b) conceptualization in terms of characteristics, such as the sense of personal identity and the mind-body aggregates; and (c) mental states that are conditioned, for example, [3.116a] by attitudes of naïvely fixating on the pleasures of the senses. One should not rely on such consciousness.

Relying on the Definitive Meaning, Not the Provisional One [iv]

The source verses state:

> **Rely on the definitive meaning, with its profound and vast implications;**
> **do not rely on the provisional meaning that is temporarily expedient.**

The definitive meaning is found in those teachings that go far beyond one's immediate perceptions, or intellectual speculation, or the scope of śrāvakas and pratyekabuddhas and that deal with profound and vast topics that fall within the scope of those of the very highest acumen, which is inconceivable to our ordinary way of thinking. It is this meaning that one should rely on.

Those teachings that arouse a sense of disenchantment with saṃsāra; that deal with the will to be free[84] as defined in the various spiritual approaches; that present things in terms of substantial versus nominal existence, or as "mind only," or as an empty state of nothingness—these are provisional teachings that are presented as temporary expedients, and so one should not rely on them.

Four Logical Principles [d]

The source verses state:

> **In mundane contexts, things are established through dependent relationships; the sense faculties, objects, avenues of consciousness, and so forth,**
> **perform functions with respect to specific objects but do not perform these with respect to other aspects of experience;**

there is valid cognition based on inference, on direct experience, or on scriptural authority;
and all phenomena can be found always to have their common and individual characteristics:
These are known, respectively, as the logical principle of dependent relationships, that of the performance of functions,
that of establishing what is reasonable, and that of the nature of things.

The term "logical principle"[85] refers here to what is logical and valid if one examines what is commonly accepted in mundane contexts to be proven as authentic purely on the conventional level. There are four cases of such principles:

(1) The first is the establishment of things through dependent relationships. It is logical that a seedling occurs in dependence on there being a seed; it is logical that formative factors and the other links of interdependent connection occur in dependence on there being ignorance;[86] and while visual consciousness does not occur by its own nature, it is logical that it occurs in dependence on there being both the visual faculty and the forms that are the sense objects involved. Such cases are examples of "the logical principle of dependent relationships."

(2) In the second case, the sense faculties, sense objects, avenues of consciousness, and so forth, contribute to performing the particular function of perceiving a specific kind of object and do not perform this with respect to anything else. Thus, it is logical that if visual consciousness occurs, [3.116b] it performs the function of seeing forms but is not appropriate for the hearing of sounds. In the case of the visual faculty, moreover, it is suitable to perform the function of generating visual consciousness but not suitable for generating auditory or other kinds of consciousness. It is logical for grains of barley to produce barley but not logical that they produce buckwheat or millet or some other grain. Such cases are examples of "the logical principle of the performance of functions."

(3) The third case may involve valid cognition based on inference, such as knowing that there is a fire from the fact that there is smoke, or realizing that there is water from the presence of water fowl; valid cognition based on the direct experience of what is perceived by the six avenues of ordinary consciousness or the mind of an advanced spiritual practitioner; or valid cognition based on scriptural authority—the infallible words spoken from

the mouth of a buddha. These are cases of "the logical principle of what is validly cognized," "the logical principle of establishing what is reasonable."

(4) As for the fourth case, it is logical for water to flow downhill (but not logical that it flow uphill), for the sun to rise in the east, for earth to be solid, for water to be wet, for fire to be hot, for wind to be motile, and so forth. The fact that phenomena are such that they have characteristics in common (including being empty and lacking any identity), as well as their individual ones, and are known to continue always to be that way by their specific natures is termed "the principle of the nature of things."

These successive topics are known as the "four logical principles." The foregoing discussion has been summarized on the basis of the source verses.

Extraordinary Keys to Understanding [2]

The explanation of the extraordinary methods for evaluating the profound meaning in the secret mantra approach is twofold: a brief discussion and a more extensive explanation.

Brief Discussion [a]

The source verses state:

> **The extraordinary approach of secret mantra is evaluated**
> **through six parameters and four modes.**

One could never arrive at a definitive conclusion concerning the definitive secrets of the extraordinary secret mantra approach of the Vajrayāna with the more superficial scriptural authority and reasoning of intellectuals; rather, these secrets are to be realized through six parameters and four modes.

Extensive Explanation [b]

The explanation is of both the six parameters and the four modes.[87]

Six Parameters [i]

The source verses state:

Given the presence or absence of a fortunate capacity regarding reality,
a single vajra word conveys distinct meanings. [3.117a]
Therefore, the provisional meaning is found in the stage of development and its ancillaries;
the definitive meaning lies in both the causal aspect of tantra and the stage of completion.

In this regard, as the source tantra of the Kālacakra cycle states:

> The language of what is intended to be interpreted, and likewise what is not;
> what is to be taken literally, and likewise what is not;
> the provisional meaning and the definitive meaning:
> tantras are characterized by six parameters.[88]

Which is to say, the vajra words[89] of the tantras, which plumb such profound depths, are embraced within these six parameters.

The first pair is that of provisional vis-à-vis definitive meaning. Out of consideration of the fact that some have the fortunate capacity to realize the significance of the reality of suchness itself, while others do not, a single tantra of vajra words conveys distinct meanings.

Of these, the provisional meaning is found in the methods for engaging on the inner level of spiritual practice—colored sand maṇḍalas, offerings, symbols, ritual hand gestures, fire rituals, development stage practice, practices to carry out specific activities, and so forth.

The definitive meaning lies in the presentations of the causal aspect of tantra[90] as the true way of abiding and the completion stage of practice.[91] These are found in the sources that discuss the control of subtle channels, subtle energies, and bodhicitta;[92] or the "universal ground"[93] (that is, the way in which mind truly abides, utterly lucid by nature), the buddha nature, the sublimely unchanging state of mahāmudrā.[94] To cite, for example, from the *Hevajra Tantra*:

> Supreme and timeless awareness abides in the body.
> All ordinary concepts have been truly eliminated.
> This is what permeates all things.
> Although it abides in the body, it is not produced by the body.[95]

The source verses state:

> **A single meaning treated by different and seemingly contradictory statements**
> **is a case of explanation requiring interpretation, in which the meaning being expressed depends on the underlying intent.**
> **Where it does not depend on this, one understands the presentation directly; this is explanation that does not require interpretation. These are two more parameters.**

(A) With respect to a single topic of development stage practice, there may be different vajra words that seem to be making contradictory statements about that topic. The meaning being expressed must be understood in relation to the underlying intent, and so this is "explanation requiring interpretation." [3.117b]

Alternatively, different intended meanings can be imbedded in a single vajra word. When this approach is adopted, there is interpretation with respect to time frame, interpretation with respect to implied meaning, and interpretation with respect to understanding.

(i) The first case is, for example, the statement

> In a single instant there is perfect buddhahood.[96]

Here the intention concerns something that will occur at some future point in time.

(ii) The second case is, for example, the lines from the tantra *Supreme Illusion*:

> Having kidnapped her from all the buddhas,
> enjoy the maiden born of the sublime deity.[97]

Here the intention is that one should constantly be experiencing emptiness endowed with the most sublime of all distinct manifestations[98]—Prajñāpāramitā, the feminine principle that embodies the transcendent perfection of sublime intelligence, the mother of all buddhas[99]—the nature of which is like that of a diviner.[100]

(iii) The third case is, for example, like the passage from the *Hevajra Tantra*, which reads:

> You should slay living beings. . . .[101]

Here the intention is that one should "slay" the fixation on personal identity that is referred to here by the name of the supreme subtle energy that sustains life force.

(B) In cases in which the meaning being expressed does not depend on the underlying intent but is clearly understood simply through the direct presentation, there is "explanation that does not require interpretation." For example, there are the statements:

> You should not slay living beings.
> You should not speak false words.[102]

The source verses state:

> **Descriptions of maṇḍalas and other topics in well-known language are to be taken literally;**
> **those that use uncommon language and are bound up in symbolism are not to be taken literally.**
> **Since the words and meanings do not fall outside the foregoing, they are the six parameters.**

Topics and terms that are described in language that is well known in mundane treatises and other such sources—ceremonies involving maṇḍalas, fire rituals, tormas, and so forth—are to be taken literally as stated. Those that use language not commonly found in mundane treatises—the secret language of tathāgatas—and that are bound up in symbolism are not to be taken literally; for example, when terms such as *koṭākhyāḥ* are used in naming the ten aspects of subtle energy, or when the tantra the *Heart Essence of Secrets* refers to the processes of union and release as the Sanskrit vowels and consonants, respectively.[103]

Since the foregoing principles are such that all words and meanings found in the secret approach do not fall outside them, [3.118a] they are referred to as the "six parameters."

Four Modes [ii]

These modes are discussed in the tantra *Compendium of the Vajra of Timeless Awareness* as the four kinds of explanation—the literal meaning, the shared meaning, the hidden meaning, and the consummate meaning.[104]

(A) The source verses state:

> **The mere reading word by word is the literal meaning.**

An explanation that is based on the mere reading of a text word by word,[105] arranged in the same way that one would employ for a text on grammar or logic, is said to be "the literal meaning," or what the *Galpo*[106] refers to as "the meaning of the words."

(B) The source verses state:

> **The shared meaning concerns the alleviating of misgivings concerning the sūtra tradition and others, and the stage of development.**

The shared meaning is concerned with three situations:

(i) In the first situation, any misgivings one had at following the sūtra tradition are alleviated. Suppose someone were to feel misgivings and think, "This is not good. Instead of following such a path as the inner level of the secret approach,[107] which is so straightforward and swift, I am following the sūtra tradition, or that of kriyā and carya."[108] The "shared meaning" would then be to point out that these latter are springboards to that path and that even in the sūtras we find such passages as:

> For those who are endowed with supreme skillful means,
> afflictive states become the supports of enlightenment.[109]

That is to say, even the sūtra tradition and others accept that, if one is of sharp acumen and endowed with an extraordinary understanding of skillful means, that very path can be straightforward and swift, so that a single, very powerful act in one's spiritual practice can ensure the accelerated development that otherwise would have taken many eons.

(ii) In the second situation, any misgivings one felt at following the inner level of the secret approach are alleviated. Suppose someone were to feel misgivings and think, "In this inner approach, one's conduct is like that of a pig or a dog, with no concern for impurity versus cleanliness, or for such things as bathing and ritual purity. Things such as union and release are like the dogma of those with extreme views, who profess that harmful actions are somehow spiritual." The response would then be to point out that one engages in this conduct with the thought, "This is to eliminate my fixations," for if one has not eliminated such fixations as those with impurity versus cleanliness, one cannot realize the significance of the true nature of phenomena; this is something accepted even in the sūtra tradition. Furthermore, as in the cases of the slaying of the evil one with the spear or the enjoyment of the captain's daughter,[110] due to one's having a virtuous mind, even if one engages in union and release, one will not be sullied by any flaw; rather, one's merit will be increased immeasurably. This, too, is something accepted even in the sūtra tradition. This is the "shared meaning" because these are common guidelines of training.[111] [3.118b]

(iii) In the third situation, the shared meaning for practitioners of the stage of development lies in those factors that are connected with the development stage—such as meditation on immeasurable mansions as supports and deities as what is supported within these. This is the "shared meaning" because these are guidelines of training that are common to the stages of both development and completion.[112]

(C) The source verses state:

> **The teachings on desire are hidden, relative truth is hidden,**
> **and the higher, middling, and lesser degrees with respect to what**
> **lies at the core are hidden meaning.**

Because the presentations of karmamudrā, ceremonies involving sexual union, and so forth, are unsuitable for public exposure, the teachings on desire are hidden. The process of "self-consecration"[113]—the completion stage practices involving subtle channels, subtle energies, and bindu, are cases of the hidden meaning of relative truth. Generally speaking, these teachings are "hidden" because they constitute what is comparable to the very core of something since they bring one to the central position between dualistic extremes. In this regard, the meaning of higher, middling, and lesser degrees with respect to what lies at the core is as explained previously.[114]

(D) The source verses state:

> **The path of utter lucidity and the fruition state of primordial unity**
> **constitute the consummate meaning. These four modes can be differentiated**
> **from a single vajra word, in accord with progressive levels of acumen.**

Serving to authenticate the foregoing is the consummation of the path of the completion stage that focuses on utter lucidity and the consummation of the fruition state (which is the realization of the primordial unity of the two levels of truth).[115]

All four of these modes need to be clearly differentiated in even a single vajra word, in accord with the levels of peoples' acumen, from greater to lesser. These are, therefore, referred to as "the four modes of explanation."

Lacking these foregoing keynote instructions,[116] no matter how meticulous one's thinking and mental investigation, one will not be capable of developing an authentic state of sublime intelligence;[117] whereas in having access to them, if one applies them to the techniques employed in the sūtras and tantras, this will arouse in one the flawless sublime intelligence that derives from contemplation.

The foregoing constitutes the commentary on the first part,
concerning a definitive treatment of the keys
for evaluating the teachings.

Part 2. Understanding Truth and Meaning

· · · ·

The second part involves three discussions: an investigation of provisional and definitive meaning in the three cycles of teaching; an investigation of the two levels of truth; and an investigation of the process of interdependent connection.

Provisional and Definitive Meaning in the Three Cycles of Teachings [I]

The first investigation is twofold: a general presentation and a specific and detailed analysis.

General Discussion [A]

The source verses state:

> **The principal topics for evaluation are the three cycles of the sacred dharma.** [3.119a]

The principal topics that are to be evaluated with the foregoing means for evaluating the teachings constitute the treasure house of the precious dharma, what is known in the Mahāyāna tradition as the "three cycles of the Buddha's word."

In this regard, from among the words of the Buddha, a clear classification of these three cycles is found in the sūtra *Definitive Commentary on Enlightened Intent*, which speaks of the first cycle being concerned with the Four Truths, the intermediate cycle with the absence of characteristics, and the final with a thorough and precise analysis of reality. *Expansive Gem* merely refers to them in passing,[118] while the sūtra the *Discourse Requested by Dhāraṇīśvararāja* speaks of them as the mode of the Four Truths, that of emptiness, and that of the very heart of attaining the state of suchness.[119] In the *Highest Continuum*, Lord Maitreya uses the terms "bringing the world to the path of peace," "bringing complete spiritual maturity," and "uttering prophecies."[120]

The exalted Nāgārjuna refers to the first cycle as teaching on identity, the intermediate as teaching on the lack of identity, and the final as undermining all bases for dogmas. In commenting on the significance of such terminology, the master Āryadeva states that the first cycle undermines all that is not conducive to spiritual merit, the intermediate cycle undermines the [false] sense of identity, and the final cycle undermines all dogmas.

As for the ways of analyzing these as provisional or definitive, let us consider the characteristics in general of provisional and definitive sūtras. As for the characteristics of a sūtra containing provisional meaning, it is a sūtra that principally teaches on the relative level of truth, which serves as a means to ensure that the path to the definitive state of excellence can arise in the experience of those who are to be guided along any of the three spiritual approaches.[121] As for the characteristics of a sūtra containing definitive meaning, it is a sūtra that principally teaches on the ultimate level of truth, so that the few to be guided who can patiently accept its profound meaning can attain nirvāṇa that is not defined by extremes,[122] by meditating on the path to definitive excellence.

The classification of these within the three cycles of teachings is twofold: (A) how this is found in the Buddha's word [3.119b] and (B) how this is found in the commentaries on his enlightened intent.[123]

(A) In the first place, according to the *Definitive Commentary on Enlightened Intent*:

> O transcendent and accomplished conqueror, at the deer park of Ṛṣipatana in the region of Varāṇasī, you first turned the wheel of the dharma, presenting the Four Truths of spiritually advanced beings[124] to those who had authentically embraced this spiritual approach. This cycle of teachings is amazing and marvelous, for you turned the wheel in an excellent manner and in a way that had not been done in this world previously by anyone, whether a god or a human being. Nevertheless, this wheel of dharma that you turned, O transcendent and accomplished conqueror, is still surpassable, is for the shorter term, is provisional in meaning, and is a context that is open to debate.
>
> Then, O transcendent and accomplished conqueror, beginning with the fact that phenomena have no finite essence, beginning with the facts that they have no origination, that they have no cessation, that they are forever a state of peace, and that they are by nature nirvāṇa, you turned the wheel of dharma a second time, by way of speaking about emptiness to those who had authentically embraced the Mahāyāna approach. This cycle is yet more amazing and marvelous; nevertheless, this wheel of dharma

that you turned, O transcendent and accomplished conqueror, is still surpassable, is for the shorter term, is provisional in meaning, and is a context that is open to debate.

Then, O transcendent and accomplished conqueror, beginning with the fact that phenomena have no finite essence, beginning with the facts that they have no origination, that they have no cessation, that they are forever a state of peace, and that they are by nature nirvāṇa, you turned the wheel of dharma a third time, concerning a thorough and precise analysis of reality, to those who had authentically embraced all spiritual approaches. This cycle is exceedingly amazing and marvelous; this wheel of dharma that you turned, O transcendent and accomplished conqueror, is unsurpassable, is not for the shorter term, is definitive in meaning, and is not a context that is open to debate.[125] [3.120a]

And in the *Discourse Requested by Dhāraṇīśvararāja*:

O children of spiritual heritage, it is thus: Suppose, for example, that someone skilled in the knowledge of gemstones, who knows how to refine them, should take from among such precious stones one that is still totally untreated. He dips it in heavily salted water and rubs it with a piece of haircloth, and so treats it thoroughly. But he does not abandon his efforts with this alone, for following that he dips it in a strong broth of foodstuffs and rubs it with woolen cloth, and so treats it thoroughly. But he does not abandon his efforts with this alone, for following that he dips it in a powerful medicinal solution and rubs it with fine silk and so treats it thoroughly. Once it is totally treated and free of all blemishes, it can then be described as a great specimen of a gemstone.

O children of spiritual heritage, in a similar way the Tathāgata, knowing the totally impure condition of ordinary beings, uses talk of impermanence, suffering, the nonexistence of identity, and uncleanness to arouse dissatisfaction in those beings who take delight in saṃsāra and to cause them to engage in the discipline that is the dharma of spiritually advanced beings. But the

> Tathāgata does not abandon his efforts with this alone, for following that he uses talk of emptiness, and the nonexistence of subtle traits, and the absence of speculation[126] to cause them to realize the ways of the tathāgatas. But once more the Tathāgata does not abandon his efforts with this alone, for following that he uses talk that constitutes the cycle of nonregression[127] and talk of the complete purity of the three focal points to cause these ordinary beings, whose fundamental temperaments are so various, to engage in the scope of the tathāgatas.[128]

(B) In the second place, the foremost among those skilled at commenting on the Buddha's enlightened intent[129] is his regent Maitreya, who made the following comments on the ultimate meaning of the sūtra teachings:[130] [3.120b]

Initially the teachings are for the purpose of using discussions that are discouraging to urge those to be guided who are fascinated with saṃsāra to enter the path to peace; next, of using discussions of emptiness to completely mature them into the Mahāyāna approach; and finally, of using discussions from the cycle that ensures no regression[131] to cause them to embrace the scope of the tathāgatas and obtain the supreme prophecy.[132] In one of his synopses, the exalted Asaṅga cites from the *Definitive Commentary on Enlightened Intent* to establish that the final cycle of teachings constitutes the consummate level of definitive meaning,[133] and Vasubandhu and others are in agreement with this. While Asaṅga and his brother,[134] however, do not state that the intermediate cycle of teachings is provisional in meaning, in the source *Reasoning for a Detailed Explanation* and its commentary, it is explicitly stated to be definitive in meaning.[135] The great spiritual guide Dharmapāla, in his *Decision concerning Conscious Awareness*,[136] explains that both of these cycles concern the definitive meaning of the teachings.

The exalted Nāgārjuna considers the three stages of refinement referred to in the *Discourse Requested by Dhāraṇīśvararāja* to be from the point of view of definitive meaning, and Āryadeva concurs with this. Among Tibetan teachers, there should be no one who does not agree that this treatment is in accord with the three stages of beginning, middle, and end found in the *Definitive Commentary on Enlightened Intent*, for in fact such is actually the case.[137] Those who upheld the genuine lineage of Maitreya and composed commentaries on these teachings[138] in later times did not contravene this tradition, while Candra,[139] in commenting on Nāgārjuna's treatise, did not employ the model of three cycles—initial, intermediate, and final—but simply used the analysis on the basis of provisional vis-à-vis definitive meaning as found in the *Discourse Taught by Akṣayamati.*[140] It would seem that—due to a failure to examine accurately the meaning of the underlying intent of this source—there have occurred cases of Tibetan teachers indulging in a lot of nonsense concerning two cycles (that is, the intermediate and the final), as to which is provisional and which definitive, and which is "higher" or "lower" than the other. In this regard, as was mentioned earlier,[141] this sūtra speaks of eight topics that distinguish provisional from definitive meaning. The others[142] apply equally to both the intermediate and final cycles of teachings as topics of definitive meaning; [3.121a] as for the eighth topic, however—that of the lack of identity—Candrakīrti assigns as the definitive meaning the mere fact that things are empty of both kinds of identity,[143] while Asaṅga, his brother, and their followers analyze this point more precisely and thoroughly, for the point here is that of the lack of any such identity as is construed by spiritually immature people. As the *Definitive Commentary on Enlightened Intent* states:

> It would be inappropriate to conceive of things in terms of identity;
> I have not taught this to spiritually immature people.[144]

And in *Aṅgulimālā* we read such passages as the following:

> Even though the transcendent and accomplished conquerors investigate all phenomena assiduously, a self in the mundane sense, neither something about the size of one's thumb,[145] . . . nor anything that can be described as "it is like this" is found by any of all the buddhas, or by any of all the śrāvakas, and once they have awakened to manifest buddhahood, they explain this fact to living beings.[146]

And in the *Journey to Śrī Laṅka*:

> Teaching concerning the buddha nature [*tathāgatagarbha*] is not equivalent to theories that those who hold extreme views entertain concerning self-identity[147] . . . [bodhisattvas] are not obsessed with self-identity.[148]

With a definitive conclusion having been reached concerning the significance of the foregoing citations, it is shown that the intermediate and final cycles of teaching are equally definitive in meaning, with the distinction that the former concerns the definitive meaning that puts an end to conceptual elaborations in the shorter term, while the latter concerns that which reveals the true way of abiding in the far-reaching sense.

Specific and Detailed Analysis [B]

This specific and detailed analysis includes five topics: the common tradition; the tradition of proponents of things having no finite essence;[149] the tradition of Yogic Practitioners;[150] the connection with the explanations of the Exalted One; and the negation of incorrect opinions concerning provisional meaning and the establishment of a single enlightened intent.

Common Tradition [1]

The source verses state:

> **All agree that the first cycle is provisional in meaning.**

Concerning the first cycle of the Buddha's teachings, all proponents of the Mahāyāna approach agree in professing that it teaches largely on the level of provisional meaning, for they classify it from the point of view of its being primarily concerned with what is relatively valid.

Tradition of Proponents of Things Having No Finite Essence [2]

The source verses state:

> **Proponents of things having no finite essence opine,**
> **"The intermediate cycle is primarily definitive in meaning,**
> **the final one largely provisional."** [3.121b]
> **They have no actual scriptural authority for this, only proving**
> **their rationale through reasoning.**

Proponents of things having no finite essence are of the opinion, "The intermediate cycle is the consummate degree of definitive meaning, while the final cycle presents primarily what is provisionally meaningful." There is no actual scriptural authority found in the sūtras that makes such an obvious distinction; they prove their rationale through reasoning, using only the most general scriptural citations that distinguish provisional from definitive meaning.

Tradition of Yogic Practitioners [3]

The source verses state:

> **"The intermediate cycle, putting an end to elaborations,**
> **is definitively meaningful in the shorter term;**
> **the final cycle, bringing a definitive conclusion concerning what is ultimate, is definitively meaningful**
> **in the far-reaching sense." So says the tradition of Yogic Practitioners.**
> **Their scriptural authority is found in the distinctions made by the Victorious One himself,**
> **and the further distinctions made by the tradition of the prophesied exalted one, who attained the third level of realization.**
> **The reasoning is found by applying the example of refining a gem and so forth.**
> **Rangjung, Dolpo, Drimé Özer, and others**
> **primarily accept this latter interpretation, others the former.**

The intermediate cycle of teachings—because it puts an end to the conceptual elaborations of thinking of the view in terms of absolute principles—is concerned with definitive meaning in the shorter term; while the final cycle—because it clearly brings a definitive conclusion that the true way in which things abide is that of individual self-knowing timeless awareness—is concerned with definitive meaning in the far-reaching sense. Such statements are found in the mainstream tradition of Yogic Practitioners, or Yogācāra.

Their scriptural authorities, as cited previously, are those conferred by the Victorious One himself,[151] making such distinctions in his discourses. In addition, in the *Discourse of the Great Drum* we read the following:

> Any and all those discourses that teach on emptiness should be understood to be intentionally interpretable, while such unsurpassable discourses as this one should be understood to be explanations that do not require interpretation.[152]

As this passage illustrates, the modes of provisional and definitive meaning are analyzed very clearly, over and over again, in the sūtras that teach on the buddha nature.

In addition, the foregoing is the tradition of one who codified the distinction between provisional and definitive meaning—the exalted Asaṅga, whose coming was prophesied and who had attained the third level of realization—and his brother.[153] [3.122a] Their reasoning[154] would appear to be that of applying such models of metaphors and their underlying meaning as the threefold refinement of a gem spoken of in the *Discourse Requested by Dhāraṇīśvararāja.*[155]

From among the masters of the Tibetan tradition, the all-knowing Rangjung Gyalwa, the omniscient Dolpopa, the omniscient Drimé Özer,[156] and others, together with their followers, would seem to have professed this latter interpretation.[157] The majority of renowned teachers in Tibet were proponents of the former interpretation.[158]

Explanation of the Exalted One [4]

As for the connection that the foregoing has with the explanations of the Exalted One,[159] the source verses state:

> **In particular, it is explained that the three successive cycles of the dharma—**
> **initial, intermediate, and final—undermine, respectively,**
> **nonvirtue, the belief in identity, and all bases for dogmatic opinions.**

In particular, the exalted Nāgārjuna and his spiritual heirs[160] state:

> What is nonvirtuous is undermined initially;
> intermediately, any sense of identity is undermined;
> and finally, all bases for dogmatic opinions[161] are undermined:
> Whoever understands this is wise.[162]

Thus, they say that what is nonvirtuous, the belief in identity, and all bases for dogmatic opinions are what are undermined respectively in the initial, intermediate, and final cycles of teachings; and teachers of the Tibetan tradition have also adopted this progressive model of the three turnings of the wheel of the Buddhadharma.

In this regard, the first cycle ensures that, by becoming unerringly involved with moral choices of acceptance and rejection on the level of what is relatively true, one is more capable of perceiving what is ultimately true. For the purpose of undermining perception based on a sense of identity, the second cycle presents ultimate truth in a quantifiable way, negating one extreme of conceptual elaboration.[163] And in order to undermine all bases for dogmatic opinions about existence, nonexistence, and so forth, the third cycle presents ultimate truth in actuality, in the sense that transcends all elaboration.

According to this model, then, the intermediate cycle previously discussed is considered by those who profess unqualified emptiness to be the final word;[164] this is even accepted by certain of those who profess qualified emptiness. As for the vast majority of those who profess qualified emptiness, they interpret the undermining of identity in the sense of proving the absence of identity (that is, an absence that is a freedom from conceptual elaboration), and the undermining of all bases of dogmatic opinions in the sense of transcending some emptiness that could be investigated intellectually.[165] [3.122b] They explain the underlying intent of these cycles[166] to be in accord, in keeping with the progression found in the previous two citations from the sūtras.[167]

Furthermore, the omniscient Rangjung[168] gives the following explanation:

> The cycle of the Exalted One[169] (which undermines all dogmas) and the cycle of the venerable Maitreya (who was prophesied by the Buddha), generally speaking, both come down to the same crucial point; for this key point is the fact that if something constitutes the final cycle of teachings, of necessity it is a cycle that demonstrates a freedom from conceptual elaboration.
>
> In certain particulars, however, these are not identical, for the former does not speak of anything but that freedom from elaboration, while the latter explains that timeless awareness, which is free from elaboration, is a particular way in which one's own individual self-knowing timeless awareness can be experienced.

> But if one were to wonder, "Does that mean that Nāgārjuna and his heirs did not accept timeless awareness free of elaboration?" such is not the case because they actually demonstrate this acceptance in such works as the "Collection of Praises" and the *Four Hundred Verses for Engaging in a Bodhisattva's Conduct.*[170]

Incorrect Opinions and Single Intent [5]

As for the dispelling of incorrect opinions concerning provisional meaning and the explanation of a single enlightened intent, the source verses state:

> **Some think of what is provisionally meaningful as untrue, as false, but this is an incorrect opinion, for the Buddha's word entails no falsehoods.**

Some, who lack the immaculate vision of sublime intelligence, think that everything spoken by the Buddha as provisionally meaningful is false in being unreliable because it is not true from the ultimate perspective. But this is an incorrect opinion due to their own ordinary minds' being ensnared by myriad layers of delusion. The words of the Buddha never entail any falsehood or deceptiveness because the provisional meaning itself is true, albeit as what is provisionally meaningful, and so leads one in an authentic manner toward the profound way in which things actually abide.

This being the case, to boast, "I am a follower of the Middle Way!" could be a case of one's implicitly denigrating other aspects of the Buddha's sublime words; and to claim, "I am a tantric practitioner!" could be a case of one's dismissing the repositories of teachings in the śrāvaka approach and so forth as though these were useless straw. In particular, the lord Mikyö Dorjé[171] said:

> Those who claim nowadays to be Nyingmapas, but who do not regard the Buddha Śākyamuni to be their teacher and have never heard of the thirty-seven factors conducive to enlightenment [3.123a] are not worthy of inclusion among the ranks of Buddhists![172]

Therefore, one should examine and investigate the possibility of one's rejecting the Buddhadharma and exercise caution!

The source verses state:

> **Because it eliminates elaborations concerning the manner in which things appear while actually demonstrating the way things actually abide,**
> **the great spiritual guide and others accept that the entire Buddhadharma has a single intent.**

The ways in which conceptual elaborations on the relative level (the manner in which things appear) are eliminated and the ultimate perspective (the way in which things actually abide) is actually demonstrated can be more obvious or more subtle, depending on the audience's specific level of acumen.[173] It is for this reason that the great spiritual guide Nāgārjuna and others accept that all avenues of teaching taught by the Victorious One have a single underlying intent. As we read in the *Source Verses on Sublime Intelligence*:

> The transcendent and accomplished conqueror,
> understanding what is real and what is not,
> refuted both existence and nonexistence
> in his advice to Kātyāyana.[174]

That is to say, since there is advice concerning freedom from the extremes of existence and nonexistence even in the initial cycle of teachings, all the Buddha's statements concerning the "existence" of things within the range of one's ordinary experience are intended to refer to what merely manifests.[175]

Furthermore:

> "Nirvāṇa, the transcendence of sorrow, alone is true"
> is what victorious ones say.
> At that point, would anyone who is wise not think
> that everything else is false?[176]

That is to say, in the intermediate cycle, everything else—from forms up to and including the state of omniscience[177]—is false due to being relative and conditioned.[178] That these are, in essence, empty of any elaborations is nirvāṇa, which is unconditioned and is taught to be solely what is true.

And from *Stages of Meditation* in the Middle Way tradition:

> Therefore, through pure sublime intelligence
> this ultimate essence in and of itself
> is thoroughly ensured as being the case,
> and so anything else, being imputed, does not have any reality.[179]

Thus, all of Nāgārjuna's statements on the topic of meditation are in accord with the final cycle of teachings. In particular, he emphasizes the meaning found in that final cycle in his "Collection of Praises," and in his *Commentary on Bodhicitta* he discusses the connection between that cycle and the profound meaning of the mantra approach, without these mutually excluding one other.[180] [3.123b]

This is also illustrated by the fact that the exalted and venerable Asaṅga also states quite clearly:

> To claim that there is a contradiction between one sūtra and another sūtra is to reject the sacred Buddhadharma.[181]

It is for this reason that the venerable Maitreya emphatically advises one not to misinterpret the tradition of the Sage,[182] which was established by the Buddha himself.[183] With folded hands, I beseech all to respect this.

Two Levels of Truth [II]

The classification of the two levels of truth involves two topics: an introductory discussion and the actual classification.

Introductory Comments [A]

The source verses state:

> **The sacred Buddhadharma was taught on the basis of two levels of truth.**

However many avenues of the sacred dharma were presented by the Tathāgata, these were all spoken on the authentic basis of there being two levels of truth. According to the *Reunion of Father and Son*:

> O Knower of the World,[184] without having of them from others
> you yourself taught these two levels of truth.
> What are they? The relative and likewise the ultimate;
> there is not in any sense a third level of truth.[185]

And as the venerable Nāgārjuna states in following this citation:

> The dharma taught by buddhas
> is authentically based on two levels of truth—
> the mundane level of relative truth
> and the level of ultimate truth.[186]

Actual Classification [B]

The actual classification is fivefold: the essence, the derivation of the terms, the characteristics and synonyms, a precise analysis, and the value of understanding these truths.

Essence [1]

The source verses state:

> **Generally speaking, these are in essence contrived and uncontrived, respectively—**
> **that which is imputed by the minds of ordinary beings and the state of spiritually advanced beings in meditative equipoise.**

Concerning these levels of truth, there are numerous ways in which the individual philosophical systems posit them and identify what they are in essence. But generally speaking, the interpretation of those who follow the Mahāyāna approach is that relative truth constitutes what is contrived and conceptually imputed, while ultimate truth constitutes what is uncontrived and not imputed. In particular, the *Entrance to the Middle Way* states (according to the Consequentialist system, the pinnacle for those who profess Buddhist philosophical systems):

> Due to all things being perceived either authentically or erroneously, [3.124a]
> any and all things can be taken two ways in essence.

> Whatever is the object of authentic perception is ultimate;[187]
> erroneous perception is said to be relative truth.[188]

That is to say, all phenomena—from forms up to and including the state of omniscience—can be thought of in terms of being perceivable in two ways in their nature or essence. Thus, there is the individual makeup[189] of things that is detected by the ordinary mind of spiritually immature beings, which engages by taking things at face value, without examining or investigating them further; and there is the essence that is discovered by spiritually advanced beings in formal meditative equipoise through nonconceptual timeless awareness.

Of these two cases, the former is termed "relative truth." Due to a lack of recognition—that is, the obscuring of the perception of suchness itself—it is termed "completely overlaid."[190] This level is taken to be true, and as long as one has not realized the significance of suchness itself, this level continues to perform a function that accords with one's misconstruing of it; because it is thus infallible for spiritually immature beings, it can be termed "truth." For as the same source states:

> Because ignorance[191] obscures the true nature, everything is
> completely overlaid.
> Whatever this contrives nevertheless appears to be true,
> which the Sage said to be "relative truth."
> Things that are contrived are on the relative level.[192]

The latter case is termed "ultimate truth." This is because the state of formal meditative equipoise for spiritually advanced beings—that is, nonconceptual timeless awareness—can be referred to as "sublime,"[193] for it engages with the actual way in which things abide, just as they are, and because that is its domain, and so it is infallible in all ways and in all that is truly meaningful, being "truth."

Derivation of Terms [2]

The source verses state:

> **As for the derivation of the terms, what is conditioned is true on**
> **the relative level itself,**
> **while one fact is true on the ultimate level.**

As for the derivation and meaning of the terms for the two levels of truth, due to the rules governing the formation of words in the Sanskrit language, the term "relative" can be explained to be interpreted to mean (1) "obscuring what is authentic"; (2) "gathered together," or "composite"; (3) "symbolic," or "conventionally designated"; (4) "all-differentiating"; and (5) "deceptively masking." [3.124b]

(1) The term "relative" refers to a lack of recognition that entails afflictive mental states and that obscures what is ultimately true—the authentic nature of things. This exerts an influence over the ongoing experience of an individual, such that the conditioned phenomena that manifest in the valid experience of one who is under that influence are "true" in a relative sense, which is why the term applies. The *Entrance to the Middle Way* gives explanations such as the following:

> Because a lack of recognition[194] obscures the true nature, everything is completely overlaid.[195]

(2) The term "relative" means that things that are gathered together[196] are ensured only due to their dependent relationships with one another, like a stack of poles leaning against one another, and not due to their very essence.

(3) According to *Clear Words*:

> Alternatively, "relative" means "symbolic"; it is an equivalent term for "conventional designation" in the mundane context. It is characterized by such factors as verbal descriptions and what is being described, or consciousness and what is known.[197]

(4) In *Blazing Logic* we read the following:

> Due to its function of thoroughly differentiating all things—forms and so forth—it is relative.[198]

(5) It is relative due to the fact that it cannot stand up under mental investigation, as the master Haribhadra states:

> Since it cannot withstand the force of thorough mental investigation, it is relative.[199]

In the case of the one level known as ultimate truth—the "truth of the sacred meaning"—what is actually sacred is the timeless awareness in the ongoing experience of spiritually advanced beings in formal meditative equipoise; what is meaningful is the emptiness that serves as that awareness's domain; and truth lies in the fact that this is infallible under any and all circumstances. That is why such terminology is used.

A parallel to what is sacred is inferential knowledge based on reasoning; to what is meaningful, the emptiness that is characterized as an unqualified negation, which serves as the domain of that knowledge; to what is truth, the fact that this is infallible in light of the reasoning that involves mental examination and investigation. Again, that is why such terminology is used. This latter aspect is termed the "approximation"[200] or "quantifiable aspect of ultimate truth."[201] In treatises of the Middle Way school, all the debate concerning the process of investigating the two levels of truth has taken place on solely the basis of this aspect, for ultimate truth in actuality[202] is not something to be investigated with the conceptual thought process.[203] [3.125a] *Blazing Logic* discusses clearly there being, from a conventional perspective, two aspects of the ultimate and their characteristics.

Characteristics and Synonyms [3]

Concerning the characteristics of, and synonyms for, these levels, the source verses state:

> **The characteristics are those of the object's being either that of a confused consciousness that does not investigate it**
> **or that of the unconfused mind of a spiritually advanced being—that is, deceptive or not deceptive.**
> **The way in which the subjective perceiver apprehends is either one of confusion or its absence.**
> **These levels are presented with many synonymous terms.**

As for the respective characteristics of these levels, what characterizes relative truth is that it is, in essence, imputed or contrived—a false state of perception, in which the meaningful objects that are discovered are discovered in light of a consciousness that is spiritually immature and does not investigate them. What characterizes ultimate truth is that it is, in essence, not imputed or contrived—an authentic state of perception, in which the meaningful objects that are discovered are discovered in light of the awareness of spiritually advanced beings.[204] As Mabja Jangchub Tsöndrü, the foremost among the spiritual descendants of Patsap,[205] explains:

> The relative level is the scope of consciousness that is confused and does not investigate things;
> the ultimate level is the scope of a spiritually advanced being's awareness that is unconfused.[206]

There are many who consider that the mere fact that confusion is involved in one's individual perception of sensory appearances qualifies this as consciousness based on confusion. That would mean that inferential knowledge based on reasoning definitely was also, but because this is knowledge that involves investigation, the qualifier "does not investigate things" is used to exclude it.[207]

In this present context, however, the criterion for whether an object is true or false lies in its being nondeceptive or deceptive, while the criterion for whether the subjective perceiver is true or false lies in the way it apprehends, being one of a lack of confusion or one of confusion.

As for the synonyms for these levels, due to the styles of individual philosophical schools, these are very numerous. According to the Middle Way tradition, to cite from *Distinguishing Center and Limit*:

> As for emptiness, in brief
> suchness, the final authentic state,
> the absence of subtle traits, the ultimate,
> and the basic space of phenomena are its synonyms.
> Because it is nothing other,[208] is unerring, . . .[209]

The venerable Vimuktisena, following the sūtras, explains that there are eleven synonyms,[210] [3.125b] while the master Candrakīrti explains that there are many synonyms.[211]

The opposites of the foregoing terms would serve as synonyms for relative truth; in addition, such terms as "merely symbolic level," "mere labeling," "merely imputed level," "mere conventional designation," and so forth are used.

Precise Analysis [4]

My precise analysis is fivefold: the actual analysis, the reasons underlying the analysis, the determination of the levels of truth as two in number, their unity or separateness; and the positions held by the various philosophical systems.

Actual Analysis [a]

This involves both a general analysis and a specific analysis of the respective levels.

General Analysis [i]

The source verses state:

> **Without investigating any foundation for analysis, on the basis of what simply can be known,**
> **one can distinguish the way in which things appear from the way they abide—that is, the relative from the ultimate.**

Generally speaking, the relative is not something that can be known in light of pure awareness, while the ultimate is not something that can be known in light of confusion. However, in the context of things being taken at face value without being examined or investigated further, the sūtras speak of what simply can be known as the foundation for an analysis of relative vis-à-vis ultimate. As is said:

> Concerning what can be known, this amounts quite simply to the two levels of truth.[212]

On this note, as is said in the *Source Verses on Sublime Intelligence*:

> the mundane level of relative truth
> and the level of ultimate truth.[213]

This means that there are two levels, that of deceptive phenomena, constituting relative truth, and that of what is undeceptive, constituting ultimate truth; alternatively, the analysis can be into the two levels of relative and ultimate truth on the basis of the way in which things appear and the way in which they abide, respectively.

Specific Analysis [ii]

For the specific analysis, the source verses state:

> **The way in which things appear is a state of confusion—the perceptions in the minds of ordinary beings;**
> **the unconfused state is accepted by most to consist of the path and its fruition.**
> **The relative is that of ordinary mortals and the spiritually advanced, or that of mundane people and advanced spiritual practitioners.**
> **The ultimate is in essence indivisible but can be analyzed as having three characteristics, or,**
> **from the perspective of topics under discussion, sixteen aspects, and so forth.**

As for the way in which things appear, there are actually two ways, a confused one and an unconfused one. In the first place, that of the confused way in which things appear, this consists of any and all ways in which what is based on confusion—sensory appearances, fixated perceptions, and consciousness—occurs in the mind of ordinary beings. Since these are deceptive and untrue, all that manifests such that it can be thought of or described, from hell realms up to buddhahood, [3.126a] is imputed by the designs of the ordinary mind and is not something one can be aware of in any actual sense,[214] and for this reason it is explained as being a state of confusion. Furthermore, things such as the four elements[215] that manifest and are capable of performing a function are considered to be what is relative in an authentic sense, while things such as a hallucination of two moons that manifest but are incapable of performing a function are considered to be what is relative in an erroneous sense.

The unconfused way in which things appear is also twofold. The timeless awareness together with its attendant qualities that is experienced on the spiritual path and is not confused with regard to the fruition state is impermanent due to the fact that it evolves; nevertheless, it is unconfused from the point of view that it leads to the fundamentally unconditioned level of being.[216] The unconfused way—due to the fruition's having been attained—consists of the timeless awareness of buddhahood together with the manifest expressions of enlightenment[217] that abide in the pinnacle pure realm.

The foregoing points are by and large posited by the Autonomist school. In this regard, what this school considers to be relative in an authentic sense is posited on the basis of the fact that they hold that one is unconfused about one's own individual perception of sense objects—that is, the direct experience of one's sense faculties in apprehending the forms, sounds, and so forth, that one perceives in one's immediate situation. But those who follow the Consequentialist school hold that these cognitive states are confused with respect to one's own individual perception of sense objects, and therefore they do not accept that there is anything relative in any authentic sense—for them, rather, if something is relative, it is erroneous. More recent generations of dialecticians have said that this is a subtle point, for the issue hinges on whether or not to hold that things are established due to their specific characteristics.[218]

Alternatively, one can discuss the two aspects of the relative as that of ordinary mortal beings and that of spiritually advanced beings. The first aspect consists of such things as the reflection of the moon in water or an echo because even spiritually immature people can determine these accurately as having the qualities of being false and deceptive. The second aspect consists of such things as forms, sounds, and so forth, on which spiritually immature people are completely fixated, because those who perceive what is true for spiritually advanced beings can thoroughly appreciate that these are fallacious, hollow, and lacking in any real substance.

As yet another alternative, the teachings speak of an analysis into the relative level for mundane people and the relative level for advanced spiritual practitioners. Śāntideva says:

> [3.126b] What is relative for advanced spiritual practitioners is
> without flaw, . . .[219]

And Candrakīrti states:

> "Being nonexistent due to this seven-step analysis, how could it exist
> in any way?"
> Thus, advanced spiritual practitioners do not find it to exist.[220]

As for the basis of what is being defined, the relative level for mundane people constitutes the more obvious things in the phenomenal world, perceived in light of confusion, in which things are taken at face value without being examined or investigated further. The relative level for advanced spiritual practitioners constitutes both the appreciation of impermanence on a more subtle level (the meaningful experience discovered by an ordinary mind of conventional values in light of some small degree of examination) and the perceptions experienced in postmeditative awareness by spiritually advanced beings (from those on the path of no more training in the śrāvaka approach to those on the spiritually advanced levels of the bodhisattva approach).[221]

As for synonyms, the former aspect is also referred to as the relative "of what is not examined," or "of spiritually immature people," or "unconnected with knowledge based on reasoning." The latter aspect is referred to as the relative level "of what is investigated," or "that entails knowledge based on reasoning for spiritually advanced beings,"[222] or "of the follower of the Middle Way."

With respect to what is ultimately true, from the point of view of its essence, this cannot be subjected to any analysis because it is in all ways of "one taste," like space, and because it transcends the purview of conventional designations. In the *Amassing of the Rare and Sublime* we read:

> O monks, this ultimate truth is unique. It is thus: it constitutes nirvāṇa, the transcendence of sorrow, which has the quality of being infallible.[223]

If one analyzes this level in a purely semantic way, a brief treatise on the levels of truth speaks of two aspects of ultimate truth, a quantifiable one and an unquantifiable one.[224] The former aspect is free to a certain extent of conceptual elaborations, as in the case of its being "unborn," which negates its having origination; the latter aspect is free of absolutely all conceptual elaborations.[225]

As for the quantifiable aspect of ultimate truth, if one analyzes it from the perspective of what is being negated, there are two aspects to the lack of identity—in the individual and in phenomena. If one analyzes it from the perspective of characteristics, there are the three avenues to complete liberation—emptiness, the absence of subtle traits, and the absence of naïve speculation—or the four avenues (the fourth, its being completely unconditioned). If one analyzes it from the perspective of the topics under discussion, there are sixteen aspects of emptiness; the phrase "and so forth" in the source verse refers to analyses into eighteen or twenty aspects. [3.127a]

Reasons Underlying the Analysis [b]

As for the reasons underlying this analysis, the source verses state:

> **Due to the difference in the way that the minds of the spiritually advanced and the spiritually immature perceive,**
> **and the classification based on mutual dependence, . . .**

Thus, the reasons underlying this analysis into two levels of truth derive from the differing ways in which the minds of two kinds of individuals—the spiritually advanced and the spiritually immature—perceive. Therefore, it is from the point of view of the subjective perceiver that truth can be analyzed into two levels not because these abide in any actual sense. For if the relative level abided in any true sense, it would not, in fact, be the relative level; and besides, this would mean that there would be two ultimate truths! For this reason, other than the fact that what is relative does not abide in any ultimate sense, there does not exist whatsoever anything "ultimate"[226] because the classification that assigns two levels of truth[227] is established on the basis of their mutual dependence.

Therefore, the statement that "ultimate truth is reality free of limitations, while everything else is relative truth" applies in the representational language used by those with such fixations; but in the tradition of the Middle Way itself,[228] there is nothing whatsoever to be classified on either side, relative or ultimate. For as long as one has not realized the significance of what is ineffable, for that long one is not even a follower of the Middle Way because one has not realized the meaning of the middle way.

Certainty of Two Levels [c]

The source verses state:

> **. . . truth is certainly twofold.**

What is true is certainly to be enumerated as twofold—what is relatively true and what is ultimately true, as we read in the *Journey to Śrī Laṅka*:

> There is the relative and the ultimate;
> there is no third alternative born of some cause.
> The relative is imputed by concepts;
> the exhaustion of that is the domain of the spiritually advanced.[229]

And according to the *Reunion of Father and Son*:

> Thus, the Tathāgata has thoroughly mastered the relative and the ultimate. The knowable amounts to this as well—relative and ultimate truth.[230]

The logic behind this, moreover, is as follows: The relative level, which emphasizes the principle of skillful method, is indispensable for making moral choices of what to undertake or avoid; whereas the ultimate level is indispensable for the nonreferential state of complete purity, [3.127b] which is foremost among all that is to be undertaken. This being the case, allowing for any fewer levels of truth would not take account of the situation, while these alone ensure the welfare of a given spiritual practitioner in its entirety because any more levels are unnecessary. Alternatively, it is certain that the minds that are the subjective perceivers of things are of two kinds, confused and unconfused. The relative level is assigned with respect to the former case, while the ultimate level is assigned with respect to the latter case. This classification is indispensable, and so it is certain that there are two levels of truth.

Two Levels of Truth: Identical or Separate? [d]

The source verses state:

> **Conventionally, this is one nature with separate facets;**
> **ultimately, there can be no discussion of being identical or separate.**

Regarding the way in which these levels of truth are identical or separate, the philosophical schools hold their individual and disparate positions. However, according to the glorious Rangjung:

> Concerning the two levels of truth explained thus, this itself is simply the way things are—phenomena and the true nature of those phenomena—and so completely free of any other consid-

> eration, so there is nothing whatsoever to be discussed concerning these being identical or separate.[231]

This means that it can be accepted that, in light of one's not having investigated the issue, on a purely conventional level, the two levels of truth constitute a single nature with separate facets, while from the ultimate perspective, there can be no discussion whatsoever of their being identical or separate in essence.

That is to say, if they were identical, this would entail many problems. Spiritually immature people would realize ultimate truth just as they do relative truth, because the situation would require that they gain freedom without any effort. As well, if the relative were, like the ultimate, not subject to any division, this would require that it be the cause of the state of complete purity; or if the ultimate were like the relative, this would require that it be subject to myriad divisions and be a framework for the increase of deeply ingrained afflictive states.

If they were separate, this situation would require that even though advanced spiritual practitioners had realized the ultimate they would nevertheless be incapable of eliminating their overt fixations on the relative level and that this ultimate level could not be the true nature of the relative. This would entail many such issues that make the possibility invalid.

It is for the foregoing reasons that the *Definitive Commentary on Enlightened Intent* states:

> The characteristics of the realm of ordinary mental states[232] and the ultimate are the characteristics of being free of being identical or separate. [3.128a] Those who conceive of them as either identical or separate have fallen into fallacious ways of thinking.[233]

Positions Held by Philosophical Systems [e]

Concerning the positions held by individual philosophical systems, the source verses state:

> **If something is destroyed or broken down, the concept of it**
> **can be either discarded or not. More obvious things and streams of consciousness are relative,**
> **while what is indivisible is ultimately true. This is the tradition of the Particularist school.**

Generally speaking, the classification of two levels of truth is something that is accepted by all Buddhist philosophical schools. Of these, followers of the śrāvaka approach[234] say:

> Whatever can be dismantled or mentally dissected
> such that the mind no longer entertains a concept—
> such as a vase or water—exists on the relative level;
> Anything else exists on the ultimate level.[235]

This means that if something is dismantled by an instrument of destruction such as a hammer or if it is mentally dissected to eliminate individually all extraneous material factors, such that the mind no longer entertains the concept of that thing that is capable of being done away with, then that thing—such as a vase, or the water it contains—is relative. When the mind still entertains something after attempts to dismantle or mentally dissect it, and it still presents itself to one's consciousness as something autonomous—as with such things as perceived forms, sounds, and so forth—this is ultimate. Both cases, however, are considered "truth," given that the things concerned exist with their respective essential qualities.

To summarize, the followers of the Particularist school hold that substantial things of the more obvious kind and ongoing streams of consciousness are relative, while indivisible moments of consciousness and indivisible particles of matter are ultimately true.[236]

The source verses state:

> **Things that are ultimately able to perform functions or not,**
> **which are characterized as specifics or generalities—this is the tradition of the Followers of the Sūtras.**

According to the *Detailed Commentary*:

> Whatever is ultimately capable of performing a function,
> that exists ultimately in this context.
> Anything else exists relatively.
> These are held to be specifically or generally characterized, respectively.[237]

Things that are capable of performing functions in an ultimate sense (such as a vase or a pillar) constitute ultimate truth, while things that are ultimately incapable of performing a function (such as space, or the generic idea of "vase," or the generic idea of "pillar") constitute relative truth. To put it concisely, these categories are held to correspond to those of things existing with specific characteristics versus those existing only with general characteristics; [3.128b] and "to exist" is held to mean "to be true." This is the tradition of the Followers of the Sūtras, or Sautrāntikas.[238]

Some more recent scholars explain that in this tradition the terms "ultimately true," "impermanent," "substantial thing," "conditioned thing," and "specifically characterized thing" are synonymous, while "relatively true," "permanent," "nonsubstantial phenomenon," "unconditioned thing," and "generally characterized thing" are synonymous.[239]

The source verses state:

> **Dualistic experiences of perceived and perceiver, of objects and perceiving subject,**
> **are considered as actually being nondual consciousness. This is the tradition of the Mind Only school.**

The perceived objects and perceiving subjects experienced by dualistic consciousness constitute relative truth, while nondualistic consciousness only is considered to constitute ultimate truth: such is the tradition of the Mind Only, or Cittamātra, school. The *Anthology on the Heart Essence of Timeless Awareness* states:

> "Nothing with facets exists;[240]
> even minute material particles are not existent.[241]
> Perceptions of individual things, moreover, are like dream images,
> experienced[242] in a state without any fixed point of reference.
> Consciousness free of object-subject dualism
> is held to be what has ultimate meaning."
> In the vast range of sources for Yogic Practitioners,
> those who follow the approach of the transcendent perfections expound in such language.[243]

If we tie this in with the three principles, things that are imputed are relative in the true sense of the term because they are nonexistent as anything substantial and are determined to be merely conventional designations.[244] Things that are dependent constitute the quantifiable aspect of what is ultimate in the true sense of the term, and the quantifiable aspect of the relative because (respectively) they can be determined to have true existence if they are examined in the light of reason and because they obscure one's perception of suchness itself.[245] What is absolute constitutes the ultimate in the true sense of the term because it is the domain for the timeless awareness of spiritually advanced beings.[246]

The source verses state:

> **Sensory appearances, which are proven to be relative, are similar to illusions,**
> **while what is ultimate, like space, cannot be found to exist. This is the tradition of the Autonomist school.**

All that appears as it does, which is proven to be relative, constitutes relative truth, like horses and elephants in an illusionist's trick. What is ultimate, which—like space—cannot be found to exist in any way whatsoever, is accepted as ultimate truth. This is the tradition of the Svātantrika, or Autonomist, school. [3.129a] In *Overcoming Confusion*, we read the following:

> What involves a frame of reference is relative; in the ultimate,
> there is freedom from anything to focus on and any attempt to focus.[247]

The analysis of the relative level according to this system is as discussed earlier.[248]

The source verses state:

> **What is imputed by ordinary consciousness is relative (accepted in accord with what is commonly accepted in the world),**
> **while freedom from conceptual elaboration is beyond imagination or expression. This is the tradition of the Consequentialist school.**

Things that are imputed by ordinary consciousness as describable, imaginable, and expressible constitute relative truth; these are accepted in accord with whatever is known through being commonly accepted in the world.[249] The fundamentally unconditioned nature that is free of all such description, imagination, and expression constitutes ultimate truth. This is the tradition of the Prāsaṅgika, or Consequentialist school; as Candrakīrti states:

> With respect to the arousal of a frame of mind that is in accord with emptiness, this can be referred to as "realizing emptiness," but it does not constitute the realization of emptiness.[250]

Otherwise, this would be similar to one's realization that the nature of space is one of providing a dimension of openness meaning that space itself and one's ordinary mind had become inseparable. In this context, the omniscient Drimé Özer remarks in his commentary to his own *Finding Ease in the Nature of Mind Itself*:

> In this context, let us analyze this clearly and in accordance with the pith instructions: Within the unique scope of the basic space of phenomena as the basis for this analysis, the manifest aspect of sensory appearances is similar to an illusion, or a mirage, or the reflection of the moon in water. That is, the nature of these appearances is that of being apparent yet nonexistent per se, and so we call this "relative truth." As is stated in the sūtra the *Discourse Requested by Druma*:
>
> > Just as the clear image of one's face appears
> > in the flawless surface of a mirror,
> > so too, O Druma, know that phenomena
> > cannot be found to have any independent nature.[251]
>
> According to what such sources say, even though an ordinary being perceives sensory appearances as though they were so very true, an advanced spiritual practitioner sees them with no such conviction, but merely as dream images. [3.129b] Being merely indeterminate yet vividly apparent, if these are not investigated, they manifest, but if investigated are known to be wholly nonexistent; this is termed "realization of relative truth," which is not undermined by the influence of those sensory appearances.
>
> If this realization becomes further refined, this ensures such miraculous powers as one's being able to pass without impediment through these appearances[252] and so forth. Without one's committing oneself to any opinion about these whatsoever,[253] these very appearances have no independent nature, and so one's

mind becomes trained in the fact that they have no separate status as "true."

Once one has gained the timeless awareness of a spiritually advanced being, even though pure realms of experience[254] and so forth manifest, one has no fixation on these as being truly existent, and so they constitute what is called "valid on the relative level." All concepts and perceptions that involve attitudes of fixating on things as truly existent constitute what is erroneous on the relative level. I hold that what is valid on the relative level is all avenues for the arising of awareness and all perceptions where these do not involve fixation on the seemingly true existence of things.

As for what is ultimate, this constitutes the way in which mind itself truly abides, without any independent nature, and inner mastery of the experience of all phenomena without any fixation on their seemingly true existence—their nature rather being like that of the reflection of the moon in water—so that one understands them in essence as having no independent nature, merely manifesting without there being any fixed basis to support perception based on confusion. Once such concepts as "exists" and "does not exist" have vanished in basic space, it is said that one has "realized the ultimate way in which things truly abide." As is said in *In Praise of the Mother* by Rāhula:

> Indescribable, inconceivable, and inexpressible, the transcendent perfection of sublime intelligence
> is unborn, unceasing, the very essence of space,
> yet experienced as the domain of one's individual self-knowing timeless awareness—
> I pay homage to the mother of victorious ones of the three times.[255]

Thus, it is accepted that one's individual self-knowing timeless awareness is what is ultimate and that to realize this constitutes the realization of ultimate truth.

In this regard, the two levels of truth are not separate from one another, like an animal's horns, even as the way in which what is relative truly abides is perceived to be comparable to the reflection of the moon in water: from the point of view of the mani-

> festation of the moon's image, there is the relative, while from the point of view of the moon's having no true existence,[256] there is the ultimate. [3.130a] Just as these two aspects are in essence identical, even as what does not exist nevertheless manifests in the water of a pond, these levels of truth are inseparable, or a primordial unity. A mind that has realized this[257] to be the case is said to have "realization of the two levels of truth."[258]

The source verses state:

> **The imputed and the dependent are relative; the ultimate is the absolute—self-knowing timeless awareness. This is the tradition of qualified emptiness.**

What is imputed and what is dependent constitute relative truth, while the ultimate is considered to be what is absolute—self-knowing timeless awareness: this is the tradition of those who profess the Middle Way interpretation of *zhentong*, or qualified emptiness.

In this regard, the omniscient Dolpopa[259] maintained that what is imputed has no true existence even on the relative level (being comparable to dream images) and what is dependent has true existence in a merely conventional sense, while the absolute is constant, stable, and truly existent. The interpretation of Serdok Paṇchen[260] accords with the position of the Mind Only school in the two former cases[261] and that of Dolpopa in the latter case. I will discuss the interpretation of the venerable Rangjung, Lord of Victorious Ones,[262] later.

As for that of the great and venerable one of Jonang,[263] all phenomena subsumed within the perceptions of dualistic consciousness—substantial and nonsubstantial things, perceived objects and perceiving subject, and so forth—are relative, while he considers self-knowing awareness (that is, the basic space of ultimate reality, timeless awareness empty of such dualism) to be what is ultimate. Thus, he does not consider the ultimate to constitute simply a freedom from elaboration but rather considers it to constitute *pure awareness* devoid of the elaborations of dualistic consciousness of object and subject. Therefore, concerning the three principles Tāranātha states, while the dependent constitutes consciousness that entails perception based on confusion, the imputed constitutes the confusion that manifests to that consciousness, and the absolute is that consciousness, empty of the confusion imposed by subject-object dualism but not empty of being, in essence, self-knowing awareness. And so what is imputed, other than constituting what is assigned on the basis of symbolic and conventional designations, has no status whatsoever as anything existent; what is dependent exists in the relative sense but does not exist ultimately; and what is absolute exists in the ultimate sense. [3.130b] In this, Tāranātha aligns himself with the enlightened intent of Dolpopa.

The source verses state:

> **In the mantra approach, there is further embellishment due to its special features.**
> **In particular, the relative consists of the appearances that manifest to dualistic consciousness,**
> **which are described as being apparent yet without true existence, like the reflection of the moon on water.**
> **The ultimate is the essence of things, emptiness in its eighteen aspects;**
> **the truth of this is nondual timeless awareness.**

The way of interpreting the two levels of truths in the mantra approach is explained as being one that is based on the Middle Way view of these truths, further embellishing this with special features, such as that of viewing sense objects and the perceiving subject as the circle of the maṇḍala and as a state of supreme bliss. The master Jñānapāda[264] speaks of the view of "profound and lucid nonduality."[265]

In this regard, the relative constitutes saṃsāra—an adventitious manifestation of what is actually nonexistent, like a mottled rope being misperceived to be a snake; the ultimate consists of mind as a profound and lucid state of nonduality, analogous to the actual rope.[266] For a mind that entails confusion, saṃsāra is comparable to the purely adventitious consciousness that mistakenly perceives the mottled rope to be a snake, while nirvāṇa's becoming fully evident is comparable to that adventitious consciousness's being dispelled, so that the perception of a snake is invalidated, and the actual nature of the rope is seen. The fact that the ordinary mind of saṃsāra is by nature nirvāṇa is analogous to the fact that the rope is by nature not a snake, but remains with its own properties.

The very fact that saṃsāra has no independent nature of its own means that it is by its actual nature nirvāṇa, and this means that the *profound* nature of saṃsāra and the *lucid* and unceasing quality of what is simply the manifestation of saṃsāra constitute what is, by nature, the maṇḍala of the support and what is supported.[267] As for the consciousness to which this clearly manifests, given that its nature is one of supreme and uninterrupted bliss, the lucid aspect of that nature is nirmāṇakāya, while the supremely blissful aspect of that nature is sambhogakāya. While these aspects constitute a lucidity, these two are acknowledged to abide as a primordial unity, similar to that of a mirror and the mirror's clarity.

In particular, the venerable and omniscient Rangjung gives the following interpretation: [3.131a]

> *Relative* [*kun rdzob*] refers to the perceptions that manifest to dualistic consciousness; while not existing in actuality, these are imputed by the conceptual process—the manifestations of the animate and inanimate universe and so forth; *truth* [*bden pa*] refers to the fact that, while all of this manifests, it has no independent nature, being like the reflection of the moon in water. Thus there is a nominal truth in what is meaningful to a confused mind.
>
> *Ultimate* [*don dam pa*] refers to emptiness as the actual nature of things—that is, emptiness of what is internal and the rest of the eighteen aspects of emptiness that are discussed; while *truth* [*bden pa*] describes naturally occurring timeless awareness, which entails none of the dualism of subject and object; this awareness is present in the ultimate sense.[268]

In this respect, the meaning of this discussion is as expressed in the glorious tantra *Compendium of the Vajra of Timeless Awareness*:

> The enlightened intent concerning the two levels of truth is as follows: there is the truth of what is relative and the truth of what is ultimately meaningful. O children of spiritual heritage, the relative consists of the inanimate[269] and the animate; the truth of that is like the reflection of the moon in water. What is ultimately true consists of the eighteen aspects of supreme emptiness; the limit of that is one of abiding.[270]

Value of Understanding These Truths [5]

As for the value of understanding these truths, the source verses state:

> **Knowing the foregoing, one is undeluded concerning the words of the Sage,**
> **puts the skillful means of moral choices—what to accept or reject—into practice,**
> **and beholds the significance of what derives from those means, reaching the far shore of saṃsāra.**

Thus, if one does not understand the way in which the two levels of truth are present, one does not understand their profound suchness. But through understanding them, one becomes undeluded concerning the unerring topics that constitute the meaning of the words spoken by the Lord of Sages.[271] So, becoming learned with respect to what is relatively true, one is aware of the skillful methods involved in all moral issues—what to accept and what to reject—in their entirety and applies this in a practical manner. And having realized what is ultimately true, one is aware of that which derives from those skillful methods—that is, nirvāṇa as defined in any of the three spiritual approaches,[272] which is totally pure by nature and entirely free of all adventitious distortions—and so reaches the level beyond saṃsāra, that of supreme nirvāṇa that is not confined to any extreme. As we read in the *Two Levels of Truth*:

> Those who understand the differentiation of the two levels of truth
> are undeluded concerning the words of the Sage.
> They are those who augment all spiritual qualities without exception
> and reach the far shore of excellence.[273] [3.131b]

Investigating the Process of Interdependent Connection [III]

The examination of the process of interdependent connection is threefold: interdependent connection with respect to the fundamentally unconditioned nature, interdependent connection with respect to saṃsāra, and interdependent connection with respect to nirvāṇa.

Interdependent Connection: The Fundamentally Unconditioned Nature [A]

The source verses state:

> **The totally pure nature of the foregoing**
> **is the way in which things are fundamentally unconditioned—**
> **interdependent connection free of limiting extremes.**

The totally pure nature of the foregoing—the relative and the ultimate, or saṃsāra and nirvāṇa—is the process of interdependent connection with respect to the way in which things are fundamentally unconditioned, or the ground of being, and that moreover is free of all limitation imposed by conceptual elaborations. The true nature of the universe of appearances and possibilities (whether of saṃsāra or nirvāṇa), its actual nature, is such that nothing has come from anywhere whatsoever, goes anywhere whatsoever, or abides anywhere whatsoever. Given that objects in the phenomenal world are sustained by their true nature, even as these phenomena appear as though originating and ceasing, they are free of all limitations due to origination, duration, and cessation, and so their nature is said to be that of the middle way. According to the *Source Verses on Sublime Intelligence*:

> Whatever occurs through being connected interdependently
> is explained as being emptiness.
> This is designated contingently;
> this itself is the path of the middle way.[274]

The foregoing statements are not at odds with utterly lucid timeless awareness[275] (which is beyond the domain of interdependent connection). This is because even though it transcends the domain of the relative level of conventional designations, what is itself ultimate manifests as the nature of that level and because the former[276] constitutes the definitive meaning, while the latter[277] is a classification based on conventional designations.

Interdependent Connection: Saṃsāra [B]

The source verses state:

What occurs dependently, externally and internally, constitutes the interdependent connection of saṃsāra.

That which arises in the usual progression—originating in dependence on causes and conditions, whether external or internal—is termed "the interdependent connectedness of saṃsāra." To explain the significance of this a bit, there are two considerations: the connection with causes and the connection with conditions.

Of the two aspects of the process, the external and the internal, the external aspect of interdependent connectedness that involves connection with causes is as follows: From a seed through a seedling and on to the fruit, the situation remains such that without one, the next does not occur. Even though there is no conscious deliberation—"I will produce this" or "I was produced by that"—on the part of these factors, if the causes are present, the results will occur. [3.132a]

Second, as for the external aspect of interdependent connectedness that involves connection with conditions, the earth element serves the function of supporting the seed; water, of moistening it; fire,[278] of maturing it; air, of stimulating its growth; space, of ensuring that this proceeds without impediment; and time, of allowing the seed to change. Thus, even though these six elements and the seed have no conscious deliberation vis-à-vis one another, the situation remains such that without a given factor, another will not occur. None of the foregoing factors is created by the things themselves, or by any other thing, or by a powerful creator god, or by time. They neither occur by their very nature, nor are they causeless. Rather, through the coming together of the elements, once the seed ceases, the seedling is ensured.

This external aspect of the process of interdependent connection is not one of permanent things. Moreover, the seed and the seedling are not one and the same, for the seedling is not *produced* by whether or not the seed ceases, because the cessation of the seed and the occurrence of the seedling are simultaneous events. Nor is this aspect of the process one of a nihilistic void, for the cessation of the seed and the occurrence of the seedling are like the rise and fall of a balance. Nor is it a case of transference, because the seed is one thing and the seedling is another.[279] In addition, a small cause can ensure a large result, such as the case of the seed of a banyan and the actual tree.[280] There is a continuity of like type, for it is impossible for the relationship of cause to effect to become random.

Of the two considerations for the internal aspect of the process of interdependent connectedness, that which involves connection with causes constitutes the process from ignorance up to and including aging and death.[281] Although there is no agent involved, and these factors have no conscious deliberation vis-à-vis one another, as long as there is a cause, the corresponding result occurs.

The internal aspect of interdependent connectedness that involves connection with conditions is as follows: With the coming together of the six elements of earth, water, fire, air, space, and consciousness, these serve their functions (from earth providing solidity to space providing the cavities and orifices of the body),[282] ensuring the formation of the "seedling" of the mind-body complex in a manner similar to a stack of spears.[283] With the coming together of the six avenues of ordinary consciousness,[284] there is consciousness. Although the body is formed with the coming together of all of these factors, there is no agent involved, and these factors have no conscious deliberation vis-à-vis one another, but the situation remains that their nature is such that when a factor is absent another does not occur. Moreover, none of these factors—from earth to the coordinating function of mind—is something with identity, [3.132b] or an ordinary being, or a life force, or a life form, or a member of the human race, or a human being. There is neither a woman, nor a man, nor even an androgyne. There is neither a self nor anyone else.

In this regard, one has the impression that these six elements constitute a single thing; or a unit; or something permanent, stable, and standing on its own; or something satisfying; or anything from an ordinary being up to a human being[285] or an "I." These and other such aspects of unknowing are termed "*ignorance*," because this constitutes a greatly benighted state and because there is a lack of understanding of suchness and an erroneous concept of it.

With that serving as the cause, the three patterns of attachment, aversion, and delusion occur; due to the influence of ignorance, there is "*formative karmic patterning*," given that such patterning becomes fully evident. Because this patterning gives rise to specific expressions of consciousness that lead toward states that are meritorious, nonmeritorious, or neutral, there are three aspects to this patterning.

This gives rise to *consciousness* that is cognizant of individual types of things; this constitutes the six avenues of consciousness. Occurring concomitantly with these are the four aggregates—of forms, sensations, perceptions, and formative factors—that perpetuate cyclic existence. There is mind, since there are ordinary fixated perceptions of "this is such-and-such"; and there is body, because there are ordinary fixated perceptions of "the specific form of this is such-and-such." These two are combined in the single term "*the mind-body complex*," because this serves as the basis for the sense faculties.

The faculties that depend on this complex are the *six sense fields*, so called because they are avenues for the arising of experience, or because such experience can arise and develop.[286] With the coming together of three factors—sense objects, sense faculties, and the coordinating function of mind—there is *contact*, because contact is made.[287] The experience of that is *sensation*, because sensations are involved. Further fixation on those brings *compulsion*, because there is deeply rooted attachment and fixation. The increase of this brings *perpetuation*, because the causes of those sensations are perpetuated. The perpetuation of those brings about *involvement in conditioned existence*, because it leads to actually taking rebirth in conditioned existence once again. From this come the mind-body aggregates—that is to say, *rebirth*—because one is reborn into whatever state of existence is appropriate. [3.133a] Once rebirth has taken place, the maturation of the mind-body aggregates brings aging, and their destruction brings death; these two factors are combined as one—*aging and death*. On account of that, there is sorrow due to attachment, because this gives rise to inner torment; verbal expressions of grief due to that; suffering due to the experience of unhappiness; mental anguish due to distressing states of mind; and so forth: secondary afflictive states render the mind completely turbulent.

These twelve links neither constitute anything from a self or an individual up to and including something that is "mine"[288] nor belong to anyone else. They are neither permanent nor impermanent, neither conditioned nor unconditioned. They are neither acausal and aconditional, nor do they exist as agents of experience. Nor are they phenomena that become exhausted, are subject to destruction, or cease to exist. They have, however, played out continuously throughout beginningless time due to other causes and other conditions; they have played out in succession without interruption, like the flow of a river.

These twelve links can also be subsumed under four categories: (1) karma, because it is like a fertile field; (2) ignorance, because it is like the sower of a seed; (3) compulsion, because it "moistens" like water; and (4) consciousness, because it is like the seed. While consciousness as the seed is ensured by these conditions, there is no agent involved, and these factors have no conscious deliberation vis-à-vis one another and do not constitute anything from a self up to and including something that is "mine." Nevertheless, if the "seed" of consciousness is supported by the "field" of karma, moistened by the "water" of compulsion, and planted by the "sower" of ignorance, it perpetually takes rebirth in wombs. But no one at all causes this to happen; it does not come about without cause; and it does not "come" from anywhere. All the same, when conditions come together—the cells of the father and mother uniting, the disembodied consciousness[289] entering, and so forth—the "seedling" of the mind-body complex forms in the womb. This, too, does not constitute anything from a self up to and including something that is "mine." It is not some subjective agent; rather, it is analogous to space, having as its nature that which characterizes an illusion.

Visual consciousness, too, comes about due to five causal factors: (1) the eye serves to provide the support, (2) forms, to provide the frame of reference, (3) illumination, to provide the cause for clear perception, (4) space, to ensure that there is no physical obstruction, [3.133b] and (5) the mental focus that gives rise to this consciousness, to perform the function of cognition. Although these factors bring about visual consciousness, that visual consciousness is not an agent, and it does not have any conscious deliberation, being like an illusion. The same is true for the other avenues of consciousness.

Therefore, although it is indeed the case that no phenomenon whatsoever passes into some future state, and no phenomenon whatsoever comes from some past state, once the coming together of causes is complete within the context of a state of confusion, things appear as though they have passed forward from past states and are produced in future states. But in the case of all these phenomena, that situation is like that of one's face appearing in a mirror even though it is not transferred to the mirror, or like the reflected image of the moon, which moves forty-two thousand *yojana*s above in the sky,[290] appearing in a vessel of water on the earth's surface, or like the burning that occurs if the causes and conditions for fire come together.

As well, this internal process of interdependent connection is not something permanent, for the mind-body aggregates at the final moment of death are one thing and those that are then born are another. Nor is this process a nihilistic void, for the aggregates that are born do not occur due to whether or not those at the final moment of death cease; rather the cessation of the aggregates at death and the occurrence of the aggregates at birth are like the rise and fall of a balance. Nor this is a case of transference, because the rebirth that takes place can be that of a different type of being.[291] In addition, a small cause can give rise to a large result, such as the case of a single moment of an extremely malicious attitude propelling the mind toward rebirth in a hell state, or a loving attitude of short duration propelling it toward rebirth as a king among the Brahma gods. There is a continuity of like type because results are experienced according to actions committed.

These processes are discussed in the *Journey to Śrī Laṅka*:

> O Mahāmati, just as a pot comes from a lump of clay, so too a blanket comes from yarn, thick cloth from carded wool, seedlings from seeds, and butter from human efforts such as churning and from curds, so too, O Mahāmati, the external aspect of the process of interdependent connection occurs such that what is later comes from what is earlier. . . . As for the internal aspect of the process of interdependent connection, [3.134a] it is as follows: ignorance, compulsion, karma, and such phenomena as these are given the name "interdependent connection."[292]

In summary, the initial failure to recognize one's own self-knowing timeless awareness constitutes a supreme state of ignorance. From that comes the formative karmic patterning for conditioned existence, leading to consciousness and all the way down to aging and death, these occurring in an uninterrupted succession, which each relying on the last, as is stated in *Letter to a Friend*:

> From ignorance comes karma,[293] from that
> consciousness, and from that the mind-body complex fully forms.
> From that come the six sense fields, and from them,
> said the Sage, contact occurs in all situations.
>
> From contact come all sensations.
> From sensations as a basis comes compulsion.
> Compulsion brings about perpetuation;
> from that comes the process of becoming, and from becoming,
> rebirth.

> Once there is rebirth, there is sorrow, illness, aging,
> feeling poverty-stricken due to desires, death, destruction,
> and so forth—
> a huge amassing of suffering comes about.[294]

With respect to these aspects of the process of interdependent connection, the expression "coming from causes" is used from the point of view that what is later comes from what is earlier, while the expression "coming from conditions" is used due to there being a process of giving rise to things from the point of view of the coming together of six elements—earth, water, fire, air, space, and consciousness—on the internal level.

I have previously discussed to a small extent the particular ways in which this process is interpreted in the Hīnayāna and Mahāyāna teachings—of it forming a continuum over one, two, or three lifetimes and so on; of how it is complete in any given instant; and so forth.

The foregoing constitutes what is called "the usual progression, the interdependent connectedness of saṃsāra."

Interdependent Connection: Nirvāṇa [C]

The source verses state:

> **Whoever beholds the interdependent connection of nirvāṇa—**
> **the reversal of the usual progression—**
> **has access to the key points of the Buddha's speech;**
> **therefore realize the significance of these through dedicated contemplation.**

Interdependent connection with respect to nirvāṇa, which is the reversal of the usual progression, has two considerations: the path and the fruition state.

In the first place, as for the spiritual path, [3.134b] given that ignorance is the root of the usual progression of the twelve links that constitute interdependent connection with respect to saṃsāra, this is removed by pure and timeless awareness. Through becoming familiar with the evolution of sublime intelligence through studying teachings to contemplating them to meditating on them, one removes the initial root factor, that of ignorance.

Once that has been removed, the other factors that depend on it are successively removed. When the causes for engaging further in conditioned existence have come to an end, one moves beyond the state of saṃsāra. *Letter to a Friend* states:

> With the stopping of rebirth, all of this stops.[295]

In this regard, since advanced spiritual practitioners who wish to attain liberation have not reinforced the karmic causes that sustain saṃsāra, any future result of saṃsāra does not come about because formative karmic patterning has stopped. This is why it is said:

> The root of saṃsāra is formative patterning;
> therefore, the wise do not engage in such patterning.[296]

As for interdependent connection with respect to the fruition state, this is the fact that the benefit that buddhas ensure for ordinary beings takes place in the manner of a dream or an illusion. That is to say, whoever beholds the fact that all phenomena simply occur through a process of interdependent connection does not view things as self, or other, or existent, or nonexistent, and does not conceive in terms of the limitations imposed by the three phases of linear time. They are not involved with such views as the *atman* theory of Brahmanical practitioners, and so have uprooted belief in the reality of the perishable mind-body aggregates. Those for whom objects in the phenomenal world are unborn and unceasing have access to the key points of the limitless collections of teachings that are the speech of the Buddha; therefore, having thoroughly assimilated the meaning of these as true, they also have access to the state of all-seeing enlightenment. The *Source Verses on Sublime Intelligence* state:

> For those who behold that things occur
> in interdependent connection, suffering
> and its all-pervasive origin stop,
> and they behold the spiritual path.[297]

Thus, having contemplated in a dedicated manner these two levels of truth and the way in which things occur through interdependent connection, [3.135a] one should not leave it at following a path of studying teachings, but rather should truly realize the significance of these topics. In the foregoing discussion I have again spoken of the significance of interdependent connection, this time according to the enlightened intent of the sūtra *Verdant Rice Seedling*.[298]

The foregoing constitutes the commentary on the second part, concerning a definitive treatment of provisional and definitive meaning according to the three approaches, the two levels of truth, and interdependent connection.

Part 3. Authentic View

I. The Need for Authentic View
II. The Way to Develop Sublime Intelligence
III. Preliminaries: The Four Axioms
IV. The Path That Avoids Dualistic Extremes
  A. General Way to Avoid Dualistic Extremes
  B. Specific Explanation of the Middle Way Tradition
    1. Identifying Emptiness
    2. Unqualified Emptiness (*rang stong*)
    3. Qualified Emptiness (*gzhan stong*)
V. Main Explanation: Two Aspects of the Lack of Identity
  A. Purpose
  B. Analysis
    1. Lack of Identity in Phenomena
      a. Key Topic
      b. Factor to Be Negated
      c. Purpose of Negating Identity
      d. Philosophical Interpretations
      e. Definitive Understanding through Middle Way Reasoning
    2. Lack of Identity in the Individual
      a. Key Topic
      b. Factor to Be Negated
      c. Purpose of Negating Identity
      d. Philosophical Interpretations
      e. Definitive Understanding through Middle Way Reasoning
    3. Relevant Issues
      a. Identicalness or Separateness
      b. Purpose
      c. Factors to Be Negated

d. Valid Cognition
e. Authentic Reasoning
4. Specific Middle Way Interpretations
a. Unqualified Emptiness
b. Qualified Emptiness
5. Advice Integrating Both Traditions
VI. Mantra Approach
A. General Position
B. Specific Position: Gargyi Wangpo
VII. Summation: The View of Unborn Primordial Unity

The third part, a definitive treatment of the view, involves seven discussions: the reasons an authentic view is necessary; the way to develop sublime intelligence as realization of the lack of identity; the preliminary overview of the four axioms; the process of following the path that avoids dualistic extremes; the main explanation of the two aspects of the lack of identity; an analysis of the distinctive view of the mantra approach; and a brief summation of the view of unborn primordial unity.

The Need for Authentic View [I]

The source verses state:

> **Given that nirvāṇa—the deathless state—is what to strive for,**
> **sublime intelligence is the remedy to eliminate ignorance, the source of obscuration.**
> **Without it this will not take place, for it ensures that one's view is pure.**
> **Conduct through skillful means brings purification,**
> **and one swiftly gains freedom in the integration of totally pure view and conduct.**

Given that the peace of nirvāṇa, the deathless state, is that goal that those who wish for liberation strive for, whether or not that is made fully evident hinges on whether or not the potential, or source, of obscuration has been eliminated. This, in turn, will not take place if one lacks the sublime intelligence that is the remedy eliminating the deluded state of ignorance. "What kind of intelligence?" one might wonder; it is sublime intelligence that realizes the lack of identity in things. It is this intelligence that ensures that one's view is totally pure and that one gains the most excellent degree of perspicacity concerning what is definitively meaningful.

In order for that to become fully evident, moreover, one is aware that one must apply the aspect of skillful means in a practical manner and in every way possible. By one's truly engaging in such means, one's conduct becomes totally pure, and this awakens in one the most excellent degree of perspicacity concerning what is provisionally meaningful.

In this way, one's totally pure view and conduct are integrated, not becoming divorced from one another. And so, it is said, one swiftly gains access to the bliss of complete freedom. [3.135b]

The source verses state:

> **In particular, because all the teachings spoken by the Victorious One**
> **are directed toward, and come down to, the basic space of phenomena,**
> **initially one should come to a definitive understanding of the view.**
> **Having properly understood the flawed attitudes of erroneous opinions, one discards these**
> **while seeking out and accepting what is definitively meaningful as one's authentic view.**

Moreover, of the two—view and conduct—the former is especially important. All of the limitless collections of teachings spoken by the Victorious One, whether of provisional or definitive meaning, are entirely directed toward, and come down to, the basic space of phenomena. And so, for one to seek out the authentic view—that which accords with this fact—through the eye of sublime intelligence becomes the direct cause for one's gaining the experience of that basic space. Initially, then, one should come to a definitive understanding of the true and abiding nature of this view. As we read in *Letter to a Friend*:

> Even though individuals with erroneous opinions may conduct themselves well,
> they will endure all manner of intolerable results.[299]

Thus, erroneous opinions, which conflict with the authentic view, together with anything associated with them, constitute the source of all flaws and faults. Initially, then, one should use the mind's powers of thorough discernment, relying on scriptural authority and reasoning, to understand the role of such opinions and, having gained certainty about this, one should discard them.

In this respect, non-Buddhist doctrines based on naïve affirmation or nihilistic denial,[300] and even Buddhist schools that profess materialist tenets,[301] are subject to the flaw of philosophical absolutism. The authentic view, therefore, lies entirely with the Middle Way path. So one should accept the profound and flawless definitive meaning of the mainstream traditions of the two "charioteers,"[302] seeking these out with a perspicacity that does not fall into any extreme, marshaling the forces of good by reinforcing one's merit, and striving with the sublime intelligence that derives from the threefold process of studying, contemplating, and meditating on teachings.

The Way to Develop Sublime Intelligence [II]

In referring to the process of developing this intelligence, the source verses state:

> **With ignorance serving as the cause, the belief in the reality of the perishable aggregates**
> **is the false perception of identity, which is the root of four mistaken ideas.**
> **The remedy to this is to develop sublime intelligence that realizes the lack of identity.**

With ignorance serving as the cause, [3.136a] there ensues the "belief in the reality of the perishable aggregates." That is, due to the deluded attitude that completely fails to understand that the collection of the mind-body aggregates has no identity, there develops the confused belief in the reality of these aggregates, that they constitute some identity.

While this belief is a mode that is perceived as a clear image in the mind,[303] ignorance is an unclear impression without any such differentiation whatsoever. So these two modes[304] are in contradiction with respect to the impression they present and the way the mind perceives them. Therefore, while ignorance does not, in actuality, develop from this belief, it nevertheless develops through the force of the potential that derives from habituation to this mistaken attitude—belief in the reality of the perishable aggregates.[305]

Furthermore, this belief in the reality of the perishable aggregates, when analyzed with respect to the three realms, functions in three ways. The belief as it is experienced within the states of the realm of desire constitutes an entirely negative influence, whereas the belief as it is experienced within the states of the two higher realms constitutes a karmically neutral obscuration.[306]

The belief in the reality of the perishable aggregates is synonymous with "false perception of identity," which is the root of four mistaken ideas. These four are: misperceiving what is impure to be pure; misperceiving what is productive of suffering to be pleasurable; misperceiving what is impermanent to be permanent; and misperceiving what has no identity to have identity. With the first three of these being accessories to the false perception of identity, these ideas all serve as the basis, or root, as it were, of all thought patterns that derive from mistaken perceptions.

In general, the term "identity"[307] is the equivalent of the Sanskrit *ātmaka*. If this term is interpreted in the broadest sense, "identity" refers to something that is able to stand on its own, without depending on anything else; it is in this sense that it is meant when referring to "the identity in phenomena." If the term is interpreted in a narrower sense, it refers to the "I," or "self," falsely perceived with reference to the mind-body aggregates; it is in this sense that the term is meant when referring to "the identity in the individual." In this regard, what is called "belief in identity" constitutes that selfsame belief in the reality of the perishable aggregates, for that itself constitutes the false perception of a self with reference to the collection of these aggregates, [3.136b] which are by nature perishable and impermanent. This misperception is itself connected with ignorance. For as long as there is ignorance, which consists of delusion concerning the Four Truths,[308] there is this misperception; and once that ignorance has been eliminated, this misperception has also been eliminated.[309]

The remedy to this misperception is sublime intelligence that realizes the lack of any identity because it serves as a counterbalancing force that is the opposite of the belief in identity, which is allied with ignorance.[310] If ignorance and the belief in identity, together with their potentials, are not uprooted and eliminated, there is no way for one to become free of the three realms. And if one lacks the sublime intelligence that realizes the lack of any identity, one is incapable of eliminating the belief in identity. Thus, one should train in that completely authentic view through the three means of studying, contemplating, and meditating on teachings, and so develop that flawless and sublime intelligence.

Preliminaries: The Four Axioms [III]

In explaining the overview of these four axioms as a preliminary step, the source verses state:

> **Conditioned phenomena are momentary and impermanent;**
> **all that is corruptible is of the nature of the three kinds of suffering;**
> **both the deeply ingrained afflictive state and the totally refined state are empty and lack identity;**
> **nirvāṇa alone is liberation, the state of peace.**
> **These are the four axioms that denote the general teachings of the Buddha's words.**
> **Contemplating them thoroughly, one arouses a sense of certainty at the outset.**

It is said that, in coming to a definitive understanding of the lack of identity through studying and contemplating teachings, if one has not aroused a sense of certainty concerning these four axioms that denote the Buddha's words—that is, the view—it will be difficult for one to develop the certainty that will finally resolve this issue of lack of identity. So one should initially examine these axioms precisely:

(1) In this regard, all conditioned phenomena[311] subsumed within the outer and inner levels[312] are found to be impermanent because there is never any situation in which they exhibit permanence. And this impermanence is not simply and completely accounted for on the more obvious level of impermanence; there is also the more subtle level of impermanence, in that the characteristics of things are such that they cease in the very moment they come about, having no independent status that allows them to last for even an instant. [3.137a] Just as the flame of a lamp can be understood to be momentary (as the oil fueling it is consumed moment by moment), likewise so can all that is conditioned. And just as it is impossible, in the case of a rider and mount, for one to proceed and the other not to, so too the sense faculties and their respective sense objects are found to be momentary because they constitute the support for momentary consciousness.

(2) That being the case, suffering can also be understood because things must disintegrate moment by moment, without any independent status that would allow them to endure. In this context, subliminal suffering—the subtle aspect of suffering—lies in the fact that conditioned things, merely by having come about, can be characterized as producing suffering. It is not appropriate to think that whatever entails suffering constitutes some agent that somehow *causes* happiness or suffering, for the thing itself has no independent status. This is why it is a contradiction for any phenomenon that is impermanent to also be something with identity or a producing agent.

Regardless of which phenomenon one considers, everything that serves as a cause to perpetuate afflictive mental states is corruptible,[313] and these things do not transcend the nature of suffering. In this regard, the suffering of actual pain, as experienced by beings in the states of animals and lower, can plainly be understood to be suffering, and so we need not prove it to be so through reasoning. The suffering of change can be understood to be actual suffering by ordinary mortal people with good powers of discernment, and so it too need not be proved to be so through reasoning. The suffering that needs to be proved to be so through reasoning is the subliminal suffering that spiritually immature people do not understand to be suffering and instead hold to be happiness.

On this note, all conditioned things come about and disintegrate moment by moment, their nature being one of impermanence, and so there is not the slightest chance of them enduring. Without the independent status that would allow them to endure, they constitute suffering itself because they disintegrate even though we do not wish them to do so. Furthermore, if we put aside the case of something that we do not wish to disintegrate nevertheless disintegrating and so constituting suffering, [3.137b] even something that disintegrates whether we wish it to or not is suffering because its disintegration is due to its lacking any independent status to prevent that disintegration.

From among the Four Truths, in the case of those of suffering and its all-pervasive origin, from the point of view of their common ground, the all-pervasive origin is considered to be the cause and suffering the effect. To give an example, if one is motivated by an afflictive state of aversion and so commits the act of taking another being's life, from that cause (that is, the all-pervasive origin) comes the effect (the truth of suffering), in this case the formation of a body in a state of hell.[314]

But while, as a general rule, these two—suffering and its all-pervasive origin—are related to one another as effect and cause, respectively, it is by no means certain that the all-pervasive origin will always be the cause and suffering always the effect. All suffering comes about through the force of impermanence, for things are such that they do not endure in their respective situations; those situations change into others and eventually things disintegrate, so that they are productive of suffering and are sources of disappointment. To give an example, when a seed as the cause is thoroughly augmented by water, fertilizer, warmth, and other factors, it does not remain in the state of being a seed. Rather, it completely disintegrates, and there ensues the state of a seedling. That, too, does not last, but completely disintegrates, and there ensues the complete state of a fruit. And that, too, does not last forever, but eventually disintegrates.

(3) All phenomena that pertain to either deeply ingrained afflictive states or the totally refined state[315] are empty and lack identity. Generally speaking, those who believe that things have a creator are mistaking an inappropriate cause to be the cause.[316] This serves as the avenue for ordinary consciousness to perceive things in an erroneous way—in fact, for all manner of afflictive mental states and flaws. And even though there are mistaken ideas of taking something that is not a cause to be a cause—such as that of taking a seedling to come about from some cause other than itself, such as impermanence—[3.138a] it is not as though these serve as the avenue for all flaws to come about, as is the case with believing in a creator.

In this regard, all of the happiness and suffering in the world comes about through the force of positive and negative karma. The fact that one commits negative actions and experiences suffering as a result, or that one commits positive actions and experiences happiness as a result—these are not due to some creator imposing these on each and every ordinary being as some ultimate essential principle. And so, although simply as a general rule it is definitely the case that the results of happiness and suffering come about due to positive and negative actions, respectively, this is not ever made to be so, as non-Buddhists believe, by some eternal, unitary, autonomous entity,[317] such as the soul of an individual or a powerful creator god. If such were the case, one would incur the effects of actions one had not committed, the effects of actions one had committed would be ineffectual, and there would be no predictability in ascertaining causes and effects—the entire framework of moral choices of acceptance and rejection, which is based on cause and effect, would be subverted. This would serve as the utterly intolerable avenue for ignoble opinions based on exceedingly warped interpretations of which actions to embrace and which to avoid.

Therefore, if one understands that all phenomena, although they are devoid of identity and have no creator, nevertheless can and do come about through a process of interdependent connection, unceasing in their manifestation, then all of the afflictive mental states pertaining to the three realms are completely undermined.

(4) If the belief in identity is thus eliminated, one gains the state of cessation—which is to say, nirvāṇa, the transcendence of sorrow. In this regard, the happiness of higher states of rebirth and so forth are temporary states of well-being, which are very limited, deceptive, unreliable, and lacking in any real essence. And so nirvāṇa alone is the liberation that is an ongoing state of well-being—the state of peace that is undisturbed by the waves of afflictive mental states. If we analyze it, however, there are many different interpretations in the Indian and Tibetan traditions of Buddhism regarding the state of nirvāṇa according to each of the three spiritual approaches,[318] and the consummate level of the truth of cessation. I will discuss the essential points of these in the section on the fruition state.[319]

Let me use an analogy to describe the role played by these four axioms that denote the general teachings of the Buddha's words. [3.138b] Just as a ruler's subjects uphold the edicts of their ruler and would not contravene them, in a similar fashion, it would be inappropriate for those who consider themselves followers of the Lord of Sages[320] ever to stray outside the guidelines of this view. So one should contemplate these axioms thoroughly and at the very outset arouse a sense of certainty concerning them.

The Path That Avoids Dualistic Extremes [IV]

There are two considerations in following this path: the general way in which to avoid dualistic extremes and a specific explanation of the Middle Way tradition.

General Way to Avoid Dualistic Extremes [A]

The source verses state:

> **Next, one follows the path that avoids dualistic extremes.**
> **One uses the sublime intelligence that understands ultimate reality as the perceiving agent**
> **to pare away conceptual elaborations concerning the object that is to be known. This is the tradition of each individual's own school.**

Be that as it may, materialists may eliminate naïve affirmation and nihilistic denial
according to their own interpretations, but they still fall into extremes of overstatement and understatement.

Once one has already cultivated one's authentic intelligence, such that it is capable of becoming totally pure, one then must follow the Middle Way path that avoids the dualistic extremes of conceptual elaborations involving either naïve affirmation or nihilistic denial. As the means to follow it, one uses the perceiving agent of sublime intelligence that knows ultimate reality to pare away conceptual elaborations concerning the object that is to be known. This is, in general, the tradition of each of the Buddhist schools of thought. Therefore, those who follow philosophical systems that profess materialism[321] may, with recourse to the scriptural authority and reasoning that pertain to their own traditions, eliminate naïve affirmation and nihilistic denial as these apply with their specific context. Nevertheless, if their positions are evaluated according to the Middle Way tradition and the reasoning that concerns the absence of conceptual elaborations, they still fall into extremes of overstatement and understatement.

Sublime intelligence, generally speaking, can be of two kinds: sublime intelligence that knows the relative and sublime intelligence that knows the ultimate; the latter is the basis of what is being characterized in this present context. Concerning that kind of intelligence, moreover, within the Mahāyāna approach we can ascertain three distinct interpretations: (1) followers of the Mind Only school understand all phenomena to be simply conscious awareness; (2) those who assert unqualified emptiness understand all phenomena to be free of conceptual elaborations; and (3) those who assert qualified emptiness understand that freedom from conceptual elaborations itself to be endowed with the potential for all manifestation.[322] [3.139a]

In general, proponents of all philosophical systems, both Buddhist and non-Buddhist, presume that they are espousing a "middle way," refuting dualistic extremes in light of their own understanding of what this means. This is because they hold that they profess, according to their own systems, a middle way that avoids two extremes—although lower approaches, in exaggerating what does not exist as existing, incur the extreme of naïve affirmation, while relatively higher approaches, in denying what exists as not existing, incur the extreme of nihilistic denial.

With respect to our own Buddhist schools:

(1) For followers of the Particularist school, the way in which the extremes of naïve affirmation and nihilistic denial are avoided is as follows: the extreme of naïve affirmation is avoided due to the fact that all conditioned things disintegrate moment by moment, while the extreme of nihilistic denial is avoided due to the fact that minute and irreducible subatomic particles are truly existent.

(2) For those who are Followers of the Sūtras, the extreme of naïve affirmation is avoided due to the fact that causes in their own individual essences are subject to cessation, while the extreme of nihilistic denial is avoided due to the fact that their accordant results ensue.[323]

(3) For those of the Mind Only school, the extreme of naïve affirmation is avoided by the fact that what is imputed has no independent nature, while the extreme of nihilistic denial is avoided by the fact that what is dependent can be proven to be truly existent.[324]

(4) For those of the Middle Way school,[325] the extreme of naïve affirmation is avoided by the fact that the nature of things is a freedom from conceptual elaboration, while the extreme of nihilistic denial is avoided by the fact that what is relative comes about through a process of interdependent connection.

(5) For those who profess qualified emptiness, the extreme of naïve affirmation is avoided by the fact that all phenomena on the relative level (which come about due to other factors) are primordially such that they cannot be proven to exist, while the extreme of nihilistic denial is avoided by the fact that the heart essence of the attainment of the state of bliss[326] (which is naturally occurring and unchanging) abides as the fundamentally unconditioned mode of being.[327]

The source verses state:

> **Therefore, these interpretations are partly truth but with much untruth.**
> **Because the way of abiding is realized to be free of conceptual elaborations and the way in which things manifest**
> **to be a process of interdependent connection, the Middle Way tradition is entirely true.**

Because they largely fall into the extremes of overstatement and understatement, the majority of the foregoing views of the respective schools of thought have some element of truth, but for the most part contain much that is untrue.[328] But because it entails the realization of things just as they are—of the fundamentally unconditioned mode of reality as a freedom from conceptual elaborations and as the utter lucidity of unconditioned basic space, and of the way in which things manifest as such, that by nature they come about through a process of interdependent connection—[3.139b] it is the Middle Way tradition that is entirely true. As we read in the *Brief Presentation of Buddhist Views*:

> In the scriptural sources of the Particularists,
> Followers of the Sūtras, and Yogic Practitioners,
> there is some small element of truth and there is untruth.
> The Middle Way tradition is entirely true.[329]

In this present context, to summarize the path that avoids dualistic extremes, there are two considerations: the way in which to dispel dualistic extremes with respect to conduct and the way in which to dispel dualistic extremes with respect to view.

1) In the first case, if one asserts that phenomena (whether of deeply ingrained afflictive states or the totally refined state[330]) that can be validated through what is considered valid cognition in the ordinary mundane sphere[331] are in fact nonexistent, one falls into the extreme of understatement.[332] On the other hand, if one asserts that phenomena (whether of deeply ingrained afflictive states or the totally refined state) that are tainted by causes of confusion in the present circumstances,[333] or are posited in schools of thought that espouse extreme views, are in fact existent, one falls into the extreme of overstatement.[334] On the Middle Way path that avoids these two extremes, one's conduct is that of training in the six transcendent perfections.[335]

2) As for the two extremes with respect to one's view, if one naïvely accepts the existence of all objects of knowledge that there are in general, and all the limitless aspects of the relative level of truth in particular, one falls into the extreme of overstatement because one is asserting that these exist even though valid cognition cannot prove that they do. On the other hand, if one naïvely asserts that, on the same relative level of truth (which can be validated through valid cognition), things are not existent once they are thoroughly investigated (using such reasoning as whether things are unitary or manifold[336]), one falls into the extreme of understatement because one is asserting that emptiness is the *cause* of things disintegrat-

ing.[337] On the Middle Way path that avoids two such extremes, one's view is such that it pares away conceptual elaborations.

Specific Explanation of the Middle Way Tradition [B]

There are three considerations in explaining the Middle Way tradition: a general discussion identifying emptiness, a specific explanation of the interpretation of "unqualified emptiness," and a specific explanation of the interpretation of "qualified emptiness."

Identifying Emptiness [1]

The source verses state:

> **The scope of its view is emptiness—**
> **the actuality of negating the two kinds of identity, and an aspect of unqualified negation.** [3.140a]

Given that the scope[338] of the view in the Middle Way tradition is that of emptiness, the significance of that term "empty" is one of "absence." What is it that is absent? The two kinds of identity. The "-ness" component signifies that this constitutes the "circumstance" of things.[339]

In this regard, according to the school of Yogic Practitioners, what is alone explained as being the actuality of what is ultimate is timeless awareness—entailing no duality of perceived object and perceiving subject, such that the two kinds of identity (as what is to be negated) have been negated. According to those who have an unqualified interpretation of emptiness, this actuality is, rather, an aspect of unqualified negation that is simply the negation of the two kinds of identity.

Unqualified Emptiness (*rang stong*) [2]

The source verses state:

> **The basis for emptiness is objects in the phenomenal world, which are also what is to be negated and the basis for such negation.**
> **The way in which these are empty, according to the unqualified interpretation of emptiness, is that they cannot be proven to exist in essence.**

If this is analyzed, there are sixteen aspects—of outer, inner, both, emptiness, and so forth—
but these can be subsumed within the four aspects of what is substantial, insubstantial, true nature, and alternate reality.

More specifically, the basis for emptiness lies in objects in the phenomenal world[340]—which is to say, all possible phenomena, as many objects of knowledge as there may be. These are, at one and the same time, what is to be negated—that is, what it is that is empty—and the basis on which there can be this negation.[341] In brief, they constitute two kinds of things—individuals and phenomena.

As for the way in which these are empty, all phenomena that could be considered as bases for negation are empty by virtue of their very essence—for example, just as form is empty of form, any given thing is empty of being that very thing; because when one evaluates it using the reasoning that investigates from the ultimate perspective, the thing in question cannot be found to be that thing. To give an example, when a vase is investigated to establish whether it is something unitary or manifold, it cannot be established to be a "vase."

To summarize, to say nothing of things that are unsuitable to be objects of ordinary consciousness,[342] as many phenomena as are suitable are all explained as being empty of their respective essences. The *Entrance to the Middle Way* states:

> Since that[343] is its nature,
> the eye is empty of the eye;
> the ear, the nose, the tongue,
> the body, and the mind are to be described likewise.[344]

The basis for emptiness lies in its sixteen aspects, such as the emptiness of outer and inner objects in the phenomenal world.[345] If these aspects are summarized, [3.140b] they fall into the four categories of what is substantial, what is insubstantial, nature, and "alternate reality."[346] As is said:

> Furthermore, O Subhūti,[347] the Mahāyāna approach of the bodhisattva consists of the following aspects of emptiness: emptiness of what is internal, emptiness of what is external, emptiness of what is external and internal, emptiness of emptiness, emptiness

> of what is great, emptiness of what is ultimate, emptiness of what is conditioned, emptiness of what is unconditioned, emptiness of what is beyond limitations, emptiness of what is without beginning or end, emptiness of what is not to be discarded, emptiness of nature, emptiness of all phenomena, emptiness of specific characteristics, emptiness of what has no frame of reference,[348] . . . and emptiness of the very essence of what has no substantiality.[349]

Of these aspects:

(1) The first aspect refers to the six internal components of the sense fields (the faculty of vision and so forth).[350]

(2) The second aspect refers to the six outer components of the sense fields (forms and so forth).[351]

(3) The third aspect refers to the foregoing outer and inner components of the sense fields but not in this case to the physical bases for the senses.[352]

(4) The foregoing explanations confirm that phenomena on the relative level are empty of any finite essence on the relative level, but the fourth aspect of emptiness is explained in order to negate any fixation that the fact that things are empty of being things itself constitutes something that is their "nature." The topic under discussion in this fourth explanation is that of emptiness in the three aspects just explained. The purpose of presenting this fourth aspect of emptiness is to negate any fixation that emptiness, moreover, "exists," or "is," something.

(5) Concerning the fifth aspect, the term "supreme" is used because there is a pervasiveness throughout the entire animate and inanimate universe, without exception.[353]

(6) The sixth aspect refers to nirvāṇa because this is the most sublime purpose concerning what is ultimate.[354] In this context, this is not held to refer to nirvāṇa that does or does not entail residual traces,[355] but to either nirvāṇa as the natural state[356] or nonlimited nirvāṇa.[357]

(7) and (8) As for the seventh and eighth aspects, what is conditioned and what is unconditioned refer, respectively, to that which entails the three phases of production, duration, and cessation, and that which does not.[358] [3.141a]

(9) Concerning the ninth aspect, "what is beyond limitations" refers to a freedom from the dualistic limitations of naïve affirmation or nihilistic denial. It applies to all three topics of emptiness, interdependent connection, and the path of the Middle Way.

(10) As for the tenth aspect, "what is without beginning or end" refers to saṃsāra.

(11) Concerning the eleventh aspect, in the expression "what is not to be discarded" "to discard" in general implies there being some "thing to be discarded," which is another word for a "flaw." To say "not to be" with regard to that implies "what is to be accepted," which is another way of saying "the phenomena that pertain to the totally refined state of enlightenment."[359]

(12) Regarding the twelfth aspect, "nature" refers to the emptiness of phenomena of any finite essence on the relative level because this constitutes the essence of phenomena on the ultimate level. Although there really is no difference between this aspect and the topic discussed as the basis for emptiness under the fourth aspect of emptiness, they are explained in these distinct ways in order to negate the fixation on emptiness per se and the fixation on that emptiness as being some "nature."

(13) As for the thirteenth aspect, "all phenomena" refers to as many phenomena as there are, whether conditioned or unconditioned.

(14) Concerning the fourteenth aspect, the "specific characteristics" referred to are as many characteristics as there are that are specific to phenomena (such as anything that is suitable to be a form and so forth)—"from forms up to and including the state of omniscience."[360]

(15) With respect to the fifteenth aspect, "what has no frame of reference" refers to the three phases of linear time. As it is said:

> The present is not something that abides,
> nor are the past or the present things that exist.[361]

This aspect of emptiness must be discussed in light of the foregoing citation; it is not to be discussed in the sense of "no frame of reference," meaning a situation in which one thing is absent in another.[362]

(16) Regarding the sixteenth aspect, the expression "the very essence of what has no substantiality" means that any substantial thing is empty of being that substantial thing itself. That emptiness being in turn empty of itself is termed "emptiness of the very essence of what has no substantiality."

Thus, a detailed analysis discusses these sixteen aspects, while a less elaborate treatment subsumes them into four categories. In the extensive and middle-length "Mother" texts,[363] we find these words following the discussion of the sixteen aspects of emptiness:

> O Subhūti, what is substantial is empty of what is substantial, [3.141b] what is insubstantial is empty of what is insubstantial, nature is empty of nature, and alternate reality is empty of alternate reality.[364]

This passage, then, speaks of four aspects of emptiness. In this regard, if we summarize all objects that there are in the phenomenal world, which are bases for emptiness, they can be subsumed within the two categories of relative and ultimate truth. As for the relative level of truth, it comprises two categories, what is substantial and what is nonsubstantial.[365] And although the ultimate level of truth cannot be analyzed from the point of view of what it constitutes in essence, from the point of view of its aspects, it can be shown to consist of both nature and what is termed "alternate reality."

The points to be understood from such a presentation are:

(1) that phenomena on the relative level have primordially never known existence, but it is not the case that timeless awareness has newly *made* them nonexistent (this is the logic that shows emptiness to be the nature of all that is relative); and

(2) while this is the case, it is not appropriate for emptiness to be an object either of a consciousness that is subjectively perceiving what is relative, or of its verbalizations (this is the logic that shows it to be "alternate reality").

"Well," one might wonder, "why is this term 'alternate reality' used?" The commentary to the *Entrance to the Middle Way* gives three reasons[366] in discussing the use of the term "alternate reality":

(1) due to the fact that, while objects in the phenomenal world—that is, things on the relative level—are not constantly present, this is constantly present;

(2) due to the reason that, while things on the relative level are not what is realized by timeless awareness, this is what is realized by that awareness; and

(3) due to the reason that, while what is relative does not transcend saṃsāra, this does transcend it.

Qualified Emptiness (*gzhan stong*) [3]

The source verses state:

> **The basis for negation is what is absolute, while the factors to be negated are what is imputed and what is dependent.**

The Yogic Practitioners profess that it is "empty of these."
They explain that this can be analyzed into fourteen aspects, which can be subsumed within two.

The basis on which there can be negation is what is absolute[367]—that is, basic space, suchness beyond the confines of conceptual elaboration. The factors to be negated are what can be characterized as imputed or dependent.[368] As to the way in which emptiness is so, given that the basis for negation is empty of the two factors to be negated, [3.142a] it is the absolute itself that is described by Yogic Practitioners—that is to say, those who uphold the tradition of qualified emptiness—to be "empty of other."[369] In this regard, Serdok Paṇchen[370] provides the following explanation:

> That which serves as the basis for emptiness is that which is dependent—that is to say, the limitless aspects of the consciousness imbued with the dualistic framework of perceived objects and a perceiving subject. The factor that is to be negated is that which is imputed, which is in turn twofold according to an analysis of what is perceived and what perceives. Each of these aspects of perceived and perceiver has two further divisions, from the point of view of the individual and that of phenomena.[371]
>
> As to the way in which these are empty, the basis for the negation is empty of the factors to be negated in the sense of being "empty of other," not in the sense of being "empty in itself." For the factors to be negated—the two aspects of what is imputed, that is, perceived and perceiver—are in essence "other" with respect to the two aspects of perceived and perceiver that pertain to consciousness based on dualistic perception (which are the bases on which negation can take place) because the former cannot be considered to be of the essence that is specific to the latter.
>
> "What," one might ask, "is the essence that *is* specific to that consciousness based on dualistic perception?" It is nondual timeless awareness itself—the bare lucidity and awareness of experiencing whatever is knowable.[372]

In general, while timeless awareness—entailing none of the duality of perceived objects and perceiving subject—is explained as being the basic space of phenomena, when its ramifications are analyzed, there are fourteen aspects of emptiness; when the significance of these are summarized, these are understood as being subsumed within two categories.[373]

These fourteen aspects as follows:

> Emptiness of what is internal, of what is external, of what is external and internal,
> and of what is great; emptiness of emptiness,
> of what is ultimate, of what is conditioned, of what is unconditioned,
> of what is beyond limitations, of what is without beginning or end,
> of what is not to be discarded, of nature,
> of characteristics, and emptiness of phenomena.[374]

In this case, the bases for these aspects of emptiness are referred to in *Distinguishing Center and Limit*:

> There is emptiness of that which experiences and what it experiences,
> of their body, and of the basis for existence;
> there is also such perception of how, what,
> and why, which are also emptiness.[375]

This passage constitutes a brief summation of all aspects of emptiness without exception. The specific contexts that are the bases for these aspects of emptiness are the inner components of the sense fields, the outer components of the sense fields, [3.142b] the body that constitutes the context for of these two, and the inanimate universe that serves as their support; that is to say, what pertains to the relative level of truth. The timeless awareness that has direct knowledge of the emptiness of these four categories is the specific context that is the basis for the emptiness of the fifth and sixth aspects;[376] this is from the point of view of the ultimate level. So the specific contexts that are the bases for emptiness in the six foregoing cases are assigned on the basis of an analysis of the two levels of truth, while the specific situations that are the bases for emptiness in the last eight cases[377] are assigned in light of their usefulness. As is said:

> Because the two kinds of virtue are to be gained,[378]
> because there is constant benefit for beings,[379]
> because saṃsāra is not to be relinquished,[380]
> because virtue becomes inexhaustible,[381]

> because, moreover, their spiritual potential becomes evident in its total purity,[382]
> because the major and minor marks of perfect form are gained,[383]
> and because the attributes of buddhahood are revealed in their purity,[384]
> bodhisattvas pursue spiritual accomplishment.[385]

The foregoing points identify the specific contexts that serve as the bases for the emptiness for the eight latter aspects of emptiness. Because bodhisattvas base their spiritual practice on these eight specific contexts, one might wonder for what purpose any given aspect is undertaken.

Because the two kinds of virtue—(1) conditioned and (2) unconditioned—are to be gained in the more consummate sense, one pursues the practice of these two kinds of virtue—conditioned and unconditioned—in the shorter term. These two kinds are the specific contexts, respectively, for the emptiness of what is conditioned and the emptiness of what is unconditioned;

(3) using the same model, because there is the specific purpose of benefiting beings, one pursues spiritual practice on the path of the Middle Way;

(4) in order not to abandon beings, one pursues practice to engage in saṃsāra;

(5) in order to ensure that virtue becomes inexhaustible in the state in which there is not residual traces,[386] one pursues the accomplishment of virtue that accords with the true nature of phenomena;[387]

(6) in order for it to be purified of adventitious distortions,[388] one pursues practice that focuses on one's naturally indwelling spiritual potential;

(7) one pursues spiritual practice in order to gain the major and minor marks of perfect form;[389] and

(8) in order to gain the attributes of buddhahood, [3.143a] one pursues practice to accomplish the powers and so forth.

The first four of these aspects of emptiness[390] are from the point of view of what is held in common with the ordinary approaches of the śrāvaka and pratyekabuddha; the latter four aspects,[391] of what is extraordinary about the Mahāyāna approach. It is in order to promote one's understanding of this that the citation states:

> . . . bodhisattvas pursue spiritual accomplishment.[392]

In addition, it is for this or that particular purpose that one pursues accomplishment with respect to this or that corresponding aspect of emptiness. To give one example, if one did not understand saṃsāra to be emptiness, one would feel disheartened and relinquish saṃsāra.

In this context, with respect to the explanations of the specific contexts that are the bases for aspects of emptiness, there are distinctions in how this interpretation differs from that found in the sources of the interpretation of unqualified emptiness—specifically, the naturally indwelling spiritual potential, as distinct from emptiness of nature; the major marks of perfect form, as distinct from the emptiness of specific characteristics; and the qualities of the level of buddhahood, as distinct from the emptiness of all phenomena.[393]

As to the way in which there is emptiness,[394] the true nature of phenomena is empty of what is "other"[395]—which is to say, dualistic consciousness from the point of view of the individual and phenomena.[396]

A concise analysis consists of two aspects—emptiness of what has no substantiality and emptiness of the very essence of what has no substantiality.[397] These two aspects, moreover, can be analyzed into their own aspects. Emptiness of what has no substantiality is designated from the perspective that there is a negation of an imputed individual and imputed phenomena as factors to be negated. Emptiness of the very essence of what has no substantiality is designated from the perspective that there is a negation of what remains in the wake of the negation of the foregoing factors to be negated—that is, the existence of the individual and phenomena as being the true nature of things. These two aspects are not two separate "emptinesses" that can each stand on its own; however, they must be designated as a means of dispelling the two extremes of overstatement and understatement with respect to each situation involving things that are actually emptiness. The point here is that one understand that these two aspects must be seen as applying to all fourteen aspects of emptiness.

The two extremes here are explained as being that of overstatement (that is, of naïvely assuming the existence of an individual and phenomena that are imputed) and that of understatement (that is, of denial that states: "The factors of the true nature of reality and the entity of the individual do not exist").[398] [3.143b]

Main Explanation: Two Aspects of the Lack of Identity [V]

The main explanation—that of an investigation of the two aspects of the lack of identity—is twofold: an articulation of the purpose of addressing the lack of identity and an investigation of this actual lack of identity.

Purpose [A]

The source verses state:

> **The hindrances to perception are the ten distracting concepts;**
> **the remedies that dispel these are the two aspects of lack of identity.**

That which acts as a hindrance to one directly perceiving emptiness consists entirely of ten digressive concepts.[399] As the *Summary of the Meaning of the Eight Thousand Verses* states:

> Due to the ten ways in which mental distraction occurs,
> the mind is distracted to other things,
> so that spiritually immature people have no chance
> to develop nondual timeless awareness.[400]

The remedy that dispels these concepts is timeless awareness that directly realizes the twenty, or sixteen, aspects of emptiness. If these aspects are summarized, they are twofold, due to an analysis into realization of the lack of identity in the individual and in phenomena.

Analysis [B]

The investigation of this actual lack of identity is fivefold: the lack of identity in phenomena; the lack of identity in the individual; the relevant issues related to both aspects; the defining of the topics for investigation through the individual interpretations of the Middle Way; and the advice concerning the integration of the underlying intent of the two mainstream traditions.

Lack of Identity in Phenomena [1]

This discussion has five topics: (a) the key topic for initially coming to a definitive conclusion; (b) what, in essence, constitutes the identity that is to be negated; (c) the reasons that negation is necessary; (d) the realizations that are specific to the individual philosophical systems; and (e) the process for reaching a definitive conclusion through reasoning in the Middle Way tradition.

Key Topic [a]

The source verses state:

> **The more obvious aspect of the lack of identity in phenomena**
> **is an issue common to Buddhists**
> **and non-Buddhists alike, and so one should come to a definitive**
> **conclusion about it at the outset.**

Concerning the lack of any identity in phenomena, there is a more obvious aspect (in which the factor to be negated—which is in fact negated—is the sense of this identity having true existence) and a more subtle aspect (in which even something having no true existence is negated). Of these two, first and foremost one should come to a definitive conclusion concerning the more obvious aspect, for the following reasons: (a) because this aspect is an issue common to Buddhists and non-Buddhists; (b) because the realization of this more obvious aspect of the lack of identity in phenomena must precede the realization of the more subtle aspect of that lack of identity; [3.144a] and (c) because once one has come to a definitive conclusion that all phenomena on the relative level are empty in and of themselves of any finite essence, this proves as a consequence that anything called "the identity in the individual"—which is imputed by an almost innate level of nonrecognition—is empty in and of itself of any finite essence.

Factor to Be Negated [b]

As for what this is in essence, the source verses state:

This is, in essence, similar to a rope being taken for a snake; there is just the fixation in the ordinary mind that this is something self-justifying that is truly existent.

The identity in phenomena, in its essence, is discussed in the commentary to the *Four Hundred Verses*, which states that this is

> a case in which something exists solely due to there being a concept of it, but is not something existent in the absence of that concept. These are cases like that of a coiled rope being unhesitatingly imputed to be a snake; this is certainly a case in which something cannot be established to exist in its very essence.[401]

In accord with this citation, it is due to the influence of this almost innate level of nonrecognition—to which one has become habituated throughout beginningless time—that all phenomena, both external and internal, all forms, and so forth, that manifest to the ordinary mind, are fixated on as though truly existent things that have their own specific and innate characteristics. In any way that this occurs, it comes down to nothing more than something being imputed by conceptual thinking—like a rope being mistaken for a snake—for things by their very nature cannot be found to exist. And so they are things that are negated through reasoning when one is focusing on suchness itself.

Purpose of Negating Identity [c]

As for the purpose of negating these,[402] the source verses state:

This is negated because it is the cause for misconstruing things to have identity, which lies at the root of the two obscuring factors.

Such overt fixation is the cause for misconstruing things to have identity, which lies at the root of the two kinds of obscuration.[403] This is discussed in the *Precious Garland*:

> As long as there is reification of the mind-body aggregates,
> for that long there is the belief in an "I."

If there is belief in an "I," there is, furthermore, karma,
and due to that there is rebirth.[404]

That is, furthermore, the foremost factor in the cognitive obscuration, as is pointed out in the *Highest Continuum*:

Whatever conceptual thoughts involve the three focal points[405]
is held to constitute the cognitive obscuration.[406]

Therefore, those who wish to attain liberation and omniscience[407] by eliminating the two kinds of obscuration [3.144b] must eliminate overt fixation on the *root* of these two kinds of obscuration. This, in turn, must be eliminated through negating the sense that objects are truly existent things. As we read in the *Four Hundred Verses*:

With one having perceived that no identity exists in sense objects,
the potential for conditioned existence will come to an end.[408]

And according to the *Detailed Commentary on Valid Cognition*:

In this context, without repudiating an object,
one is unable to eliminate it.[409]

Philosophical Interpretations [d]

Concerning the ways in which the various philosophical systems understand this issue, the source verses state:

Although the Particularists and Followers of the Sūtras do not have a completely perfect understanding of suchness,
they come to their definitive conclusion on the basis of temporary objects in the phenomenal world.
The rationale is that nothing whatsoever is found through investigation;
for to consider this to mean a lack of true existence is their general tradition.

What is simply the most obvious aspect of the lack of identity in phenomena is found in all philosophical systems, for it is explained in such texts as the *Ornament of the Middle Way*[410] that this is found even among non-Buddhists. But even though this will suppress the more obvious aspect of the cognitive obscuration (which is in direct opposition to it), it is not the view that becomes the path to omniscience. It is not possible for one to directly perceive the lack of identity in the subjective perceiving agent[411] by familiarizing oneself simply with this because it is devoid of the basis for positive qualities that is in accord with liberation.[412]

Concerning this issue, the followers of the Sāṃkhya school believe objects in the external world to be mind and further believe that dualistic consciousness becomes a nondual state with the dissolution of mind into primal matter.[413]

In the systems of the Particularists and the Followers of the Sūtras, there are no explanations that bring one to a definitive conclusion on the basis of all limitless objects in the phenomenal world, and so they lack a completely perfect understanding of suchness as it pertains to the lack of identity in phenomena. Nevertheless, their explanations bring a definitive conclusion on the basis of ephemeral objects in the phenomenal world, and so they must have a partial understanding.

That is to say, source texts of the Particularist school explain that external objects on the coarse level have no true existence; while the sources of the Followers of the Sūtras do not stop there but make the distinction of a duality between what is material and what is a mental determinant[414] and explain that mental determinants, too, have no true existence. The rationale for this, moreover, is as follows: whenever a given phenomenon is examined in the light of sublime intelligence from the ultimate perspective [3.145a] and nothing whatsoever is actually found, that fact alone means that it does not truly exist. This, in fact, is the general tradition for these systems,[415] and so it is said:

> Whatever can be dismantled or mentally dissected
> such that the mind no longer entertains a concept—
> such as a vase or water—exists on the relative level. . . .[416]

And generally speaking, as soon as a given phenomenon is accepted to be relative, it must be accepted that it does not truly exist; this is in fact the tradition of all who profess a Buddhist system of philosophy. And in a source of the Followers of the Sūtras, we read:

Due to this, in any way that something is imputed,
it does not exist in the ultimate sense.[417]

There are a great number of such scriptural citations explaining that exclusionary mental determinants have no true existence.[418]

The source verses state:

The Mind Only school's own tradition holds that they realize both aspects of the lack of identity;
but if a follower of the Middle Way evaluates this, because nondual consciousness is held
to be ultimate, there still remains a rudimentary sense of identity in phenomena.

To say nothing of the lower philosophical systems, even the Mind Only school of the Mahāyāna approach holds that, according to its own tradition, both aspects of the lack of identity are realized. But if this is evaluated with the reasoning of the Middle Way, the two aspects of the lack of identity have not yet been brought to consummation since there remains a rudimentary sense of identity in phenomena because consciousness per se, devoid of the dualism of perceived objects and perceiving subject, is held to be ultimate. Nevertheless, the obvious and subtle aspects of identity in the individual and the more obvious aspect of identity in phenomena have been eliminated.

In particular, those Mind Only proponents who hold sense data to be valid,[419] even though they accept that objects in the external world do not exist, also accept sensory appearances to be mind, and so do not accept the emptiness of both perceived objects and perceiving subject. Therefore, they accept the lack of identity in the individual in a completely perfect way, but their way of establishing emptiness on the internal level has not been fully developed. This is because even though they accept that any identity that is entirely imputed does not exist, they do not establish the identity that is imputed to be a perceiving agent does not exist.[420]

Definitive Understanding through Middle Way Reasoning [e]

As for the way in which one comes to a definitive conclusion through the reasoning of the Middle Way school, [3.145b] the source verses state:

Although there are many lines of reasoning in the Middle Way, the tradition of the Exalted One uses five
to usher in certainty concerning the integration of emptiness and interdependent connection.
Candra speaks of two models: once perceived objects are negated,
the proof that they do not exist negates the perceiving subject;
and the logic that a single relative thing is empty means that all phenomena are empty.

In the Middle Way school, there are many traditions of individual masters, such as Asaṅga and his brother,[421] for lines of reasoning that bring one to a definitive conclusion concerning the lack of identity in phenomena. However, the tradition associated with the Exalted One, Nāgārjuna, uses five—four that investigate, respectively, the essence, the cause, the result, and both the latter, and a fifth that is the reasoning concerning interdependent connection. I have explained earlier in this work[422] the way in which these lines of reasoning usher in the state of timeless awareness in which emptiness and the process of interdependent connection are integrated.

Candrakīrti discusses two distinct methods that have been developed for coming to a definitive conclusion concerning the lack of identity in phenomena. He states:

> If no object of knowledge exists, the negation of consciousness is ensured;
> at the outset [the Buddha] negated objects of knowledge.[423]

Accordingly, one method is to begin by negating the objective pole of consciousness, following which the evidence that perceived objects do not exist negates the subjective pole of consciousness. On the other hand, as is said:

> Whatever is the seeing of the one
> is the seeing of everything.[424]

This, the other method, is one of coming to a definitive conclusion that a given single relative phenomenon is empty in and of itself, so that by the very same reasoning one comes to a definitive conclusion that as many objects of knowledge as there are—subsumed within the two levels of truth—are all empty in and of themselves of any finite essence.

This process of coming to a definitive conclusion is from the point of view of someone progressing from a purely mundane path to embarking on the path of the Middle Way, without having been conditioned by any other philosophical system, Buddhist or otherwise. It does not apply to other cases because those who have already become involved in other systems of thought may have reached a definitive conclusion that coarser objects in the external world do not truly exist, [3.146a] but due to the conditioning of their belief systems, the reasoning they employ cannot be reassigned to some other specific situation.[425]

Lack of Identity in the Individual [2]

The investigation of the lack of identity in the individual also has five topics: (a) the key topic for initially coming to a definitive conclusion; (b) what, in essence, constitutes the identity that is lacking; (c) the reasons that such negation is necessary; (d) the realizations that are specific to the individual philosophical systems; and (e) the process for reaching a definitive conclusion through reasoning in the Middle Way tradition.

Key Topic [a]

The source verses state:

> **The issue that distinguishes non-Buddhists from Buddhists**
> **is that of identity in the individual.**

As just mentioned, even among non-Buddhists there is realization on a more obvious level of the lack of identity in phenomena, as well as some degree of virtuous conduct. So the real distinction between non-Buddhists and Buddhists must be made on the basis of whether or not there is acceptance of identity in the individual because the lack of identity in the individual constitutes the unique and extraordinary feature for all those who profess some system of Buddhist philosophy.

In this regard, identity in the individual has two expressions: a more obvious expression as imputed by belief systems, and a more subtle one that is imputed by an instinctual sense of fixated perception. What is called the "self" is that which is the object misconstrued by this instinctual fixation—that is, belief in the reality of the perishable aggregates. If one has not realized that this "self" is empty in and of itself of any finite essence, one is incapable of completely realizing the lack of identity in phenomena. And so if one has not completely realized the lack of identity in the individual, one cannot have realized the lack of identity in phenomena.[426]

Factor to Be Negated [b]

As for what, in essence, constitutes such identity, the source verses state:

> **In essence, this is the instinctual fixation on "I" and "mine."**

In essence, what is known as the "self" of the individual is something that all ordinary beings, even down to animals, are naturally born with. It is simply this conceit of thinking "I," which is the object of fixation for an instinctual sense of "I" and "mine." According to the commentary to the *Four Hundred Verses*:

> In this regard, what is called the "self" is what is imputed on the basis of the mind-body aggregates. . . .[427] In this regard, what is called "identity" is that which would naturally be the case in things such that in its essence it did not rely on any other factor.[428] [3.146b]

This, indeed, cannot be found to exist in the ultimate sense, as it is presumed to by holders of extreme views, as something permanent, unitary, and autonomous. However, just because this perception is capable of functioning on the conventional level, it is not the case that this does not exist simply as an imputation. This is because such thoughts as "given that I am following the path to liberation, this is, in fact, that path to liberation"[429] or "my path to liberation," and various other conventions of perceiving what is "mine," are well known in the world and pose no problem.[430] As *Entrance to the Middle Way* states:

> Just as the Buddha, although free of any belief in the reality of the transitory aggregates,
> taught in terms of "I" and "mine,"
> similarly, even though things[431] have no independent nature,
> they are taught as "existing" in a purely provisional sense.[432]

Purpose of Negating Identity [c]

As for the reasons that such negation is necessary, the source verses state:

> **It is negated because from it comes the sense of "other," from which all opinionated views derive.**

While this can be established as a convention, it cannot be found to exist in the ultimate sense, and so must be negated through reasoning. All emotionally afflicted views and all afflictive mental states (such as attachment and so forth) derive from overt fixation on "I" and "mine" with respect to this "self." The *Detailed Commentary on Valid Cognition* states:

> If there is an existent self, there is a sense of "other."
> From self and other come attachment and aversion.
> All flaws derive
> from a complete involvement with these.[433]

And as *Entrance to the Middle Way* explains:

> Once there is first fixation on the identity of "I,"
> attachment develops to things that are "mine." . . .[434]
> . . . Having used their intelligence to see that afflictive mental states and flaws all, without exception,
> derive from belief in the reality of the perishable aggregates,
> and having understood that the self is the object of that belief,
> advanced spiritual practitioners negate the self.[435]

Philosophical Interpretations [d]

As for the realizations that are specific to the individual philosophical systems, the source verses state:

> **While there are differences in the way in which realization takes place, all four philosophical systems bring realization.**

The significance of emptiness, and the conventional terms used concerning this, are found nowhere other than in the Middle Way school. And so, given a distinction that is to be made—between a general way in which realization takes place and a consummate degree of this— [3.147a] those who follow all four systems of Buddhist philosophy realize at least the lack of identity in the individual. For if this lack of identity in the individual is presented in a complete way in the source texts of the Particularist school, it goes without saying that the Followers of the Sūtras also accept this.[436]

Therefore, through gaining familiarity with the lack of identity in the individual as definitively presented in the source texts of the Particularists and Followers of the Sūtras, one comes to experience this lack directly. And through becoming familiar with that experience, one becomes capable of making fully evident the state of nirvāṇa (in the sense that the potential for fixated perception of individual selfhood has been eliminated).

However, these systems accept that the two aspects of the lack of identity[437] are substantial things because they accept these to be ultimately true (based on the reasoning that they are capable of performing functions in the ultimate sense). As for the bases on which they characterize these things, with the negation of any agent above and beyond the internal factors[438] (as the specific case in point), they specify either of two things that are irreducible.[439] And with the negation of any materially existent thing above and beyond objects in the external world (as the specific case in point), they specify substantial things that are irreducible particles of matter.[440]

While it is axiomatic that those of the Middle Way school have realization of the foregoing to a consummate degree, even those of the Mind Only school have a similar degree of realization.[441]

Definitive Understanding through Middle Way Reasoning [e]

Concerning the way in which one comes to a definitive conclusion through the reasoning of the Middle Way school, the source verses state:

> **The five aggregates are not the self, the self does not possess them,**
> **nor do they act as supports one for the other. Some twenty alternatives**
> **are negated by lines of proof such as the reasoning based on the chariot.**

Generally speaking, the object that serves as the frame of reference for concepts that involve the belief in a self consists of the five mind-body aggregates that are subsumed within one's ongoing experience. These constitute the objective pole that expresses itself in the way that the mind perceives, believing in the identity of "I" while focusing on that object. It is for this reason that the idea of believing in a self functions at all times with respect to any of the five aggregates subsumed within one's ongoing experience.[442] In all kinds of other situations, there are thoughts of what pertains to the self—"This is my friend, my family, my house, my land," and so forth; because if someone else causes harm to any of these, [3.147b] there is the thought, "So-and-so has harmed *me*." Nevertheless, the objective pole in the way that the mind perceives—that on which the thought fixates —is nonsubstantial and an abstract concept.

Forget about identity in the individual not existing in light of reasoning that investigates from the ultimate perspective; identity in the individual does not even exist in light of reasoning that investigates from the conventional perspective! An individual, a person, is held to exist only to be in accord with what is commonly accepted in the world, taking things at face value without examining them or inquiring further. But this is not under any circumstances existent in the sense of being a material and substantial thing. Therefore, while this is not existent on either of the two levels of truth, it is accepted to "exist" as something imputed merely on the level of what is relatively valid.[443]

In negating the object of that, the Buddha spoke, for example, of some twelve kinds of reasoning that negate in a general way the objects of belief in the reality of the perishable aggregates. These, however, must be learned from other sources. As for the specific negation of the objects of the twenty aspects of belief in the reality of the perishable aggregates, in general the transcendent and accomplished conqueror[444] spoke in the sūtras about the "twenty beliefs in the reality of the perishable aggregates" as follows: belief concerning any one of the five aggregates (making five);[445] belief that any one of the five aggregates is a possession of the self, by way of being partnered with it, or a secondary attribute (making ten); belief that the self serves as the support, with any one of the five aggregates being supported by it (making fifteen); and belief that any one of the five aggregates serves as the support, with the self being supported by it (making twenty). As is said in *Letter to a Friend*:

> "Forms," it is said, "are not the self." Nor does the self
> possess forms, nor do forms depend on the self,

> nor does the self depend on forms. In a similar fashion,
> understand that the four remaining aggregates are empty.[446]

That is to say, in one's analyzing the five mind-body aggregates, in each case none of these is the self. The self (which is not some substantial thing) does not possess any of the five aggregates. With respect to the five aggregates vis-à-vis the self, or the self vis-à-vis the five aggregates, in no case is the one associated with the other. So in the case of these twenty alternatives, to prove the nonexistence of a self [3.148a], the master Nāgārjuna and his heirs use the reasoning of the chariot and so forth to negate identity in the individual, as was discussed previously.[447] To describe the form this takes clearly, it is as stated in the first version of *Stages of Meditation* by Kamalaśīla:

> The individual is not thought of as something aside from the mind-body aggregates, or the components of ordinary perception, or the sense fields. The individual is also not the essence of the aggregates and so forth. This is because the aggregates and so forth are, in essence, impermanent and manifold, and because the individual is imputed by others to be, in essence, permanent and unitary.
>
> It is not suitable for that (or, alternatively, an individual that cannot be described[448]) to be an existent thing because there is no other form it could take as an existent thing.
>
> Therefore, it is thus: one should investigate the fact that what is called "I" and "mine" in the world[449] is confusion, pure and simple.[450]

This identity is a fixated concept of selfhood based on the conceit of thinking in terms of "I," imputed with respect to the aggregates that perpetuate one's body. If it could truly be found to exist, would it be identical to, or separate from, the aggregates of forms and so forth? One might suppose it would be identical, but this is not the case, because their characteristics are not in harmony. The aggregates are impermanent, compounded of manifold factors, and subject to external influences, while the self, it is presumed, would be something permanent, unitary, and autonomous.

In this regard, it is not the case for the following reasons:

(a) because the aggregates can be determined through reasoning to be *impermanent* and conditioned, while the self is supposedly provable through some experience of one's taking it to be *permanent*, such as assuming that what one recognizes it as now is what one perceived it to be previously;

(b) because the aggregates can be determined through reasoning to be *manifold* groups of forms, sensations, and so forth, while the self is supposedly provable through some experience of one's taking it to be *unitary*, such as assuming, "I endure as a single entity"; and

(c) because the aggregates can be determined through reasoning to be *subject to external influences* such as origination and disintegration, while the self is supposedly provable through some experience of one's taking it to be *autonomous*, of the inward sense of "I." [3.148b]

One might suppose that it can be determined to be separate from the aggregates, but this is not the case:

(a) because the fixated concept of selfhood could not function with respect to anything other than the aggregates; and

(b) because it would thus be deprived of the characteristics of the aggregates and so be nonsubstantial and, if it were therefore nonsubstantial, this would contradict its being capable of performing functions.[451]

On this note, the *Source Verses on Sublime Intelligence* state:

> If the self were the aggregates,
> it would be subject to origination and disintegration.
> If it were other than the aggregates,
> it would lack the characteristics of the aggregates.[452]

In addition, substantial things amount to just these five aggregates—forms, sensations, perceptions, formative factors, and aspects of consciousness; one cannot directly detect in the slightest a self that is separate from these. Because the vision and the other sense faculties are the subjective perceivers of the external components of the sense fields (visual forms and so forth) as their objects, and because even reflexive consciousness[453] is the subjective perceiver of consciousness as its object, it is not logical that any of these be the self. Because the nature and effects of such an identity—not subsumed within the aggregates—would be unable to be perceived, there is no line of reasoning that can support there being such, and it cannot even be provable through valid inference.[454]

One might suppose that this mental attitude of thinking in terms of "I" is a valid state of subjectively perceiving in terms of a self as its object. But since this is just a concept that embodies an overt form of fixation, it does not constitute direct experience, and because it cannot be supported by any valid line of reasoning whatsoever, it also does not constitute valid inference.[455] Rather, it amounts to nothing more than the conceit of thinking in terms of "I" without any real reason for doing so, due to the influence of a familiarization process that has extended throughout beginningless time, similar to the case of a rope's being mistaken for a snake.

Therefore, given that the self and the individual are imputed on the basis of what is merely the collection of the mind-body aggregates, if they are examined with authentic sublime intelligence, no substantial thing that is an identity can be found. In the sūtras it is stated:

> O monks, any spiritual practitioners or brahmins[456] whose belief is one of thinking in terms of "self" [3.149a] are all focusing solely on the five aggregates that perpetuate saṃsāra. That being the case, all fixated perception of a self is solely with respect to the lack of such identity.[457]

And:

> Thus, just as the name "chariot"
> is given to an assemblage of parts,
> similarly on the basis of the mind-body aggregates,
> there is the relative term "ordinary being."[458]

If such investigation negates there being any "I" that can be found to exist by its very nature, this also negates anything "mine" that can be found to exist by its very nature. This is similar to the fact that since one cannot conceive of the child of a barren woman, one also cannot conceive of that child's having its own eyes and so forth. In the *Source Verses on Sublime Intelligence*, we read the following:

> If the "I" itself is not existent,
> how could "mine" exist?[459]

And in *Entrance to the Middle Way*:

> Because there are not actions without agents,
> there is, therefore, no "mine" that exists without "I."

And, therefore, seeing "I" and "mine" to be empty,
advanced spiritual practitioners gain total freedom.[460]

The source verses state:

In *Distinguishing Center and Limit*, there are ten ways of being wise, as remedies
to ten ways of believing in identity in the individual. There are many other such ways of reasoning.

In the regent Maitreya's source *Distinguishing Center and Limit*, there is discussion of some ten ways of believing in identity. The text states that identity in the individual can be (1) misperceived as something unitary; (2) believed to be the cause that gives rise to all other things; (3) believed to be an agent of experience that appreciates sense objects; (4) believed to be a creator; (5) believed to have control over sense objects; (6) believed to be permanent; believed to be the basis (that is, the support) for (7) deeply ingrained afflictive states or (8) the totally refined state;[461] (9) believed to be a spiritual practitioner; or (10) believed to be that which is not free and then free.[462]

Given these beliefs, the text speaks of the ten ways of becoming learned as their remedies:[463]

(1) The remedy to the first belief is to become learned about the mind-body aggregates; because these are by their nature collections of myriad factors, [3.149b] this serves as a remedy to the belief in something unitary.

(2) To become learned about the components of ordinary perception[464] serves as the remedy to the second belief; given that the significance of these components lies in their being causes, to become learned about these eighteen components becomes the remedy to believing in a self as being a cause.[465]

(3) One's becoming learned about the sense fields serves as the remedy to the third belief; there is no existent self as that which enjoys sense objects because the process of appreciating sense objects is due to the interdependent connection between the twelve constituents of the sense fields.[466]

(4) To become learned about interdependent connection serves as the remedy for the fourth belief; things are not created by a self because they are the manifestation of what is simply the interdependent connection between causes and conditions.

(5) To become learned about what is or is not in accord with the nature

of things serves as a remedy to the fifth belief; things are not controlled by a self in any way whatsoever because they proceed from a process of harmonious cause and effect.[467]

(6) To become learned about the faculties becomes the remedy to the sixth belief; there is no individual as the governing condition[468] because the twenty-two faculties serve as the supports that govern our experience.[469]

(7) To become learned about time serves as the remedy to the seventh belief; there is no permanent self because the three phases of linear time ensure that things are subject to origination and cessation.

(8) To become learned about the Four Truths acts as the remedy to the eighth belief; there is no identity in the individual that is the basis for either deeply ingrained afflictive states or the totally refined state because the first two truths constitute the basis for deeply ingrained afflictive states, while the latter two constitute the basis for the totally refined state.

(9) To become learned about spiritual approaches serves as the remedy to the ninth belief.[470]

(10) To become learned about what is conditioned and unconditioned serves as the remedy to the tenth belief.[471]

Given that there are a great many ways of reasoning such as the foregoing, one should learn about these from the traditions of the scriptural sources.[472]

Relevant Issues [3]

An explanation of the relevant issues related to both aspects of the lack of identity consists of five topics: [3.150a] an examination of the identicalness or separateness of these two aspects; the purpose of explaining these two aspects; the factors to be negated in these two cases; the valid cognition that ascertains these; and an investigation of authentic ways of reasoning.

Identicalness or Separateness [a]

The source verses state:

> **Because all phenomena lack identity, in essence**
> **these aspects are inseparable. The factors to be negated being**
> **true existence and the "I," or self,**
> **the aspects are assigned as this vis-à-vis that from distinct points**
> **of view.**

Given that the two aspects of lack of identity in the individual and in phenomena are distinct aspects that are identical in essence, the reasoning behind this is as follows: Because all visible and audible phenomena[473] are such that they lack identity, from the point of view of their essence, there cannot be the slightest division whatsoever. By way of example, a given phenomenon as a basis for specific features—a vase, say—may not be something that can actually be fixated on as a substantial thing, but under the circumstances (from the point of view of its being merely something imputed), it can be identified as a basis for specific features. Something such as a vase, then, does not ever have an "I" or "self"; this is the lack of identity in an individual. And the vase cannot be found to truly exist in the slightest; this is the lack of identity in a phenomenon. This is because there is, in essence, no distinction to be made between the fact that no identity can be found in this and the fact that no true existence can be found. Therefore, all phenomena lack any identity as an individual *and* lack any identity as a phenomenon. Nevertheless, from the point of view of distinguishing an "I" or self as the factor to be negated, there is the lack of identity in the individual, while from the point of view of distinguishing true existence as the factor to be negated, there is the lack of identity in phenomena. These are assigned as this vis-à-vis that from the perspective of distinguishing the factors to be negated; so the division is due to there being aspects.

Purpose [b]

As for the purpose for explaining these two aspects, the source verses state:

> **The purpose of this is in order to care for two types of people.**

One might wonder, "If the two aspects of lack of identity are in essence inseparable, what is the point in analyzing two aspects?" The reasoning is as follows: The Victorious One[474] spoke of the lack of identity in the individual in order to care for those of the śrāvaka and pratyekabuddha types in the Hīnayāna approach, and of the lack of identity in phenomena in order to care for those of the bodhisattva type in the Mahāyāna approach. [3.150b]

In this regard, it was definitely necessary to teach the lack of identity in the individual for those of the Hīnayāna type, for if this were not taught, they could not become free of saṃsāra. But he taught only the lack of identity in the individual for them because they are not suitable recipients to be taught the lack of identity in phenomena in addition, and so there would have been no point even if he had taught this. But for those of the Mahāyāna type, he taught the lack of identity in phenomena because of the necessity of their attaining omniscience.

Factors to Be Negated [c]

As for an investigation of the object to be negated in these two cases, the source verses state:

> **Although the actual factors to be negated cannot possibly be known,**
> **due to confusion on the part of the subjective perceiver, they are imputed as being perceived as the one and the other.**

The actual things to be negated that are the objects in the case of these two aspects of lack of identity cannot possibly be objects that can be known. It is impossible for an identity in the individual to exist as something permanent, unitary, and autonomous, and in the case of any visible or audible phenomenon whatsoever, it is likewise impossible for there to be a single phenomenon that can be found to exist by its very nature, or that can be found to truly exist.

Nevertheless, since the mind that is the subjective perceiver is confused, it fixates on the one and the other, which gives us the factors to be negated with respect to the two aspects of lack of identity. Because these are erroneous notions of taking what does not exist to exist, they are done away with. Therefore, since the factors to be negated cannot possibly be objects, there is nothing to be eliminated, and so it is the elimination of such erroneous notions (as what is to be negated in the subjective perceiver) that is explained as "negating identity." If the factors to be negated could be found to actually be objects, one would be unable to eliminate them, no matter how hard one tried! No one at all can negate anything that actually exists as such, just as no one at all can confirm anything that does not actually exist as such.

Valid Cognition [d]

As for the valid cognition that ascertains these points, the source verses state:

The special attitude that derives from inferential knowledge based on reasoning
is the primary kind of valid cognition that ascertains what is ultimately the case.
If one summarizes the categories of reasoning that rely on logical arguments,
these are proofs of negation, due to a failure to observe something supportive or an observation of something contradictory. [3.151a]

Generally speaking, the special attitude that derives from inferential knowledge based on reasoning is the primary kind of valid cognition that ascertains the ultimate level of truth.[475] In this regard, there are many detailed analyses that rely on lines of reasoning. If one summarizes these, however, all of them are definitely and solely proofs based on negation, which negate that what is to be negated is something true; according to the criteria employed by logicians, therefore, any proof based on affirmation is impossible. To give an example, the statement "*X* is like an illusion because it is interdependently connected" presents the appearance of being an explicit proof of affirmation; but it does not lead one to any certainty concerning what is ultimately the case, and to the extent that anything is affirmed, it is that *X* is empty of any true existence.[476]

Proofs of negation are of two kinds—due to either a failure to observe something supportive[477] or an observation of something contradictory.[478] The proof of interdependent connection belongs to the latter type, the others to the former.[479]

Authentic Reasoning [e]

As an explanation of authentic ways of reasoning that investigate what is ultimately the case, the source verses state:

The key point of all reasoning that investigates what is ultimately so
is investigation that identifies a basis for attributes and then seeks out
that which does not contradict its essential quality and that which contradicts its particular attributes.
Therefore, the freedom from being unitary or manifold negates any finite essence,

while the negation of production in any of four ways negates particular attributes.
These two models are foremost; the rest are simply secondary.
The root of all of these is found in the homage to the Middle Way.

The key point to all reasoning that investigates what is ultimately the case is as follows: First one identifies some basis for attributes,[480] whatever it might be under the circumstances, and then undertakes to seek out that which does not contradict it or its essential quality,[481] and to seek out that which contradicts it or its particular attributes.

To give an example, if one explains, "The characteristics, or essential quality, of a vase is that it has a roundish body and a flattened base and is capable of performing the function of containing water,"[482] one then must investigate such issues as the following: "Then it must follow that the mouth of the vase is its roundish body, because of its being the vase."

Therefore, from among these lines of reasoning, those that are foremost in being capable of bringing one to a definitive conclusion that both objects on the external level and consciousness on the internal level do not truly exist are two—that of freedom from being unitary or manifold[483] negates any finite essence [3.151b] and that of the negation of production in any of four ways[484] negates particular attributes. The many other variations on lines of reasoning that are explained in the Middle Way sources are simply secondary to these.

The root, so to speak, of all of these lines of reasoning is found in the homage to the Middle Way by the lord protector Nāgārjuna:

> . . . revealing that which occurs in interdependent connection,
> without cessation, without origin,
> without being denied, without being affirmed,
> without coming, without going,[485]
> without ultimate distinctness, and without ultimate identity,
> and revealing the thorough subsiding of elaborations to be peace.

In accord with this citation, there are four basic lines of reasoning:

(1) The subjects under discussion—external and internal things—are without cessation in the final analysis or duration in the interim because they are initially unborn.

(2) The subjects under discussion—external and internal things—cannot be found to be separate things because they are not identical.

(3) The subjects under discussion—external and internal things—do not come, because they cannot be found to have gone.

(4) The subjects under discussion—external and internal things—cannot be denied because they cannot be affirmed.

These four models are the basic lines of unsurpassable reasoning.

Specific Middle Way Interpretations [4]

An ascertainment of the significance of what is investigated, according to the distinct Middle Way interpretations, is twofold—that of unqualified emptiness and that of qualified emptiness.

Unqualified Emptiness [a]

The source verses state:

> **In the Autonomist tradition, all substantial things are proven not to truly exist;**
> **emptiness is proven so as to eliminate concepts of fixating on them.**
> **The Consequentialists negate conceptual elaborations but do not try to prove a freedom from elaboration.**

Concerning the way in which one comes to a definitive conclusion by investigating things with such reasoning, those who follow the Autonomist system of the Middle Way school begin by proving that all substantial things do not truly exist. Following this, they understand that the concepts of fixating on that lack of true existence are factors to be eliminated, and so they come to a decision, and so prove, that the lack of true existence, or emptiness, is itself emptiness. The sublime intelligence that thus dispels both extremes—of existence and nonexistence—is not the consummate view since it still involves concepts. [3.152a]

While Consequentialists negate the multitudes of conceptual elaborations with many variant forms of reasoning, they do not try to prove a freedom from elaboration, since to do so would constitute an incurable poison.[486]

The meaning of the foregoing points has been discussed previously to a small extent.[487]

Qualified Emptiness [b]

The source verses state:

> **In particular, in the extraordinary tradition of Yogic Practitioners,**
> **it is realized that there is nothing other than mind and that mind does not exist.**
> **The nondual basic space of phenomena is endowed with the seven vajra properties.**

From among the proponents of the philosophical systems of the Middle Way, the tradition of those who are Middle Way Yogic Practitioners[488] is adorned with many secret key points that are special and extraordinary. As to the way in which they come to a definitive conclusion about their view by studying teachings and contemplating, as the great regent[489] states:

> Once they are intelligently aware that there is nothing other than mind,
> they then realize that mind is also nonexistent.
> When those with intelligence are aware that these two are nonexistent,
> they dwell in the basic space of phenomena that is unencumbered with these.[490]

In accord with this citation, they begin by coming to a decision concerning all phenomena—that these cannot be found to exist as anything other than, or apart from, mind alone. On account of that proof, the objective pole of experience is found to lack any independent nature. Having then come to a decision that the subjective pole also lacks any independent nature, they come to a definitive conclusion concerning the basic space of phenomena—empty of both the objective and subjective poles, flawless and utterly lucid by nature, endowed with the seven vajra properties.[491]

In discussing the definitive conclusion that is gained through contemplation, the source verses state:

The heart essence of all ordinary beings and buddhas
is free of elaboration, in no way resembling any identity of an individual.
This is the inseparability of saṃsāra and nirvāṇa, free of the mere lack of identity in the individual,
transcending being manifest or nonmanifest, and even interdependent connection.

What is referred to as "suchness itself," or "the very heart of attaining the state of bliss,"[492] is that which permeates and is present in ordinary beings, in buddhas—in all phenomena—in a state of evenness. This is present in ordinary beings in the manner of what lies at their very heart and in buddhas in the manner of being fully evident, [3.152b] and so is termed "the very heart of buddhahood" because in essence it undergoes no change.[493] Yet it in no way resembles some permanent, unitary, and autonomous identity of an individual since it constitutes a freedom from all limits imposed by elaboration. While there can be no division into a duality of saṃsāra versus nirvāṇa within its very essence, it can be classified into three phases with respect to context.[494] It is freed from being merely the view of emptiness (that of lack of identity in the individual), primordially ensured as what is uniquely and ultimately true. And it is freed from being either manifest or nonmanifest, substantial or nonsubstantial; it is truly unconditioned—what is termed "unconditioned ultimate truth." Since this ultimacy is said to transcend even interdependent connection, the ultimate is not classified as interdependently connected.

The source verses state:

Empty of adventitious flaws, it is not empty of unsurpassable qualities.
There is nothing to be removed or added, for it is realized through naturally occurring pure awareness.

Because this selfsame heart essence is empty of all adventitious flaws or distortions yet not empty of unsurpassable qualities (being spontaneously endowed with these), from the point of view of its essence, there are no distortions to be removed or qualities to be added. This itself is not realized merely though a limited amount of studying and contemplating teachings; it is said that it is realized in stages through the flawless awareness—one's individual self-knowing pure awareness, or naturally occurring pure awareness—that derives from meditation.

The source verses state:

> **It is said that ordinary mortals, śrāvakas, pratyekabuddhas, and beginning bodhisattvas**
> **do not have mastery of the view concerning the buddha nature.**
> **This is not an object of inference, because it is beyond language and concepts.**
> **Since this mode is difficult for any mind other than that of a spiritually advanced being to comprehend,**
> **it has become a topic of controversy, but I will not elaborate here.**

The fact that this mode of being is difficult to fathom is attested to in the commentary to the *Highest Continuum*:

> To summarize, these four kinds of individuals are considered to lack the vision to behold the very heart of attaining the state of suchness."[495] "What are these four kinds?" you ask. They are ordinary mortal beings, śrāvakas, pratyekabuddhas, and bodhisattvas who have newly embarked on their spiritual approach. [3.153a] This is as is said:[496]
>
> > O transcendent and accomplished conqueror, the very heart of attaining the state of suchness is not within the realm of experience of those who have fallen into the belief in the reality of the perishable aggregates, or those who have overt desire for[497] what is mistaken, or those whose minds stray completely from emptiness.[498]

As the foregoing citation indicates, not only we who remain at the level of ordinary mortal beings, but even śrāvakas, pratyekabuddhas, and bodhisattvas who have newly embarked on their spiritual approach (who are beginning practitioners on the path of accumulation[499]) do not have mastery of the view of the true nature of reality that is the very heart of attaining the state of bliss. Given that this fact has been clearly expressed by the Lord of Sages, the Lord Regent,[500] and others, this is not an object to be evaluated by the conventional methods and reasoning of intellectuals, such as some kind of valid cognition that is arrived at on the basis of the power of the thing itself,[501] or some inferential knowledge based on reasoning. This is because this way in which things truly abide is beyond the domain of language and conceptual thought.

This being so, with the exception of buddhas and spiritually exalted bodhisattvas,[502] it is difficult for the minds of others to embrace this mode that lies at the very heart of things, in the true sense of what the term implies. And since this seems contradictory within the framework of language and concept,[503] in the perceptions of half-baked intellectuals who in these times are renowned as supposed "Middle Way proponents"—whose understanding and personal merit are limited and who are lacking in any truly profound intelligence—as profound as this way in which things truly abide may be, to that extent they simply use it as a basis for their unfounded suppositions and denials, thus subverting the four reliances and turning this into a topic of controversy. Therefore, I will not elaborate here on the secret key points of this tradition's philosophical system; rather, if one wishes to gain understanding of these points, one should learn them from the scriptural sources of the great spiritual traditions of India and Tibet.

Advice Integrating Both Traditions [5]

As for advice concerning the integration of the underlying intent of the two mainstream traditions, the source verses state:

> **Having realized the individual methods of the two mainstream traditions,**
> **one integrates them as a single underlying intent , free of the flaws of exaggeration or denigration.**
> **One is endowed with flawless vision concerning the sūtras and tantras.** [3.153b]

Two masters—Nāgārjuna and Asaṅga—were great spiritual guides who unquestionably dwelled on the level of the spiritually advanced, who adorned this human world, and whose coming was indisputably prophesied by the Victorious One. Although there is no question of any hierarchy of higher or lower between their enlightened intentions, the fact that there may *seem* to be one is due solely to one's lack of good fortune and to one's highly restricted intelligence.[504]

That being the case, once one has understood the distinct approaches found in the sources of the two masters who codified these mainstream traditions, if one can integrate these through realizing that the enlightened intent of both is, in the final analysis, one and the same—the meaning of the Middle Way—one is freed from the many flaws of misinterpreted suppositions or denials. One becomes endowed with the flawless vision of the view concerning all sūtras and tantras. Understanding these two approaches—the one more short-term, the other more ultimate; the one more obvious and externally oriented, the other more subtle and internally oriented; the one putting an end to conceptual elaboration, the other focusing on the ultimate point of meditation[505]—one comes to realize the unerring intent of buddhahood, free of the conceptual imputations found in the minds of ordinary mortal beings, with one's view of both the sūtras and the tantras being unaffected by any flaw of seeing supposed contradictions therein.

Mantra Approach [VI]

An analysis of the distinctive view of the mantra approach is twofold: the presentation of the position held in general by masters of the Middle Way and that of the specific position held by Gargyi Wangpo.[506]

General Position [A]

The source verses state:

> **In the mantra approach, the interpretation of unqualified emptiness is that the subjective aspect is distinguished as the skillful factor of bliss,**
> **but that there is no difference in the objective aspect as freedom from elaboration.**
> **For the interpretation of qualified emptiness, even the objective aspect is not merely freedom from elaboration;**
> **rather, it is posited to be endowed with the most sublime of manifestations, comparable to divination with a mirror.**
> **Some say that other than the mere freedom from elaboration, because of the skillful methods involved,**
> **the difference is like that between an ordinary fire and one of sandalwood.**

One might wonder, "In which interpretation of the Middle Way is the view of the secret mantra approach to be found?" In this regard, individual masters have advanced many positions that incline to their own personal inclinations. Nevertheless, the explicit message of this approach is entirely in accord with the final cycle of the Buddha's teachings and that is by and large what is taught in the authoritative source texts from the land of spiritually advanced beings.[507] [3.154a] It was only in Tibet that the interpretations of the Middle Way renowned as "unqualified emptiness" and "qualified emptiness" arose as distinct positions.

Those who follow the interpretation of unqualified emptiness posit that the subjective aspect is to be taken as superior[508] due to the skillful influence of supreme bliss. With respect to the objective aspect of emptiness as the freedom from elaboration, they maintain that there is no distinction between the approach of mantra and that of the transcendent perfections.[509]

Those who follow the interpretation of qualified emptiness agree with the foregoing concerning the subjective aspect. With respect to the objective aspect of emptiness, however, they posit that this is not merely a freedom from elaboration, but emptiness endowed with the most sublime of manifestations, transcending even the most subtle subatomic structure yet comparable to the visions that occur through the process of divination with a mirror.[510]

And there are some who say that, while the approaches of mantra and the transcendent perfections are in accord simply concerning the essence of emptiness as a freedom from elaboration, the mantra approach is superior as to the way in which realization takes place, because of the special feature of the skillful means it entails. Speaking generally, the Sakya school and others categorize their view on the basis of both specific phenomena and their true nature; that is, from the point of view of the true nature of phenomena free of elaboration, there is no difference between the approach of mantra and that of the transcendent perfections, but there is a distinction in the mantra approach of the kāyas and timeless awareness as specific phenomena. The former point is the basis for the enlightened intent of the venerable Sakya Paṇḍita,[511] and he had no objection to the latter.[512]

Specific Position: Gargyi Wangpo [B]

The source verses state:

In the Middle Way of the mantra approach, the profoundly lucid unity of bliss and emptiness,
the position of the vajra of enlightened speech, who bore the mark of light,
is that there are four special attributes—the function of the central channel, the skillful means to experience emptiness,
the influence exerted with respect to the ground of being, and the attainment of the kāya of primordial unity.

Since origination and cessation are eliminated from that inseparable unity of supreme and unchanging bliss and emptiness as freedom from elaborations, it is profound and lucid. This unity, endowed with four characteristics[513] is the basis for what is characterized as the Middle Way in the mantra approach. There are four special attributes that are associated with it:

(1) the function of the central channel,[514] that is, the path of skillful methods such as that of focusing intently on the *avadhūti*;[515]

(2) other skillful methods to elicit the experience of emptiness, such as the techniques of instantaneous or gradual dissolution;[516] [3.154b]

(3) the influence exerted by establishing a connection, within the context of the ground of being—the way in which things truly abide—between the ground for refinement and the factors that bring refinement;[517] and

(4) the accomplishment of the consummate kāya of primordial unity that is the specific manifestation.

These four are posited by the vajra of enlightened speech, the sixth bearer of the crown marked with light—the scholar from the north, Jamyang Chökyi Nangwa.[518]

Summation: The View of Unborn Primordial Unity [VII]

As for a brief summation of the view of unborn primordial unity, the source verses state:

If this were not present as the fundamentally unconditioned nature, viewing it as such would not make it so,
and when emptiness is realized, cause and effect are spontaneously ensured.
Whatever is the ceaseless process of interdependent connection
is itself the supreme seal of unborn primordial unity.

Just as washing a lump of coal will never make it a conch shell,[519] if the true nature of buddhahood were not present as the reality that is the fundamentally unconditioned way that things truly abide, it would be impossible for it to become so through a process of investigation involving scriptural authority and reasoning, or through viewing it as such through a process of conceptual meditation.

On the basis of the three kinds of sublime intelligence,[520] one realizes emptiness in direct experience—not allowing the significance of the utter lucidity of emptiness to remain merely an object of intellectual understanding. At that point timeless awareness, which as a consequence is undeluded concerning the significance of cause and effect, is spontaneously ensured, so that its radiance arises as the unceasing process of interdependent connection. As this does not in any way deviate from the realization, in one's direct experience, of its fundamentally unconditioned and unborn nature, there is the primordial unity of skillful method and sublime intelligence. This is termed the "transcendent perfection of sublime intelligence" (*prajñāpāramitā*) or the "supreme seal" (*mahāmudrā*), which is the consummate meaningful state to be realized according to the sūtras and tantras.

The foregoing constitutes the commentary on the third part,
concerning a definitive treatment of the view
that is the principal factor.

Part 4. Foundations of Spiritual Practice

I. Impact of Study and Contemplation
II. Four Contemplations
  A. Reorienting the Mind Away from This Lifetime
    1. Foundation for Reorientation
      a. Identifying Opportunities and Endowments
      b. Great Purpose
      c. Difficulty of Obtaining the Support
    2. Contemplation of Impermanence
      a. Recollection of Death
      b. Rebirth in Other States
  B. Reorienting the Mind Away from Saṃsāra
    1. Karma
      a. General Contemplation
      b. Specific Issues
    2. Saṃsāra
      a. Eights Kinds of Suffering
      b. Three Kinds of Universal Suffering
  C. Reorienting the Mind Away from Quiescence and Naïve Happiness
  D. Reorienting the Mind Away from Dualistic Consciousness

The fourth part, a definitive treatment of the four contemplations that reorient the mind, is twofold: a general presentation of the impact of studying and contemplating teachings, and a specific delineation of the four contemplations that reorient the mind.

Impact of Study and Contemplation [I]

The source verses state:

> **The impact of study and contemplation is that of arousing an uncontrived faith**
> **in the teachings and the upholders of the teachings without sectarian bias.**
> **Without falling into any extreme, one conducts oneself with precision[521] concerning the effects of karma.**
> **The excellent speech of the buddhas serves as one's advisor, so that one feels a growing sense of freedom in one's ongoing experience.** [3.155a]
> **Nonetheless, there are the four contemplations that reorient the mind, which are methods from the tradition of pith instructions**
> **that dramatically reorient an ordinary person's mind.**

Having studied teachings in the foregoing way, without any prejudice, and having contemplated their meaning precisely through reasoning, one awakens in one's ongoing experience a sublime intelligence born of such study and contemplation. The impact of this is one of arousing faith, uncontrived yet informed and without any sectarian bias, in the general teachings of the victorious ones (both the Hīnayāna and Mahāyāna approaches) and in the special spiritual mentors who uphold these teachings.

Without falling into some extreme of inflexible prejudicial thinking or zealous adherence to one's own personal belief system or dogma, one conducts oneself in a forthright manner, behaving precisely with respect to the process of karmic causality, without confusing moral issues of what to accept or reject.[522] The excellent speech of the victorious ones—that is, all the sūtras and tantras—serves as one's advisor, as one does not let these teachings remain mere words but applies them to one's experience, feeling a growing sense of freedom. This is the impact that getting to the very root of hearing and contemplating teachings has on one.

This being the case, one will not be able to hear and contemplate teachings properly without relying on a deliberate and precise contemplation of such topics as one's hard-won state of opportunities and endowments. Even if one is able to do so, one's experience will not be affected in an ongoing way.

So one should carefully contemplate the four contemplations that reorient the mind, which are methods found in the tradition of pith instructions that dramatically reorient an ordinary individual's mind.[523]

Four Contemplations [II]

This discussion is fourfold: reorienting the mind away from this lifetime, reorienting the mind away from saṃsāra, reorienting the mind away from a state of quiescence and naïve happiness, and reorienting the mind away from dualistic consciousness.

Reorienting the Mind Away from This Lifetime [A]

This involves two considerations: contemplation of the hard-won state of opportunities and endowments (which is the support for meditation that reorients the mind), and contemplation of impermanence (which is the actual method for reorienting the mind).

Foundation for Reorientation [1]

The source verses state:

> **The precious support, endowed with eight opportunities and ten endowments,**
> **has great purpose and is difficult to obtain (as determined by cause, result, and analogy).**

This has three parts: identification of the opportunities and endowments; the great purpose of that state; and contemplation of the difficulty of obtaining it.

Identifying Opportunities and Endowments [a]

The eight opportunities are provided [3.155b] when one is free of the eight states devoid of such opportunity. Of these eight states, four are states within the human realm that are devoid of opportunity:

(1) that of people in "border regions," that is, places in which the four branches of the spiritual community are not present;[524]

(2) that of people whose faculties are incomplete, due to mental or physical impairment, deafness, and so forth;[525]

(3) that of those with erroneous opinions, who hold that there is no continuity from previous to future lifetimes, or consequences to one's actions, or who deny the validity of the Three Jewels; and

(4) that of those in worlds in which buddhas have not appeared and the teachings of the victorious ones are not present.

The four nonhuman states devoid of opportunity are (5)–(7) the three lower states of rebirth and (8) that of the long-lived gods. These long-lived gods are explained in *Letter to a Friend* to be those of both the state devoid of perception and the realm of formlessness;[526] of these, the former are found in one region of the state of the Mahāphala gods (associated with the fourth degree of meditative stability),[527] as though in a hermitage outside a populated area,[528] while the latter are ordinary mortal beings who have been reborn in the realm of formlessness.[529] The *Account of the Eight States Devoid of Opportunity* explains the long-lived gods to be those gods of the desire realm, who are constantly distracted by activities driven by their desires.[530]

Of the ten endowments, five derive from one's own situation:

> To be a human being, to be reborn in a central region, to have all one's faculties intact,
> not to have made wrong ethical choices, and to have faith in a spiritual foundation.[531]

"To be reborn in a central region" means to be reborn where the four branches of the spiritual community are active. "To have all one's faculties intact" means that one is not physically or mentally handicapped, and one's limbs, sight, hearing, and so forth, are complete. "Not to have made wrong ethical choices" means that one has not committed, or caused anyone to commit, any of the acts that bring immediate consequences at death.[532] "To have faith in a spiritual foundation" means to have faith in the ethical codes of the sacred dharma, as the foundation that gives rise to all positive qualities, whether mundane or transcendent; here the term "ethical codes" refers to any and all of the Three Repositories.[533] These five factors are called "endowments that derive from one's own situation" because they are circumstances supporting spiritual practice that pertain to one's own personal experience.

The five endowments that derive from others are as follows:

The coming of a buddha, the teaching of the sacred dharma,
the establishment of a tradition of teachings, the adherence of followers,
and the kindness shown for the sake of others.[534]

"The coming," or advent, "of a buddha" refers to one who has truly awakened to buddhahood [3.156a] after a process of spiritual development spanning three incalculably long eons. "The teaching of the sacred dharma" refers to the teachings presented by such a buddha or by followers of that buddha who are arhats. "The establishment of a tradition of teachings" refers to the fact that, from the time a buddha awakens to enlightenment and teaches until that buddha passes into nirvāṇa, the practice of the teachings is unimpaired by way of making the ultimate aspect of the teachings fully evident. "The adherence of followers" of the tradition thus established refers to people being aware that the realization of those teachings has the power to make the sacred dharma evident to ordinary beings, and so following those teachings as they were given in accord with such realization.[535] "The kindness shown for the sake of others" refers, for example, to sponsors and patrons donating monastic robes. These five factors are called "endowments that derive from others" because they are circumstances supporting spiritual practice that pertain to the personal experience of others.

Great Purpose [b]

Next, one contemplates the great purpose of this state. To have the eight opportunities and ten endowments is called having a "precious human existence" because it is extremely difficult to obtain and once obtained gives one an enormous advantage, for one is then capable of attaining all the limitless states of higher rebirth and the definitive excellence of enlightenment. In *Letter to Students* we read the following:

The path that is obtained by human beings with great mental fortitude,
and that serves as a support for conveying beings along the path of those gone to bliss,
is not obtained by gods, nāgas, demigods,
garuḍas, vidyādharas, kiṃnaras, or mahoragas.[536]

Therefore, one contemplates in the following way: "I have obtained, at least for the present, the noble working basis that is the most special one throughout the three realms.[537] If I do not then use this support, which has such a great purpose and which is the cause for higher states of rebirth and the definitive excellence of enlightenment, I will be more grievously deluded than someone who returns empty-handed from the fabled Isle of Jewels."

Difficulty of Obtaining the Support [c]

To contemplate the difficulty of obtaining this support, consider the difficulty from the point of view of the causes of such a rebirth. In general, to obtain any more fortunate state of rebirth requires some degree of sincere and positive action, such as ethical discipline. [3.156b] In particular, to obtain these freedoms and opportunities in their entirety requires a great many fundamentally positive factors: you must lay the foundation with completely pure ethical discipline, support this with such qualities as generosity, and provide momentum with flawless prayers of aspiration. Consider the fact that, if such factors are necessary, it seems that there are very few cases in which such causes are established, from which one can deduce that, as a consequence, the results—more fortunate states of rebirth in general and these freedoms and opportunities in particular—are difficult to obtain.

As for the difficulty from the point of view of the resultant states of rebirth, generally speaking, the *Foundation of Scriptural Transmission* states that when beings die and pass from lower or higher states of rebirth, those who go on to a lower state of rebirth are comparable to the motes of dust covering the great earth, while those who go on to higher states are only comparable to the few motes that gather on your fingernail.[538] One considers the fact that any merely higher state, when compared to lower states (which bear no resemblance to it) seems to be just within the realm of possibility, while this special state of freedom, even when compared to higher states (which share many common features with it), is exceedingly rare.

As for one contemplating the difficulty of obtaining this state through the use of analogy, Śāntideva points out:

> Similar to the case of a turtle whose neck might enter the hole
> of a yoke buffeted on a very turbulent ocean,
> the state of a human being is said to be very difficult to obtain.[539]

Alternatively, one gains certainty by referring to any number of other analogies, such as that of a star in the daytime or the *udumbara* flower.[540]

Contemplation of Impermanence [2]

The contemplation of impermanence is twofold: the recollection of death (since one will not remain long in this world) and the contemplation of how change occurs when one passes on to another state.

Recollection of Death [a]

The source verses state:

> **There are three primary topics: death is certain; when one will die is unknown;**
> **and when death occurs, anything that is not spiritual will be of no avail.**
> **There are secondary considerations: death cannot be prevented, life cannot be extended, and there is never enough time;**
> **the time of death is unpredictable, it happens under many circumstances, and life is fragile;**
> **and death does not allow us to take our companions, body, or wealth.**
> **One recalls death by applying these nine rationales.**

There are three primary considerations in contemplating death and impermanence: the certainty that one must definitely die (due to the proof of death lying in the fact that one has been born); [3.157a] the uncertainty of when death will occur (due to the proof as proved by the fact that people die unpredictably, both young and old); and the fact that when death occurs, only what is spiritual will be of any benefit (as established through scriptural authority). Each of these involves three secondary considerations.

There are three rationales for the fact that one is certain to die:

(1) the Lord of Death[541] is certainly coming for one and no means whatsoever can prevent that;

(2) one's life span cannot be extended, and each moment day and night there are factors that shorten it;

(3) even while one is still living, death can come suddenly, without there

ever being enough time to carry out all of the plans one has, both secular and spiritual.

There are three rationales for the fact that it is unknown when one will die:

(4) the length of one's life in this human world is unpredictable, unlike that in other worlds, which is more or less fixed;[542]

(5) there are a great many conditions that can cause death (diseases inside one's body, negative forces and the elements in the external world, and so forth), so that in just staying alive, one is pointed toward death with no other guarantee;

(6) one's body is fragile, like a bubble on water, and the slightest injury could end one's life.

There are three rationales for the fact that only what is spiritual will be of any benefit, for none of the following will be of any use at death:

(7) even though one might have hundreds or thousands of family members, friends, attendants, or servants, one cannot take a single one of them with one at death;

(8) even one's cherished body, which has been with one all along, must be left behind, like so much earth or stone;

(9) even though one might have incalculable wealth, one cannot take even a single needle with one.

One recalls death by applying these nine rationales.

Rebirth in Other States [b]

The source verses state:

> **Once one has died, one will be reborn in either of two destinies;**
> **having contemplated the foregoing, one reorients one's mind away from this lifetime.**

Given the certainty that one will also die swiftly, one has no chance of remaining in this life, and after death one does not become nothing but must take rebirth. [3.157b] And given that there are only two possible destinies, and no other, one will be reborn in either a more or less favorable state. This process is one that is subject to the external influences of karma, not something over which one has any control, and so one takes rebirth under the impetus of one's positive or negative karma.

Therefore, one contemplates the suffering of lower states of rebirth, thinking, "What would it be like if I were to be reborn in some lower state?" As Nāgārjuna tells us:

> Bring to mind what a day would be like in the realms
>   of the hells,
> whether exceedingly hot or cold.
> Bring to mind as well the tormented spirits
> who are tortured by hunger and thirst.
>
> Observe and bring to mind the forms of animal life
> who are subject to so many sufferings due to their ignorance.
> Avoid the causes of these states and engage in the causes for
>   happier ones.
> When one hears of the state of human rebirth in Jambudvīpa,
>   difficult to obtain,
> one should strenuously put an end
> to the causes of lower states of rebirth.[543]

There are incalculable forms of suffering, foremost among them those of the hot and cold hells. Again, according to Nāgārjuna:

> If one's own fear is aroused by seeing depictions of the hell realms,
> hearing of them, recalling them, reading of them, or making one's
>   own depictions,
> what can be said about those who are actually experiencing the
>   unbearable consequences of their actions? . . .[544]
> . . . Whatever pain one would endure in this life by being pierced
>   violently
> with three hundred spears for a day
> would not even come close to, and could not compare with,
> the smallest suffering in the hell realms.[545]

Tormented spirits are also subject to many kinds of suffering, due to hunger and thirst and so forth:

> Among tormented spirits there is constant and incurable suffering
> caused by the distress of their unfulfilled desires.

> Understand that they undergo unbearable suffering
> caused by hunger, thirst, cold, heat, fatigue, and fear.[546]

Animals are subject to such suffering as that of the predation of one species on another:

> In animal states of rebirth there are various sufferings, [3.158a]
> such as being slaughtered, bound, beaten, and so forth.
> These beings, who have abandoned the virtue that leads to peace,
> undergo the utterly unbearable pain of preying on one another.[547]

In the foregoing ways, one recalls death and contemplates the sufferings of falling into lower states of rebirth. Thus, one reorients one's mind away from this lifetime and arouses the attitude that one's real concern is for one's future destiny.

Reorienting the Mind Away from Saṃsāra [B]

There are two ways in which one's mind is reoriented away from saṃsāra: the contemplation of the consequences of karma (which are the causes of happiness and suffering) and the contemplation of the shortcomings of saṃsāra.

Karma [1]

This has two further parts: the contemplation of karmic consequences in general, and the contemplation of such specific issues as the degree of gravity.

General Contemplation [a]

The source verses state:

> **Such is the process of karma: it is ineluctable; its results are greatly magnified;**
> **actions not committed have no effect; and the effects of actions committed never expire on their own.**

Generally speaking, whether you are an ordinary mortal individual or a spiritually advanced being,[548] all positive experiences that carry with them any pleasant sensation—down to even the slightest pleasure caused by a cool breeze for beings reborn in a hell realm—occur due to positive karma reinforced in the past; it is not in accord with the nature of things that happiness be due to negative karma. And all negative experiences that carry with them any unpleasant sensation—down to even the slightest suffering that could occur in the experience of an arhat[549]—occur due to negative karma one has reinforced in the past; for it is not in accord with the nature of things that suffering be due to positive karma. As the *Precious Garland* states:

> All suffering comes from nonvirtue,
> and so do all lower states of rebirth.
> From virtue come all fortunate states of rebirth
> and the happiness within all those rebirths.[550]

Karma is marked by four characteristics: (1) the certainty of the consequences of one's actions, (2) the greatly magnified results that come about, (3) the fact that one is never subject to the effects of actions one has not committed, and (4) the fact that the effects of those one has committed never expire on their own.

(1) All the various kinds of happiness and suffering derive from the corresponding positive and negative kinds of karma, without the slightest conflation; neither are these causeless, nor are they due to such dissonant causes as primal matter or a powerful creator.[551] [3.158b] Rather, the general states of happiness and suffering come from the general kinds of virtuous and nonvirtuous actions, while myriad specific states of happiness and suffering come about individually from myriad specific actions of the corresponding kinds, without the slightest conflation. The certainty one gains concerning the predictable and ineluctable process of karmic consequences is referred to as the "authentic view" for Buddhists and is extolled as the foundation for all positive qualities.

(2) A great degree of happiness results from a small degree of virtuous karma, while a great degree of suffering results from a small degree of nonvirtuous karma; and so the kind of magnification from cause to effect that takes place on this inner level is not found in the process of causation in the external world.[552] As is said in *Didactic Aphorisms*:

Due to a small harmful action being committed,
something very destructive[553] occurs in the next world.
This brings about great ruination;
it is like poison having been ingested.

Due to a small meritorious action being committed,
some great happiness is brought about in the next world.
This brings about things of great purpose;
it is like an abundant harvest of grain ripening.[554]

(3) If one has not reinforced the karma that serves as the cause of either happiness or suffering, one will never experience those pleasant or painful effects. In this regard, the Teacher[555] stated that while those who enjoy the fruits of reinforcing positive karma over incalculably long eons do not necessarily need to amass all the causes of those results, they still must amass them to some degree.[556]

(4) The virtuous and nonvirtuous actions one has committed bring about their corresponding effects, wanted and unwanted, respectively. As is stated in the *Foundation of Scriptural Transmission*:

The effects of actions do not expire on their own,
even after a hundreds eons.
When circumstances come together and the time is ripe,
their effects occur for ordinary beings.[557]

Specific Issues [b]

As for the contemplation of such specific issues as the degree of gravity, the source verses state:

The degree of gravity is greatly influenced by the focus, intention,
underlying support, and actual content of an action—
these bring about results due to complete maturation, results
consistent with causes, and governing results. [3.159a]

In this regard, there are certainly three avenues through which one engages in conduct,[558] whether excellent or ignoble. And although it cannot be stated categorically that all positive and negative actions committed through these three avenues fall entirely within ten kinds of actions, when summarizing broadly and roughly the major ways in which actions are virtuous or nonvirtuous, the Transcendent and Accomplished Conqueror[559] spoke of ten kinds of negative actions and also spoke of ten kinds of positive actions, for he saw that the key points of rejecting the negative actions and instead accomplishing something truly meaningful were subsumed within these ten.[560] As the *Treasury of Abhidharma* states:

> To summarize in a broad way,
> any and all kinds of virtue and nonvirtue
> are spoken of as ten kinds of actions.[561]

And in the *Detailed Analysis of Scriptural Transmission*:

> Guarding one's speech, thoroughly controlling one's mind,
> and not committing any harmful actions physically—
> by training oneself well in these three kinds of activity,
> one gains the path taught by the Seer.[562]

These ten kinds of activity are very well known, so I will not explain them here in detail, having already discussed them earlier.[563]

As to the degrees of gravity involved, the main text of *Levels*[564] speaks of six factors that affect the way in which actions bear weighty consequences. As for the *overt mental state*, this is one's motivation, which comes from a strong attitude that involves one of the three emotional poisons or their absence.[565] *Familiarity* with an action is due to one's committing either a virtuous or a nonvirtuous action many times over, with a familiarity born of having engaged in it over a long time. The *essential quality* of an act is reflected by the fact that, of the seven kinds of physical and verbal actions, the former kinds are of greater gravity than the latter, while in the case of the three kinds of mental actions, the latter are of greater gravity than the former.[566] The *focus* of the act refers to beneficial or harmful actions committed toward the Buddha, dharma, saṅgha, or your guru, for example. A *unilateral commitment to counterproductive factors* refers to the fact that one is unilaterally committed to negative actions, and not positive ones, throughout one's lifetime; while the *elimination of counterproductive factors* [3.159b] refers to one's rejection of negative influences and involvement in positive actions, free of desire and attachment. As *Letter to a Friend* states:

> Actions performed constantly, with strong feeling, without any remedy,
> or in which the primary focus is imbued with positive qualities—
> these factors contribute to five major kinds of virtuous and nonvirtuous actions.
> Therefore, strive to engage in virtuous activity![567]

In this citation, the number five refers to two kinds of primary focus—a focus endowed with enlightened qualities (such as the Three Jewels) and a focus of someone who has benefited one (that is, one's father and mother).

Actions are powerful due to any of four factors—the focus, the intention, the underlying support, and the actual content of an action.

(1) This is a factor because if one commits even a minor beneficial or harmful action, without any strong intention, toward the Three Jewels, or one's guru, or likewise one's parents, the corresponding merit or ignobleness is nonetheless great. In particular, bodhisattvas are very powerful foci for one's virtuous (or nonvirtuous) actions. If someone were, out of anger, to imprison all beings in the ten directions in a dark dungeon, it would still be an action of incalculably greater harm for that person to stand with his or her back turned to a bodhisattva and say, "I won't look at that villain!" It would be an act of far greater harm to be furious with and feel malice toward a bodhisattva and say something spiteful than to tear down and burn as many stūpas as there are grains of sand in the river Ganges. By the same token, it is also said that they are sublime foci for one to reinforce one's spiritual merit.

(2) The sūtra *Mound of Precious Gems*[568] states that there would be more merit in someone who never loses sight of the intention to gain omniscience casting a single flower with the motivation of bodhicitta than in all beings in the three-thousandfold universe each erecting a stūpa as large as Sumeru and paying honor to these in all ways that honor can be paid, for tens of millions of eons.

In this regard, one should also understand that there are other variables, such as one's intention—whether the goal is more sublime or more common, [3.160a] or the focus is on one's own or others' benefit—or the degree of intensity or weakness of the action, or the length or shortness of the duration of the action. With regard to negative conduct, moreover, the more powerful actions are those that involve intense attitudes of afflictive mental states and that take place over longer periods of time, and among all of these factors, anger is an extremely powerful one. *Entering the Way of a Bodhisattva* states:

> Whatever excellent conduct has been reinforced
> for a thousand eons—
> generosity, honoring of the sugatas, and so forth—
> can all be destroyed by a single act of anger.[569]

In this regard, it is said that it is extremely grievous to indulge in anger toward someone upholding pure ethics,[570] and even more so toward a bodhisattva.[571]

(3) A ball of iron, although small, will sink to the bottom, but it will float on the surface if fashioned into a large bowl. By analogy, it is said that harmful actions have more or less gravity depending on whether they are committed in an unskillful or skillful manner. In this respect, it is further said that the gravity is lessened when one has the skill to create virtue by using the remedy to harmful actions previously committed—regretting them, resolving not to commit them again, and not hiding the fact that one has committed them. But it is a grievous thing not to do the foregoing, and instead to arrogantly presume that it is skillful to engage deliberately in such actions without regard for the consequences.

In the case of virtuous actions, as well, there are variables that successively bring about considerable changes in their benefits and advantages—the skillfulness of understanding the key points of such actions, the fact that one is upholding vows, and the fact that one is endowed with a significant degree of meditative absorption.

(4) To share the generosity of spiritual teachings in being generous to beings and to honor buddhas with one's spiritual practice are far superior to acts of material generosity and offering. One can understand the other cases on the basis of this illustration.

The foregoing paths of action bring about (1) results due to complete maturation, (2) results consistent with causes, and (3) governing results:

(1) Each of the ten paths of action has three degrees, depending on the three degrees—great, middling, or small—of the three emotional poisons that are their basis. [3.160b] In this regard, the main text of *Levels of Realization* states that in the case of each of the ten kinds of actions—killing and so forth—a great degree of emotional poison leads to rebirth in hell states, a middling degree to rebirth in preta states, and a small degree to rebirth in

animal states[572] (the sūtra *Ten Levels of Realization* reverses these results in the cases of the middling and small degrees).[573]

(2) Even though one is reborn from lower states to a human one, there are consequences that follow one. As is said:

> Killing brings a shortening of life,[574]
> causing harm leads to many threats,
> theft causes a loss of wealth, and
> behaving in immoral ways produces many enemies.
>
> Speaking lies leads to censure,
> divisive speech deprives one of companions,
> abusive language means one will hear unpleasant things, and
> purposeless talk causes one to hear dishonorable words.
>
> Covetous attitudes mean that the hopes in one's mind are
> dashed,
> malicious intent ensures fear, and
> dogmatic belief systems lead to wrongheaded opinions.[575]

(3) These are flaws that occur in the external environment. As is said:

> Externally, little is impressive and there are many threats,
> dust storms, bad odors, and uneven ground,
> poor soil, environmental upheavals,
> and poor or failed harvests.[576]

As for the relative power of virtuous actions, using the foregoing discussion as a model, the complete maturation is such that virtuous actions of a small, middling, or greater degree lead to rebirth, respectively, as a human, a god of the realm of desire, or a god in the realm of form or formlessness.[577] The results that are consistent with the cause and the governing results apply in the reverse manner to those for nonvirtuous actions.

As for the distinction between those actions that provide momentum and those that bring completion,[578] virtue is the karma that provides momentum for more favorable states of rebirth, while nonvirtue is the karma that provides momentum for lower states of rebirth. The karma that brings completion is more unpredictable; those in more favorable states of rebirth can still have defects of major and minor parts of the body, incomplete faculties, ugly complexion, shortness of life, many illnesses, poverty, and so forth, which are accounted for by nonvirtuous karma. There are also animals and pretas who possess great wealth, which is accounted for by virtuous karma. Thus, there are four alternatives: in states in which virtue has provided the momentum, there are both situations in which virtue has brought about completion, and nonvirtue has brought about completion, [3.161a] just as in states in which nonvirtue has provided the momentum, there are both situations in which nonvirtue has brought about completion, and virtue has brought about completion.

Of the two kinds of karma—that which is certain to be experienced and that which is not—that which is certain to be experienced is action that has been consciously committed and reinforced, while that which is not certain to be experienced is action that has been consciously committed but not reinforced. As for the distinction between committed and reinforced, "committed" means that which is thought of or, even if not thought of, is carried out through physical and verbal action; "reinforced" refers to actions other than those of the ten kinds and so forth that are committed in dreams, while "not reinforced" refers to actions of the ten kinds that are committed in dreams and so forth.

With respect to that which is certain to be experienced, from the point of view of the time frame in which results are experienced, there are three alternatives. "That which is experienced in one's immediate perception" is the result of actions that is experienced in this lifetime. "That which will be experienced upon rebirth" refers to a result that is experienced in the next lifetime. "That which will be experienced in other contexts" refers to what is experienced in the lifetime after that or later.

One should contemplate all the foregoing processes very thoroughly.

Saṃsāra [2]

Contemplation of the sufferings of saṃsāra is twofold: contemplation of eight kinds of suffering and contemplation of three kinds of universal suffering.

Eight Kinds of Suffering [a]

The source verses state:

> **Birth, aging, illness, death, being separated from what is appealing,**
> **encountering what is unappealing, striving for what one desires and not finding it,**
> **and the suffering of the aggregates that perpetuate saṃsāra: . . .**

While it is patently easy to understand that the nature of lower states of rebirth is one of suffering, there is also no true happiness in higher states, for in general the nature of saṃsāra in its entirety is one of suffering. As the lord protector Maitreya points out:

> Just as there is no pleasant odor in filth, there is no real happiness in the five states of ordinary being;[579]
> the sufferings of these states are like that of being in constant contact with fire, weapons, or corrosive salt.[580]

Of these sufferings, eight are primary:

(1) Birth is fraught with suffering, birth entails tendencies toward the perpetuation of ignoble states of existence, birth is a context for further suffering, [3.161b] birth provides a context for afflictive mental states, and birth leads to unwanted separation.[581] Given that this is the very nature of birth, it entails these five attendant kinds of suffering.

(2) There are five sufferings attendant on death: the body degenerates, strength wanes, faculties weaken, the enjoyment of sense objects fades, and life itself is completely undermined.

(3) There are five sufferings attendant on falling ill: the body's constitution changes, pain and mental discomfort increase, there is no power to enjoy pleasant sense objects, what is unwanted must be endured,[582] and one comes close to losing one's life.

(4) One contemplates the five sufferings that are attendant on dying. There is separation from four aspects of the richness of living—family, entourage, material wealth, and one's own body—as well as the actual suffering of dying and the intense experience of unwanted sensations.

(5) There are five aspects to the suffering of encountering what is unappealing: there is the pain and mental distress aroused simply by one's encountering those who are like enemies; there is the further terror of punishment and physical injuries inflicted by them; there is the fear of being slandered; there is the fear of dying in a state of anxiety; and there is the fear of being apprehensive that after death one will fall into a lower state of

rebirth due to having flouted what is spiritual.

(6) One contemplates the five aspects to the suffering of being separated from what is appealing: mental anguish is aroused if one is separated from companions, for one is devastated at losing them; one cries aloud in anguish; physical harm is done to one's body;[583] one's mind is tormented by the longing brought on by memories of former sense pleasures; and one's experiences of enjoyment no longer feel complete.

(7) There are five topics to contemplate concerning the suffering of striving for what one desires and not finding it; these are similar to those in the preceding case of being separated from what is appealing. In essence, this is the suffering of taking up farming but having your crops fail, or going into business but failing to turn a profit, and so forth. [3.162a] This is the suffering of disappointment that comes from seeking and striving for whatever one hopes for, only to fail to attain it.

The foregoing are definitely experienced by all beings subsumed within the four methods of rebirth but are primarily associated with human beings, so much so that some classify them solely as "the sufferings of the human condition."

(8) In brief, there are five topics involved in contemplating the fact that the five mind-body aggregates that perpetuate saṃsāra are described as "suffering." Over and over, one contemplates the following topics: (a) that these constitute a context for the suffering in a situation becoming fully manifest, (b) that they constitute a context for the suffering that takes place on the basis of that situation having become fully manifest, (c) that they constitute a context for overt suffering, (d) that they constitute a context for the suffering of change, and (e) that their nature is one of subliminal suffering. To elaborate:

(a) Due to these aggregates having been taken up,[584] the sufferings of the rest of one's life are ushered in.

(b) With the aggregates already in place, they serve as the basis for such attendant sufferings as those of aging and falling ill.

(c) and (d) Since these two kinds of suffering are entailed in the perpetuation of ignoble states of existence, they develop accordingly.

(e) The mere fact that the mind-body aggregates, which perpetuate saṃsāra, are ensured means that they do so with a nature that is one of subliminal suffering, because everything that is subliminally conditioned due to the external influences of karma and afflictive mental states from previous lifetimes constitutes suffering on a subliminal level.

If one does not arouse a genuine sense of disenchantment with saṃsāra, whose nature is that of the mind-body aggregates that perpetuate it, one will not arouse an equally genuine attitude of seeking liberation and will also have no real chance of arousing supreme compassion toward the ordinary beings who wander in saṃsāra. Hence, this contemplation is crucial regardless of which approach one embarks upon, Hīnayāna or Mahāyāna.

Three Kinds of Universal Suffering [b]

As for contemplation of the three kinds of universal suffering, the source verses state:

> **. . . For everyone, moreover,**
> **there is nothing reliable, nothing satisfying, and this has been going on forever.**
> **Contemplating the three kinds of suffering, the mind reorients itself away from saṃsāra.**

Letter to a Friend states that six flaws pertain to all beings who are in saṃsāra: nothing is predictable, one can never know satisfaction, bodies are cast off again and again, the relentless continuity of rebirth asserts itself over and over, circumstances change from high to low and back again, [3.162b] and one is on one's own, without real companionship.[585]

If these points are summarized, there are three considerations: (1) there is nothing in saṃsāra upon which one can depend, (2) no matter how much of its happiness one may enjoy, there is no end point at which one will truly be satisfied, and (3) this process has proceeded relentlessly throughout beginningless time.

(1) This has four implications:

(a) It is inappropriate to depend on having attained a body, for bodies are cast off again and again.

(b) It is inappropriate to depend on circumstances being either beneficial or harmful, for one's father could be reborn as one's child, one's mother as one's spouse, one's enemy as one's friend, and so forth, without any predictability.[586]

(c) It is inappropriate to depend on the achievement of any prosperity, for one only falls from a high place to a low one.

(d) It is inappropriate to depend on companionship, for one will go forth[587] unaccompanied.

(2) As one has moved entirely within the cycle of existence, with no evi-

dent starting or ending point, one might have become a powerful master among gods or humans and enjoyed boundless sense pleasures. Nevertheless, this has been like trying to slake your thirst with salt water or scratch an incurable itch, for one has never known the slightest real satisfaction. Thus, one's compulsive urges only increase more and more.

(3) This refers to the relentless process of continuity, that is, the succession of rebirths with no evident end point. Other sufferings felt by human beings are discussed in *Advice for the Multitude*:

> All the sufferings of lower states, without exception,
> seem to be the case for human beings, too.
> There is intense pain comparable to that of the hells
> and poverty like that of denizens in the world of the lord of death.[588]
>
> In this state,[589] there is also the suffering of animals,
> for the powerful oppress
> and tyrannize the powerless.
> This is like a flowing river.[590]

And in the *Four Hundred Verses* we read the following:

> For the highly placed there is mental suffering,
> while for the lowly it is born of the body;
> each and every day, the two kinds of suffering[591]
> bring destruction in the world.[592]

Furthermore, the minds of demigods are tormented by their envy of the splendor and wealth of the gods, on the basis of which they fight with the gods, only to experience as well the many sufferings of their bodies being hacked and beaten. [3.163a] It is said that even though they are endowed with intelligence, they are obscured by the consequences of their karma and so are incapable of beholding what is true in those circumstances.

Gods in the realm of desire undergo the sufferings of dying and falling from that state, the suffering of becoming demoralized,[593] and such sufferings as being hacked, beaten, killed, driven away, and so forth.[594] Gods in the two higher realms[595] do not have overt suffering but nonetheless are subject to afflictive mental states and are obscured, and so suffer due to dying and falling from those states, having to take ignoble states of rebirth due to their lacking freedom to remain in their states.

To summarize, one contemplates the fact that, regardless of where one is reborn in any state within the three realms, high or low, the process is one of constantly floundering about in a ocean of the three kinds of suffering—overt suffering, the suffering of change, and subliminal suffering. One thus reorients one's mind away from saṃsāra.

Reorienting the Mind Away from Quiescence and Naïve Happiness [C]

As for reorienting the mind away from quiescence and naïve happiness, the source verses state:

> **Through seven practical instructions concerning cause and effect, the basis for arousing an attitude**
> **of concern for the welfare of others is established by an even-minded attitude and a sense of empathy.**
> **Seeking enlightenment as one's goal, with loving-kindness, great compassion,**
> **and altruistic motivation, one reorients one's mind away from quiescence and naïve happiness.**

Having thus contemplated the shortcomings of saṃsāra, one sees the whole of conditioned existence as being like a pit of fire. If those whose minds are completely consumed by the wish for liberation—which will cause afflictive mental states and suffering to thoroughly subside—were to train in the path of the three higher trainings,[596] they would indeed gain the liberated state of freedom. But although they would not revert from this state to something like the splendor of higher states of rebirth,[597] it nevertheless constitutes a state in which flaws have only partially been removed and positive qualities only partially attained, and so their own benefit is not complete. For this very reason, the benefit they can bring to others amounts to something quite limited. In the final analysis, they are exhorted by buddhas and see that it is only logical that they must embark on the Mahāyāna approach. Given that the awakening attitude, bodhicitta, is the avenue through which one enters that approach, it is once that has awakened in one's ongoing experience that one is considered a Mahāyāna practitioner. [3.163b] Concerning this point, the *Cluster of Stems* states:

> O child of spiritual heritage! Bodhicitta is like the seed of all the Buddhadharma.[598]

In this regard, regardless of what conditions come together, a grain of barley is not suitable to be the cause of rice or any other plant, being the specific cause of its own seedling, while the water and fertilizer and so forth that the grain absorbs are also causes of the barley seedling.[599] In a similar fashion, from among the causes of the "seedling" of buddhahood, bodhicitta is the specific cause (comparable to the seed grain), while the sublime intelligence that realizes emptiness is the specific cause (comparable to water, fertilizer, and so forth) of the three degrees of enlightenment.[600] It is for these reasons that the *Highest Continuum* says:

> Dedication to the sublime approach is the seed, while sublime intelligence
> is the mother that gives birth to the buddhas and the dharma.[601]

Thus, it describes dedication to the sublime spiritual approach as being comparable to one's father's seed, while the sublime intelligence that realizes the lack of identity is comparable to one's mother. To extend the analogy, since it is impossible for a Tibetan father to sire a Chinese or Mongolian child, the father is the cause that defines the child's ethnicity; but since a Tibetan mother can bear children of various ethnicities, she serves as the common cause.[602]

As Nāgārjuna says in his praise of the transcendent perfection of sublime intelligence:

> You upon whom buddhas, pratyekabuddhas,
> and śrāvakas definitely rely,
> you alone are the path to liberation;
> it can certainly be said that "there is no other."[603]

That is to say, even śrāvakas and pratyekabuddhas rely on that intelligence, which is why the perfection of sublime intelligence is referred to as the "mother."[604] And so, because it is the "mother" of both Hīnayāna and Mahāyāna "children," the distinction between the Hīnayāna and the Mahāyāna is not made on the basis of the sublime intelligence that realizes emptiness, but rather is made on the basis of bodhicitta and its truly magnificent conduct.

Therefore, given that it is necessary to train in the awakening attitude of bodhicitta from the outset, there are two methods of practical instructions concerning this, which are both lineages transmitted through the Noble Lord.[605] [3.164a]

The instructions transmitted by Tumtön Lodrö Drak, who was a student of Sharawa,[606] involve five stages of cause and effect. These entail one pursuing the following train of thought:

"Given that I must attain buddhahood, as the cause of buddhahood, (1) bodhicitta is necessary. As the cause of that, (2) compassion is necessary. As the cause of that, (3) loving-kindness is necessary. As the cause of that, (4) knowledge of what has been done for me and a desire to repay that kindness are necessary. And as the cause of that, (5) knowledge of all beings having been my parents is necessary.

"All beings have been my parents. How very kind they have been! Why shouldn't they all be free of suffering and instead be happy and joyful? In order to bring them to happiness, I will attain buddhahood. And having attained buddhahood, I will furthermore bring all beings to that state of buddhahood!"

Alternatively, it is said that one trains one's mind[607] through seven practical instructions concerning cause and effect, which were transmitted by Tsangpa Rinpoché, a student of Jayulwa.[608] If one adopts the point of view of these instructions, they state that buddhahood itself, as that which is to be attained, does not come about without cause or condition. Rather, it comes about from (1) bodhicitta as its cause. This in turn comes about from (2) completely pure altruistic motivation. This comes from (3) supreme compassion. This comes from (4) supreme loving-kindness. This comes from (5) a sense of empathy.[609] This comes from (6) knowledge of what has been done for one and a desire to repay that kindness. And this comes from (7) cultivating the idea of beings as one's mother.

In this regard, the basis for arousing an attitude of concern for the welfare of others lies in establishing an even-minded attitude in oneself that is free of attachment or aversion toward beings. Initially one cultivates this even-mindedness toward those whom one regards as neutral—that is, who have done one neither good nor harm. Then one extends this attitude toward those who are loved ones and friends, then to those who are enemies who harm one, and then to all beings.

With respect to the foregoing, one contemplates as follows: "From the perspective of ordinary beings, they are all alike in wishing to be happy and not wishing to suffer. Thus, it is not reasonable that I should treat certain of them as close to me and try to help them, [3.164b] while holding others at a distance and trying to harm them (or at the very least not trying to help them)." One also thinks, "From my own perspective, given that I have been in saṃsāra throughout beginningless time, there is no being whomsoever who has not been my friend a hundred times over, so to whom should I be attached and to whom should I feel averse?" This is as stated in the intermediate version of *Stages of Meditation*.[610]

One then develops a sense of empathy toward everyone.[611] That is to say, one thinks of each and every being's having been one's mother, recalls their kindness, and therefore contemplates the necessity of repaying that kindness by ensuring their release from saṃsāra. Since it is held that the means to liberate them from saṃsāra is for one to seek the state of supreme enlightenment as one's goal, one should train one's mind in cultivating its causes—attitudes of loving-kindness, compassion, and altruistic motivation.

Loving-kindness

Of these, the focus for loving-kindness is beings who are lacking in happiness. The forms it takes are the thoughts, "Why shouldn't they find happiness?" "May they find happiness!" and "I will ensure that they find happiness." The benefits and advantages of this are boundless, as is illustrated by the following passage from the *Precious Garland*:

> Even if one were to give away
> three hundred vessels of food three times each day,
> the merits of this could not compare in the slightest
> to even an instant of loving-kindness.
>
> Gods and human beings will treat one lovingly,
> they will also protect one,
> one will have mental happiness, many other kinds
> of happiness,
> will not be harmed by poisons or weapons,
>
> will realize one's goals effortlessly,
> and be reborn in the world of purity.

And so even if one does not gain liberation,
one gains these eight qualities of loving-kindness.[612]

As for the stages in meditation, initially one should meditate on loved ones and friends, then on those to whom one feels neutral, and then on enemies. One then meditates, step by step, on all beings. [3.165a]

As to the way in which one meditates, just as one would arouse compassion by contemplating over and over the way in which beings are afflicted by suffering, here one contemplates over and over the way in which beings are devoid of happiness, lacking any virtue, whether corruptible or not.[613] Once one has become familiar with this, the wish that they find happiness will occur as a matter of course. Furthermore, one brings to mind all kinds of virtue and mentally confers these on beings.[614]

Compassion

The focus for compassion is beings who are afflicted by any of the three kinds of suffering. The forms it takes are the thoughts, "Why shouldn't they be free of those sufferings?" "May they be free of them!" and "I will ensure that they are free of them." As for the stages in meditation, initially one should meditate on loved ones and friends, then on those to whom one feels neutral, then on enemies, and on all beings in the ten directions. (Such successive meditations on impartiality, loving-kindness, and compassion, distinguishing their respective objects, were set forth by the master Kamalaśīla, following the model found in the sūtras of the abhidharma class;[615] these are exceedingly profound key points.)

As to the way in which one cultivates compassion, it is by contemplating the ways in which these beings (who have been one's mother), having fallen into conditioned states of existence, experience general and specific forms of suffering. As to the measure of having successfully aroused compassion, the first version of *Stages of Meditation* says the following:

> At whatever point compassion is engaged as a matter of course, expressing itself as the wish to rid all beings forever of suffering (as though they were one's unhappy children with whom one feels a sense of empathy), so that one takes on that same quality oneself—at that point this is perfected, and so can be called "supreme compassion."[616]

From this one can also understand the measure of having successfully aroused loving-kindness.

Altruistic Motivation

Having thus cultivated loving-kindness and compassion, [3.165b] one finally thinks, "Alas! These beings, who are dear to me and with whom I feel empathy, are thus lacking in happiness and tormented by suffering. I will do whatever it takes to ensure that they find happiness and are liberated from suffering." As for accepting the responsibility to liberate them, one trains one's mind, even if only by giving lip service, so that one never loses sight of the intention that they gain higher states of rebirth in the shorter term, while one's desire is that they be brought solely to supreme enlightenment and not just to some more limited state of mere liberation.[617] This is what constitutes the especially superior states of higher altruistic motivation.

In this regard, spiritually advanced beings of the śrāvaka and pratyekabuddha approaches do not regress back into saṃsāra, their minds abiding innately in the absence of conceptual elaborations, and are endowed with entirely authentic qualities of enlightenment, so that from our perspective as ordinary mortal individuals, they are indeed truly awe-inspiring. However, by comparison to the way in which buddhas and bodhisattvas eliminate the two kinds of obscuration;[618] to the way in which their timeless awareness unfolds as awareness of the true nature of things just as it is and awareness of things in their multiplicity; to the way in which they are endowed with limitless qualities of enlightenment; to the way in which the force of their innate compassion and the dynamic energy of their spiritual power and might (which are all difficult to realize) are present in them; and to the way in which their enlightened activity ensues to carry out benefit for beings in all places and at all times—by comparison to these inconceivable aspects, the freedom experienced by śrāvakas and pratyekabuddhas is so very much smaller in scope. By analogy, the difference is greater than that between Sumeru and a mustard seed!

Therefore, one contemplates over and over, "I will attain perfect enlightenment and the sublime state of liberation, for this is by nature such that all processes of elimination and realization have been completely perfected for my own benefit, while enlightened activity for the benefit of others is inexhaustible. Come what may, may I attain buddhahood!" In this way, one reorients one's mind away from the inferior goals of quiescence and naïve happiness.

Reorienting the Mind Away from Dualistic Consciousness [D]

As for reorienting one's mind away from the dualistic mode of consciousness, the source verses state:

> **Investigating the significance of the unborn nature of all phenomena**
> **with discernment, one reorients one's mind away from dualistic consciousness.**

Using one's discerning powers of sublime intelligence, [3.166a] again and again one examines and investigates the significance of the fact that the nature of all phenomena—those of the deeply ingrained afflictive state and those of the totally refined state—is primordially unborn. From this comes the timeless awareness of a spiritually advanced being, and one's mind is reoriented away from the confusion, in its entirety, of how things appear at present to dualistic consciousness. The objects in this case consist of topics discussed previously, such as the two levels of truth, while the subjective perceiver of these consists of this selfsame discerning quality. Its important role in the development of sublime intelligence born of contemplation is spoken of in the *Chapter of Kāśyapa*:

> O Kāśyapa, it is thus. To use an analogy, suppose two trees are rubbed together by the wind, which causes them to burst into flame. Once this has happened, both trees are burned up. In a similar fashion, O Kāśyapa, if one has authentic discernment, this causes the faculty of sublime intelligence in a spiritually advanced being to develop, and once this has developed, that selfsame authentic discernment is "incinerated."[619]

This passage states that the sublime intelligence of a spiritually advanced being develops from this discernment. In the intermediate version of *Stages of Meditation*, moreover, we read the following:

> In this way, sublime intelligence is used to thoroughly investigate thus. Whenever, concerning a given thing, an advanced spiritual practitioner[620] does not definitively apprehend the very essence itself of that thing from the ultimate perspective, at that point

he or she enters into a nonconceptual state of meditative absorption. He or she also realizes the very nonexistence of the very essence of all phenomena.

When one does not meditate using sublime intelligence to examine precisely the very essence of a thing but rather engages in meditation solely by completely eliminating all conceptual processes, that will never do away with conceptual thought and also will never lead[621] to realization of the very nonexistence of the very essence because the perspective of sublime intelligence is absent.

In this way, if the fire of knowing what is authentic, just as it is, comes from authentic discernment itself, then the wood of conceptual thought will be incinerated, just like the fire brought on by rubbing wooden sticks together.

This is what the transcendent and accomplished conqueror proclaimed.[622]

As for the important role that contemplation plays in meditation, moreover, we may quote from holy masters of the past, who said: [3.166b]

Gathering together in one's mind the teachings one has heard previously, over and over one must contemplate them, evaluate them, and truly understand them. Someone who allows the teachings to be forgotten and trains only in some focusing of the mind is left without any allies. The most excellent kind of great meditator makes the most excellent teacher; a middling "great meditator" makes only a middling teacher. It must be the case that by however much one meditates, by that much one's understanding of the teachings grows greater.

If one thus gains a stable degree of certainty through contemplation, then even if harmful companions should say to one, "All thinking, whether virtuous or nonvirtuous, just consists of thoughts, so these are all to be eliminated," one's response would be, "That is not what is said in the teachings and that is not what true spiritual mentors accept." Then one will not listen to what such a person says.

Failing that, if one has a little faith but no intelligence, one will cry when one looks at someone crying and laugh when one looks at someone laughing—that is, one will be like water following the easiest course, thinking, "That's the truth!" regardless of what someone says and being led off to wherever that takes one.[623]

The foregoing constitutes the commentary on the fourth part, concerning a definitive treatment of the four contemplation that reorient the mind.

This concludes the commentary on the seventh book, a developmental analysis of the higher training in sublime intelligence, from The Encompassing of All Knowledge, *also entitled* The Precious Treasury of Sublime Teachings: The Compendium of the Methods of All Spiritual Approaches *and* A Treatise That Thoroughly Presents the Three Higher Trainings.

Book Eight, Parts One and Two

The Higher Training in Meditative Absorption

The Source Verses

Part 1. Foundations of Meditative Absorption

Necessity of Meditative Absorption [I]

The actual significance of what one has studied and contemplated is put into practice through meditation;[624]
by analogy, although a farmer may reap a fine harvest, it is meant to be eaten.

Identifying Meditative Absorption [II]

Seek for certainty about the themes for the vast range of meditative absorption—
in the Hīnayāna and Mahāyāna approaches—in the two aspects of calm abiding and profound insight.

Extensive Explanation of Meditative Absorption [III]

Essence of Meditative Absorption [A]

In essence, these are a one-pointed state of attention
and the discernment that thoroughly analyzes phenomena.

Definition of Terms [B]

As for the derivation of these terms, with the *calm*ing [*zhi*] of distraction, there is *abiding* [*gnas*] to the highest degree,
and the *profound*ly [*lhag*] special quality of things is seen with the *insight* [*mthong*] of the vision of sublime intelligence.

Necessity of Both Aspects [C]

Similar to a lamp's being unstirred by wind and burning brightly,
when both aspects come together, the true way of abiding itself is realized.

Developmental Process [D]

The developmental process involves a relationship of support and supported.

Training in Meditative Absorption [E]
Extensive Explanation [1]
Training in Calm Abiding [a]
Supportive Circumstances [i]

One dispenses with all that is counterproductive by relying on the circumstances for calm abiding—
dwelling in a conducive place, having few wants, knowing contentment,
observing pure discipline, and avoiding distractions and concepts.

Stages of Calm Abiding [ii]

An analysis includes the mind of the realm of desire, the states of meditative stability, the formless realm, and the state of cessation.

Process of Cultivation [iii]

Physical Posture [aa]

The process of meditation involves sitting comfortably in a physical posture that has eight points.

Settling the Mind [bb]
General Framework [1']

In general, the focus can be any of four—pervasive, purifying one of former behavior, involving knowledge, or purifying one of afflictive states—and accords with the individual.

Specific Stages of Meditation [2']

Settling with a Support [a']

As for specific ways of settling the mind, these may involve an impure or pure physical support.

Settling without a Support [b']

Without a physical support, one settles one's mind on a partial impression up to a complete one,
or uses some external or internal focus on the body or something related to it.

Essence of Meditation [c']

Once the waves of thought dissolve into the ocean that is the basis of all ordinary experience,
one strives at meditative equipoise that is the very essence of meditation.

Identifying Experiences [cc]

Introduction [1']

There are two ways to identify experiences that develop from these methods.

Extensive Explanation [2']

Mainstream Sources [a']

Five Flaws and Eight Remedial Techniques [i']

According to mainstream sources, the five flaws are: three kinds of faintheartedness,
the forgetting of instructions, two kinds each of laxity and agitation, nonapplication,
and overapplication. These are remedied by eight techniques:

intention, effort, confidence, and thorough pliancy (which prevent the first flaw);
meditative absorption without forgetfulness (endowed with three special features);
alert effort, and equanimity (once evenness has ensued).

Six Powers, Four Ways of Focusing, and Nine Steps in Settling [ii']

Through six powers—listening, contemplation, mindfulness, alertness, diligence, and familiarization—
involving situations of tension, interruption,
no interruption, and spontaneity,
nine steps of settling the mind (settling on a focus and so forth) develop.

Personal Advice [b']

In the tradition of personal advice, understanding is gained through illustrative analogies of five experiences—
movement, attainment, familiarization, stability, and consummation.

Measuring Success [iv]
Attaining Calm Abiding [aa]

With the consummation of thorough pliancy, calm abiding is ensured—
the space within which well-being, clarity, and the absence of any concepts about subtle traits blend.

Purpose [bb]

This is the basis of all meditative stability in the traditions of sūtra and tantra.
It suppresses all afflictive states and suffering.

Training in Profound Insight [b]
Supportive Circumstances [i]

The causal circumstances for profound insight are to rely on holy masters,
to hear many teachings, to think correctly, and so to seek the view.

Analysis of Profound Insight [ii]

Its specific expressions are said to be the more obvious state of quiescence also found in non-Buddhist traditions,
the topics that pertain to the Truths (in the śrāvaka and pratyekabuddha approaches),
the view of emptiness (in the pāramitā approach), and the influence of bliss (in the tantric approach).
The ordinary preparatory phases parallel those of the mundane path;
however, these are not pursued by those in the tantric approach and others.

Essential Experiences [iii]

An analysis may involve three categories: analytical insight, thoroughly analytical insight,
and insight as the avenue for four essential experiences of examination and investigation.
Insight can derive from the ordinary distinctions one makes, from a thoroughgoing search, and from discernment.
It can involve six explorations—of meaning, things, characteristics, influences, time, and logical principles.
(There are four logical principles that concern dependent relationships, performance of function, establishment of what is reasonable,
and the nature of things.) These six are used to analyze things in detail,
from visual forms to omniscience.
These can be understood in three ways: meaning, reality just as it is, and things in all their multiplicity.
The preparation and the main practice are subsumed, respectively, within discernment and an unwavering state.

Cultivating Profound Insight [iv]

As for the way insight is cultivated in meditation, having used sublime intelligence to investigate
the fact that things lack identity, one rests in equipoise in a state free of conceptual elaborations.
The bases for the investigation—the nonconceptual images—

are focused on as bases of attributes, while any false assumptions
concerning their specific attributes are eliminated.
The nature of what is perceived is known to be empty, like space;
what is to be examined—the origin, location, shape, and so forth, of the
perceiving consciousness—
and the discerning function itself are like fire sticks consumed by fire.
Nothing is found, for things dissolve into basic space, and one rests
without any fixated perception.

Measure of Attainment [v]

The gaining of thorough pliancy is explained as being the point at which
there is attainment.

Training in Integration [c]
Actual Training Process [i]

Although followers of the Middle Way interpret the process of
development in distinct ways,
they agree on what is to be developed—the integration of calm abiding
and profound insight.
Unwavering and developmental meditation is paramount in all three
cases.

Integration [ii]

When one is meditating with a construct, integration involves
a precise analysis of the image on which one is focusing.
Once one gains profound nonconceptual insight, there is integration
when these have become identical in essence.

Result of Integration [iii]

That is the consummation of authentic meditative absorption—
the attainment of nirvāṇa that is not confined, but free of the bonds of
conditioned existence and the state of peace.

Summary of General Principles [2]
Alternative Approaches [a]
Calm Abiding [i]

In brief, unattractiveness, loving-kindness, the counting of exhalations and inhalations,
the elimination of specific perceptions, the use of subtle channels and energies, visualization, mantra repetition,
and being at rest in the natural state of relaxation—all these amount to situations in which the attention is focused.

Profound Insight [ii]

One may thoroughly investigate what is characterized and what serves to characterize it, or general and specific characteristics;
one may investigate interdependent connection, use the five logical proofs, be directly introduced to one's true nature
through scriptural citations, logical reasoning, the transmission of blessing through symbols, and so forth. These are means to arouse
the superb discerning function of one's sublime intelligence, accommodating the acumen of individuals.

Investigative and Settling Meditation [b]

Investigative and settling meditation are both alike in accomplishing calm abiding and profound insight.

Auxiliary Explanation [c]

Initially, with the meditative stability of an inexperienced practitioner,
one experiences indications such as smoke. With the thorough analysis of what is ultimately meaningful,
the phenomena of dualism merge as equal in taste, and the most sublime state of meditative stability is ensured.
With focus on suchness itself, one realizes all phenomena to be emptiness, and that is further realized to be the state of peace by nature.

The foregoing constitutes the first part,
concerning a presentation of the stages in meditation
to cultivate calm abiding and profound insight,
the common foundation of meditative absorption.

Part 2. Meditation in the Cause-Based Dialectical Approach
Preliminaries to Meditation [I]

As preliminaries to meditation, one observes discipline and develops sublime intelligence,
is capable of both mental and physical isolation, rejects the eight concerns,
maintains the twelve disciplines of spiritual training,
and abandons the five kinds of wrong lifestyle. . . .

Actual Process of Meditation [II]
Hīnayāna Approaches [A]
Śrāvaka Approach [1]
Brief Discussion [a]

. . . then, the process of meditation
consists of seven stages for those who follow the śrāvaka schools.
These are subsumed within five points—focus, content, essence, result, and context.

Extensive Explanation [b]
Beginning Practitioners [i]

Those who are beginners meditate on the general and specific remedies to desire
(that is, skeletons and the eight mental images); they examine their bodies;
they see sensations to be productive of suffering and without any true substance, like hollow reeds;
they focus their attention on the breath, and they meditate on the ultimate fact that no identity exists;
and they see mental states and aspects of consciousness to be like illusions.
They employ the applications of mindfulness, using sublime intelligence to examine
the fourfold characteristics that are specific and general.
They engage the Four Truths, cultivating the initial phase of the path of accumulation.
This model serves for the remaining stages.

Nonvirtue is prevented from arising or guarded against, while the opposite applies to virtue.
One employs meditative absorption that involves intention, exertion, attention, and investigation.

Four Anticipatory Phases [ii]

During the four phases that anticipate the decisive breakthrough,
one applies two groups of five factors—confidence, diligence, mindfulness, meditative absorption, and sublime intelligence—
to the sixteen topics pertaining to the Four Truths.

Path of Seeing [iii]

On the path of seeing, there are seven aids to enlightenment: mindfulness, thorough analysis of phenomena,
diligence, joy, thorough pliancy, meditative absorption, and impartiality.

Path of Meditation [iv]

The path of meditation is explained as eightfold: correct view, thought, speech,
action, livelihood, effort, mindfulness, and meditative absorption.

Pratyekabuddha Approach [2]

Pratyekabuddhas employ the foregoing and, in addition, the process of interdependent connection,
and focus their attention on the three avenues to complete liberation.

Mahāyāna Approach [B]
Individual Meditator [1]

Those who have awakened their affinity for the Mahāyāna uphold the two aspects of bodhicitta.

Preliminaries to Meditation [2]
Four Immeasurable Attitudes [a]

The initial step is that of the four immeasurable attitudes
(loving-kindness and so forth).
Beginning practitioners focus on beings; those who are advanced
in practice
focus on phenomena; those who have gained patient acceptance have
no fixed frame of reference.

Path of Accumulation [b]

As preliminaries, one maintains discipline, controls the senses,
exercises moderation in eating, exerts oneself in spiritual practice
in the late evening and early morning,
takes joy in maintaining alertness, is enthusiastic without regret,
enjoys the seven riches of spiritually advanced beings, engages in
the ten kinds of spiritual activity,
and relies on inspiration and other positive causes of liberation; . . .

Actual Stages of Meditation [3]
General Stages of Mental Training [a]

One trains one's mind with the four axioms, the five factors conducive
to liberation,
recollection of the Victorious One and so forth, the nine perceptions
of impurity,
the eight thoughts of a superior spiritual practitioner,
and the thorough purification of one's sphere of activity.

Formal Meditation Sessions and in Postmeditation [b]
Formal Meditation vis-à-vis Postmeditation [i]

In the specific phase of formal practice, the significance of the
Middle Way is paramount,
and that involves investigation as a preliminary.
Autonomists rest in the significance of an unqualified negation,
comparable to space.

For Consequentialists, the basic space of phenomena (as what to become familiar with) and the mind that becomes familiar
are inseparable, like water poured into water.
For those who profess qualified emptiness, the state is nonconceptual and utterly lucid.
They all agree on the key point of there simply being a freedom from elaboration.

General Discussion of Postmeditation [ii]

In the postmeditation phase one meditates successively on the thirty-seven factors that contribute to enlightenment;
their significance has extraordinary dimensions of vastness and profundity.

Summary [c]

In summary, through four applications—perfecting all aspects,
culminating, sequential, and instantaneous—
one gains accomplishment of the "mother," the unsurpassable and transcendent perfection.

The foregoing constitutes the second part,
concerning a presentation of the specific stages in meditation
in the cause-based dialectical approach.

This concludes [the first two parts of] the eighth book,
a developmental analysis of the higher training in meditative absorption,
from The Encompassing of All Knowledge,
also entitled The Precious Treasury of Sublime Teachings:
The Compendium of the Methods of All Spiritual Approaches
and A Treatise That Thoroughly Presents the Three Higher Trainings.

The Higher Training in Meditative Absorption

On the basis of sublime intelligence that derives from contemplation, one gains certainty, having put an end to naïve assumptions concerning the general and specific characteristics of phenomena, as well as the topics entailed in the profound view.[625]

Once this certainty has been gained, one should put it into practice and apply it in one's ongoing experience through meditation; hence, Book 8 concerns a developmental analysis of the higher training in meditative absorption. This book has four parts, which present: (1) a presentation of the stages of cultivating calm abiding and profound insight, which constitute the common foundations of meditative absorption, (2) a presentation of the specific stages of meditation in the cause-based dialectical approach, (3) a general presentation that emphasizes the tantric approach—that is, the stages of meditation in the secret mantra approach of the Vajrayāna,[626] and (4) a specific presentation that emphasizes the esoteric instructions.[627] [3.167a]

Part 1. Foundations of Meditative Absorption

. . . .

The first part involves three discussions: the reasons for which the cultivation of meditative absorption is necessary, an identification of the meditative absorption that is to be cultivated, and a more extensive explanation of that absorption.

Necessity of Meditative Absorption [I]

The source verses state:

> **The actual significance of what one has studied and contemplated**
> **is put into practice through meditation;**
> **by analogy, although a farmer may reap a fine harvest, it is meant**
> **to be eaten.**

Thus, the actual significance of the sublime intelligence that has been developed through study and contemplation should be incorporated into one's experience through meditation, in which one's focus turns inward. For no matter how profoundly one has studied and contemplated, in the absence of meditation, this will not bring about freedom from bondage.

To give two analogies: A farmer may reap a fine harvest, but unless it is consumed, one's hunger will not be assuaged, for it is meant to be eaten. Alternatively, no matter how skilled one is at reading and thinking about and knowing about medical prescriptions, that skill will not assuage the pain of one's disease, for the medicinal regimen must be followed.

Identifying Meditative Absorption [II]

The source verses state:

> **Seek for certainty about the themes for the vast range of meditative absorption—**
> **in the Hīnayāna and Mahāyāna approaches—in the two aspects of calm abiding and profound insight.**

In citing the pronouncement of the transcendent and accomplished conqueror,[628] the *Definitive Commentary on Enlightened Intent* states that all the states of meditative absorption in the Hīnayāna and Mahāyāna approaches are subsumed within the aspects of calm abiding and profound insight:

> Whatever presentations there are concerning the many expressions of meditative absorption for śrāvakas, for bodhisattvas, and for tathāgatas, one should know that all of these are subsumed within calm abiding and profound insight.[629]

Thus, for those who are motivated to develop meditative absorption, but who cannot thoroughly investigate its endless categories, the universal themes for the vast range of states of meditative absorption are twofold—those of calm abiding and profound insight. Therefore, one begins by seeking to gain certainty concerning these two aspects.

One might wonder, "What is the necessity for doing so?" As the *Definitive Commentary on Enlightened Intent* states, all qualities found in the Hīnayāna and Mahāyāna approaches, whether they are mundane or transcendent,[630] are the results of calm abiding and profound insight. [3.167b] As this source states:

> O Maitreya, you should know that all virtuous factors, both mundane and transcendent—whether they pertain to śrāvakas, or to bodhisattvas, or to tathāgatas—are the results of calm abiding and profound insight.[631]

Extensive Explanation of Meditative Absorption [III]

This explanation has five topics: the essence of these aspects, a definition of the terms, the reason that two aspects are necessary, the developmental process involved, and the way in which one trains in the significance of the individual aspects.

Essence of Meditative Absorption [A]

The source verses state:

> **In essence, these are a one-pointed state of attention**
> **and the discernment that thoroughly analyzes phenomena.**

As to what these aspects constitute in essence, calm abiding is essentially a one-pointed state of attention that is focused within an authentic framework, while profound insight is essentially the discerning and sublime intelligence that thoroughly analyzes phenomena and comprehensively investigates suchness itself. As we read in the *Cloud of the Rare and Excellent*:

> Calm abiding is simply a one-pointed state of mind; profound insight is discernment.[632]

And as Vasubandhu states, by way of commentary on this text:

> One should know that calm abiding and profound insight are to be understood to be a sequence because they constitute, respectively, mind settling in mind[633] and a thorough analysis of phenomena, both relying on an authentic state of meditative absorption; neither can be the case in the absence of meditative absorption. Such are the characteristics of calm abiding and profound insight.[634]

And as the intermediate version of *Stages of Meditation* explains:

> With the calming of distractions due to external sense objects, one takes delight in engaging with a focus, continuously and as a matter of course, and rests in mind itself, which is imbued with thorough pliancy;[635] this is termed "calm abiding." "Profound insight" constitutes whatever thorough investigation of suchness itself takes place when one is focused on that state of calm abiding.[636]

Definition of Terms [B]

The source verses state:

> **As for the derivation of these terms, with the *calm*ing [*zhi*] of distraction, there is *abiding* [*gnas*] to the highest degree,** [3.168a]
> **and the *profound*ly [*lhag*] special quality of things is seen with the *insight* [*mthong*] of the vision of sublime intelligence.**

As for the etymology and meaning of the Sanskrit terms, in the word *śamatha*, the component *śama* means "calm" [Tib. *zhi ba*], while *tha*[637] means "abiding" [Tib. *gnas pa*]. Thus, "calm abiding" means that once the mind distracted by forms and other sense objects has become calm, it abides one-pointedly in any given state of meditative stability that one is cultivating.

In the word *viśeṣapaśya*,[638] the component *viśeṣa*[639] means "special quality" [Tib. *khyad par*] or "profound quality" [Tib. *lhag pa*], while *paśya*[640] means "having insight" [Tib. *mthong ba*] or "seeing" [Tib. *lta ba*]. Thus, "profound insight" means that there is insight due to the perspective of sublime intelligence that sees the profoundly special quality of things—that is, their true nature.

Necessity of Both Aspects [C]

The source verses state:

> **Similar to a lamp's being unstirred by wind and burning brightly,**
> **when both aspects come together, the true way of abiding itself is realized.**

One might wonder why both aspects are needed, with neither calm abiding nor profound insight being sufficient on its own. To give an analogy, if a lamp is both unstirred by wind and burning brightly, one can see things clearly, whereas one cannot see if the lamp is, for example, stirred by wind, even though it is bright. Similarly, if one is endowed with both sublime intelligence that ascertains the meaning of suchness itself in an unmistaken manner and meditative stability in which the mind can abide at will on its focus, one will perceive that suchness clearly. However, even though one has meditative stability (which ensures that the mind abides without wavering), without the sublime intelligence for understanding the way things actually are, one could not possibly realize the way in which they truly abide. And even though one has the view of realizing the absence of any identity,[641] without meditative absorption in which the mind abides one-pointedly, one could not possibly perceive the way things actually are with any clarity. Therefore, all the sūtras and tantras advise the way of integrating these aspects, for the underlying intention is that one will realize suchness itself when both aspects—those of calm abiding and profound insight—come together.

Developmental Process [D]

The source verses state:

> **The developmental process involves a relationship of support and supported.**

The developmental process of calm abiding and profound insight involves a relationship between them of, respectively, a support and what is supported, similar to that between oil and the lamp it fuels. [3.168b] According to *Engaging in the Conduct of a Bodhisattva*:

> Having understood that profound insight utterly imbued with calm abiding
> will completely overcome afflictive mental states,
> one first seeks calm abiding....[642]

Therefore, one begins by establishing calm abiding and, based on that, cultivates profound insight. There is a reason for this order: it is because profound insight consists of using discerning and sublime intelligence to perceive, just as it is, the true way in which mind abides; and in order for such perception to take place, it must certainly be the case that the mind being perceived is pliable and has been brought under control, which depends on there being calm abiding to begin with.

Training in Meditative Absorption [E]

The explanation of how one trains in the significance of the individual aspects is twofold: a more extensive explanation of the individual aspects, and a summary of the general principles.

Extensive Explanation [1]

This explanation is threefold: the way of training in calm abiding, in profound insight, and in these aspects in conjunction with one another.

Training in Calm Abiding [a]

The first explanation is fourfold: reliance on the circumstances that are supportive of calm abiding; analysis of the stages of calm abiding; the process of how these stages are cultivated in meditation; and the measure of success gained through meditation, together with its benefits and advantages.

Supportive Circumstances [i]

The source verses state:

> **One dispenses with all that is counterproductive by relying on the circumstances for calm abiding—**
> **dwelling in a conducive place, having few wants, knowing contentment,**
> **observing pure discipline, and avoiding distractions and concepts.**

That is to say, for those who wish to accomplish calm abiding, it is crucial that they rely on the causes, or circumstances, for it. As the Lord [Atīśa] says in his *Lamp on the Path to Enlightenment*:

> With the factor of calm abiding impaired,
> though one were to meditate with intense effort
> even for thousands of years,
> one would not accomplish meditative absorption.
>
> Therefore, rely entirely on all the factors outlined
> in the *Chapter on the Circumstances for Meditative Absorption*.[643]
> With respect to any pure focus whatsoever,[644]
> one's mind should settle in a virtuous context.[645]
>
> Once an advanced spiritual practitioner accomplishes calm abiding,
> levels of deeper discernment are also accomplished.[646] [3.169a]

One might wonder, "What are these circumstances?" According to the intermediate version of *Stages of Meditation*:

> To dwell in a conducive place, to have few wants, to be content, to completely avoid having many activities, to observe pure discipline, and to completely avoid the concepts and distractions of desire and so forth.[647]

And in the *Ornament of the Mahāyāna Sūtras* we read:

> The place in which an intelligent person will practice
> is where everything fine is provided, with a fine dwelling,
> a fine environment, fine companions,
> and the things that delight an advanced spiritual practitioner.[648]

That is to say, *everything fine is provided* means that it is easy to come by food and clothing. *A fine dwelling* is where one is not subject to such threats as bandits and thieves. *A fine environment* is one in which one will not fall ill. *Fine companions* are those whose view and conduct are in accord with one's own. *The things that delight* are such things as the absence of busyness caused by people and the absence of the hardship of noise.

In such ways, one:

(1) *dwells in a conducive place*;
(2) *has few wants* for fine food and clothing;
(3) *knows contentment* with these being simply adequate;
(4) completely avoids having many activities, such as business matters,

and *observes pure discipline*, without any flaw or breach of one's vows (both those of individual liberation and the bodhisattva path); and

(5) completely *avoids concepts* concerning desires, keeping in mind that they create many problems in this lifetime.

In addition, one should rely completely on the advice given by the lord Atīśa in his *Chapter on the Circumstances for Meditative Absorption*, where he discusses the circumstances or supports for calm abiding, as well as counterproductive factors.

Stages of Calm Abiding [ii]

The source verses state:

> **An analysis includes the mind of the realm of desire, the states of meditative stability, the formless realm, and the state of cessation.**

If we analyze calm abiding according to the working bases,[649] or kinds of beings, we find that there are four categories of stages that are included (1) within the mind of the realm of desire, (2) within the states of meditative stability, [3.169b] (3) within the states of meditative equipoise associated with the formless realm, and (4) within the meditative equipoise of cessation.[650] The ways in which these stages unfold can be found in earlier and later discussions throughout this work.[651]

Process of Cultivation [iii]

The process by which these stages of calm abiding are cultivated is threefold: establishment of physical posture, presentation of the means of settling the mind, and identification of the experiences that develop from these methods.

Physical Posture [aa]

The source verses state:

> **The process of meditation involves sitting comfortably in a physical posture that has eight points.**

When one is cultivating calm abiding, physical posture is very important from the outset. In this regard, one sits on a comfortable seat, with one's posture having eight points. As described in the *Stages of Meditation*,[652] these are as follows: one's legs are fully crossed or half-crossed; ones' eyes are half-closed and focused beyond the tip of one's nose; one's body is held erect; one's shoulders are even; one's nose serves as the guide for one's gaze;[653] one's lips and teeth are slightly parted; one's tongue rests against one's hard palate; and one's breathing is allowed to occur quite naturally, without any effort.

Settling the Mind [bb]

The presentation of the means of settling the mind is twofold: a general discussion of the focus employed, and the actual discussion of the specific stages of meditation.

General Framework [1']

The source verses state:

> **In general, the focus can be any of four—pervasive, purifying one of former behavior,**
> **involving knowledge, or purifying one of afflictive states—and accords with the individual.**

Generally speaking, the transcendent and accomplished conqueror[654] spoke of four kinds of focus used by advanced spiritual practitioners:

(1) As for a pervasive focus,[655] there are four alternative ways in which one's goal can be realized. The first two are those of (a) resting without any process of mental investigation or (b) using a focus in which one does use mental investigation. One may also meditate on (c) the "limit of things"[656] (both things in their multiplicity and their true nature just as it is) or (d) the significance of any of these[657] and thus effect a transformation, which are ways of validating the purpose of the practice.[658]

(2) As for a focus that purifies one of former behavior, there are five alternatives. One's behavior in one's earlier life might have been due to a predominance of desire, anger, delusion, pride, or discursiveness. The respective remedies are to meditate on what is unattractive, loving-kindness, interde-

pendent connection, a detailed analysis of one's mind-body complex, or the coming and going of the breath.[659] [3.170a]

(3) As for a focus involving knowledge, there are again five alternatives—that is, knowledge concerning the mind-body aggregates, the components of one's ordinary experience, the sense fields, the twelve links of interdependent connection, or what is appropriate and inappropriate.[660]

(4) As for a focus that purifies one of afflictive mental states, there are two alternatives—the higher and lower levels of the coarser state of calm abiding,[661] or the sixteen topics (impermanence and the rest) pertaining to the Four Truths.[662]

From among all the foregoing alternatives, which focus is used by any given individual must accord with one's acumen. If one is an individual subject to a predominance of one influence or another (from desire to discursiveness), one should use the corresponding definitive theme (from unattractiveness to the coming and going of the breath). If one is an individual who has behaved in a balanced way, or who is subject to few afflictive mental states, one may focus one's attention using any of the foregoing themes.

Specific Stages of Meditation [2']

The actual discussion of the specific stages of meditation is threefold: settling with a physical support, settling without such a support, and settling in the very essence of meditation.[663]

Settling with a Support [a']

The source verses state:

> **As for specific ways of settling the mind, these may involve an impure or pure physical support.**

With regard to the specific ways of settling the mind, what is important at the outset is training that uses a physical support. One may settle one's mind using some impure object, such as a small stick of wood or a pebble, to focus one's attention. Alternatively, one may use a pure object—a painted or sculpted image (such as an image of the Buddha), a sacred syllable, a symbolic emblem,[664] and so forth.

Settling without a Support [b']

Concerning the way in which one settles one's mind without a support, the source verses state:

> **Without a physical support, one settles one's mind on a partial impression up to a complete one,**
> **or uses some external or internal focus on the body or something related to it.**

Once one has gained some sense of one's mind's abiding on a physical support, one calls to mind some object that is not such a support, such as the image of an enlightened being's form. Initially the impression is partial, as one focuses one's attention on some specific part (such as the face or hands); this is called "having a partial focus." Once one has become familiar with that, one can focus one's attention on a general impression of the complete form; this is called "having a complete focus."

In his analytical overview of the foregoing stages, [3.170b] the master Bodhibhadra explains in his *Essay on Meditative Absorption* that calm abiding is subsumed under either of two methods: that of (1) directing one's attention outwardly or that of (2) directing it inwardly.

(1) The outward directing of one's attention can be of two kinds, special or ordinary; the former involves focusing on either a form of enlightened being or a sacred syllable.

(2) The internal directing of one's attention can also be of two kinds, that of (a) focusing on one's body or (b) settling one's mind on something related to the body.

(a) There are three ways to focus on the body: as the form of a deity, as a symbolic emblem, or as a skeleton.

(b) There are five ways to focus on something related to the body: on the breathing, on some minute characteristic of the body,[665] on a sphere of light,[666] on rays of light, or on feelings of joy and well-being.[667]

Although other works contain any number of ways to classify what one focuses on, these nevertheless all fall into the two categories of those that involve a physical support and those that do not.

Essence of Meditation [c']

As for settling in the very essence of meditation, the source verses state:

> **Once the waves of thought dissolve into the ocean that is the basis of all ordinary experience,**
> **one strives at meditative equipoise that is the very essence of meditation.**

Once one has become familiar with the foregoing methods, without bringing to mind any support for one's focus, one settles into a state in which all mental activity associated with object or subject has thoroughly subsided. With this, all the waves of thoughts proliferating and resolving dissolve thoroughly and in their entirety into the "ocean" that is the basis of all ordinary experience.[668] This is meditative equipoise that is the very essence of meditation, and so constitutes the consummate state of calm abiding. One should, therefore, strive at that.

Identifying Experiences [cc]

There are two points to identifying the experiences that develop from the foregoing methods: a brief presentation by way of introduction, and a more extensive explanation of the significance of individual experiences.

Introduction [1']

The source verses state:

> **There are two ways to identify experiences that develop from these methods.**

There are two traditions for identifying the meditative experiences that arise from these processes—that is, of settling with a physical support, settling without a support, and settling in the very essence of meditation.

Extensive Explanation [2']

The extensive explanation is twofold: according to the tradition of mainstream sources and according to the tradition of personal advice.[669]

Mainstream Sources [a']

The first tradition involves two models: that of relying on eight remedial techniques to eliminate five flaws, and that of accomplishing nine steps in settling the mind (which involve six powers and four ways of focusing). [3.171a]

Five Flaws and Eight Remedial Techniques [i']

The source verses state:

> **According to mainstream sources, the five flaws are: three kinds of faintheartedness,**
> **the forgetting of instructions, two kinds each of laxity and agitation, nonapplication,**
> **and overapplication. These are remedied by eight techniques:**
> **intention, effort, confidence, and thorough pliancy (which prevent the first flaw);**
> **meditative absorption without forgetfulness (endowed with three special features);**
> **alert effort, and equanimity (once evenness has ensued).**

If we consider the way in which calm abiding is explained in the great tradition of mainstream sources, it is said that one relies on eight remedial techniques to eliminate five flaws, which act as impediments that obstruct the development of meditative experiences. According to *Distinguishing Center and Limit*:

> Abiding in that state with flexibility
> ensures that all one's goals are fulfilled.
> This comes about due to the causes on which it depends—
> using eight remedial techniques to eliminate five flaws.

Faintheartedness, forgetting instructions,
mental laxity and agitation,
nonapplication, and overapplication—
these are held to be the five flaws.

The context, remaining within that,
cause, and effect;
not forgetting the framework;
being alert to laxity or agitation;
taking steps to ensure that they are actually eliminated;
and entering into a genuine state of repose when calm ensues.[670]

From the foregoing citation, the words *abiding in that state* mean that, in order to do away with counterproductive influences, one exerts oneself diligently and remains in that state. This leads to meditative absorption that brings physical and mental *flexibility*.[671] This is the basis, or context, for supernormal powers (such as powers of deeper discernment) that bring realization of all one's goals, and so *ensure that one's goals are fulfilled*. Such a state of meditative absorption develops due to *the causes on which it depends—using eight remedial techniques* and *eliminating five flaws*.

Of these five flaws:

(1) *Faintheartedness* is a flaw when one is trying to apply oneself to meditative absorption because it ensures that one does not, in fact, apply oneself. It can be of three kinds: lethargy (which includes sleepiness), obsession with ignoble activities, or diffidence.[672]

(2) *Forgetting instructions* is a flaw once one is diligently pursuing meditative absorption, [3.171b] for one's mind cannot settle in equipoise if one forgets the focus.

(3) *Mental laxity and agitation* are impediments to settling in equipoise since both of these make the mind inflexible. Each of these can be of two kinds. There is obvious laxity, when one loses the sense of holding one's attention to the focus and instead feels a sense of losing consciousness, in which that focus is no longer clear; and there is subtle laxity, when there is still some clarity, but the strength of the mind holding the focus wanes. There is obvious agitation, when the mind is fascinated with sense objects and cannot be reined in with remedies; and there is subtle agitation, when the mind is stirring slightly, without abiding in an unwavering way.

(4) *Nonapplication*[673] is a flaw when either laxity or agitation occurs, for it ensures that neither subsides.

(5) *Overapplication* is a flaw once one is free of laxity or agitation since it means one cannot abide in equanimity.

When laxity and agitation are counted as one, there are five flaws; when they are considered separately, there are six, as described in the *Stages of Meditation*.[674]

One uses eight techniques of elimination as remedies to these flaws:

(1)–(4) Four of these techniques—intention, effort, confidence (as the cause), and thorough pliancy (as the result to which that cause leads)—put a stop to the first flaw, faintheartedness.[675]

(5) The remedy for forgetfulness is meditative absorption that ensures one is *not forgetting instructions*. Such absorption is endowed with three features, in that it involves an intensity, due to the mind's being extremely lucid; a nonconceptual quality, due to the mind's abiding one-pointedly on its focus; and an experience of well-being that takes the form of a blissful sensation.

(6) By one's *being alert to* whether or not *laxity or agitation* are taking place, then should either occur, one exerts oneself in any means to dispel the problem—focus, gaze, conduct, and so forth.[676]

(7) Rather than failing to apply remedies for laxity or agitation, one applies them with an attitude of making *effort*.

(8) Once meditative stability ensues faultlessly and one is resting in equipoise, rather than continuing to make effort in application, one trains in *equanimity*, no longer applying any remedy.

Six Powers, Four Ways of Focusing, and Nine Steps in Settling [ii']

The source verses state:

> **Through six powers—listening, contemplation, mindfulness,**
> **alertness, diligence, and familiarization—** [3.172a]
> **involving situations of tension, interruption,**
> **no interruption, and spontaneity,**
> **nine steps of settling the mind (settling on a focus and so**
> **forth) develop.**

One relies on six powers that promote one's growth: these are the powers of listening to teachings, contemplation, mindfulness, alertness, diligence, and familiarization. The first power ensures the first step in settling the mind; the second power, the second step; the third power, the third and fourth steps; the fourth power, the fifth and sixth steps; the fifth power, the seventh and eighth steps; and the sixth power, the ninth step.

These steps involve four attendant attitudes: those of involvement with tension, involvement with interruption, involvement without interruption, and spontaneous involvement. During the first two steps of settling the mind, one is involved with the first situation; during the third through the seventh steps of settling, with the second situation; during the eighth step of settling, with the third situation; and during the ninth step of settling, with the fourth situation. These steps are therefore said to "involve situations with four attendant attitudes."

The nine steps of settling the mind that develop through these powers and attitudes are those of settling, settling continually, and so forth. Of these nine steps:

(1) settling the mind involves drawing one's mind in from any external focus and directing it toward some inner focus;

(2) settling continually involves the mind that was thus directed initially continuing to settle on its focus without becoming distracted by anything else;

(3) settling repeatedly involves one's being aware if the mind becomes distracted outwardly and causing it to settle once more on its focus;

(4) settling more intimately involves settling in a more subtle way, ensuring that the mind is drawn naturally from a broader scope to a more concentrated one;

(5) guiding the mind involves a feeling of inspiration when one reflects on the positive qualities of meditative absorption; [3.172b]

(6) pacifying the mind involves one's seeing distraction to be a fault, so as to pacify any resistance one still has to developing meditative absorption;

(7) pacifying it thoroughly involves pacifying feelings such as desirous attitudes or unhappiness;

(8) settling the mind one-pointedly involves striving in order to be able to settle effortlessly; and

(9) settling in equipoise, once the mind has achieved evenness, involves one's allowing that to occur with equanimity; thus, the final of the nine steps in settling the mind is awakened.

The nine steps of settling the mind are discussed in the *Ornament of the Mahāyāna Sūtras*,[677] while the six powers and the four attendant attitudes are explained in the *Levels of the Śrāvaka*.[678]

Personal Advice [b']

As for an explanation according to the tradition of personal advice, the source verses state:

> **In the tradition of personal advice, understanding is gained**
> **through illustrative analogies of five experiences—**
> **movement, attainment, familiarization, stability, and**
> **consummation.**

In the tradition of those who employ personal advice, the process by which calm abiding develops is subsumed within five stages of meditative experience:

(1) the first stage is the experience of mind in *movement*, comparable to water cascading down a rock face;

(2) the second stage is the experience of *attainment*, comparable to a torrent in a deep ravine;

(3) the third stage is the experience of *familiarization*, comparable to a meandering river;

(4) the fourth stage is the experience of *stability*, comparable to an ocean free of waves; and

(5) the fifth stage is the experience of *consummation*, with the mind abiding in a state of limpid clarity in which no circumstance whatsoever can cause it to stir; this is comparable to the flame of a lamp unstirred by any breeze.

One should understand that each of the analogies is an attempt to illustrate the actual experience taking place.

Measuring Success [iv]

An explanation of the measure of success gained through meditation, and related topics, is twofold: the way to attain calm abiding and the attendant states of mental focus, and an explanation of the purpose of such attainment.

Attaining Calm Abiding [aa]

The source verses state:

> **With the consummation of thorough pliancy, calm abiding is ensured—**
> **the space within which well-being, clarity, and the absence of any concepts about subtle traits blend.**

That is to say, even though one may have achieved the four attendant attitudes and the nine steps of settling the mind, if one has not gained a thorough pliancy of mind and body, one has not yet reached the consummate state of calm abiding. According to the *Commentary on Enlightened Intent*: [3.173a]

> "O transcendent and accomplished conqueror! As long as a bodhisattva's mind is such that the attention is directed inwardly but thorough pliancy of body and thorough pliancy of mind have not been attained, what does such attention constitute?"
>
> "O Maitreya! This is not calm abiding. Rather, one should describe this as a case of someone who has an approximation of, and a dedicated interest that is entirely in accord with, calm abiding."[679]

And in the *Ornament [of the Mahāyāna Sūtras]* we read the following:

> Once familiar with that, they no longer use application.
>
> This then brings about a consummate degree
> of thorough pliancy of body and mind,
> which is termed "involving deliberation."[680]

In this context, the phrase "involving deliberation" refers to calm abiding.[681]

In brief, calm abiding is explained as being the thorough pliancy that involves flexibility of body and mind. Before it is attained, any state of meditative absorption still falls within the realm of desire; this is not yet actual calm abiding, and so is referred to as "the one-pointed mind of the realm of desire."

As for thorough pliancy, the *Compendium of Abhidharma* states:

> "What is thorough pliancy?" one might ask. It is flexibility of body and mind, because the continuity of the physical and mental tendencies that perpetuate ignoble states of existence has been interrupted; its function is that of removing all obscurations.[682]

The physical and mental tendencies that perpetuate ignoble states of existence are such that one is incapable of engaging at will in positive actions, whether physical or mental. Their remedy lies in a thorough pliancy of body and mind, for due to being free of both kinds of such tendencies, one's body and mind are extremely flexible in engaging in positive actions. There is flexibility of body, for once one has made effort to eliminate the afflictive states that reinforce physical tendencies that perpetuate ignoble states (and interfere with the process of eliminating those tendencies), one is free of bodily inflexibility (such as physical sensations of heaviness) and instead feels one's body to be buoyant and light, like a ball of cotton. There is flexibility of mind, for once one has made effort to eliminate the afflictive states that reinforce mental tendencies that perpetuate ignoble states, one is free of mental inflexibility (in which the mind is incapable of engaging wholeheartedly within any positive framework) and can engage without any impediment. [3.173b]

According to the *Levels of the Śrāvaka,*[683] of these two kinds of flexibility, the thorough pliancy of mental flexibility develops first, and due to its influence, a subtle energy (that causes thorough pliancy of body to develop) stirs and becomes pervasive throughout the body, so that one is freed of physical tendencies that perpetuate ignoble states, resulting in the development of thorough pliancy of body. (This thorough pliancy of body is not just a mental state; there is a remarkable and extremely pleasant physical sensation throughout one's body.)

As for the way in which these states develop, at first thorough pliancy is subtle and hard to detect; then it becomes more obvious and easily recognized; then it develops to a great degree, with a powerful sense of well-being and joy overtaking one's body and mind. According to the *Levels of the Śrāvaka,*[684] once this has developed, one meditates by adopting an attitude of equanimity toward the joy that could otherwise make one's mind too excited. At a certain point, due to the influence of a thorough pliancy that ensues, as light as a shadow, one gains calm abiding.[685] As for the measure of success in the calm abiding that comes with the consummation of this thorough pliancy, without any obstacle due to distraction, outwardly or inwardly, one's mind rests inherently on its focus in a stable way, abiding limpidly since it is free of laxity or agitation.

Thus, the attainment of the aforementioned attendant attitudes ensures that one attains four factors to some small degree: (1) a mind state included within the realm of form,[686] (2) thorough pliancy of body, (3) thorough pliancy of mind, and (4) one-pointed focus. With these come calm abiding on a more obvious level (or what could be termed the spiritual path that embodies the aspects of the Truths[687]), which has the capacity to refine away afflictive states. If one then turns inward, resting in equipoise, thorough pliancy of body and mind develop very swiftly; the five obscurations (such as fascination with objects of desire or sleepiness)[688] do not, for the most part, occur; and even when one arises from a formal state of meditative equipoise, one is, at least from time to time, endowed with a thorough pliancy of body and mind. This explanation, found in the *Levels of the Śrāvaka*,[689] concerns the indications that one is imbued with this state of mental engagement.[690]

It is also explained that there is the sense of well-being that comes from thorough physical and mental pliancy. This pliancy also leads to exceptional meditative experiences of clarity, such as being able to perceive things on the atomic level, and to an absence of conceptual thinking about any of the ten kinds of characteristics that one might perceive in things (that is, the five kinds of sense objects (visual forms and so forth), the three times, and male and female genders), [3.174a] so that one has an experience as though one were blending with space. This experience is such that during formal meditative equipoise one has no perception of having a body, while one's mind blends with space; in postmeditation, one has experiences such as the impression that one's body suddenly reappears.

Purpose [bb]

The source verses state:

> **This is the basis of all meditative stability in the traditions of sūtra and tantra.**
> **It suppresses all afflictive states and suffering.**

The consummate state of calm abiding that comes with the attainment of thorough pliancy is the basis that gives rise to, or supports, all the states of meditative stability discussed in the sūtras and tantras, whether these states involve conceptual frameworks or not. It is like a fertile field for someone who wishes to grow crops. This state of meditative absorption alone is itself capable of suppressing and pacifying all the overt manifestations of afflictive states and suffering. And that is not all, for the realization of the authentic state of suchness (that is, the lack of identity in things), just as it is, must depend entirely on one's resting in equipoise. As the first version of *Stages of Meditation* states:

> A mind that is not resting in equipoise cannot know what is authentic, just as it is. The transcendent and accomplished conqueror proclaimed, moreover, "It is through resting in equipoise that one knows what is authentic, just as it is."[691]

Training in Profound Insight [b]

The second explanation, how one trains in profound insight, is fivefold: reliance on the circumstances that are supportive of profound insight; an analysis of the specific expressions of profound insight; an analysis of the essential experiences of profound insight; the way in which it is cultivated in meditation; and the measure of attainment.

Supportive Circumstances [i]

The source verses state:

> **The causal circumstances for profound insight are to rely on holy masters,**
> **to hear many teachings, to think correctly, and so to seek the view.**

In this regard, the intermediate version of *Stages of Meditation* states:

> "What are the circumstances that support profound insight?" one might ask. They are: to rely on holy masters, to seek any and every way to study the teachings in depth, and to think correctly.[692]

That is to say, one relies on learned people who have fathomed the meaning of the scriptures [3.174b] and listens to their teachings on the flawless mainstream traditions. Through the sublime intelligence that comes from listening to and contemplating these teachings, one develops the view that constitutes the realization of the very nature of things. These are the indispensable causal circumstances that are supportive of profound insight, for it is impossible for the realization that constitutes that profound insight to awaken without one's having the completely authentic view.

With respect to such a view, one must seek to develop this by relying on the definitive meaning of the teachings rather than the provisional meaning. And so, having understood the distinction between the definitive and provisional meanings,[693] one must master the profound meaning of the scriptures that deal with that definitive meaning, which, in the present context, is to say that one should discover the view that constitutes the realization of the profundity of emptiness by relying on the extensive traditions established by the two guides.[694]

Analysis of Profound Insight [ii]

As for a more detailed analysis, the source verses state:

> **Its specific expressions are said to be the more obvious state of quiescence also found in non-Buddhist traditions,**
> **the topics that pertain to the Truths (in the śrāvaka and pratyekabuddha approaches),**
> **the view of emptiness (in the pāramitā approach), and the influence of bliss (in the tantric approach).**
> **The ordinary preparatory phases parallel those of the mundane path;**
> **however, these are not pursued by those in the tantric approach and others.**

In this regard, if one considers profound insight from the point of view of its expressions from lower to higher levels of spiritual development, the following expressions are spoken of:

(1) The expression of insight as a more obvious state of calm abiding—which is found in common with non-Buddhist systems—is the more mundane level of insight that eliminates overt manifestations of afflictive mental states.

(2) In the śrāvaka and pratyekabuddha approaches, the expression of profound insight is the view that focuses on impermanence and the rest of the sixteen topics pertaining to the Four Truths.

(3) In the Mahāyāna approach of the transcendent perfections, it is the view that focuses on emptiness.

(4) In the systems of the tantric approach, that same view is imbued with a blissful quality.

The three latter expressions constitute profound insight that transcends the mundane sphere, in that it completely eliminates even the underlying potential for afflictive states.

The way in which the main states of meditative stability are accomplished through the seven preparatory phases that are expressions of calm abiding[695] is, in fact, the one that was explained in the section on the mundane path.[696] However, those who are following the tantric path—and the words "or others" refer to those with the exceptional view of the pāramitā approach—are not motivated to practice deliberately to achieve these phases.

Essential Experiences [iii]

As for an analysis of the essential experiences involved, the source verses state: [3.175a]

> **An analysis may involve three categories: analytical insight,**
> **thoroughly analytical insight,**
> **and insight as the avenue for four essential experiences of**
> **examination and investigation.**
> **Insight can derive from the ordinary distinctions one makes,**
> **from a thoroughgoing search, and from discernment.**
> **It can involve six explorations—of meaning, things,**
> **characteristics, influences, time, and logical principles.**
> **(There are four logical principles that concern dependent**
> **relationships, performance of function, establishment of what**
> **is reasonable,**
> **and the nature of things.) These six are used to analyze things**
> **in detail,**
> **from visual forms to omniscience.**

At this point, my discussion will not place emphasis on the profound states of insight that pertain to the advanced paths and levels;[697] rather, I shall emphasize the profound insight that is cultivated in meditation while one is an ordinary mortal individual. An explanation of such an analysis involves three categories:

(1) In the *Definitive Commentary on Enlightened Intent*,[698] two aspects are those of analytical insight and thoroughly analytical insight. Each of these two is further divisible into two modes, those of thoroughgoing examination and thoroughgoing investigation, making for the third category, that of what is known as "profound insight involving four essential experiences."

Of these, analytical insight focuses on things in all their multiplicity, precisely analyzing the mind-body aggregates, sense fields, and components of perception. Thoroughly analytical insight focuses on reality just as it is,[699] leading to realization of the lack of identity in the individual and the lack of identity in phenomena. The two modes of examination and investigation involve mentally analyzing things in a more obvious and more subtle way, respectively.

As for the way in which these aspects of profound insight are realized, the *Definitive Commentary on Enlightened Intent* states:

> with thorough examination, certain examination, thorough evaluation, and intimate evaluation.[700]

If we apply the same detailed divisions to investigation, we arrive at a total of sixteen degrees of insight.[701] A precise classification of these can be found in the *Levels of the Śrāvaka*.

A similar treatment is found in the *Compendium of Abhidharma*:

> "What is profound insight?" one might ask. It is the analysis, the thorough analysis, the thoroughgoing examination, and the thoroughgoing investigation of phenomena, because it is the remedy for tendencies that perpetuate ignoble states of existence and the ordinary distinctions one makes, keeps one away from what is erroneous, and allows one's mind to settle in what is without error.[702] [3.175b]

(2) As for profound insight through three avenues of engagement, we read in the *Definitive Commentary on Enlightened Intent*:

> "O transcendent and accomplished conqueror! How many expressions of profound insight are there?"

> "O Maitreya, there are three: that which derives from the ordinary distinctions one makes, that which derives from a thoroughgoing search, and that which derives from discernment."[703]

If we define these three expressions of profound insight with reference to meditation on the absence of identity, for example, the first expression involves focusing on the identification of this absence of identity, so that the ordinary distinctions entailed are called to mind; but it does not involve much attention to come to a definitive conclusion. The second expression involves coming to such a conclusion, in order to gain certainty about what was hitherto uncertain. The third expression involves the same kind of investigation as used before but concerning the significance of what has already been ascertained.

(3) As for "profound insight that involves six explorations," this derives from a thoroughgoing search of six factors—meanings, things, characteristics, influences, time, and logical principles—and from the discernment one gains through having examined them. Of these factors:

(a) the exploration of meaning here refers to the inquiry "The meaning of such-and-such a word is such-and-such";

(b) the exploration of things refers to such inquiries as "This thing is something internal, while that thing is something external";

(c) the exploration of characteristics has two aspects, what is more common and what is more particular, as in the inquiry "These are the characteristic specific to something, while these are its more general characteristics";

(d) the exploration of influences involves the examination of negative factors (from the point of view of their flaws and drawbacks) and positive ones (from the point of view of their qualities and benefits); and

(e) the exploration of time involves the inquiry "Such-and-such happened in the past, such-and-such will happen in the future, such-and-such is the case at present."

(f) The exploration of logical principles entails four such lines. Of these:

(i) The logical principle of dependence focuses on results coming about in dependence on their causes and conditions. It also involves investigations of what is relative or ultimate, and the respective bases for these contexts. [3.176a]

(ii) The logical principle of function focuses on the functions that are specific to phenomena, such as the function of fire's being that of burning. It involves such explorations as "This is a given phenomenon; this is a function; this phenomenon performs this function."

(iii) The logical principle that establishes what is reasonable involves the proof of a point without contradicting the process of valid cognition. It involves investigation by considering, "Does this point in question conform to any of the three kinds of valid cognition, whether direct experience, correct inference, or reliable scriptural authority?"[704]

(iv) The logical principle of the nature of things involves investigating things by concentrating on their nature's being what is commonly accepted in the world (such as fire's being hot and water's being wet), on the inconceivable nature of reality, and on the true and abiding nature of things,[705] without considering extraneous issues.[706]

One can apply these six methods of exploration to any given phenomenon within the deeply ingrained afflictive state and the totally refined state—from forms up to and including the state of omniscience—to analyze them in detail and gain realization thereby.

The source verses state:

> **These can be understood in three ways: meaning, reality just as it is, and things in all their multiplicity.**
> **The preparation and the main practice are subsumed, respectively, within discernment and an unwavering state.**

While these examinations can be classified as sixfold, for an advanced spiritual practitioner, there are three topics to be understood: the meaning of what is uttered, reality just as it is, and things in all their multiplicity.

In categorizing these topics, from the point of view of the first topic, the method of exploration is of the first kind.[707] From the point of view of the second topic, the methods of exploration are of things and characteristics (both general and specific). From the point of view of the third topic, the methods of exploration are of the latter three kinds,[708] plus that of general characteristics.

The avenues to the four kinds of profound insight discussed earlier[709] are threefold,[710] while the methods of exploration are explained as being the foregoing six. Thus, the three avenues and six methods of exploration are subsumed within the foregoing four kinds of profound insight.

Alternatively, profound insight can be considered as twofold, divided into a preparatory phase and the actual state. So profound insight can be subsumed under two categories: profound insight as a discerning function of thought (in the context of the preparatory phase) and profound insight as a completely unwavering state (in the context of the actual state). [3.176b]

Cultivating Profound Insight [iv]

As for the way in which profound insight is cultivated in meditation, the source verses state:

> **As for the way insight is cultivated in meditation, having used sublime intelligence to investigate**
> **the fact that things lack identity, one rests in equipoise in a state free of conceptual elaborations.**
> **The bases for the investigation—the nonconceptual images—**
> **are focused on as bases of attributes, while any false assumptions concerning their specific attributes are eliminated.**

If one has not discovered the view of things lacking identity, one will stray from the ultimate point of suchness itself, regardless of which method of meditation one employs; so one must discover that view. However, even with an understanding of that view, if one does not meditate by resting one's mind on the basis of that understanding, one will not cultivate the experience of suchness. Therefore, having used sublime intelligence to investigate the fact that things lack identity, one rests in equipoise in basic space, free of all conceptual elaborations.

With respect to this point, if one engages a great deal in analytical meditation and the abiding aspect of one's meditation diminishes, one can engage more in resting meditation and nurture that abiding aspect. If one engages in a great deal of resting meditation and becomes disinclined to engage in analytical meditation, one should engage in the latter. For it is explained that it is more powerful for one to meditate by balancing calm abiding and profound insight in equal measure.

In this regard, the usual model common to most systems of Buddhist thought[711] is that once one has completed an investigation of the topic of meditation using discerning intelligence, one rests in equipoise in this freedom from conceptual elaboration. The model of the Gedenpa school,[712] however, is that when maintaining the main practice of meditative equipoise, one should continue to clarify, further and further, the way in which one's mind deliberately apprehends.[713]

As for the actual cultivation of profound insight in meditation, if one has begun by cultivating calm abiding, the many forms that are perceived within the scope of one's meditative absorption—whether or not these accord with external circumstances—are termed "nonconceptual images." If one then cultivates profound insight in meditation, one meditates by using those reflections (which arise on the strength of one's calm abiding) as the bases for examination by one's discernment. But the mind is entirely directed inwardly; there is no examination that actually focuses on externals in a deliberate way.[714]

When one investigates those images, which constitute the scope of one's meditative absorption, initially one must use the discernment of one's sublime intelligence [3.177a] to focus on the individual phenomena under investigation, because one cannot eliminate any false assumptions concerning the specific attributes of things until one has ascertained the bases of these attributes. Therefore, one first clearly brings to mind a given object about which one's false assumptions must be eliminated. Then one uses the authentic discerning function of one's sublime intelligence to examine it, coming to the definitive conclusion that it is apparent yet has no independent nature. One then focuses without wavering on that as the object of one's meditative absorption, and so realizes that the object upon which one is completely focused *is* apparent yet has no independent nature.[715] Meditative absorption and sublime intelligence are thus integrated with an identical focus. This is what is meant when the *Compendium of Abhidharma* states:

> involving the congruency of meditative absorption and sublime intelligence . . .[716]

The source verses state:

> **The nature of what is perceived is known to be empty, like space;**
> **what is to be examined—the origin, location, shape, and so forth, of the perceiving consciousness—**
> **and the discerning function itself are like fire sticks consumed by fire.**
> **Nothing is found, for things dissolve into basic space, and one rests without any fixated perception.**

Suppose that, while resting in equipoise vis-à-vis visual forms and so forth, one uses the discerning function of one's sublime intelligence to realize that the nature of those forms and so forth is empty; this is not due to one's calling to mind such things as the ordinary characteristics of those forms. By initially familiarizing oneself with this, one becomes aware that the nature of what is merely perceived is emptiness, comparable to the realm of space, without any fixed frame of reference. This is to immerse oneself in the genuine state in which there is no conceptual framework of perceived objects; one meditates on what is external as the inseparability of appearance and emptiness.

When one experiences the onset of a given state of one's inner perceiving consciousness—such as aversion—in one's ongoing experience, one examines this with the discerning function of one's sublime intelligence, trying to determine what cause it could have come from in the first place; what location (whether internal or external) it could reside in for the duration; and what shape, color, and so forth, it might have in its essence. One should rest in equipoise, experiencing the significance of finding nothing whatsoever through such examination. This method is applied upon the onset of any of the six primary afflictive states.[717] And that is not all, [3.177b] for in becoming aware of any thoughts that occur, including neutral ones and so forth,[718] one applies this method accordingly. This is to immerse oneself in the genuine state in which there is no conceptual framework of a perceiving consciousness; one meditates on what is internal as the inseparability of awareness and emptiness.

Finally, the objects to be examined and even discerning sublime intelligence itself dissolve into basic space so that nothing can be found any longer (analogous to a fire stick's being consumed by the fire it produces), and one should rest in that state without any subjective perception. The foregoing points are presented in distilled form in *Pith Instructions on the Middle Way* by the Noble Lord, which states:

> In this way, the mind of the past has ceased and so dispensed with; the mind of the future has not yet developed or occurred; the mind of the present moment is likewise extremely difficult to examine.[719] Since there is a similarity to space, with no color and an absence of any shape, if one uses the weapon of reasoning in investigating and analyzing mind—whether from the perspective that it cannot be found to exist, or that it is free of being one thing or many, or that it is unborn, or that it is utterly lucid by nature, and so forth—you will realize that it cannot be established to exist.

Thus, given that mind cannot be found to exist in essence as some "thing" of either of two kinds[720] and so simply does not exist as such, even discerning sublime intelligence itself[721] cannot be established to exist as such. To give an analogy, the fire that results from two sticks' being rubbed together consumes them both, and in the wake of them vanishing, even the fire that consumed them dies out in and of itself. Similarly, once it has simply been established that all phenomena (with both shared and specific characteristics) do not exist as such, even that sublime intelligence itself is not something manifest, but rather is an utter lucidity, free of all conceptual elaborations,[722] not something that can be found to exist as anything at all in essence. And so everything that could constitute a circumstance[723] of mental dullness, agitation, and the like has been eliminated.

Under those circumstances, there is no thinking about anything at all, no fixation on anything at all; for all deliberate recollection and formulation of thought has been eliminated. One's consciousness should rest[724] for as long as enemies and thieves—that is, ordinary distinctions and thoughts[725]—do not arise.[726]

Measure of Attainment [v]

As for the measure of one's attainment of profound insight, [3.178a] the source verses state:

> **The gaining of thorough pliancy is explained as being the point at which there is attainment.**

When one meditates using the discerning function of one's sublime intelligence to investigate things individually, as long as thorough pliancy has not been attained, one has a valid approximation of profound insight, but with the onset of that pliancy, one's insight is completely authentic. The essence of thorough pliancy and the way in which it comes about were explained in the context of calm abiding. If one is able to usher in this thorough pliancy on the specific strength of one's having practiced analytical meditation, the *Definitive Commentary on Enlightened Intent*[727] and Śāntipa's *Pith Instructions on the Transcendent Perfection of Sublime Intelligence*[728] speak of this as the point at which insight is attained. This applies to both kinds of profound insight—that which focuses on phenomena in all their multiplicity and that which focuses on reality just as it is.

Training in Integration [c]

Training in the integration of calm abiding and profound insight is threefold: the actual training process, the point at which integration occurs, and the result of this process.

Actual Training Process [i]

The source verses state:

> **Although followers of the Middle Way interpret the process of development in distinct ways,**
> **they agree on what is to be developed—the integration of calm abiding and profound insight.**
> **Unwavering and developmental meditation is paramount in all three cases.**

That is to say, as far as the accomplishment of nondual timeless awareness—in which calm abiding and profound insight are integrated—is concerned, various masters of the Middle Way school discuss different ways in which this is developed. Nevertheless, they agree that what is to be developed is the integration of that abiding and insight.

In this regard, the master Bhāvaviveka gives the following explanation: Having fostered calm abiding by focusing on unattractiveness, loving-kindness, and so forth, one follows this by developing profound insight through the influence of precise investigation using reasoning.[729] The master Śāntideva explains that, having first fostered calm abiding by cultivating bodhicitta, one follows this by developing the sublime intelligence of profound insight by focusing on emptiness.[730] In the intermediate version of *Stages of Meditation*, the master Kamalaśīla states that one first develops calm abiding by focusing on an image of the Sage,[731] for example, and then gains profound insight through a precise investigation of the nature of that same focus.[732] [3.178b] According to the master Candra,[733] calm abiding and profound insight are accomplished on the basis of the view that derives from investigating suchness itself.

Given that all these interpretations, moreover, are completely accurate and constitute unerring paths, they all agree in holding that one meditates in a methodical and developmental way, given the cause-and-effect relationship that involves three steps: calm abiding, profound insight, and their integration. And for all these masters, what is paramount is the unwavering quality of one-pointed attention.

Integration [ii]

The source verses state:

> **When one is meditating with a construct, integration involves**
> **a precise analysis of the image on which one is focusing.**
> **Once one gains profound nonconceptual insight, there is**
> **integration**
> **when these have become identical in essence.**

"Well," one might wonder, "at what point do calm abiding and profound insight become integrated?" When one is cultivating that abiding and that insight by meditating with some construct,[734] both the calm abiding (the nonconceptual mind focused on the image) and the profound insight (the realization that analyzes phenomena precisely) are equally engaged as a matter of course—that is, they are in actual fact integrated. In this present discussion, though, when one gains both calm abiding that is completely nonconceptual and profound insight that is also completely nonconceptual, these two abide identical in essence, and so there is truly what is termed "integration."[735] As the first version of *Stages of Meditation* states:

> At whatever point one is focused on the absence of any finite essence in all phenomena, such that one's consciousness is engaged yet free of mental dullness, agitation, and the like, and without the overt application of any remedy, at that point one has completed the path that brings about the integration of calm abiding and profound insight.[736]

Result of Integration [iii]

The source verses state:

That is the consummation of authentic meditative absorption—
the attainment of nirvāṇa that is not confined, but free of the
bonds of conditioned existence and the state of peace.

Such meditative absorption, which integrates calm abiding and profound insight, is truly authentic meditative absorption. This is what Maitripa refers to in his *Commentary on the "Ten Topics of Suchness"*: [3.179a]

> with authentic meditative absorption, just as intended, . . .[737]

The path that connects and integrates calm abiding and profound insight is that of truly authentic meditative absorption, just as it is intended to be, for as is said:

> This is the actuality that ensures accomplishment of that integration.[738]

It is the consummation of this that leads to nirvāṇa that is not confined, but free of the bonds of conditioned existence and the state of peace.[739] According to the *Definitive Commentary on Enlightened Intent*:

> When people have become familiar
> with profound insight and calm abiding,
> they become free of the bonds that perpetuate ignoble states of existence
> and the bonds of making ordinary distinctions.[740]

When one arises from meditative equipoise, with the perspective that all phenomena are like dream images, one exerts oneself in skillful ways to honor buddhas and bodhisattvas, treat ordinary beings with compassion, dedicate one's fundamentally positive qualities on a vast scale, and so forth.

Summary of General Principles [2]

A summary of the general principles of meditative absorption is threefold: a summary of alternative approaches, a discussion of the means of accomplishment through investigative and settling meditation, and an auxiliary explanation of the three situations involved in meditative stability.

Alternative Approaches [a]

This involves a summary of the alternative approaches for calm abiding and a summary of the alternative approaches for profound insight.

Calm Abiding [i]

The source verses state:

> **In brief, unattractiveness, loving-kindness, the counting of exhalations and inhalations,**
> **the elimination of specific perceptions, the use of subtle channels and energies, visualization, mantra repetition,**
> **and being at rest in the natural state of relaxation—all these amount to situations in which the attention is focused.**

In brief, in the more ordinary approach,[741] one may meditate on the nine perceptions of unattractiveness,[742] train one's mind in loving-kindness and compassion,[743] or count the phases of one's breathing (exhalation, inhalation, and retention). In the Vajrayāna approach, there are many means available to one: the pith instructions on consolidation (isolating, and thus eliminating, the perceptions of specific sense objects), the empty framework[744] of the subtle channels, the advanced practices for harnessing the subtle energies, the melting bliss[745] of bindu, the visualization of deities, or the repetition of mantras. Or one can rest in the natural state of relaxation—the uncontrived and unfettered state of genuine being. All these alternatives, while accommodating the various degrees of acumen in individuals, [3.179b] amount to means that usher in the focusing of the mind's attention and develop calm abiding.

Profound Insight [ii]

The source verses state:

> **One may thoroughly investigate what is characterized and what serves to characterize it, or general and specific characteristics;**
> **one may investigate interdependent connection, use the five logical proofs, be directly introduced to one's true nature**

through scriptural citations, logical reasoning, the transmission of blessing through symbols, and so forth. These are means to arouse
the superb discerning function of one's sublime intelligence, accommodating the acumen of individuals.

According to the principles of valid cognition,[746] for example, one may investigate such issues as what serves as a basis for certain characteristics, what is characterized, and what serves to characterize it. In the abhidharma teachings, one may thoroughly investigate the general and specific characteristics of phenomena. One may gain understanding of the process of interdependent connection, both the usual progression and its reversal.[747] One may eliminate wishful thinking through use of the five major logical proofs, focusing on causes, results, both, things in their essence, and interdependent connection.[748] Or one may be introduced directly to one's own true nature, beholding it in all its nakedness, due to many means involving scriptural citations, logical reasoning, the transmission of blessing, or the use of symbols. All such approaches are a developmental spectrum of means to arouse the superb discerning function of one's sublime intelligence, in accord with the acumen of individuals. Given that any of these means will develop calm abiding and profound insight, any in itself will ensure that the goal is realized; there is no need for a single individual to employ all these methods.

Investigative and Settling Meditation [b]

As for the means by which calm abiding and profound insight are accomplished through investigative and settling meditation, the source verses state:

Investigative and settling meditation are both alike in accomplishing calm abiding and profound insight.

As discussed previously, calm abiding and profound insight are accomplished by alternating the two modes of investigative meditation and settling meditation. Since either mode, if carried through to its consummation, will ensure both aspects of meditative absorption, in the final analysis, investigative and settling meditation are alike.

Auxiliary Explanation [c]

As for an auxiliary explanation of the three situations involved in meditative stability, the source verses state:

> **Initially, with the meditative stability of an inexperienced practitioner,**
> **one experiences indications such as smoke. With the thorough analysis of what is ultimately meaningful,**
> **the phenomena of dualism merge as equal in taste, and the most sublime state of meditative stability is ensured.**
> **With focus on suchness itself, one realizes all phenomena to be emptiness, and that is further realized to be the state of peace by nature.**

If one summarizes the situations involved in the development of meditative stability, there are said to be three: [3.180a]

(1) Initially, with the meditative stability of an inexperienced practitioner, one experiences the onset of the "indications of empty form"—smoke and the like[749]—which are signs that the mind's attention has turned slightly inward, away from distraction by externals.

(2) Then, with the meditative stability that thoroughly analyzes what is ultimately meaningful, one sees the interdependent connection between illusion-like phenomena and one's ordinary conceptual elaborations subside, so that one realizes the identical "taste" of things.[750] One is able to rest with one's mind directed inwardly and authentically in experiencing the equal taste of all phenomena of the dualistic state of consciousness, thus ensuring an unmistaken state of mind that is the most sublime meditative stability.

(3) Finally, with the meditative stability that focuses on suchness itself, one understands all phenomena subsumed within dualistic consciousness to be emptiness, and on the strength of that understanding further realizes the state of peace, primordial by its very nature, so that the true nature of everything as effortless is ensured.

The foregoing constitutes the commentary on the first part,
concerning the stages for cultivating calm abiding and profound insight,
which are the foundation common to all states of meditative absorption.

Part 2. Meditation in the Cause-Based Dialectical Approach

I. Preliminaries to Meditation
II. Actual Process of Meditation
  A. Hīnayāna Approaches
    1. Śrāvaka Approach
      a. Brief Discussion
      b. Extensive Explanation
        i. Beginning Practitioners
        ii. Four Anticipatory Phases
        iii. Path of Seeing
        iv. Path of Meditation
    2. Pratyekabuddha Approach
  B. Mahāyāna Approach
    1. Individual Meditator
    2. Preliminaries to Meditation
      a. Four Immeasurable Attitudes
      b. Path of Accumulation
    3. Actual Stages of Meditation
      a. General Stages of Mental Training
      b. Formal Meditation Sessions and in Postmeditation
        i. Formal Meditation vis-à-vis Postmeditation
        ii. General Discussion of Postmeditation
      c. Summary

Part 2. Meditation in the Cause-Based Dialectical Approach

The second part, a presentation of the specific stages of meditation in the cause-based dialectical approach, is twofold: an explanation of the preliminaries to meditation and a presentation of the actual process of meditation.

Preliminaries to Meditation [I]

The source verses state:

> **As preliminaries to meditation, one observes discipline and develops sublime intelligence,**
> **is capable of both mental and physical isolation, rejects the eight concerns,**
> **maintains the twelve disciplines of spiritual training,**
> **and abandons the five kinds of wrong lifestyle. . . .**

In the context of meditation, there are five indispensable factors that are the preliminaries at the outset, serving as the foundation, or root, of all meditation. One engages in meditation through the following:

(1) the underlying basis, which is the observance of discipline and development of the three kinds of sublime intelligence;[751]

(2) the circumstance that promotes meditation, which is the fact that one is capable of both physical and mental isolation;[752]

(3) the eschewing of counterproductive circumstances, that is, the eight mundane concerns;[753]

(4) the supportive circumstances, that is, the twelve disciplines one maintains in one's spiritual training; and

(5) the circumstance of a pure lifestyle, that is, the complete abandonment of the five kinds of wrong lifestyle.

(1) As to the first of these preliminaries, one observes any of the seven kinds of ordination for individual liberation,[754] [3.180b] thus avoiding all manner of harmful actions of body, speech, and mind. Following that, one hears teachings by listening to scriptures that accord with the actual realization of what is true. One uses reasoning to thoroughly investigate the meaning of what one has heard, developing the sublime intelligence that derives from contemplation (which is to say, the correct functioning of the thinking process). In this way, one proceeds to apply oneself to meditation

by focusing one's attention one-pointedly on the meaning of what one has contemplated.

One might wonder, "What is sublime intelligence that derives from hearing teachings, contemplating, and meditating?" The Particularist school holds that the sublime intelligence that derives from hearing teachings has only the words as its objects; that which derives from contemplation has both the words and their meaning as its objects; and that which derives from meditation has only the meaning as its object. But Vasubandhu points out that a single state of sublime intelligence cannot focus on both the words and the meaning at once; thus, while that which derives from hearing teachings constitutes the aspect of sublime intelligence that focuses on the words and that which derives from meditation constitutes the aspect that focuses on the meaning, it is impossible for there to be sublime intelligence deriving from contemplation that focuses on both the words and the meaning at the same time.[755]

Therefore, it is logical that hearing teachings involves listening to authoritative and reliable scriptural sources; sublime intelligence that derives from contemplation constitutes that which comes from using reasoning to arrive at a definitive conclusion concerning the meaning of what one has heard; and sublime intelligence that derives from meditation constitutes that which comes from meditating one-pointedly on the meaning of what one has contemplated. Therefore, these are aspects of sublime intelligence that involve, respectively, gaining certainty concerning the meaning on the basis simply of the language employed; gaining this on the basis of lines of reasoning; and gaining this certainty concerning the meaning on the strength of meditation, without relying on language or concepts.

(2) One might wonder, "What is the working basis on which these aspects of sublime intelligence that derive from hearing teachings, contemplating, and meditating can be developed?" In order for these aspects of a deep immersion in spiritual practice to develop, people, whether they are lay or monastic practitioners, must physically distance themselves from the busyness of societal ties and mentally distance themselves from inappropriate trains of thought and other distractions. But for those who are not content with monastic robes and the simple fare obtained through begging, [3.181a] and who are very covetous, desiring fine things and many possessions, these aspects of deep immersion in the spiritual path—deriving from hearing teachings, contemplating, and meditating—will not develop.

(3) Given that the path of a spiritually advanced being will not develop

for someone who is caught up in the eight mundane concerns, one should eschew these concerns in order to promote access to that path. As one reads in *Letter to a Friend*:

> You who are wise in the ways of the world, the eight mundane concerns
> are those called gain and loss, pleasure and pain,
> fame and notoriety, and praise and blame.
> Please treat these as equally unworthy objects of your attention![756]

(4) Of these disciplines:

(a) Three are remedies to attachment to food:

(i) living on alms (that is, keeping only enough food for one day and not hoarding any extra);

(ii) eating at one sitting (that is, having sat down to eat, eating one's fill without eating anything further once having arisen from one's seat); and

(iii) not eating after midday (that is, having first eaten one's fill of what food has been given one, not eating later even if more should be given).

(b) Three are remedies to attachment to clothing:

(iv) wearing only the three monastic robes (that is, wearing only the three garments of vest, skirt, and shawl and not hoarding anything extra);

(v) wearing only coarse wool (that is, wearing only robes fashioned entirely from rough wool); and

(vi) wearing inferior clothing (that is, wearing older clothing, not newer clothing that is less than a year old, and wearing robes made from inferior cloth discarded by others).

(c) Four of these disciplines are remedies to an attachment to a dwelling place:

(vii) living in solitude (that is, building oneself a hut out of earshot from the nearest village and not staying in any other dwelling, whether in a community or a temple);

(viii) frequenting charnel grounds (that is, staying in charnel grounds and using shrouds for clothing and living solely off the food offered to the dead); [3.181b]

(ix) dwelling in the forest (that is, living at the foot of a tree in a solitary place); and

(x) living without a roof over one's head (that is, living in a simple hut without any more permanent structure protecting one).

(d) Two of these disciplines are remedies to an attachment to a comfortable bed:

(xi) making do with whatever bed is available (that is, refraining from fashioning one's sleeping quarters over and over); and

(xii) sleeping sitting up (that is, passing the night in an upright position).

(5) As is said in a sūtra:

> It is difficult for householders to train in the view
> when they always have so many opinions;
> it is difficult to maintain a spiritual practice
> when one is dependent on other lifestyles.[757]

This means that, for those who have taken monastic ordination, there is the danger of them adopting five kinds of wrong lifestyle, and so they should take care and avoid these. The five are lifestyles that involve the following:

(a) ingratiation (that is, speaking sweetly to others in order later to receive gain and honors);

(b) flattery (that is, praising something owned by another because one wishes to obtain it);

(c) self-promotion (that is, speaking of one's qualities in order to advance one's own interests);

(d) profiteering (that is, using one's gain to seek further gain by boasting about one's previous gains or giving a little to receive a lot in return); and

(e) hypocrisy (that is, pretending to control one's senses and be restrained in order to receive gain and honors).

In addition, engaging in agriculture, trading, or the selling of religious articles and texts are wrong kinds of lifestyle that incur a heavy burden.[758] Thus, if one pursues them, the manifest states of realization associated with the spiritual path that have not arisen in one will not arise, while those that may have arisen will swiftly fade. So avoid these lifestyles completely and adopt a lifestyle that is completely pure.

Actual Process of Meditation [II]

A discussion of the actual process of meditation is twofold: the stages of meditation in the Hīnayāna approaches of śrāvakas and pratyekabuddhas, and the stages of meditation in the Mahāyāna approach of the transcendent perfections.

Hīnayāna Approaches [A]

This discussion is also twofold: the stages of meditation in the śrāvaka approach and the stages of meditation in the pratyekabuddha approach.

Śrāvaka Approach [1]

This discussion involves two topics—a brief discussion continuing from the preceding remarks and an extensive explanation of the significance of these stages.

Brief Discussion [a]

The source verses state:

> **. . . then, the process of meditation**
> **consists of seven stages for those who follow the śrāvaka schools.**
> **These are subsumed within five points—focus, content, essence, result, and context.**

The first of the successive discussions of the process of meditation in the more common and extraordinary approaches [3.182a] concerns those who follow the śrāvaka schools. They meditate on the first four paths[759] in seven stages. According to the *Treasury of Abhidharma*:

> The seven stages, in order, are thoroughly analyzed as follows:
> those of beginning practitioners,
> those of the phases that anticipate the decisive breakthrough,
> that of meditation, and that of seeing.[760]

That is to say: on the path of accumulation, (1) in the initial phase, one cultivates the four applications of mindfulness; (2) in the intermediate phase, one cultivates the four aspects of authentic renunciation; (3) and in the final phase, one cultivates the four bases of supernormal powers. On the path of linkage, (4) during the anticipatory phases of meditative warmth and the peak experience, one cultivates the five governing powers; (5) during the phases of patient acceptance and the highest state of mundane experience, one cultivates the five strengths. (6) On the path of seeing, one cultivates the seven aids to enlightenment. (7) On the path of meditation, one cultivates the eightfold path of spiritually advanced beings.[761]

All of these stages should be understood to be subsumed within five points—(A) the scope of one's focus, (B) the content (or process of meditation involved), (C) the essence, (D) the result, and (E) the context that delineates when one engages in the respective meditations.[762]

Extensive Explanation [b]

This explanation is fourfold: the stages of meditation for beginning practitioners, in the four anticipatory phases, on the path of seeing, and on the path of meditation.

Beginning Practitioners [i]

The source verses state:

> **Those who are beginners meditate on the general and specific remedies to desire**
> **(that is, skeletons and the eight mental images); they examine their bodies;**
> **they see sensations to be productive of suffering and without any true substance, like hollow reeds;**
> **they focus their attention on the breath, and they meditate on the ultimate fact that no identity exists;**
> **and they see mental states and aspects of consciousness to be like illusions.**

For beginning practitioners in the śrāvaka approach:

(A) The *scope of their focus* is that of meditation that focuses on four topics: the body, sensations, mind, and phenomena. In this regard, as the general remedy for desire, they meditate on their own and others' bodies—and, in fact, all sensory appearances—as being skeletons, and thus neutralize their desire. As the *Treasury of Abhidharma* states:

> skeletons in all situations that involve attachment.[763]

As specific remedies, they meditate on eight mental images, such as a decomposing corpse, a swollen corpse, a maggot-ridden corpse, and so forth.[764] [3.182b] Once they are free of desire, from time to time they use the application of mindfulness that scrutinizes the body to meditate on their bodies as being, for example, like hollow reeds.

They next meditate on the idea that regards sensations—whether pleasurable, painful, or neutral—as being productive of suffering, and the idea that these are like hollow reeds, without any real substance.

Then these practitioners calm their thought processes by focusing their attention on the coming and going of the breath; and while the usual flow of thoughts in the mind constitutes the relative level of truth, when they examine this, the ultimate level of truth lies, for these śrāvaka practitioners, in indivisible moments of consciousness,[765] and so within that context they meditate on the fact that nothing has identity.

Next, they meditate on everything subsumed within the categories of mental states and aspects of consciousness—everything that seems to embody something either internally or externally—to determine that the nature of all of these is such that they have no true identity, are impermanent, are like illusions, and forth.

"Why," one might ask, "do they take these topics as their focus?" It is in order to undermine the following concepts in the minds of those whose thinking is erroneous: that the body is the actual abode of the personal self; that sensations are the basis for the self's experiences; that the mind is the actual self; and that phenomena are the basis for the self's experience of either deeply ingrained afflictive states of mind or the totally refined state of enlightenment.

In this regard, there are three aspects to what constitutes one's "body": the inner aspect, the outer aspect, and the aspect that partakes of both. The first aspect consists of the eyes and other corporeal sense organs that are the internal components of one's perceptual field. The second aspect consists of visual forms and other tangible sense objects that are the external components of one's perceptual field. The third aspect consists of the bases for one's own sense organs and the corporeal sense organs of others, for causes and perceptual fields interact in a way that effects change in both.

Each of the remaining three topics[766] also has three aspects; one can understand these through consideration of the bases and the scopes of focus that apply in their respective cases.

The term "phenomena" here includes all mental events other than sensations, as well as distinct formative factors[767] and forms that fall within the sense field of one's subjective consciousness,[768] as well as unconditioned phenomena.[769] [3.183a]

The source verses state:

> **They employ the applications of mindfulness, using sublime intelligence to examine**
> **the fourfold characteristics that are specific and general.**
> **They engage the Four Truths, cultivating the initial phase of the path of accumulation.**
> **This model serves for the remaining stages.**

(B) As to the *content* of their meditation, they focus on the specific characteristics of the body and the other topics (what any given thing essentially is, of what elements it is composed, what derives from these elements, and so forth) and the general characteristics of things (that they are impermanent, productive of suffering, empty, without true identity, and so forth). Alternatively, they focus on four topics: that the body is unclean, that sensations produce suffering, that the mind is impermanent, and that phenomena have no true identity.

(C) In its *essence* this meditation brings an understanding due to one's sublime intelligence (which discerns both the general and specific characteristics of the body and the other topics) and one's mindfulness (which ensures one does not forget the scope on which one is focusing or the content). The term "application of mindfulness" is used because one thus considers the general and specific characteristics with sublime intelligence, while mindfulness keeps one's mind directed again and again toward its focus.

(D) The *result* (or alternatively, the purpose) of this meditation is that of causing one to come to terms with the Four Truths. The first topic[770] causes one to come to terms with the truth of suffering because through precise analysis one gains a thorough appreciation of the body as a subliminal state of suffering that perpetuates ignoble states of existence. The second topic[771] causes one to come to terms with the truth of the all-pervasive origin of suffering because one realizes that the primary factor in this all-pervasive origin—compulsion[772]—is the cause and condition for the three kinds of sensations (pleasurable and so forth), and so one wishes to eliminate that factor. The third topic[773] causes one to come to terms with the truth of the cessation of suffering because one determines that consciousness (which is devoid of personal identity) disintegrates moment by moment, and so one wishes to make that cessation fully evident, for there is no fear of any "self" being annihilated with the attainment of nirvāṇa. The fourth topic[774] causes one to come to terms with the truth of the spiritual path [3.183b] because one determines that afflictive states (such as attachment) are factors to be eliminated, while aspects of the totally refined state of enlightenment (such as faith) are factors to be relied upon, and so one wishes to follow the path. This is what is meant in *Distinguishing Center and Limit*:

> Because of the perpetuation of ignoble states, because of the causes of craving,
> because of the ground of being, and because of the absence of delusion,
> one come to terms with the Four Truths, and so . . .[775]

(E) As to the *context* in which one engages in these meditations, it is during the initial phase of the path of accumulation when—having completed the process of hearing teachings and contemplating—one meditates on what is unattractive and follows the coming and going of the breath with mindfulness, thus rendering one's mind flexible through the process of calm abiding and meditating in order to initiate the process of developing profound insight.

These five points just discussed serve as the model for the remaining sections in the explanation that follows.[776]

The source verses state:

> **Nonvirtue is prevented from arising or guarded against, while the opposite applies to virtue.**
> **One employs meditative absorption that involves intention, exertion, attention, and investigation.**

Once a state of meditative absorption has been achieved, one cultivates the four aspects of authentic renunciation.

(A) The *scope of one's focus* includes those factors that are to be eliminated (that is, deeply ingrained afflictive states of mind), those factors to be encouraged (that is, aspects of the totally refined state of enlightenment) that have already developed, and the development of those positive factors that have not yet developed.

(B) The *content* is that of ensuring that harmful, nonvirtuous factors that have not yet developed do not develop, while those that have developed are eliminated and their recurrence guarded against; and, in opposite fashion, of ensuring that virtuous factors that have not yet developed do develop, while those that have developed flourish. To these ends, one arouses one's intention, brings exertion to bear, focuses one's attention intently, and immerses oneself thoroughly in the process.

(C) These aspects, in their *essence*, constitute the diligence that ensures that factors to be eliminated decline, while the remedies to these factors gain in strength.

(D) The purpose, or *result*, of these aspects is that all factors to be eliminated decline without exception, and one avails oneself of all the remedies without exception.

(E) As for the *context* demarcating this process, one cultivates these aspects of authentic renunciation during the intermediate phase of the path of accumulation. This is due to the fact that, having meditated by relying in the appropriate manner on the topics for the application of mindfulness, [3.184a] one sees the flaw of those factors that are to be eliminated and the advantages of their remedies, and so arouses the diligence to begin making choices, rejecting the former and embracing the latter.

One might wonder why the term "aspect of authentic renunciation" is employed. It is because it signifies that these aspects eliminate all that is spiritually counterproductive.

Once these aspects are in place:

(A) The *scope of one's focus* in cultivating the four bases of supernormal powers includes creating emanations and other powers of transformation that are achieved through meditative absorption. The process of meditation is described in *Distinguishing Center and Limit*:

> This comes about due to the causes on which it depends—
> eliminating five flaws and using eight remedial techniques.[777]

That is to say, one meditates as discussed earlier, employing the eight remedial techniques.[778]

(C) As for what these constitute in their *essence*, they are in general states of meditative absorption that are fourfold from the point of view of being supportive factors. Meditative absorption that involves *intention* is carried out on the basis of *exertion* as a dedicated application, due to which one reaches a state of one-pointed *attention*; while due to another aspect of meditative absorption that involves *investigation*, thoroughly analyzing in detail the spiritual teachings given by others, one reaches that same state of one-pointed mind.

(D) The purpose, or *result*, of these bases is that one wishes to make any given supernormal power fully evident, and brings it into full evidence by directing one's mind accordingly.

(E) As for the *context*, one cultivates these bases during the final phase of the path of accumulation.

One might ask why meditative absorption is referred to here as a "basis of supernormal powers." The term signifies that this absorption serves as a support for one to acquire all spiritual qualities.

Four Anticipatory Phases [ii]

As for the stages of meditation in the four anticipatory phases, the source verses state:

> **During the four phases that anticipate the decisive breakthrough,**
> **one applies two groups of five factors—confidence, diligence,**
> **mindfulness, meditative absorption, and sublime intelligence—**
> **to the sixteen topics pertaining to the Four Truths.**

The foregoing meditative absorption brings one to the path of linkage, which anticipates the decisive breakthrough[779] and has four phases: warmth, the peak experience, patient acceptance, and the highest state of mundane experience. During these four phases, one focuses on the sixteen topics that pertain to the Four Truths (those of impermanence and so forth),[780] applying two groups of five factors: the five governing powers—confidence, diligence, mindfulness, meditative absorption, and sublime intelligence—and the five strengths that are the transmutation of these.[781] [3.184b]

In this regard:

(A) The *scope of one's focus* in cultivating the five governing powers is that of the Four Truths, because these topics constitute aspects of those truths insofar as they link one to the path of spiritually advanced beings.[782]

(B) As for the *process of meditation*,[783] one meditates with *confidence*, such that this gives one the conviction that these truths address what is to be understood and what is to be eliminated; with *diligence*, such that one's enthusiasm is aroused in order for one to come to a realization of what these truths actually entail; with *mindfulness*, such that one does not forget the topics on which to focus (that is, what these truths actually entail); with *meditative absorption*, such that one's attention is focused in a one-pointed manner; and with *sublime intelligence*, such that the topics of these truths are individually and precisely analyzed.

(C) This process, in its *essence*, consists of the five governing powers of confidence, diligence, mindfulness, meditative absorption, and sublime intelligence.

(D) The *result* is the swift attainment of the path of seeing and the accomplishment of the four steps in the path of meditation.

(E) As for the *context*, one cultivates these powers during the two phases of warmth and the peak experience.

If one wonders why the term "governing power" is used, it is because these factors give one governance over that which supports the state of definitive excellence—that is, over the mundane factors associated with the completely refined state of enlightenment.

Next, in the cultivation of the five strengths:

(A) The *scope for one's focus* and (B) the *content* employed are similar to the foregoing case.

(C) In their *essence*, these strengths constitute an increase in the force of confidence and the rest of the five powers, such that they become solely remedial, without any admixture of a lack of confidence of any of the counterproductive factors; this is what the term "strength" signifies.

(D) Their *result* is the onset of the phases of patient acceptance and the highest state of mundane experience, and the accomplishment of the path of seeing.

(E) As to the *context*, one cultivates these strengths during the phases of patient acceptance and the highest mundane state. As *Distinguishing Center and Limit* states:

> For the governing powers and the five strengths
> there are two pairs of anticipatory phases.[784]

The meaning of the term has just been discussed in the discussion of their essence.

Path of Seeing [iii]

As to the stages of meditation on the path of seeing, the source verses state:

> **On the path of seeing, there are seven aids to enlightenment:**
> **mindfulness, thorough analysis of phenomena,**
> **diligence, joy, thorough pliancy, meditative absorption, and**
> **impartiality.**

(A) The *scope of one's focus* in cultivating the seven aids to enlightenment (which are the factors to be cultivated on the path of seeing) is that of what the Four Truths of spiritually advanced beings actually entail. [3.185a]

(B) As for the *process of meditation*,[785] authentic *mindfulness* as an aid to enlightenment ensures that, when one focuses on suffering, one seeks to remove it; when one focuses on the all-pervasive origin of suffering, one seeks to be free of desire and attachment for it; when one focuses on the cessation of suffering, one seeks to experience that fully; and when one focuses on the path that leads to the cessation of suffering, one seeks to cultivate it. The process for the remaining six aids is similar.

(B) In their *essence*, these aids are as follows: (1) *mindfulness* is not forgetting the scope of the path of seeing; sublime intelligence is (2) a *thorough analysis* of the suchness of phenomena; (3) *diligence* is enthusiasm for what is virtuous; (4) incorruptible *joy* is a beneficial influence on the mind and body; (5) *thorough pliancy* is flexibility of mind and body; (6) *meditative absorption* is a one-pointed state of attention; and (7) *impartiality* is the mind's engagement without the fluctuation due to mental lethargy or agitation.

(C) As to the way in which these function as aids,[786] mindfulness is an aid that provides a sense of abiding because its influence is one of ensuring that the other aids do not stray from their focus. A thorough analysis of phenomena is an aid by its very nature because it is, in essence, the nonconceptual state that constitutes the nature of the path of seeing. Diligence is an aid to one's will to be free of saṃsāra, for through relying on it, one feels a certainty about one's release from suffering. Joy is an aid that constitutes a benefit and advantage, for it comes about as the result of the other aids. The remaining three aids (thorough pliancy and the rest) are aids in negating afflictive states because it is thorough pliancy that brings about the absence those states, meditative absorption that constitutes the absence of those states, and impartiality that is, in its essence, the absence of those states. The foregoing is referred to in the following lines from *Distinguishing Center and Limit*:

> An aid by nature, an aid providing a sense of abiding,
> the third an aid to the will to be free,
> the fourth an aid that is a benefit and advantage,
> and three that are aids in negating afflictive states.[787] [3.185b]

(D) The purpose and *result* of these aids is one of bringing about the removal of all factors without exception that are to be eliminated on the path of seeing.

(E) As for the *context*, once one attains the path of seeing, the nature of that state itself is that of these seven aids to enlightenment.

Path of Meditation [iv]

As to the stages of meditation on the path of meditation, the source verses state:

> **The path of meditation is explained as eightfold: authentic view, thought, speech,**
> **action, livelihood, effort, mindfulness, and meditative absorption.**

(A) The *scope of one's focus* and (B) the *content* involved in cultivation of the eightfold path of spiritually advanced beings (which is the factor that is to be cultivated on the path of meditation) are as described previously.

(C) The branches of this path are, in their *essence*, as follows:

(1) *authentic view* is the thorough determination, in postmeditation, of what characterizes the realization one gains during formal meditative equipoise;

(2) *authentic thought* is the motivation to speak so as to convey to others what one has oneself realized;

(3) *authentic speech* is the verbal ability, on the basis of that motivation, to actually convey to others what one has realized;

(4) *authentic action* is action that is totally purified of such acts as the taking of life;

(5) *authentic livelihood* is mental and verbal activity that is totally pure of such activities as ingratiation or hypocrisy;

(6) *authentic effort* is diligence in applying remedies in order to remove all the factors without exception that are to be eliminated on the path of meditation;

(7) *authentic mindfulness* consists of not forgetting the purpose of calm abiding, of holding one's attention intently, and of impartiality;

(8) *authentic meditative absorption* is meditation for the purpose of dispelling obscurations that impede one's experience of supernormal states of perception and other special spiritual qualities.

These branches are considered to be present on the path of seeing insofar as they are attained on the basis of the potential of formal meditative equipoise of that path; they are considered in their essence to constitute the path of seeing in that they become fully evident on that path.

These eight branches function as four kinds of aids. That is to say, *authentic view* is the aid that involves thorough determination; [3.186a] it constitutes the investigation "This is what has been realized during formal meditative equipoise." *Thought* is the aid that promotes understanding because it constitutes the motivation to speak in ways that completely define what one has realized. *Speech*, *action*, and *livelihood* are aids that inspire conviction, for they inspire confidence concerning view, discipline, and a completely pure livelihood, respectively. The three branches of *effort*, *mindfulness*, and *meditative absorption* are aids that are remedies to counterproductive influences because they function as remedies to the afflictive states that are to be eliminated on the path of seeing, to the afflictive states that contribute to mental laxity and agitation, and to influences that are counterproductive to the attainment of such special spiritual qualities as supernormal states of perception, respectively. As is said:

> Involving thorough determination, promoting understanding,
> bringing conviction (in the case of three branches) in the minds
> of others,
>
> and serving as remedies to counterproductive influences—
> these are the eight branches of the path.
> It is held that others are made aware
> of view, discipline, and few material needs.[788]

> There are remedies to counterproductive influences
> that involve afflictive states, secondary afflictive states, and mastery.[789]

(D) The *result* of these branches is that, due to one's cultivating them, all possible factors to be eliminated are removed.

(E) As to the *context*, they are cultivated at the point that one has attained the path of meditation.

In this regard, proponents of the Particularist school explain that the seven aids to enlightenment constitute the path of meditation since they are associated with what derives from meditation. For this school, the eightfold path of spiritually advanced beings constitutes the path of seeing because the path of seeing is the "wheel of dharma," and the eightfold path (due to its facilitating swift progress and so forth) can be likened to a precious wheel.[790]

On the path of no more training,[791] one has the incorruptible knowledge that suffering has been understood, its all-pervasive origin eliminated, its cessation made fully evident, and the path cultivated. As well, one has the incorruptible knowledge: "Suffering has been understood; now there is nothing more to understand" and so forth, [3.186b] up to "The path has been cultivated; now there is nothing more to cultivate." But other than these successive states of knowledge, that negative factors have been exhausted, and that suffering will not occur again, there is nothing upon which to meditate as some additional focus with a specific object or structure.[792]

Pratyekabuddha Approach [2]

As for the stages of meditation in the pratyekabuddha approach, the source verses state:

> **Pratyekabuddhas employ the foregoing and, in addition,**
> **the process of interdependent connection,**
> **and focus their attention on the three avenues to complete**
> **liberation.**

Pratyekabuddhas, having traversed their path by relying on the aspects of the totally refined state of enlightenment that were just discussed and on the process by which things occur through interdependent connection, maintain the focus of their attention on the three avenues to complete liberation.

In this regard, speaking generally, there are three ways in which pratyekabuddhas train in their path:

(1) Some of those who belong to the pratyekabuddha type serve the buddhas who appear during one hundred eons. Having thus matured themselves for the state of a pratyekabuddha's enlightenment, they then become learned in six topics[793] in order to attain that state.

(2) Some serve the buddhas that appear over an indeterminate period of time and listen to spiritual teachings by relying on holy masters. Having reflected on these teachings accurately, in the presence of spiritual masters, they undergo the experiences of the anticipatory phases of the path of linkage. However, unable in that lifetime to gain full realization of these teachings or the fruition of their spiritual practice, they become learned in the six topics in order to attain that state in a future lifetime.

(3) While similar to the foregoing on other points, some gain full realization of these teachings in the presence of spiritual masters and fully experience one or the other of the first two stages of fruition. However, unable to fully experience the latter two stages of fruition, they become learned in the six topics in order to experience these stages fully in a future lifetime.

Of these three models, the first are those who are solitary like a rhinoceros,[794] while the latter two are those who participate in groups.[795] [3.187a]

In any of these cases, in the lifetime following that one, they are reborn in worlds in which there are no buddhas or śrāvakas. Upon going to cemeteries and seeing the bones there, they immediately feel disenchanted with saṃsāra. They think "Alas! Where did these bones come from? They came from aging and death. Where did aging and death come from? They came from birth . . . " and so forth, examining in succession the twelve links in the process of interdependent connection. Wondering "How can I become liberated from this?" they then cut through the root of those twelve links, undermining the process of interdependent connection by arresting ignorance, karmic patterning, and so on, through the arresting of aging and death. Once they understand that all phenomena occur merely through a process of interdependent connection, they meditate on the twelve links of interdependence and the sixteen topics pertaining to the Four Truths. They thus fully experience the five paths in a single session, and so maintain an ongoing focus on the process of interdependence and complete liberation.

In this regard, the following explanation is given:

(1) Of the three avenues to complete liberation that concern the knowable, emptiness is the lack of identity; the absence of subtle traits is the nonexistence of anything the self takes to be its own; and the absence of naïve

speculation is the lack of any fixed frame of reference.

(2) In terms of the path, of the three avenues to complete liberation, emptiness is the cessation of suffering; the absence of subtle traits is the path; and the absence of naïve speculation constitutes suffering and its all-pervasive origin.

(3) In terms of the fruition, of the three avenues to complete liberation, emptiness and the absence of subtle traits pertain to the state in which there are no residual traces, whereas the absence of naïve speculation pertains to the state that still involves residual traces.[796]

Mahāyāna Approach [B]

An explanation of the stages of meditation in the Mahāyāna approach of the transcendent perfections is threefold: the individual who engages in such meditation, the preliminaries to such meditation, and the actual stages to be carried out in meditation.

Individual Meditator [1]

The source verses state:

> **Those who have awakened their affinity for the Mahāyāna**
> **uphold the two aspects of bodhicitta.**

An individual who is an aspirant for following the Mahāyāna path of the transcendent perfections is someone in whom the affinity for the Mahāyāna approach has awakened and who upholds the training involved in the two aspects of bodhicitta—relative and ultimate. [3.187b]

As for the nature of that spiritual affinity, the sūtra *Discourse of Queen Śrīmālā* states:

> The potential for attaining the state of suchness permeates all beings.[797]

And the *Highest Continuum* says:

> Because the kāya of perfect buddhahood is pervasive,
> because the state of suchness is indivisible,

> and because all beings possess spiritual affinity,
> beings are forever endowed with buddha nature.[798]

As these passages demonstrate, this affinity abides innately and pervasively in all beings.

If one analyzes this spiritual affinity, it is twofold: that which is naturally abiding and that which is perfectly developed. As to what these constitute in essence, the incomparable Dakpo has the following to say:

> First, as to the naturally abiding aspect of spiritual affinity, it is the capacity to develop the qualities of buddhahood, partakes of a timeless quality, and is obtained by the true nature of reality.
>
> As to the perfectly developed aspect of that affinity, it is that capacity to develop the qualities of buddhahood that is attained by one's having become familiar with fundamentally positive qualities.
>
> Thus, these two aspects provide the good fortune for one to awaken to buddhahood.[799]

Synonymous terms are "spiritual affinity," "potential," "natural state," and "fundamental being."[800]

In considering specific situations, the *Ornament of the Mahāyāna Sūtras* discusses five alternatives,[801] which is to say:

(1) the fact that someone has the spiritual affinity for the Mahāyāna approach is the proximate cause of buddhahood;

(2) given that the spiritual affinities of śrāvakas and pratyekabuddhas eventually lead to the attainment of buddhahood, they are the more long-term causes;

(3) of those whose affinity is uncertain, for some it is the more direct cause, (4) for others the more long-term cause;[802] and

(5) even in the case of those whose spiritual affinity is said to be "cut off," this is only in consideration of the length of time required, not that they will somehow never attain enlightenment; for them, then, it is the extremely long-term cause.[803]

Therefore, because beings have these kinds of spiritual affinity, this scripture states that ordinary beings are endowed with the quintessential potential for buddhahood.

Nevertheless, the affinities for both the śrāvaka and pratyekabuddha approaches are more rudimentary, whereas that for the Mahāyāna is far more sublime than all the others; in the former cases, the affinity is fully expressed by the refining away of the afflictive obscurations alone, while the latter is only fully expressed with the refining away of both levels of obscuration.[804] [3.188a]

The Mahāyāna affinity can be either awakened or remain unawakened; how these situations are to be understood is discussed in the sūtra *Discourse on the Ten Attributes*:

> The affinity of intelligent bodhisattvas
> can be known from indications,
> just as fire can be known from the presence of smoke,
> or water from that of water fowl.[805]

As this source states, one can know these situations from the signs or indications. The signs that this affinity has been awakened are that one's actions and speech are naturally gentle, without one's having had to rely on remedies; that one's mind holds little hypocrisy or deceit; and that one is loving and sincere toward beings. Again, from the sūtra *Discourse on the Ten Attributes*:

> Not being a rough or crude person,
> completely rejecting hypocrisy and deceit,
> and being utterly sincere toward all beings—
> such is a bodhisattva.[806]

In addition, one feels compassion for beings before undertaking any activity; is inspired by the Mahāyāna teachings; has forbearance, not being daunted by undertaking difficult challenges; and engages wholeheartedly in the fundamentally positive attributes entailed in the transcendent perfections. This is stated in the *Ornament of the Mahāyāna Sūtras*:

> Even before one undertakes training,
> to have compassion, inspiration, and forbearance,
> and to pursue what is positive wholeheartedly,
> are to be known as the indications of spiritual affinity.[807]

The signs that one's spiritual affinity, although latently present, has not yet been awakened are described in the *Highest Continuum*:

> If one lacks sensitivity to one's fundamental being, one's buddha nature,
> one will never be sufficiently dissatisfied with suffering,
> or desire nirvāṇa,
> or strive for it, or even aspire to it.[808]

That is to say, this is like the situation of the vast majority of ordinary people.

As to the circumstances under which one's spiritual affinity is awakened, it is awakened when one is free of counterproductive conditions and influenced by conducive ones; as long as the opposite is the case, one's affinity will remain unawakened. [3.188b] There are four conditions that are counterproductive: to be reborn in a state devoid of spiritual freedom;[809] to be heedless;[810] to engage in morally wrong actions; and to be subject to the harm caused by obscurations. There are two conditions that are conducive: the external condition of others teaching one the sacred dharma; and the internal condition of one's reflecting on these teachings correctly and being inspired by what is spiritually positive.

Hence, this affinity is crucial since individuals in whom it has awakened are capable of following the Mahāyāna path and applying it in their ongoing experience.

Preliminaries to Meditation [2]

The explanation of the preliminaries to meditation is twofold: the training of one's mind in the four immeasurable attitudes and the process of gaining ongoing experience through the ordinary path of accumulation.

Four Immeasurable Attitudes [a]

The source verses state:

> **The initial step is that of the four immeasurable attitudes (loving-kindness and so forth).**
> **Beginning practitioners focus on beings; those who are advanced in practice**

focus on phenomena; those who have gained patient acceptance have no fixed frame of reference.

For those who wish to train on the path of the transcendent perfections, the initial step is to train in the four immeasurable attitudes (loving-kindness and so forth), which constitute the training for bodhicitta as aspiration. According to the *Intermediate Length "Mother"*:

> O Subhūti, thus a great and heroic bodhisattva should cultivate supreme loving-kindness, supreme compassion, supreme joy, and supreme impartiality.[811]

And from the *Sublime Heart Essence*:

> O Śāriputra, thus there are four pure states—those of loving-kindness, compassion, joy, and impartiality that are not preceded by the authentic arousal of bodhicitta and that do not entail such arousal. These states entail the overt formative patterns that contribute to conditioned existence.
>
> There are four immeasurable attitudes—those of loving-kindness, compassion, joy, and impartiality that are preceded by the authentic arousal of bodhicitta and that do entail such arousal. These states entail the formative patterns that contribute to the path to nirvāṇa.[812]

In this tradition, the distinction is simply one of the immeasurability entailed.[813] And as the *Categories of the Levels* states: [3.189a]

> The four immeasurable attitudes develop both with a conceptual frame of reference (whether that of beings or the true nature of reality) or without a frame of reference.[814]

That is to say, having understood the distinction between there being a conceptual frame of reference or not, one trains either within the scope of such a framework or within the scope of the immeasurable attitude in itself.[815]

These attitudes are developed through four conditions:

(1) the causal condition is that of one's naturally abiding spiritual affinity—that is, one's fundamental being;

(2) the governing condition is a spiritual mentor who instructs one in the teachings concerning the four immeasurable attitudes;

(3) the referential condition is the scope of the respective attitude that has become fully evident;[816] and

(4) the immediate condition is one's prior familiarity with the benefits and advantages of cultivating these four immeasurable attitudes and the shortcomings of not doing so.

The processes by which these attitudes develop are explained as being threefold, depending on the specific scope of the focus:

(1) those who are beginning practitioners, who have not realized the absence of identity in things, develop the four immeasurable attitudes by focusing on beings;

(2) those who are advanced in practice—who have realized 75 per cent of that absence[817]—develop these attitudes by focusing on phenomena; and

(3) those who have gained patient acceptance, who have realized both aspects of that absence, develop these attitudes through a process that involves no frame of reference.

With respect to the foregoing processes, the *Levels of the Bodhisattva* says:

> To have beings as the frame of reference is a process held in common with non-Buddhist holders of extreme views. To have phenomena as the frame of reference is a process held in common with all śrāvakas and pratyekabuddhas. To have no fixed frame of reference is a process that has nothing in common with any of the foregoing.[818]

Path of Accumulation [b]

The source verses state:

> **As preliminaries, one maintains discipline, controls the senses,**
> **exercises moderation in eating, exerts oneself in spiritual practice**
> **in the late evening and early morning,**
> **takes joy in maintaining alertness, is enthusiastic without regret,**
> **enjoys the seven riches of spiritually advanced beings, engages in**
> **the ten kinds of spiritual activity,**
> **and relies on inspiration and other positive causes of**
> **liberation; . . .**

From the point that they first embark on the Mahāyāna path of accumulation [3.189b] until they reach the path of linkage, beginning practitioners—completely motivated by the wish to attain enlightenment—maintain completely pure discipline; control their senses; exercise moderation in eating; exert themselves in spiritual practice, foregoing sleep in the late evening and early morning; take joy in maintaining alertness in issues requiring moral choices; and are extremely enthusiastic and have no regret at their positive actions.[819]

The seven riches are as stated:

> *Faith* in the basis of truth, pure *ethical discipline*,
> *hearing* of many teachings, familiarity with *giving*,
> knowing *modesty* concerning others, having great *self-respect* concerning oneself,
> and having *sublime intelligence* in abundance; these are the seven riches of spiritually advanced beings.[820]

The ten kinds of spiritual activity are spoken of in *Distinguishing Center and Limit*:

> Copying texts, making offerings, giving generously,
> listening to teachings, reading them, memorizing them,
> explaining them, reciting texts aloud,
> contemplating and meditating—
> these embody the ten kinds of activity,
> the qualities of which are incalculable.[821]

The practical application of these is discussed, for example, in the excellent writings of Situ Rinpoché Chökyi Gyaltsen.[822]

In addition, the preliminaries involve one's efforts to increase one's spiritual progress through any and all positive acts—such as arousing one's inspiration and other positive factors that serve as causes of one's liberation—without any bias or prejudice. One then can embark on the stages of the path in the actual practice of meditation.

Actual Stages of Meditation [3]

The actual stages to be cultivated in meditation are threefold: the stages for training one's mind in general, the specific processes of meditation in formal practice and postmeditation, and a summary that simply mentions four applications.

General Stages of Mental Training [a]

The source verses state:

> **One trains one's mind with the four axioms, the five factors conducive to liberation,**
> **recollection of the Victorious One and so forth, the nine perceptions of impurity,**
> **the eight thoughts of a superior spiritual practitioner,**
> **and the thorough purification of one's sphere of activity.**

For those on the path of accumulation, in general it is the four axioms that denote the Buddha's words and other similar topics that are to be cultivated in meditation. [3.190a] Of these, the way in which one meditates on the four axioms is to arouse bodhicitta; to then meditate (1) on all that is conditioned being impermanent, (2) on the nature of what entails corruptibility being that of saṃsāra and suffering, (3) on all phenomena as lacking identity, and (4) on nirvāṇa as a state of peace; one then concludes with dedication.[823]

As for "recollection of the Victorious One and so forth," this refers to one's recollection of the Buddha, dharma, saṅgha, one's ethical discipline, giving, one's body, death, birth, and the inhalation and exhalation of ones' breath.

The nine perceptions of impurity are of a corpse decomposing, ridden with maggots, mottled with dark blotches, rotting, putrefying, being devoured by wild animals, scattered in pieces, being cremated, and disintegrating.[824]

The eight thoughts of a superior spiritual practitioner are to think as follows:

(1) "At some point, may I be capable of removing the suffering of beings!"

(2) "At some point, may I be capable of bringing great wealth to beings who are afflicted by poverty!"

(3) "At some point, may I be capable of ensuring benefit for beings with this flesh-and-blood body!"

(4) "At some point, may I be capable of ensuring benefit for beings, even if it means my remaining in a hell realm for a long time!"

(5) "At some point, may I be capable of fulfilling the hopes of beings with great wealth, both mundane and transcendent!"

(6) "At some point, having awakened to buddhahood, may I truly be capable of bringing beings out of their suffering!"

(7) "In all my lifetimes, may I never take a rebirth that does not benefit beings, or engage solely in experiencing the ultimate,[825] or speak words that do not satisfy all beings, or adopt a livelihood (or a body or intelligence or wealth or power) that does not benefit others, or take any joy in what harms others!" [3.190b]

(8) "May the fruits of beings' harmful actions ripen for me, while the fruits of my positive actions ripen for them!"

As for the thorough purification of one's sphere of activity, the *Ornament of the Mahāyāna Sūtras* states:

> When heirs of the victorious ones act in any way whatsoever,
> their perceptions[826] functioning in a variety of ways,
> they are aware of things as they are and, with appropriate words,
> make this evident in their ideas in order to benefit beings.[827]

This passage should be understood to mean that which accords with a thorough purification of the sphere of one's ordinary activity. When bodhisattvas enter a building, they arouse bodhicitta and think, "May all beings gain the citadel of liberation!" Using this as a model, when they lie down to sleep, they think, "May beings attain the kāyas of buddhahood!" If they dream, they think, "May beings realize all phenomena to be like dream images!" Once they awaken, they think, "May beings awaken from their ignorance!" As they arise, they think, "May beings gain the enlightened forms of buddhas!" When they don clothing, they think, "May beings don the raiment of modesty and self-respect!" As they tie their sashes,[828] they think, "May beings unite themselves with fundamentally positive qualities!" If they sit on seats, they think, "May beings attain the vajra seat!"[829] Thinking in such ways, they feel, "I arouse bodhicitta!" Practicing in such ways, one trains one's mind.[830]

Formal Meditation Sessions and in Postmeditation [b]

As for the specific processes of meditation in formal practice and postmeditation, there are two considerations: the specific phases of formal practice vis-à-vis postmeditation and a general discussion of the postmeditation phase.

Formal Meditation vis-à-vis Postmeditation [i]

The source verses state:

> **In the specific phase of formal practice, the significance of the Middle Way is paramount,**
> **and that involves investigation as a preliminary.**
> **Autonomists rest in the significance of an unqualified negation, comparable to space.**
> **For Consequentialists, the basic space of phenomena (as what to become familiar with) and the mind that becomes familiar**
> **are inseparable, like water poured into water.**
> **For those who profess qualified emptiness, the state is nonconceptual and utterly lucid.**
> **They all agree on the key point of there simply being a freedom from elaboration.**

In the specific case of the meditation that is unique to those who follow the Mahāyāna approach, during the phase of formal practice, it is the significance itself of the profound Middle Way (concerning which they have come to a definitive conclusion through hearing and contemplating teachings) that is their paramount concern in meditation. [3.191a]

In this regard, those who profess the Autonomist interpretation begin by arousing bodhicitta and pursuing an investigation with the discerning function of their sublime intelligence. They then rest in equipoise, in a mode of "one taste" within the essence of emptiness comparable to space, an unqualified negation in which all extremes due to conceptual elaboration have been removed, so that there is no concept even of whether or not the very mind that is becoming familiar with the practice has anything with which to become familiar. Given that the conventional designation of "primordial union"[831] is not used in this interpretation, the postmeditation phase in this context is one of not blocking what manifests in light of ordinary awareness, while overtly conceiving of developing one's merit within a state in which, in light of timeless awareness, there is no fixed frame of reference whatsoever. It is this that they term the "primordial union of the two levels of truth"; they also term it the "development of merit that is imbued with sublime intelligence that does not conceive of the three focal points."[832]

Those who profess the Consequentialist interpretation begin with the arousal of bodhicitta and an investigation with sublime intelligence. They then arrive at a nondual state, like that of water poured into water, without the mind that becomes familiar and the basic space of phenomena with which it becomes familiar being separate and distinct. Although they use the conventional designation of "sublime intelligence that realizes the basic space of phenomena," in actuality they have no classification of something to be known versus that which knows it, and so they do not employ even the conventional designation of "primordial union." As for the postmeditation phase, their way of thinking about it is like that in the context of the Autonomists.

As for those who profess qualified emptiness [*gzhan stong*], they begin with the arousal of bodhicitta and a brief investigation in which there is no frame of reference of things having any inherent nature. They then abide in the state of supreme utter lucidity, spontaneously present without involving any conceptual thinking. They rest in equipoise of that naturally lucid self-knowing awareness—timeless awareness that is devoid of the duality of perceived object and perceiving subject—and this by way of not thinking in terms of, or fixating in any way whatsoever on, ordinary distinctions of such elaborations as "exists," "does not exist," "is," or "is not." As for the postmeditation phase, they take as many tangible phenomena as there are as objects but do not fixate on any of the ordinary distinctions of conceptual elaboration whatsoever. This they term the "primordial union of the manifest and emptiness," [3.191b] and it is within this context that they engage in the development of merit on a vast scale. The phase of formal practice they refer to as the "primordial union of lucidity and emptiness" because it is empty of any conceptual thinking, while not straying from what is, in its essence, lucid pure awareness.

The foregoing three interpretations agree on the key point of simply resting in equipoise within basic space, which is a freedom from conceptual elaboration.

General Discussion of Postmeditation [ii]

The source verses state:

> **In the postmeditation phase one meditates successively on the thirty-seven factors that contribute to enlightenment;**
> **their significance has extraordinary dimensions of vastness and profundity.**

In the phase of postmeditation, once one has arisen from that of formal practice, on the lesser degree of the path of accumulation, one practices the applications of mindfulness by regarding the body, sensations, mind, and phenomena as having no inherent nature in any authentic sense, meditating on their very essence without conceiving of them individually: this is the aspect of *profundity*. And one meditates on the body as being like an illusion, sensations as being like dream images, the mind as being like utterly lucid space, and phenomena as being adventitious like clouds: this is the aspect of *vastness*.[833] Likewise, one meditates successively on the thirty-seven factors that contribute to enlightenment.[834] These are enumerated here just as they are in the context of the śrāvaka approach; however, their significance as factors that contribute to enlightenment in the Mahāyāna approach is such that, as the immediately preceding discussion illustrates, there are extraordinary dimensions with respect to the profundity of their scope and the vastness with which that scope is applied.

Summary [c]

As for a summary that simply mentions the four applications,[835] the source verses state:

> **In summary, through four applications—perfecting all aspects,**
> **culminating, sequential, and instantaneous—**
> **one gains accomplishment of the "mother," the unsurpassable and transcendent perfection.**

If we condense all the limitless stages of the paths of the Mahāyāna approach into a summary, the consummate fruition to be attained is that of omniscience; the means to attain that is knowledge of the path; and as an auxiliary entailed in the moral choices one makes in that context, knowledge of the ground (that is, knowledge of counterproductive factors in one's existing situation and of a detailed analysis of remedies). These three aspects of knowledge constitute the context within which one puts an end to erroneous assumptions. [3.192a]

The four applications involved in spiritual practice are:

(1) the "application that perfects all aspects" is one of meditation in turn on some 173 topics, which subsume within them the significance of the definitive conclusions that one has reached through hearing and contemplating teachings concerning the foregoing aspects of knowledge;

(2) the "culminating application" is one of developing one's realization (based upon meditation that summarizes the foregoing aspects of knowledge) to a consummate level;

(3) the "sequential application" is one of meditating as before but on all topics at once, in order to gain stability from the foregoing application; and

(4) once that stability has been gained, the "instantaneous application" is one of meditating on the topics of the three aspects of knowledge in a single instant of timeless awareness, so that it is certain that immediately following this the fruition state will become fully evident.

Once one has pursued spiritual practice in the foregoing manner, one will straightforwardly accomplish what is renowned as the unsurpassable Prajñāpāramitā (the transcendent perfection of sublime intelligence), the supreme mother, dharmakāya—that is, the three kāyas and their attendant enlightened deeds.

The foregoing constitutes the commentary on the second part,
concerning a presentation of the specific stages in meditation
in the cause-based dialectical approach.

This concludes the commentary on [the first two parts of] the eighth book,
a developmental analysis of the higher training in meditative absorption,
from The Encompassing of All Knowledge,
also entitled The Precious Treasury of Sublime Teachings:
The Compendium of the Methods of All Spiritual Approaches
and A Treatise That Thoroughly Presents the Three Higher Trainings.

Appendix: Outline of Book Seven and Book Eight, Parts One and Two

Book Seven

[Part 1. Keys to Understanding]

I. Sublime Intelligence Deriving from Contemplation
II. Specific Keys to Evaluating the Teachings
  A. Brief Enumeration by Way of Introduction
  B. Extensive Explanation of the Significance of These Keys
    1. Ordinary Keys to Understanding
      a. Provisional and Definitive Meaning
      b. Direct and Indirect Intention
        i. Four Cases of Direct Intention
        ii. Four Cases of Indirect Intention
        iii. Differences between Direct and Indirect Intention
      c. Four Reliances
        i. Relying on the Meaning, Not the Words
        ii. Relying on the Teachings, Not the Individual
        iii. Relying on Timeless Awareness, Not Ordinary Consciousness
        iv. Relying on the Definitive Meaning, Not the Provisional One
      d. Four Logical Principles
    2. Extraordinary Keys to Understanding
      a. Brief Discussion
      b. Extensive Explanation
        i. Six Parameters
        ii. Four Modes

[Part 2. Understanding Truth and Meaning]

I. Provisional and Definitive Meaning of the Three Cycles of Teachings
- A. General Discussion
- B. Specific and Detailed Analysis
  - 1. Common Tradition
  - 2. Tradition of Proponents of Things Having No Finite Essence
  - 3. Tradition of Yogic Practitioners
  - 4. Explanation of the Exalted One
  - 5. Incorrect Opinions and Single Intent

II. Two Levels of Truth
- A. Introductory Comments
- B. Actual Classification
  - 1. Essence
  - 2. Derivation of Terms
  - 3. Characteristics and Synonyms
  - 4. Precise Analysis
    - a. The Actual Analysis
      - i. General Analysis
      - ii. Specific Analysis
    - b. Reasons Underlying the Analysis
    - c. Certainty of Two Levels
    - d. Two Levels of Truth: Identical or Separate?
    - e. Positions Held by Philosophical Systems
  - 5. Value of Understanding These Truths

III. Investigating the Process of Interdependent Connection
- A. Interdependent Connection: The Fundamentally Unconditioned Nature
- B. Interdependent Connection: Saṃsāra
- C. Interdependent Connection: Nirvāṇa

[Part 3. Authentic View]

I. The Need for Authentic View

II. The Way to Develop Sublime Intelligence

III. Preliminaries: The Four Axioms

IV. The Path That Avoids Dualistic Extremes
- A. General Way to Avoid Dualistic Extremes

B. Specific Explanation of the Middle Way Tradition
1. Identifying Emptiness
2. Unqualified Emptiness (*rang stong*)
3. Qualified Emptiness (*gzhan stong*)
V. Main Explanation: Two Aspects of the Lack of Identity
A. Purpose
B. Analysis
1. Lack of Identity in Phenomena
a. Key Topic
b. Factor to Be Negated
c. Purpose of Negating Identity
d. Philosophical Interpretations
e. Definitive Understanding through Middle Way Reasoning
2. Lack of Identity in the Individual
a. Key Topic
b. Factor to Be Negated
c. Purpose of Negating Identity
d. Philosophical Interpretations
e. Definitive Understanding through Middle Way Reasoning
3. Relevant Issues
a. Identicalness or Separateness
b. Purpose
c. Factors to Be Negated
d. Valid Cognition
e. Authentic Reasoning
4. Specific Middle Way Interpretations
a. Unqualified Emptiness
b. Qualified Emptiness
5. Advice Integrating Both Traditions
VI. Mantra Approach
A. General Position
B. Specific Position: Gargyi Wangpo
VII. Summation: The View of Unborn Primordial Unity

[Part 4. Foundations of Spiritual Practice]

I. Impact of Study and Contemplation
II. Four Contemplations

A. Reorienting the Mind Away from This Lifetime
1. Foundation for Reorientation
a. Identifying Opportunities and Endowments
b. Great Purpose
c. Difficulty of Obtaining the Support
2. Contemplation of Impermanence
a. Recollection of Death
b. Rebirth in Other States
B. Reorienting the Mind Away from Saṃsāra
1. Karma
a. General Contemplation
b. Specific Issues
2. Saṃsāra
a. Eights Kinds of Suffering
b. Three Kinds of Universal Suffering
C. Reorienting the Mind Away from Quiescence and Naïve Happiness
D. Reorienting the Mind Away from Dualistic Consciousness

Book Eight

[Part 1. Foundations of Meditative Absorption]

I. Necessity of Meditative Absorption
II. Identifying Meditative Absorption
III. Extensive Explanation of Meditative Absorption
A. Essence of Meditative Absorption
B. Definition of Terms
C. Necessity of Both Aspects
D. Developmental Process
E. Training in Meditative Absorption
1. Extensive Explanation
a. Training in Calm Abiding
i. Supportive Circumstances
ii. Stages of Calm Abiding
iii. Process of Cultivation
aa. Physical Posture
bb. Settling the Mind
1' General Framework

[Part 2. Meditation in the Cause-Based Dialectical Approach]

- a. Brief Discussion
- b. Extensive Explanation
  - i. Beginning Practitioners
  - ii. Four Anticipatory Phases
  - iii. Path of Seeing
  - iv. Path of Meditation

2. Pratyekabuddha Approach

B. Mahāyāna Approach

1. Individual Meditator
2. Preliminaries to Meditation
   - a. Four Immeasurable Attitudes
   - b. Path of Accumulation
3. Actual Stages of Meditation
   - a. General Stages of Mental Training
   - b. Formal Meditation Sessions and in Postmeditation
     - i. Formal Meditation vis-à-vis Postmeditation
     - ii. General Discussion of Postmeditation
   - c. Summary

Glossary

The emphasis in this glossary is on the Tibetan terminology; the Sanskrit equivalents have been provided where available.

English	Tibetan	Sanskrit
absence of identity	bdag med	anātman, nairātmya
absence of naïve speculation	smon pa med pa	apraṇihita
absence of subtle traits	mtshan ma med pa	animitta
absolute	yongs grub	pariniṣpanna
abstract concept	don spyi	arthasāmānya
acumen	dbang po	indriya
advanced spiritual practitioner	rnal 'byor pa/ma	yogin/yoginī
adventitious distortions	glo bur gyi dri ma	āgantuka mala
afflictive (mental) state	nyon mongs pa	kleśa
afflictive obscuration	nyon mongs pa'i sgrib pa	kleśāvaraṇa
aging and death	rga shi	jarāmaraṇa
agitation	rgod pa	auddhatya
alertness	shes bzhin	samprajanya
alternate reality	gzhan gyi dngos po	parabhāva
altruistic motivation	lhag pa'i bsam pa	adhyāśaya
analytical insight	rnam par 'byed pa	vicaya
application that perfects all aspects	rnam kun mngon rdzogs kyi sbyor ba	sarvākārābhisaṁbhoda prayoga

authentic action	yang dang pa'i las kyi mtha'	samyakkarmānta
authentic effort	yang dag pa'i rtsol ba	samyagvyāyāma
authentic livelihood	yang dag pa'i 'tsho ba	samyagājīva
authentic meditative absorption	yang dag pa'i ting nge 'dzin	samyaksamādhi
authentic mindfulness	yang dag pa'i dran pa	samyaksmṛti
authentic speech	yang dag pa'i ngag	samyagvāk
authentic thought	yang dag pa'i rtog pa	samyaksaṃkalpa
authentic view	yang dag pa'i lta ba	samyagdṛṣṭi
Autonomist	rang rgyud pa	Svātantrika
bases for dogmatic opinions	lta gzhi	
basic space of phenomena	chos kyi dbyings	dharmadhātu
belief in identity	bdag 'dzin	ātmagrāha
belief in the reality of the perishable aggregates	'jig tshogs la lta ba	satkāya dṛṣṭi
calm abiding	zhi gnas	śamatha
causal condition	rgyu'i rkyen	hetu pratyaya
certain examination	nges par rtog pa	
cognitive obscuration	shes bya'i sgrib pa	jñeyāvaraṇa
complete purity of the three focal points	'khor gsum yongs dag	trimaṇḍalapariśuddha
components of ordinary experience	khams	dhātu
compulsion	sred pa	tṛṣṇa
conceptual elaboration	spros pa	prapañca
conceptualization	rtog pa	kalpita
conceptually imputed	sgro btags pa	samāropita
conditioned	'dus byas	saṃskṛta
confidence	dad pa	śraddha
confusion	'khrul pa	bhrānta

consciousness	rnam shes	vijñāna
Consequentialist	thal 'gyur pa	Prāsaṅgika
contact	reg pa	sparśa
contemplation	bsam pa	cintā, bhāva
contrived	bcos pa	kṛtrima
conventional designations	tha snyad	vyāvahāra
coordinating function of mind	yid	manas
corruptible	zag bcas	āsrāvin
culminating application	rtse mo'i sbyor ba	mūrdha prayoga
deeply ingrained afflictive states	kun nas nyon mongs pa	samkleśa
definitive excellence	nges par legs pa	niḥśreyasa
definitive meaning	nges don	nītārtha
dependent	gzhan dbang	paratantra
diligence	brtson 'grus	vīrya
direct intention	dgongs pa	abhiprāya
direct intention concerned with equalness	mnyam pa nyid la dgongs pa	samatābhiprāya
direct intention concerned with eventualities	dus gzhan la dgongs pa	kālāntarābhiprāya
direct intention concerned with implied issues	don gzhan la dgongs pa	arthāntarābhiprāya
direct intention concerned with the attitudes of individuals	gang zag gi bsam pa la dgongs pa	pudgalāntarābhiprāya
discerning internal dialogue	so sor rtog pa'i yid kyi brjod pa	
dualism of perceived objects and perceiving subject	gzung (ba yul dang) 'dzin (pa sems)	grāhya grāhaka
effort	rtsol ba	prayatna
eight remedial techniques	gnyen po 'du byed brgyad	aṣṭapratipakṣa saṃskāra

eight thoughts of a superior spiritual practitioner	skyes bu chen po'i rnam par rtog pa brgyad	
eightfold path of spiritually advanced beings	'phags lam yan lag brgyad	aṣṭārya mārga
emptiness	stong pa nyid	śūnyatā
emptiness of all phenomena	chos thams cad stong pa nyid	sarvadharma śūnyatā
emptiness of emptiness	stong pa nyid stong pa nyid	śūnyatā śūnyatā
emptiness of nature	rang bzhin stong pa nyid	prakṛti śūnyatā
emptiness of specific characteristics	rang gi mtshan nyid stong pa nyid	svalakṣaṇa śūnyatā
emptiness of the very essence of what has no substantiality	dngos po med pa'i ngo bo nyid stong pa nyid	abhāva svabhāva śūnyatā
emptiness of what has no frame of reference	mi dmigs pa stong pa nyid	anupalambha śūnyatā
emptiness of what is beyond limitations	mtha' las 'das pa stong pa nyid	atyanta śūnyatā
emptiness of what is conditioned	'dus byas stong pa nyid	saṃskṛta śūnyatā
emptiness of what is external	phyi stong pa nyid	bahirdhā śūnyatā
emptiness of what is external and internal	phyi nang stong pa nyid	adhyātma bahirdhā śūnyatā
emptiness of what is great	chen po stong pa nyid	mahāśūnyatā
emptiness of what is internal	nang stong pa nyid	adhyātma śūnyatā
emptiness of what is not to be discarded	dor ba med pa stong pa nyid	anavakāra śūnyatā
emptiness of what is ultimate	don dam pa stong pa nyid	paramārtha śūnyatā
emptiness of what is unconditioned	'dus ma byas stong pa nyid	asaṃskṛta śūnyatā
emptiness of what is without beginning or end	thog ma dang tha ma med pa stong pa nyid	anavarāgra śūnyatā
equanimity	btang snyoms	upekṣa
erroneous opinions	log pa'i lta ba	mithyā dṛṣṭi
examination	brtag pa	kalpanā
experience of attainment	thob pa'i nyams	

experience of consummation	mthar phyin pa'i nyams	
experience of familiarization	goms pa'i nyams	
experience of movement	g.yo ba'i nyams	
experience of stability	brtan pa'i nyams	
explanation requiring interpretation	dgongs pa can	bhāvika
explanation that does not require interpretation	dgongs pa can ma yin pa	abhāvika
exploration of characteristics	mtshan nyid 'tshol ba	
exploration of influences	phyogs 'tshol ba	
exploration of logical principles	rigs pa 'tshol ba	
exploration of meaning	don 'tshol ba	
exploration of things	dngos po 'tshol ba	
exploration of time	dus 'tshol ba	
factor to be negated	dgag bya	pratiṣedha
factors that bring refinement	sbyong byed	
faintheartedness	le lo	kausīdya
faith	dad pa	śraddha
familiarization	'dris pa	saṃstuta
finite essence	ngo bo	bhāva
five experiences	nyams lnga	pañcānubhava
five flaws	nyes pa lnga	pañcadoṣa
five governing powers	dbang po lnga	pañcendriya
five kinds of wrong lifestyle	log 'tsho lnga	
five strengths	stobs lnga	pañcabala
fixated perception	'dzin pa	grāha
flattery	gzhog slong	
focus involving knowledge	mkhas pa'i dmigs pa	paṇḍitālambana
focus that purifies one of afflictive mental states	nyon mongs sbyong ba'i dmigs pa	kleśaviśuddhālambana

focus that purifies one of former behavior	spyad pa rnam sbyong gi dmigs pa	
Followers of the Sūtras	mdo sde pa	Sautrāntika
forgetting of instructions	gdams ngag brjed pa	upadeśa sampramoṣa
form	gzugs	rūpa
formal meditation session	mnyam bzhag	samāhita
formative factor	'du byed	saṃskāra
formative karmic patterning	'du byed pa	saṃskāra
four applications	sbyor ba bzhi	catvāra prayoga
four applications of mindfulness	dran pa nyer bzhag bzhi	catvāri smṛtyupasthāna
four aspects of authentic renunciation	yang dag spong ba bzhi	catvāri samyak prahāṇa
four attendant attitudes	yid (la) byed (pa) bzhi	catvāri manaskāra
four axioms that denote the Buddha's words	bka' btags kyi phyag rgya bzhi	
four bases of supernormal powers	rdzu 'phrul gyi rkang pa bzhi	catvāra ṛddhipāda
four immeasurable attitudes	tshad med bzhi	catvārāpramāṇa
four logical principles	rigs pa bzhi	catasro yuktayaḥ
four modes	tshul bzhi	
four reliances	rton pa bzhi	catvāri pratisaraṇa
Four Truths of spiritually advanced beings	'phags pa'i bden pa bzhi	catvārārya satya
four ways of focusing	yid byed bzhi	catvāri manaskāra
fundamental being	khams	dhātu
fundamentally unconditioned nature	gshis	
generally characterized thing	spyi mtshan	sāmānya lakṣaṇa
giving	gtong ba	tyāga
governing condition	bdag po'i rkyen	adhipati pratyaya
governing results	bdag po'i 'bras bu	adhipati phala

gradual dissolution	rjes gzhig	
ground for refinement	sbyong gzhi	
guiding the mind	(sems) 'dul bar byed pa	(citta) damaka; (citta) praśamana
habitual patterns	bag chags	vāsanā
hearing teachings	thos pa	śruta
hidden meaning	sbas pa'i don	guhārtha
highest state of mundane experience	'jig rten chos mchog	laukikāgradharma
human being	shed bu	mānava
hypocrisy	tshul 'chos	
identity in phenomena	chos kyi bdag	dharmātman
identity in the individual	gang zag gi bdag	pudgalātman
ignorance	ma rig pa	avidyā
immediate condition	de ma thag pa'i rkyen	samanantara pratyaya
impartiality	btang snyoms	upekṣa
impermanent	mi rtag pa	anitya
imputed	kun brtags	parikalpita
indirect intention	ldem (por) dgongs (pa)	abhisaṁdhi
indirect intention concerned with characteristics	mtshan nyid la ldem por dgongs pa	lakṣanābhisaṁdhi
indirect intention concerned with edification	gzhug pa la ldem por dgongs pa	avatāraṇābhisaṁdhi
indirect intention concerned with remedies	gnyen po la ldem por dgongs pa	pratipakṣābhisaṁdhi
indirect intention concerning transformation	bsgyur ba la ldem por dgongs pa	pariṇāmanābhisaṁdhi
inferential knowledge based on reasoning	rigs shes rjes dpag	
ingratiation	kha gsag	
instantaneous application	skad cig ma'i sbyor ba	kṣaṇika prayoga
instantaneous dissolution	ril 'dzin	

intention	'dun pa	chanda
interdependent connection	rten cing 'brel bar 'byung ba	pratītyasamutpāda
internal dialogue	yid kyi brjod pa	
internal dialogue as an all-absorbing state of sensation	kun tu tshor ba'i yid kyi brjod pa	
interpretation with respect to implied meaning	don la dgongs pa	arthābhiprāya
interpretation with respect to time frame	dus la dgongs pa	kālābhiprāya
interpretation with respect to understanding	bsam pa la dgongs pa	
intimate evaluation	nye bar 'jal ba	
investigation	dpyod pa	vicāra
investigative meditation	dpyad sgom	
involvement in conditioned existence	srid pa	bhāva
involvement with interruption	chad cing 'jug pa	
involvement with tension	sgrims te 'jug pa	
involvement without interruption	chad pa med par 'jug pa	
joy	dga' ba	muditā
karmically neutral	lung ma bstan	avyākṛta
knowing modesty	ngo tsha shes pa	lajjin
lack of identity	bdag med	anātman, nairātman
laxity	bying ba	nimagna
levels of deeper discernment	mngon par shes pa	abhijñā
life force	srog	jīva
life form	skye ba po	jantu
line of reasoning	gtan tshigs	hetu
listening	thos pa	śruta
literal meaning	yi ge'i don	akṣarārtha

logical principle	rigs pa	yukti
logical principle of dependent relationships	ltos pa'i rigs pa	apekṣa nyāya
logical principle of establishing what is reasonable	'thad pa sgrub pa'i rigs pa	upapattisiddha nyāya
logical principle of the nature of things	chos nyid kyi rigs pa	dharmatā nyāya
logical principle of the performance of functions	bya ba byed pa'i rigs pa	kṛtakāra nyāya
logical principle of what is validly cognized	tshad ma'i rigs pa	pramāṇa nyāya
manifold	du ma	aneka
material	rdzas	dravya
materialist	dngos por smra ba	vāstavādin
meaning of the words	tshig gi don	padārtha
meditative absorption	ting nge 'dzin	samādhi
meditative equipoise	mnyam par 'jog pa	samāhita
meditative equipoise of cessation	'gog pa'i snyoms 'jug	nirodha samāpatti
meditative stability	bsam gtan	dhyāna
meditative warmth	drod	uṣman
member of the human race	shed las skyes	manuja
mental determinant	ldog pa	apoha
mental dullness	bying ba	
Middle Way	dbu ma	Madhyamaka
Middle Way Yogic Practitioner	rnal'byor spyod pa'i dbu ma pa	Yogācāra Mādhyamika
mind of the realm of desire	'dod (pa'i) sems	
Mind Only	sems tsam	Cittamātra
mind-body aggregates	phung po	skandha
mind-body complex	ming gzugs	nāmarūpa
mindfulness	dran pa	smṛti

mundane level	'jig rten pa	laukika
naïve affirmation	rtag pa(r lta ba)	śāśvata dṛṣṭi
natural state	rang bzhin	svabhāva
nihilistic denial	chad pa(r lta ba)	uccheda dṛṣṭi
nine steps in settling the mind	sems gnas dgu	nava cittasthīta
nirvāṇa that is not defined by extremes	mi gnas pa'i mya ngan las 'das pa	apratiṣṭhita nirvāṇa
no independent nature	rang bzhin med pa	
nonapplication	'du mi byed pa	asaṃskāra
nonlimited nirvāṇa	mi gnas pa'i mya ngan las 'das pa	apratiṣṭhita nirvāṇa
nonsubstantial phenomenon	dngos med	abhāva
nonvirtue	mi dge ba	akuśala
not to be taken literally	sgra ji bzhin ma yin pa	ayathāruta
object of knowledge	shes bya	jñeya
one-pointed mind of the realm of desire	'dod sems rtse gcig pa	
ordinary being	sems can	sattva
ordinary consciousness	rnam shes	vijñāna
overapplication	'du byed pa	saṃskāra
overstatement	sgro btags pa	samaropa
pacifying the mind	(sems) zhi bar byed pa	(citta) śamana
pacifying the mind thoroughly	(sems) rnam par zhi bar byed pa	(citta) vyupaśamana
Particularist	bye brag tu smra ba	Vaibhāṣika
path of accumulation	tshogs kyi lam	sambhāra mārga
path of linkage	sbyor ba'i lam	prayoga mārga
path of meditation	sgom pa'i lam	bhāvanā mārga
path of no more training	mi slob pa'i lam	aśaikṣa mārga
path of seeing	mthong lam	darśana mārga
patient acceptance	bzod pa	kṣānti

peak experience	rtse mo	mūrdhan; mūrti
perception	'du shes	saṃjñā
permanent	rtag pa	nitya
perpetuation	len pa	upādāna
perpetuation of ignoble states of existence	gnas ngan len pa	dauṣṭhulya
pervasive focus	khyab pa'i dmigs pa	spharaṇālambana
phases that anticipate the decisive breakthrough	nges 'byed cha mthun	nirvedhabhāgīya
philosophical absolutism	mthar 'dzin (gyi lta ba)	antagrāha dṛṣṭi
postmeditation	rjes thob	pṛṣṭhalabdha
potential	sa bon	bīja
primordial unity	zung 'jug	yuganaddha
profiteering	rnyed pa 'tshol ba	
profound insight	lhag mthong	vipaśyanā
profound insight involving four essential experiences	ngo bo nyid bzhi'i lhag mthong	
profound insight that involves six explorations	tshol ba drug gi lhag mthong	
profound insight through three avenues of engagement	rjes su zhugs pa'i sgo gsum gyi lhag mthong	
proponents of things having no finite essence	ngo bo nyid med par smra ba	niḥsvabhāvavādin
provisional meaning	drang don	neyārtha
pure ethical discipline	tshul khrims	śīla
qualified emptiness	gzhan stong	
qualified negation	ma yin dgag	paryudāsa pratiṣedha
quantifiable aspect of ultimate truth	rnam grangs pa'i don dam bden pa	paryāya paramārtha satya
reality just as it is	ji lta ba	
reasoning	rigs pa	yukti
rebirth	skye ba	jāti

referential condition	dmigs pa'i rkyen	ālambana pratyaya
relative in an authentic sense	yang dag pa'i kun rdzob	samyak saṃvṛti
relative in an erroneous sense	log pa'i kon rdzob	mithyā saṃvṛti
relative level	kun rdzob	saṃvṛti
relative truth	kun rdzob kyi bden pa	saṃvṛti satya
results consistent with causes	rgyu mthun gyi 'bras bu	niṣyanda phala
results due to complete maturation	rnam smin gyi 'bras bu	vipāka phala
self-promotion	thob 'jal	
self-respect	khrel yod	āpatrāpya
sensation	tshor ba	vedana
sense field	skye mched	āyatana
sensory appearances	snang ba	ābhāsa
sequential application	mthar gyis sbyor ba	anupūrva prayoga
settling continually	(sems) rgyun du 'jog pa	(citta) pravāha saṃsthāpana
settling in equipoise	mnyam par 'jog pa	samāhita
settling meditation	'jog sgom	
settling more intimately	(sems) nye bar 'jog pa	(citta) upasthāpana
settling repeatedly	(sems) bslan te 'jog pa	(citta) ākṛṣya saṃsthāpana
settling the mind	sems 'jog pa	citta saṃsthāpana
settling the mind one-pointedly	(sems) rtse gcig tu byed pa	(citta) ekāgrakaraṇa
seven aids to enlightenment	byang chub yan lag bdun	sapta bodhyaṅga
seven riches of spiritually advanced beings	'phags pa'i nor bdun	saptāryadhāna
seven vajra properties	rdo rje'i gnas bdun	
shared meaning	spyi'i don	samudāyārtha
six parameters	mtha' drug	
six powers	stobs drug	ṣaḍbala
six sense fields	skye mched	āyatana

specifically characterized thing	rang mtshan	svalakṣaṇa
spiritual affinity	rigs	gotra
spiritually advanced being	'phags pa	ārya
spiritually immature being	byis pa	bālaka
spontaneous involvement	lhun gyis grub par 'jug pa	
stage of completion	rdzogs rim	sampannakrama
stage of development	bskyed rim	utpattikrama
states of meditative equipoise associated with the formless realm	gzugs med kyi snyoms 'jug	ārūpyasampatti
subject to external influences	gzhan bdang can	paratantra
subjective perceiver	'dzin pa (sems)	grāhaka
sublime intelligence	shes rab	prajñā
subliminal suffering	khyab pa 'du byed kyi sdgu bsngal	saṃskāra dukhatā
substantial thing	dngos po	bhāva
suchness itself	de bzhin nyid	tathatā
teaching on identity	bdag ston pa	
teaching on the lack of identity	bdag med par ston pa	
things in all their multiplicity	ji snyed pa	
thirty-seven factors conducive to enlightenment	byang chub phyogs kyi chos so bdun	saptatriṃśa bodhipakṣaka dharma
thorough analysis of phenomena	chos rnam rab 'byed	
thorough evaluation	rab tu 'jal ba	
thorough examination	rab tu rtog pa	
thorough pliancy	shin (tu) sbyangs (pa)	praśrabdhi
thorough purification of one's sphere of activity	spyod yul yongs su dag pa	gocara pariśuddha
thoroughgoing examination	yongs su rtog pa	parikalpa

thoroughgoing investigation	yongs su dpyod pa	paricāra
thoroughly analytical insight	rab tu rnam par 'byed pa	pravicaya
three avenues to complete liberation	rnam (par) thar (pa'i) sgo gsum	trivimokṣamukha
timeless awareness	ye shes	jñāna
to be taken literally	sgra ji bzhin pa	yathāruta
totally refined state	rnam par byang ba	vyavadāna
transcendent and accomplished conquerer	bcom ldan 'das	bhagavat
transcendent perfection	pha rol tu phyin pa	pāramitā
true nature of phenomena	chos nyid	dharmatā
two levels of truth	bden pa gnyis	dvau satya
ultimate truth	don dam gyi bden pa	paramārtha satya
unconditioned	'dus ma byas	asaṃskṛta
uncontrived	ma bcos pa	akṛtrima
undermining all bases for dogmas	lta gzhi kun zlog	
understatement	skur ba 'debs pa	abhyākhyāna
universal ground	kun gzhi	ālaya
unqualified emptiness	rang stong	
unqualified negation	med dgag	prasajya pratiṣedha
unquantifiable aspect of ultimate truth	rnam grangs ma yin pa'i don dam bden pa	aparyāya paramārtha satya
utter lucidity	'od gsal	prabhāsvara
valid cognition	tshad ma	pramāṇa
valid inference	rjes dpag tshad ma	anumāna pramāṇa
very heart of attaining the state of bliss	bde bar gshegs pa'i snying po	sugatagarbha
way of abiding	gnas lugs	
Yogic Practitioners	rnal 'byor spyod pa	Yogācāra

Abbreviations

Dg. K.	sDe dge woodblock edition of the bKa' 'gyur. PDF version on Tibetan Buddhist Resource Center website, tbrc.org.
Dg. T.	sDe dge woodblock edition of the bsTan 'gyur. PDF version on Tibetan Buddhist Resource Center website, tbrc.org.
NGB	*rNying ma'i rgyud 'bum* (mTshams brag edition). PDF version on Tibetan Buddhist Resource Center website, tbrc.org.
P	*A Comparative Analytical Catalogue of the Kanjur Division of the Tibetan Tripitaka: Edited in Peking during the K'ang hsi Era, and At Present Kept in the Library of the Otani Daigaku*. Kyoto. 3 vols. The Otani Daigaku Library, Kyoto, 1930–1932. Otani University Shin Buddhist Comprehensive Research Institute: Tibetan Works Research Project, 2005. http://web.otani.ac.jp/cri/twrp/tibdate/Peking_online_search.html.
Toh.	*A Complete Catalogue of the Tibetan Buddhist Canons*. Edited by Hakuju Ui, Munetada Suzuki, Yenshô Kanakura, and Tôkan Tada. Sendai, Japan: Tôhoku Imperial University, 1934.
fol., ff.	folio, folios
l.	line
v., vv.	verse, verses

Notes

1. The "ten pillars of study" (Tib. *bshad brgyud 'degs pa'i ka chen bcu*, or "ten great pillars who upheld lineages of explanation") are a group of translators and teachers whose activities were instrumental in founding traditions emphasizing the exegesis of the Buddhist teachings: Tönmi Sambhota, Bairotsana, Kawa Paltsek, Chokro Lui Gyaltsen, Zhang Yeshé Dé, Lochen Rinchen Zangpo, Dromtönpa Gyalwai Jungné, Ngok Lotsawa Loden Sherab, Sakya Paṇḍita, and Gö Khukpa Lhetsé. The "eight chariots of practice lineages" are the traditions of the Nyingma, Kadampa-Gelukpa, Sakya, Marpa Kagyü, Shangpa Kagyü, Zhijé-Chö, Jordruk, and Dorjei Nyendrup. These are discussed in Kongtrul, *The Treasury of Knowledge: Book Eight, Part Four: Esoteric Instructions*, 26–28.
2. Kongtrul, *The Autobiography of Jamgön Kongtrul*, 131.
3. That is, *The Treasury of Knowledge*.
4. This introductory section is contained in Book 1 of *The Treasury of Knowledge*; see Kongtrul, *The Treasury of Knowledge: Book One: Myriad Worlds*, 79–89.
5. This section has been translated as Kongtrul, *The Treasury of Knowledge: Book One: Myriad Worlds*.
6. The preceding three sections have been translated as Kongtrul, *The Treasury of Knowledge: Books Two, Three, and Four: Buddhism's Journey to Tibet*.
7. See Kongtrul, *The Treasury of Knowledge: Book Five: Buddhist Ethics*.
8. See Kongtrul, *The Treasury of Knowledge: Book Six, Parts One and Two*; Kongtrul, *The Treasury of Knowledge: Book Six, Part Three: Frameworks of Buddhist Philosophy*; and Kongtrul, *The Treasury of Knowledge: Book Six, Part Four: Systems of Buddhist Tantra*.
9. See Kongtrul, *The Treasury of Knowledge: Book Seven and Book Eight, Parts One and Two: Foundations of Buddhist Study and Practice* (present volume); Kongtrul, *The Treasury of Knowledge: Book Eight, Part Three: The Elements of Tantric Practice*; and Kongtrul, *The Treasury of Knowledge: Book Eight, Part Four: Esoteric Instructions*.
10. See Kongtrul, *The Treasury of Knowledge: Books Nine and Ten: Journey and Goal*.
11. Kongtrul, *The Autobiography of Jamgön Kongtrul*, 263–64.
12. A translation of Book 6, Parts 1 and 2 by Gyurme Dorje is forthcoming; see Kongtrul, *The Treasury of Knowledge: Book Six, Parts One and Two: Indo-Tibetan Classical Learning and Buddhist Phenomenology*. A translation of Book 6, Part 3 by Elizabeth Callahan has already appeared as Kongtrul, *The Treasury of Knowledge: Book Six, Part Three: Frameworks of Buddhist Philosophy*, and Book 6, Part 4 (translated by Elio Guarisco and Ingrid McLeod) as *The Treasury of Knowledge: Book Six, Part Four: Systems of Buddhist Tantra*.

13. Kongtrul, *The Treasury of Knowledge: Books Nine and Ten: Journey and Goal*, 473.
14. Ruegg, "Purport, Implicature, and Presupposition," 321–22, n. 1.
15. That is, on the person hearing the statement being required to interpret it.
16. Thera, *Kalama Sutta*, secs. 9–10.
17. At the Tsadra Foundation Fellows and Grantees Conference in March of 2011, Dr. Artemus Engle gave the following interpretation of this term, drawn from his work on the *Bodhisattvabhūmi* of Asaṅga:

    Asaṅga's description of the four applications (S: *catasro yuktayaḥ*, T: *rigs pa bzhi*) appears in his explanation of the second of two methods for engaging in the practice of reflection. It is here that we find Asaṅga stating that the term *yukti* is synonymous with *yoga* (T: *sbyor ba*) and *upāya* (T: *thabs*), any of which could be rendered in this context as an "application," a "means," or an "expedient." It is for this reason that I have translated the term as "application," rather than the more commonly seen rendering "reason."

18. Guenther and Trungpa, *The Dawn of Tantra*, 1–2.
19. Kongtrul, *The Treasury of Knowledge: Books Two, Three, and Four: Buddhism's Journey to Tibet*, 151–52.
20. Longchen Rabjam, *The Precious Treasury of Philosophical Systems*, 15–16.
21. Kongtrul, *The Treasury of Knowledge: Books Nine and Ten: Journey and Goal*, 8–10.
22. Tsongkhapa authored a verse text with this title; Kongtrul was obviously impressed with this model, for he authored a commentary to Tsongkhapa's short source text and included both in his monumental collection *Treasury of Spiritual Instructions* (*gDams ngag mdzod*).
23. Kongtrul, *The Treasury of Knowledge: Books Nine and Ten: Journey and Goal*, 473.
24. Ibid., 63–105.
25. The source verses of *The Treasury of Knowledge* read "one trains with precision" (*zhib mor **sbyong***), but the verses as cited by Kongtrul in the commentary, as well as the prose commentary itself, read "one conducts oneself with precision" (*zhib mor **spyod***).
26. This is the stage of one's experiences and perceptions initially becoming framed in conceptual terms.
27. That is, perception of things in more "generic" terms, of their general characteristics, without having yet achieved a more precise determination of their specific characteristics.
28. The choice of such objects as vases and blankets is based simply on these being familiar everyday objects in traditional Tibetan culture.
29. "The way things actually abide" (Tib. *gnas lugs*) is a term for the ultimate nature of things, as distinct from the way they appear in one's ordinary perception.
30. That is, it may constitute either a mundane or a transcendent thought process.
31. The Tibetan term (*gung rab*) refers to teachings of the Buddha, contained in the Tibetan canon known as the Kangyur.
32. *Most Majestic State of Meditative Absorption*, (Toh. 127), Dg. K., mDo sde, vol. Da, p. 40, l. 3. The woodblock text of *The Treasury of Knowledge* has, in error, *ston pa* (teacher) for *stong pa* (emptiness).
33. This term (Tib. *gsob*) indicated something that gives a superficial sense of presence but lacks any real substance, for example, a stuffed lion skin. The term appears in the list as found in the source sūtra but is omitted in the passage as cited by Kongtrul in *The Treasury of Knowledge*.

34. Tib. *shed las skyes pa*; Skt. *manuja*. Literally, "born of Manu"; Manu was the original human being in ancient Indian mythology.
35. Tib. *shed bu* or *shed bdag*; Skt. *mānuja*. Literally, "child of Manu."
36. *Discourse Taught by Akṣayamati*, (Toh. 175), Dg. K., mDo sde, vol. Ma, p. 299, lines 2–3 and p. 300, lines 1–2.
37. Nāgārjuna, *In Praise of the Inconceivable Middle Way*, (Toh. 1128), Dg. T., bsTod tshogs, vol. Ka, p. 156, l. 7 to p. 157, l. 1. In the source, the third line reads: "that is a meaning that leads one on, [taught] on the relative level."
38. That is, those teachings that discuss issues peripheral to the true nature of phenomena itself.
39. These are three aspects of meditative absorption that bring about the attainment of the complete liberation of nirvāṇa; they are associated with the Cittamātra position that all that is knowable is subsumed under the three headings of imputation, dependence, and the absolute. The three avenues are:
(1) emptiness as an avenue to complete liberation, which is the realization that conceptually imputed phenomena do not exist;
(2) the absence of subtle traits as an avenue to complete liberation, which is the realization that what is absolute and unconditioned has no subtle traits such as shape, color, and so on;
(3) the absence of naïve speculation as an avenue to complete liberation, which is the elimination of reliance on dependent, conditioned phenomena due to the knowledge that such reliance produces only suffering.
On these three avenues, see Longchen Rabjam, *The Precious Treasury of Philosophical Systems*, 145:

> Of the three avenues to complete liberation that concern the knowable, emptiness is the nonexistence of a self; the absence of characteristics is the nonexistence of anything the self takes to be its own; and the absence of speculation is a nonreferential state. In terms of the path, of the three avenues to complete liberation, emptiness is the truth of cessation; the absence of characteristics is the truth of the path; and the absence of naïve assumption constitutes the truths of suffering and its universal origin. In terms of the fruition, of the three avenues to liberation, emptiness and the absence of characteristics pertain to the state in which there are no residual traces, whereas the absence of naïve assumption pertains to the state that still involves residual traces.

40. That is, the absence of deliberate and contrived mental attitudes based on naïve expectations or hesitations concerning the true nature of phenomena.
41. *Discourse Taught by Akṣayamati*, (Toh. 175), Dg. K., mDo sde, vol. Ma, p. 299, l. 3 and p. 300, lines 2–3. *The Treasury of Knowledge* has the title of this source, in error, as *The Discourse Requested by Akṣayamati*, which is a separate source (Dg. K., vol. Cha, ff. 175b–182b).
42. Nāgārjuna, *In Praise of the Inconceivable Middle Way*, (Toh. 1128), Dg. T., bsTod tshogs, vol. Ka, p. 156, l. 7. In the source, the first line reads: "The very essence of all phenomena . . ."
43. Maitreya, *Highest Continuum*, chap. 1, v. 158, (Toh. 4024), Dg. T. , Sems tsam, vol. Phi, p. 122, l. 7 to p. 123, l. 1. In the source text, the last line reads: "so that whoever had them . . ."

44. The term "provisional in meaning" (Tib. *drang ba'i don*; Skt. *neyārtha*) literally means "meaning that draws one along," that is, guides one to a further level of understanding without necessarily being the final, or definitive, statement in itself.
45. That is, the definition of what is provisional is not simply that it is taught for some purpose, because all teachings are for a purpose; otherwise, certain enlightened activities of buddhas would be meaningless.
46. That is, with respect to its appreciation of the true nature of phenomena.
47. *Most Majestic State of Meditative Absorption*, (Toh. 127), Dg. K., mDo sde, vol. Da, ff. 1b–170b is an important Mahāyāna sūtra.
48. See Kongtrul, *The Treasury of Knowledge: Books Nine and Ten: Journey and Goal*, 578, n. 243:

> These are factors that contribute to the attainment of any of the three levels of enlightenment—that of śrāvakas, that of pratyekabuddhas, or the unsurpassable enlightenment of buddhahood attained by bodhisattvas. These thirty-seven factors are:
> (1)–(4) the four applications of mindfulness,
> (5)–(8) the four aspects of correct renunciation,
> (9)–(12) the four bases of supernormal powers,
> (13)–(17) the five controlling powers associated with the completely refined state of enlightenment,
> (18)–(22) the five strengths associated with the completely refined state of enlightenment,
> (23)–(29) the seven adjuncts to enlightenment, and
> (30)–(37) the eightfold path of noble ones.

49. Vajrapāṇi, *Detailed Explanation of the Summary of the Concise Tantra Extracted from the One Hundred Thousand Verses of the Definitive Expression*, (Toh. 1402), Dg. T., rGyud, vol. Ba, p. 166, l. 2 and lines 3–4.
50. That is, in the section entitled "The Extraordinary Keys to Understanding (in the Mantra Approach)."
51. These are attempts to translate the Tibetan terms *dgongs pa* and *ldem dgongs*. "Intention" conveys an honorific term for the activity of the enlightened mind of a buddha—the functional equivalent of an ordinary being's thinking process. In the context discussed here, it refers to the specific motive or intention that informs a buddha's teaching.
52. The woodblock of *The Treasury of Knowledge* has, in error, "conventional" (*tha snyad*) for "different" (*tha dad*).
53. That is, some meaning other than the obvious one contained in the statement.
54. Vipaśyin was a buddha in a former eon, the first of "seven successive buddhas" spoken of in the Buddhist teachings—Vipaśyin, Śikhin, Viśvabhū, Krakucchanda (the first buddha of the present eon), Kanakamuni, Kāśyapa, and Śākyamuni (the fourth buddha of the present eon, in which some 1,002 buddhas will appear in total). The statement cited is a case of the Buddha Śākyamuni describing his attainment of buddhahood as that of "becoming" Vipaśyin.
55. That is, the fact that all buddhas awaken to the same ultimate realization of dharmakāya, and so are equal in that respect.
56. As Kongtrul's discussion indicates, these correspond to the three principles by which

the Cittamātra school of Buddhist philosophy describes the entire range of phenomena—imputation, dependence, and the absolute.

57. "Imputation" (Tib. *kun brtags*; Skt. *parikalpita*) refers to the adventitious mental process of assigning labels and describing things in terms of categories. Something that is imputed, being nothing more than a conceptual label imposed by the ordinary mind, does not exist even conventionally, let alone ultimately.
58. Imputed things are nonexistent in their very essence with respect to their characteristics because they are phenomena that are imputed to exist when in fact they do not, like a mottled rope being mistaken for a snake.
59. "Dependent" (Tib. *gzhan dbang*; Skt. *paratantra*) refers to things that are empirically verifiable and brought about through causes and conditions, such that they then serve as bases for the foregoing process of imputation. The impure aspect of this dependence constitutes the animate and inanimate universe, manifesting because of the mind's myriad habit patterns; these manifestations are "dependent" by virtue of the fact that they are dependent on other conditions, namely, karma and habit patterns. The pure aspect of dependence constitutes pure realms of experience, such as Sukhāvati (the Realm of Bliss associated with the buddha Amitābha); these are "dependent" in that they rely on circumstances that are due to the mind being purified of its obscurations.
60. Because phenomena that are dependent (*gzhan dbang*) come about through the influence (*dbang*) of causes and conditions other (*gzhan*) than themselves, not only is there no snake existing in the mottled rope (see the example in n. 58 of an imputed phenomenon), but even the mottled rope itself, being nothing more than a collection of many individual strands, cannot be found to exist in its own right.
61. This line of reasoning, which refutes the belief that things originate through any of the following four alternatives, is central to the Madhyamaka (Middle Way) school of Buddhist philosophy and was elaborated by, among others, the Indian master Candrakīrti in his *Entrance to the Middle Way*. See Padmakara Translation Group, *Introduction to the Middle Way*, 165–278 and Wangchuk Dorje, the Ninth Karmapa, *The Karmapa's Middle Way*, 185–314.
62. Because it has already been established that things are not produced from themselves, nor from other things, some combination of the foregoing two alternatives does not constitute a viable option.
63. Because this would mean, for example, that anything could arise from anything, and that things would be independent of time.
64. *Manifest Adornment of Timeless Awareness*, (Toh. 100), Dg. K. mDo sde, vol. Ga, ff. 276a–305a. The passage as cited does not appear in this source, although similar statements are found in it and throughout the mDo sde (Sūtra) section of the Kangyur.
65. "Absolute" refers to both the "unchanging absolute"—the basic space of phenomena as the true nature of phenomena that is ultimately real, neither dependent nor imputed—and the "unerring absolute"—timeless awareness as experienced by spiritually advanced beings in meditative equipoise.
66. That is, what is "absolute" does not constitute some "thing" with any finite essence in the ultimate sense; by way of analogy, just as in the example of the mottled rope's being mistaken for a snake, neither the rope nor the snake exists on the basis of the individual strands.
67. *Definitive Commentary on Enlightened Intent*, (Toh. 106), Dg. K., mDo sde, vol. Ca, p. 33, lines 1–2.

68. Vasubandhu, *Treasury of Abhidharma*, chap. 7, v. 34, (Toh. 4089), Dg. T., mNgon pa, vol. Ku, p. 45, l. 1.
69. Dharmatrāta, *Didactic Aphorisms*, chap. 4, v. 73, (Toh. 326), Dg. K., mDo sde, vol. Sa, p. 503, l. 7 and (Toh. 4099), Dg. T., mNgon pa, vol. Tu, p. 87, l. 7. In the source, the last line reads: "anyone will be without blame, will be a brahmin [that is, a spiritual practitioner]."
70. These are two of the "twelve links of interdependent origination"—ignorance, formative patterning, ordinary consciousness, formation of the mind-body complex, sense fields, contact, sensation, compulsion, perpetuation, becoming, birth, and aging-and-death—that describe the process by which the mind remains caught within the cycle of saṃsāra. "Compulsion" refers to the mental tension of constant effort in avoiding unpleasant and painful sensations and seeking pleasant ones; "perpetuation" is the mental process that serves as the cause for taking rebirth in saṃsāra.
71. Tib. *kun gzhi*; Skt. *ālaya*. A primary function of mind or consciousness that is karmically neutral but that perpetuates habitual patterns and so serves as a support for both karmic potentials and their natural consequences.
72. These constitute a model of ordinary mind that was formulated by a branch of the Cittamātra school of Buddhist philosophy. They are: (1)–(5) the avenues of sense consciousness (visual, auditory, olfactory, gustatory, and tactile); (6) the coordinating mental faculty that organizes sense data and develops conceptual frameworks; (7) the afflictive aspect of consciousness, which imposes a sense of individual identity; and (8) the basis of all ordinary experience.
73. That is, the faculties of sight, hearing, smell, taste, touch, and conceptual thought as avenues of sensory and mental experience.
74. That is, on the person hearing the statement necessarily having to interpret it.
75. Asvabhāva, *Explanatory Essays Commenting on the "Compendium of the Supreme Spiritual Approach,"* (Toh. 4051), Dg. T., Sems tsam, vol. Ri, p. 465, l. 7 to p. 466, l. 1.
76. That is, the Nyingma master Longchen Rabjam (kLong chen rab 'byams, 1308–1364). In his conclusion to *The Treasury of Knowledge*, Kongtrul acknowledges his debt to the writings of Longchen Rabjam as a major source in his composition of *The Treasury of Knowledge*. See Kongtrul, *The Treasury of Knowledge: Books Nine and Ten: Journey and Goal*, 463.
77. Source not identified. While statements of indirect intent are by definition only provisionally true, they do not constitute falsehoods since they lead those who hear and understand them to deeper and more accurate levels of understanding.
78. The issue of reliance here is not one of "all or nothing." Those factors on which one should not "rely" may nonetheless be useful and supportive in the shorter term; the question is one of what one can ultimately place one's trust in. For example, in considering the three objects of refuge—buddha, dharma, and saṅgha—only the first, the state of buddhahood, represents the ultimate source of refuge, with the dharma and saṅgha being more "temporary" (in that they are only necessary as sources of refuge until one becomes a buddha oneself), but this does not mean one is not to rely on them.
79. That is, the provisional meaning.
80. *Discourse on the Supreme Passing Beyond Sorrow*, (Toh. 119), Dg. K., mDo sde, vol. Ña, p. 197, lines 1–2.
81. That is, the nonexistence of identity in the individual personality and the nonexistence of identity in any phenomenon.

82. The "very heart of being as the attainment of the state of bliss"—that is, the "buddha nature" that is the true nature of all living beings.
83. That is, to exaggerate anything into something it is not or denigrating it as something it is not; specifically, to naïvely ascribe existence or nonexistence. The Tibetan idiom is literally "to adorn with feathers or hurl abuse."
84. On this term, see Kongtrul, *The Treasury of Knowledge: Books Nine and Ten: Journey and Goal*, 12:

> In order for this twofold process [of spiritual development culminating in the attainment of buddhahood] to take place, one must first have felt a sense of dissatisfaction with the present set of circumstances one is in—a profound dissatisfaction with the entire state of conditioned existence that goes beyond a dissatisfaction with any personal issues that might need to be dealt with in the meantime. This lies at the very root of the path in Buddhism; the terms used to describe it (Skt. *niḥsaraṇa*; Tib. *nges par 'byung ba*) are often rendered as "renunciation," but the English word, with its negative connotations of aversion to, and fear of, the world at large, does poor justice to the sense of the original terms. This sense of dissatisfaction does not find its expression in a puritanical attitude of repression and self-denial but rather as an inspired will to become free of the limitations imposed by our present state of ignorance of our true nature and the confusion and frustration this imposes on our mind.

85. Skt. *yukti*; Tib. *rigs pa*. Under most circumstances this term refers to the use of reasoning to establish a proof or come to a conclusion; in this context, the term could be glossed as equivalent to "application" (Skt. *prayoga*; Tib. *sbyor ba*) or "(skillful) method" (Skt. *upāya*; Tib. *thabs*). The point is that there is a logic to things because of certain principles by which they function or are simply experienced the way that they are.
86. See n. 70.
87. See the glossary in Tsang Nyön Heruka, *The Life of Marpa*, 233–34 and 255–56:

> Four methods by which the dharma is expressed or taught: in words (T: tshig gi tshul), through the general or outer method (T: phyi yi tshul), in a hidden way (T: sbas pa' tshul), and through the ultimate method (T: mthar thug gi tshul).
>
> . . . Six perspectives on the teachings that a Buddhist student uses in understanding them: literal meaning (S: neyārtha; T: drang-don), true meaning (S: nītārtha; T: nges-don), implied (S: saṃdhyā-bhāṣā; T: dgongs-pa-can), not implied (S: na saṃdhyā-bhāṣā; T: dgongs-pa-can ma-yin-pa), explicit (S: yathāruta; T: sgra ji-bzhin-pa), and not explicit (S: na yathāruta; T: sgra ji-bzhin-pa ma-yin-pa). These are often used in conjunction with the "four methods."
>
> His Holiness Dilgo Khyentse Rinpoche composed the following dohā to explain the meaning of these ten terms:
>
> > The *literal meaning* mainly expresses relative truth with appearances.
> > Disciples are gradually shown the true meaning.
> > The *true meaning* shows naked absolute truth beyond appearances.
> > This is the oral instruction for fortunate ones with sharp faculties.

To cut the root of existence, it is said, "Kill your parents."
The meaning itself—cultivating and refraining from attachments—is *implied.*
The real meaning is said to be "conquering with remedies the cultivation of attachments."
Not implied is said to show this clearly with words.

In each of the four orders of tantra, beginning with the maṇḍala, fire offering, and so forth,
Explicit dharma language is proclaimed.
Bound by signs not proclaimed by śāstras in the world,
Not explicit is bound by words difficult to understand.

The actual root texts are explained word-for-word with definitions, according to syntax.
That is the *meaning of words.*
The path of mantrayāna, the perfection of ground, path, and fruition,
Is only proclaimed in anuttara; this is the *general meaning.*

The extraordinary union and destruction, āli, kāli, and so on,
Are shown by code words; this is the *hidden meaning.*
The unsurpassable secret of the actual path and fruition
Is clearly shown by both words and meanings; this is the *ultimate meaning.*

88. *Source Tantra of the Wheel of Time*, cited in Puṇḍarīka, *Stainless Light*, (Toh. 845), Dg. K., Dus 'khor 'grel bshad, vol. Śrī, p. 63, l. 1 and (Toh. 1347), Dg. T., rGyud, vol. Tha, p. 273, l. 1.
89. The term "vajra word" (Tib. *rdo rje'i tshig*; Skt. *vajrapāda*) refers to the use of language in the Vajrayāna tradition, where it is an inspired expression of deep inner realization, and a word is suggestive of multiple levels of interpretation beyond its literal, lexical meaning.
90. The Sanskrit term *tantra* (Tib. *rgyud*) literally means "continuum" and can be discussed from the point of view of causal and resultant aspects. The causal aspect is the true and ultimate nature that remains constant for all ordinary beings as well as buddhas, and which undergoes no change during the process by which the former become the latter. This corresponds to what, in the sūtra tradition, is termed *tathāgatagarbha* or *sugatagarbha*—the "buddha nature." The resultant aspect of tantra is the state of complete enlightenment that "results" when purely adventitious factors that obscure that true nature have been removed.
91. The completion stage in Vajrayāna practice has two phases, a "thematic" one (Tib. *mtshan bcas*) based on conceptual structures that involve visualization, breathing exercises, and physical postures; and a "nonthematic" phase (Tib. *mtshan med*) that focuses on a formless and direct experience of the true nature of mind. Both phases are considered to constitute definitive meaning.
92. That is, the thematic phase of the completion stage.
93. According to the Kagyü school of Tibetan Buddhism (and in particular the third Karmapa, Rangjung Dorjé, whose writings were a major source for Kongtrul in his composition of *The Treasury of Knowledge*), the Tibetan term *kun gzhi* (Skt. *ālaya*),

here rendered as "universal ground," must be interpreted according to context. It often connotes a more negative sense of a "basis for all ordinary experience," as a subtle aspect of ordinary mind that lies at the root of saṃsāra, sustains the imprints of karmic patterning, and allows for the continuity between the commission of an action and the experience of its results, a continuity that often remains valid over lifetimes. Here, however, the term refers to the ground of being that underlies both the ordinary consciousness of saṃsāra and the timeless awareness of nirvāṇa. In his treatise *Distinguishing Ordinary Consciousness from Timeless Awareness*, Rangjung Dorjé notes that such Mahāyāna sūtras as the *Journey to Śrī Laṅka* do not make a distinction when using this term, with the result that there are many points of potential misinterpretation in reading such sources. There is a need to distinguish between *kun gzhi/ālaya* as the universal ground of being and as merely the basis of all ordinary experience within saṃsāra.

94. That is, the nonthematic phase of the completion stage.
95. *Hevajra Tantra*, (Toh. 417), Dg. K., rGyud, vol. Ṅa, p. 3, l. 6 to p. 4, l. 1.
96. Source not identified.
97. *Supreme Illusion*, (Toh. 425), Dg. K., rGyud, vol. Ṅa, p. 339, l. 4. The lines in the source read slightly differently:

    Kidnap her from all the buddhas
    and enjoy the divine and sublime maiden.

98. This term (Tib. *rnam pa kun gyi mchog dang ldan pa'i stong pa nyid*; Skt. *sarvākara varopeta śūnyatā*) is a term that derives from the Kālacakra tradition. It emphasizes the aspect of emptiness as a rich field of possibility, not a blank state or a bleak void.
99. Sublime intelligence (Tib. *shes rab*; Skt. *prajñā*) is considered to be the feminine principle in Mahāyāna and Vajrayāna Buddhism. The transcendent perfection of this intelligence is personified as a goddess (Tib. *Shes rab kyi pha rol tu phyin ma*; Skt. *Prajñāpāramitā*), who is the "mother" of all buddhas in the sense that the enlightenment of all who attain to buddhahood is "born" of the realization of this transcendent perfection.
100. That is, realization of emptiness reveals what has previously been hidden from one's direct understanding and experience.
101. *Hevajra Tantra*, (Toh. 417), Dg. K., rGyud, vol. Ṅa, p. 34, l. 6.
102. Source not identified.
103. *Heart Essence of Secrets*, chap. 12, v. 3c–d, (Toh. 832), Dg. K., rÑiṅ rgyud, vol. Kha, p. 245, l. 6 and NGB, vol. 20. p. 190, l. 7:

    Through one's applying the seals of ā li kā li,
    everything, everything is accomplished.

    The term *ā li kā li* refers to the vowels and consonants of the Sanskrit alphabet, arranged in two strings of syllables that are recited much in the manner of a mantra in Vajrayāna rituals. The terms "union and release" are code words for processes that are particularly discussed in the Mahāyoga tradition of the Nyingma school and the father tantra classes of the Sarma schools. "Union" (Tib. *sbyor ba*; Skt. *prayoga*) in the ultimate sense refers to the resolution of dualistic consciousness in the nondual state of timeless awareness; this is the underlying principle for the practices of karmamudrā and jñānamudrā, which involve a physical or imagined consort, respectively. "Release" (Tib. *sgrol ba*; Skt. *uttāraṇa*) refers specifically to the ability gained in advanced Vajrayāna practice that allows one to skillfully release the consciousness of another being from its body and guide it to a higher state of existence; this is admissible only when the one thus liberated would otherwise cause great harm through further actions in that lifetime. To confuse union and release with ordinary expressions of sexual desire and aggression is to miss the point utterly; it is due to the potential for grave misinterpretation that these teachings and practices have historically been closely guarded.

104. See *Compendium of the Vajra of Timeless Awareness*, (Toh. 447), Dg. K., rGyud. vol. Ca, p. 570, l. 5. The actual passage in the source tantra reads: "The four kinds of explanation are those of the literal meaning, the common meaning, the hidden one, and the final one."

105. The computerized edition of *The Treasury of Knowledge* reads "(the mere reading of a text) word by word" (*tshig gi 'bur non*); the woodblock edition reads "(the mere reading of) the meanings of the words" (*tshig gi 'bru don*).

106. Source not identified.

107. That is, anuttarayoga tantra, the highest and innermost of the classes of tantra in Vajrayāna.

108. Kriyā tantra and carya tantra are two classes that pertain to the "outer" level of Vajrayāna practice.

109. Source not identified.

110. These are well-known incidents from former lifetimes of the Buddha, when still a bodhisattva on the path toward complete enlightenment.

111. That is, common to the traditions of both sūtra and tantra.

112. There are themes that bridge between the stages of development and completion, such that methods used in the former stage have the threefold effect of "purifying" one (Tib. *sbyang ba*) to prepare one to embark on practice of the latter stage, of "maturing" one (Tib. *smin pa*) to be more capable of such practice, and of "finding their completion" (Tib. *rdzogs pa*) in the latter stage.

113. Tib. *rang byin gyis rlob pa*; Skt. *svādiṣṭhāna*. This term refers to practices such as that of inner heat (Tib. *gtum mo*; Skt. *caṇḍālī*), in which the harnessing of subtle energies in the body to generate deeper states of realization parallels the process of karmamudrā, in which one relies on a consort in sexual practices designed to harness those energies. Self-consecration, which is also termed "one's own body endowed with skillful means" (Tib. *rang lus thabs ldan*), is often presented as a preliminary training to practices involving a consort, termed "another's body as the source of sublime intelligence" (Tib. *gzhan lus shes rab*), but it can be considered a complete practice in itself.

114. The "hidden" quality referred to is a case of "self-secrecy" rather than something deliberately being hidden, or withheld, from someone; the true nature of phenomena is such that its profound implications are inaccessible to a mind unprepared by training. While such analyses of degrees do not in actuality apply to this true nature—which constitutes the "core," or heart essence, of the teachings, one can apply useful models (such as the one found in the *Highest Continuum*, which speaks of three situations—the impure situation of ordinary beings, the pure situation of bodhisattvas, and the utterly pure situation of buddhas) from the perspective of the degree to which a given being can appreciate and directly experience the true nature of reality.

115. These two levels of truth are discussed in the following part of Book 7.

116. Tib. *man ngag*; Skt. *upadeśa*. This term is used particularly in Mahāyāna and Vajrayāna contexts. It refers to concise presentations of key points that contain all that is required for an attuned mind to make spiritual progress, without more extensive study and preparation necessarily being obligatory.
117. That is, sublime intelligence that constitutes a complete understanding of all implications of the Buddha's teachings.
118. See, by way of comparison, *Expansive Gem*, (Toh. 506), Dg. K., rGyud, vol. Da, p. 580, l. 6 to p. 581, l. 1:

> O transcendent and accomplished conqueror, did you turn the wheel of the dharma in an excellent manner? Did you vanquish the hordes of Māra, together with their mounts? Did you light the lamp of the dharma? Did you raise the victory banner of the dharma? Did you beat the drum of the dharma? Did you loudly blow the conch shell of the dharma? O transcendent and accomplished conqueror, did you appear in the world as a buddha? Do you have knowledge of unsurpassable omniscience?
>
> O transcendent and accomplished conqueror, please then turn the wheel of the dharma, and establish the treasure of the dharma, in this human world a second and a third time!

119. Tib. *de bzhin gshegs pa'i snying po*; Skt. *tathāgatagarbha*. That is, the "buddha nature" of all beings, which constitutes the ultimate nature of mind.
120. Maitreya, *Highest Continuum*, chap. 2, v. 41, (Toh. 4024), Dg. T, Sems tsam, vol. Phi, p. 127, l. 3 (referring to the nirmāṇakāya of buddhahood):

> Enlightened embodiments that cause the world to be brought to the path of peace,
> cause beings to reach full spiritual maturity, and cause prophecies to be uttered:
> such embodiments are ever-present in this world,
> just as the realm of visible forms abides within the realm of space.

According to the Indian commentaries on the *Highest Continuum*, these lines imply a progression that links the three cycles of the Buddha's teachings to their intended audiences. Those who are brought to the path of peace are ordinary mortal individuals who enter the spiritual path, for whom the first cycle of teachings (dealing with the four truths) is most appropriate. Those who are brought to complete spiritual maturity are spiritually advanced beings (Tib. *'phags pa*; Skt. *ārya*)—that is, those who attain the path of seeing as defined in the particular Buddhist approach they are following—toward whom the intermediate cycle (dealing with emptiness) is geared. Those for whom prophecies are uttered are bodhisattvas on the eighth spiritual level (the prophecies concern their imminent attainment of buddhahood), for whom the third cycle (dealing with a thorough and precise analysis of reality) is most relevant.

121. The "definitive state of excellence" (Tib. *nges legs*; Skt. *niḥśreyasa*) is a term for the state of enlightenment, as defined by any of the three spiritual approaches—of the śrāvaka, the pratyekabuddha, or the bodhisattva.
122. In the śrāvaka and pratyekabuddha approaches, the Sanskrit term *nirvāṇa* signifies the individual's personal release from suffering, with the result being the state of quiescence experienced by an arhat; from the Mahāyāna perspective, this is seen as the

extreme of personal salvation—a static state in which one lacks the capability to benefit others. The Mahāyāna definition of nirvāṇa is that of a transcendence of either of two extremes—that of continued bondage to the conditioned state of saṃsāra, and that of mere personal salvation.

123. That is, the *śāstras*, or treatises, composed by masters of the Indian Buddhist tradition.

124. Skt. *ārya*; Tib. *'phags pa*. These are practitioners who have attained the path of seeing according to any of the Buddhist models of śrāvaka, pratyekabuddha, or bodhisattva.

125. *Definitive Commentary on Enlightened Intent*, (Toh. 106), Dg. K., mDo sde, vol. Ca, p. 48, l. 5 to p. 49, l. 4. The speaker is the bodhisattva Paramārthasamudgata, who is addressing the Buddha.

126. These are the "three avenues to complete liberation." Concerning these, see Longchen Rabjam, *The Precious Treasury of Philosophical Systems*, 145:

> Of the three avenues to complete liberation that concern the knowable, emptiness is the nonexistence of a self; the absence of characteristics is the nonexistence of anything the self takes to be its own; and the absence of speculation is a nonreferential state. In terms of the path, of the three avenues to complete liberation, emptiness is the truth of cessation; the absence of characteristics is the truth of the path; and the absence of speculation constitutes the truths of suffering and its universal origin. In terms of the fruition, of the three avenues to liberation, emptiness and the absence of characteristics pertain to the state in which there are no residual traces, whereas the absence of speculation pertains to the state that still involves residual traces.

127. That is, the third cycle, which presents a thorough and precise analysis of reality.

128. The *Discourse Requested by Dhāraṇīśvararāja* is mentioned in Roerich, *The Blue Annals*, Book 2, 459. The title may refer to a section within a larger sūtra, the *Discourse That Definitively Presents the Supreme Compassion of the Tathāgatas*, (Toh. 147), Dg. K. mDo sde, vol. Pa, ff. 142a–242b; or it may be an alternative title for this sūtra. The passage cited by Kongtrul is worded somewhat differently in the source, although identical in substance:

> O children of spiritual heritage, it is thus: Suppose, for example, that someone extremely skilled in the procedures for the refining of gemstones should take from among such stones one that has not yet been refined. He washes it in water heavily infused with sodium chloride and polishes it with a piece of black felt, thus polishing it. But he does not stop his diligent industry simply at this point, for following that he washes it in a strong solution of mercury and polishes it with a piece of serge, thus polishing it. But he does not stop his diligent industry simply at this point, for following that he washes it in a powerful medicinal solution and polishes it with a finely woven cloth, thus polishing it. Once it is polished and free of kinds of flaws in a gem, it can then be called a gemstone.
>
> O children of spiritual heritage, in a similar way the Tathāgata, being aware of the totally impure condition of ordinary beings, uses talk that arouses dissatisfaction—of impermanence, suffering, the nonexistence of identity, and unattractiveness—to cause those beings who take overt delight in saṃsāra to be dissatisfied with it, and to cause them to embrace the discipline that is the dharma of spiritually advanced beings. But the Tathāgata does not stop his

> diligent industry simply at this point, for following that he uses talk of emptiness, and the nonexistence of subtle traits, and the absence of speculation to cause them to master internally the ways of the tathāgatas. But once more the Tathāgata does not stop his diligent industry simply at this point, for following that he uses talk that constitutes the cycle of nonregression and talk of the complete purity of the three focal points to cause these ordinary beings to engage in the scope of the tathāgatas. These ordinary beings, whose origins and temperaments are so various, embrace this together, internally master the true nature of the tathāgatas, and so are known as those who are unsurpassable as sources worthy of honor.

129. Specifically, the authors of the *śāstras* of the Indian Buddhist tradition.
130. That is, the sūtras of definitive meaning, especially those concerning buddha nature.
131. That is, the third and final cycle of the Buddha's teachings.
132. That is, the certainty that they will attain complete enlightenment. The prophecy referred to is conferred by a buddha on a highly realized bodhisattva to indicate that the attainment of buddhahood is imminent.
133. See Asaṅga, *Synopsis of the Definitive Conclusion concerning the Levels of Yogic Practitioners*, (Toh. 4038), Dg. T., Sems tsam, vol. Zi, p. 131, lines 1–3 (citing the same passage from *Definitive Commentary on Enlightened Intent* that Kongtrul cited earlier):

> This cycle is exceedingly amazing and marvelous; this wheel of dharma that you turned, O transcendent and accomplished conqueror, is unsurpassable, is not for the shorter term, is definitive in meaning, and is not a context that is open to debate.

134. According to Tibetan tradition, Vasubandhu was the younger brother of Asaṅga, who converted Vasubandhu from a Vaibhāṣika point of view to Asaṅga's own Yogācāra perspective.
135. Vasubandhu, *Reasoning for a Detailed Explanation*, (Toh. 4061), Dg. T., Sems tsam, vol. Shi, pp. 57–268. The commentary referred to is probably Guṇamati, *Explanation of "Reasoning for a Detailed Explanation,"* (Toh. 4069), Dg. T., Sems tsam, vol. Si, pp. 278–601. I have not located the actual passages to which Kongtrul refers.
136. I have not located this source. The Sumatran master Dharmapāla was one of the primary sources for Atīśa's teachings on the arousal and deveopment of bodhicitta.
137. Although Kongtrul makes this statement with confidence, he is making an oblique reference to the fact that it has traditionally been the case that the Gelukpa (or Gedenpa) school has considered the intermediate cycles of the Buddha's teachings to be definitive in meaning and the final cycle to be more provisional. While the issue of definitive vis-à-vis provisional is not as key in the Kagyü school, for example, both this school and the Nyingma tend to regard the intermediate cycle as being definitive in the shorter-term context of the spiritual path and the development of authentic view, while the final cycle is definitive in the more far-reaching sense that concerns the practice of meditation and the fruition state.
138. That is, the five treatises of Maitreya.
139. That is, Candrakīrti.
140. See Candrakīrti, *Clear Words*, (Toh. 3860), Dg. T., dBu ma, vol. 'A, p. 26, l. 4 to p. 27, l. 2, which contains the same passage from the *Discourse Taught by Akṣayamati* that

Kongtrul cites earlier in this part. *Clear Words* is Candrakīrti's commentary on the actual text of Nāgārjuna's *Source Verses on Sublime Intelligence*; in his own commentary to his *Entrance to the Middle Way* (a commentary on the meaning of Nāgārjuna's *Source Verses*), Candrakīrti simply states that the sūtra "discusses this topic in greater detail." *Explanation of "Entrance to the Middle Way,"* (Toh. 3862), Dg. T., dBu ma, vol. 'A, p. 564, l. 6.

141. That is, in the first part of Book 7.

142. That is, the first seven topics of (1) engagement with the fruition state, (2) ultimate reality, (3) the totally pure state of total enlightenment, (4) the exhaustion of karma and afflictive states, (5) the nonduality of saṃsāra and nirvāṇa, (6) the direct perception of profundity that is difficult to assimilate thoroughly, and (7) mind functioning with certainty.

143. That is, the identity of any given phenomenon and the identity of the individual personality.

144. *Definitive Commentary on Enlightened Intent*, (Toh. 106), Dg. K., mDo sde, vol. Ca, p. 26, l. 7. To teach about buddha nature (or even, according to some interpretations, about the basis of all ordinary experience, the eighth avenue of ordinary consciousness) to those who are unprepared may lead to their misinterpreting this to be some identity, or self, or soul.

145. A section of the source text is omitted here, which lists variant theories by non-Buddhist schools on the properties of a supposed self or soul:

> Not that of a grain of millet or a rice kernel or a mustard seed or a sesame seed, nor something red or blue or yellow or white, nor something short or long or very long or the like, nor something that can be said to shine in one's heart region or shine in one's navel region or head or eyes or ears (like the burning heart of the reddish flame of a lamp fueled with oil), nor any other such thing—that is, none of the many concepts that mundane people may entertain in thinking about the self, nor any quality of this being something eternal, something stable, something constant.

146. *Discourse to Benefit Aṅgulimālā*, (Toh. 213), Dg. K., mDo sde, vol. Tsha, p. 302, lines 2–4.

147. A section of the passage is omitted:

> O Mahāmati, the tathāgatas, the arhats, the completely perfect buddhas use such words as "emptiness," "final authentic state," "transcendence of sorrow," "unborn," "absence of subtle traits," "absence of speculation," and so forth, the meaning of which words is to teach concerning the buddha nature. Thus, in order to eliminate the situation of spiritually immature people becoming terrified at having no self-identity, the avenue to the buddha nature is taught, revealing to them a nonconceptual state that is a whole range of experience without ordinary perceptions. But concerning this, O Mahāmati, great and courageous bodhisattvas of the future and those of the present . . .

148. *Journey to Śrī Laṅka*, (Toh. 107), Dg. K., mDo sde, vol. Ca, p. 171, lines 4–7.

149. This term refers to a branch of the Madhyamaka, or Middle Way, school of Buddhist philosophy, whose basic supposition is that phenomena lack any true existence whatsoever. In *Buddhist Philosophy in Theory and Practice*, Herbert V. Guenther refers to

them as "Mādhyamikas who disclaim the existence of anything as such," (130) and notes (223, n. 1):

> This [term] is short for *bden-grub-kyi ngo-bo-nyid med-par smra-ba*. The current rendering is to use the Sanskrit term: *niḥsvabhāvavādin*. This term is usually left untranslated or, if a translation is attempted, it is based on the mistaken assumption that words are understood by their etymology instead of by their use due to stipulation. Moreover, lexical translations have singularly failed to adduce any reason why the Sanskrit term *svabhāva* should be translated into Tibetan as *rang-bzhin* in one case, and as *ngo-bo-(nyid)* in another. The fact that the Tibetan translators of Sanskrit texts thought about what might be intended by the texts which they translated—which lexical translators painstakingly avoid doing—forced them to use different words for one term.... [Here the word is] *ngo-bo-(nyid)* which corresponds to our 'fact' and 'facticity'. The Mādhyamikas did not deny the 'fact' of things, but they denied that this fact was itself something existing as such (*bden-grub*). In other words, they most vigorously eschewed any substantival kind of ontology.

150. The Sanskrit term *Yogācāra* has been translated here as "Yogic Practitioner." The term *yoga* has gained prominence in recent times (and is now accepted as an English word in most dictionaries) but is often misunderstood in its Buddhist context because of the popularity of hatha yoga and other non-Buddhist schools in the modern West. Early Tibetan translators chose an interpretive translation that invites some consideration: *rnal 'byor*, meaning to come into contact with (*'byor ba*) the genuine state of being (*rnal ma*). Any connotation of "union" (as "yoga" is often translated, given that the Sanskrit root (*yuj*) means "to yoke together") is devoid of a sense of union *with* something *other*, such as some godhead or abstract absolute principle; rather, it is mind that is united with its own true nature in a nondual manner. Proponents of the Yogācāra school were obviously not alone among Buddhists in practicing "yoga" (in the sense that the Buddhist tradition understands this term), any more than the Sautrāntikas were the only "followers of the sūtras." In *The Treasury of Knowledge: Book Six, Part Three: Frameworks of Buddhist Philosophy*, 176–77, Kongtrul offers the following interesting etymology:

> The *Eight Thousand Stanza Perfection of Wisdom Sūtra* says:
>
> > O sons and daughters of the victors: all these three realms are simply mind (*sems tsam*).
>
> Since they practice correctly bringing to mind the meaning of this quotation as it reflects [the actuality of] things (*dngos po dang mthun pa*), they are also known as Yogācāras.

In her insightful note to this statement, Elizabeth Callahan (ibid., 349, n. 522) states the following:

> Early uses of this term designated Buddhist practitioners in general, but it later came to be associated with the works attributed to Maitreya, Asaṅga, and Vasubandhu, possibly having been derived from the title of Asaṅga's *Yogāchārabhūmi* (*rNal 'byor spyod pa'i sa, Bhūmis of Yogic Practice*).... This

became the most common term in India for followers of the thought of Maitreya, Asaṅga, and Vasubandhu, followed by "Proponents of Consciousness" (*Vijñānavādin, rNam shes smra ba*).

151. That is, the Buddha Śākyamuni.
152. *Discourse of the Great Drum*, (Toh. 222), Dg. K., mDo sde, vol. Dza, p. 214, l. 7 to p. 215, l. 1.
153. That is, Vasubandhu.
154. In the Buddhist tradition, establishing the authenticity of a school of thought, or even of a particular position being put forth, requires both scriptural authority (passages from the teachings of the Buddha, as just presented above) and lines of reasoning based on accepted principles.
155. Cited earlier in this part of Book 7.
156. That is, the third Karmapa, Rangjung Dorjé, Dolpopa Sherab Gyaltsen (Dol po pa Shes rab rgyal mtshan, 1292–1361), and Longchen Rabjam Drimé Özer. These masters are seminal authors in, respectively, the Karma Kagyü, Jonang, and Nyingma schools of the Tibetan Buddhist tradition. In his conclusion to *The Treasury of Knowledge*, Kongtrul acknowledges his debt to these masters as his primary sources in composing his treatise. See *The Treasury of Knowledge: Books Nine and Ten: Journey and Goal*, 463.
157. That is, of the first cycle of teaching being primarily provisional in meaning, with the intermediate and final cycles being equally definitive (with the proviso that the intermediate cycle is more concerned with the relatively shorter term of the path, the final cycle more with the far-reaching consequences of the buddha nature that imbues all beings).
158. That is, of the intermediate cycle being consummately definitive and the final cycle primarily provisional. This is primarily an oblique reference to masters of the Gelukpa school.
159. Here this epithet is a reference to the Indian Buddhist master Nāgārjuna.
160. Especially his principal student, Āryadeva.
161. The source text simply reads: "all dogmatic opinions . . ."
162. Āryadeva, *Four Hundred Verses*, chap. 8, v. 190, (Toh. 3849), Dg. T., dBu ma, vol. Tsha, p. 18, lines 5–6.
163. That is, the second, or middle cycle, of the Buddha's teachings, with its emphasis on emptiness, negates the naïve assumption of things existing inherently. As useful a step as this is in approaching the direct experience of reality, to remain fixated on the idea that "nothing exists" is an obstacle that must in turn be overcome through the teachings of the final cycle.
164. That is, the definitive meaning of the Buddha's teachings.
165. This model of the three cycles of the Buddha's teachings considers the first to be concerned with undermining what is nonmeritorious, the second with undermining the belief in identity in the individual and in phenomena, and the third with undermining all erroneous views and opinions concerning the true nature of reality.
166. That is, the intermediate and the final cycles, as described in the *Discourse of the Great Drum* and the *Discourse Requested by Dhāraṇīśvararāja*.
167. The distinction made in this section of the commentary (as found, for example, in the writings of the *zhentong* master Dolpopa Sherab Gyaltsen) is between an interpreta-

tion of "emptiness as an exclusion of distinct aspects," which is provisionally useful on the path for eliminating ordinary (and erroneous) concepts, and "emptiness as endowed with the most sublime of all possible manifestations" as described in, for example, the Kālacakra cycle.

168. That is, the third Karmapa, Rangjung Dorjé.

169. That is, Nāgārjuna.

170. Source not identified. The eighth Karmapa, Mikyö Dorjé (Mi bskyod rdo rje, 1507–1554), cites the same passage in his commentary on the *Ornament of Manifest Realization*. The "Collection of Praises" refers to a number of Nāgārjuna's works found in the Tengyur (vol. Ka). For translations of these, see Brunnhölzl, *In Praise of Dharmadhātu*, 117–29 and 313–23. The *Four Hundred Verses* is a work by Nāgārjuna's principal student, Āryadeva, which focuses on the application of the view of the Middle Way in one's conduct.

171. That is, the eighth Karmapa, Mikyö Dorjé, who was noted for his often controversial statements regarding the interpretations of other teachers and schools.

172. Source not identified. The criticism would seem to be leveled against certain (but by no means all) Nyingma teachers and practitioners whose emphasis on devotion to Guru Rinpoché, or Padmākara, eclipsed an appreciation of the Buddha as the original teacher in this present age.

173. That is, the degree to which a given being is capable of understanding a spiritual teaching.

174. Nāgārjuna, *Source Verses on Sublime Intelligence*, chap. 15, v. 7, (Toh. 3824), Dg. T., dBu ma, vol. Tsa, p. 17, l. 1. Kātyāyana was one of the Buddha's principal students following the śrāvaka approach, for whom the teachings of the first cycle were very appropriate. In his own commentary to his source verses, Nāgārjuna refers to a sūtra entitled *Advice to Kātyāyana*, in which the Buddha refutes both existence and nonexistence (*Universal Fearlessness: A Commentary on the "Source Verses on Sublime Intelligence,"* (Toh. 3829), Dg. T., dBu ma, vol. Tsa, p. 121, l. 7); this sūtra (or sutta) is part of the Pāli canon, nowadays the source of teachings for the Theravāda school of Buddhism. In their commentaries on Nāgārjuna's verses, both Buddhapālita (*Buddhapālita: A Commentary on the "Source Verses on Sublime Intelligence,"* (Toh. 3842), Dg. T., dBu ma, vol. Tsa, p. 489, lines 4–5) and Bhāvaviveka (*Lamp of Sublime Intelligence: A Commentary on the "Source Verses on Sublime Intelligence,"* (Toh. 3853), Dg. T., dBu ma, vol. Tsha, p. 319, l. 1) cite a passage (from *Advice to Kātyāyana*) that states:

> O Kātyāyana, this world is caught in two alternatives. The majority are either caught in existence or in nonexistence.

There is a similar passage in the Mahāyāna sūtra *Journey to Śrī Laṅka*, (Toh. 107), Dg. K., mDo sde, vol. Ca, p. 224, l. 6:

> O Mahāmati, those of this world are caught in two alternatives. That is to say, they are caught in existence, or they are caught in nonexistence.

For the Pāli source, see Bhikkhu Bodhi, *The Connected Discourses of the Buddha*, vol. 1, p. 544:

> "This world, Kaccāna [that is, Kātyāyana] for the most part depends upon a duality—upon the notion of existence and the notion of nonexistence. . . .

'All exists': Kaccāna, this is one extreme. 'All does not exist': this is the second extreme. Without veering toward either of these extremes, the Tathāgata teaches the Dhamma by the middle: . . ."

175. The term "what merely manifests" (Tib. *snang tsam*) is synonymous with "relative truth" and "provisionally meaningful." It refers to the interpretation found in the Middle Way school of relative truth and the entire range of sensory appearances—that these "merely manifest" within one's perception without having to be assumed to have any autonomous existence in their own right.
176. Nāgārjuna, *Sixty Verses on Reasoning*, v. 35, (Toh. 3825), Dg. T., dBu ma, vol. Tsa, p. 42, l. 5. The last two lines of the source text itself read somewhat differently, although with the same meaning:

    At that point, would anyone who is wise think
    that everything else is not false?

    But in his commentary to Nāgārjuna's source, Candrakīrti cites the verse as Kongtrul does here. *Commentary on "Sixty Verses on Reasoning,"* (Toh. 3864), Dg. T., dBu ma, vol. Ya, p. 43, l. 7 to p. 44, l. 1.
177. This is a stock expression encompassing all possible phenomena within saṃsāra and nirvāṇa. "Forms" refers not only to objects of the visual faculty but to all components of one's subjective and objective experiences of the material world, including forms, sounds, odors, tastes, tactile sensations, the physical body, and the sense faculties; the state of omniscience is a synonym for buddhahood, which, according to the intermediate cycle of the Buddha's teachings, is not to be reified as some "thing."
178. What is conditioned (Tib. *'dus byas*; Skt. *saṃskṛta*) is anything produced by causes and conditions other than itself, and dependent on those for its continued "existence," however nominal.
179. Nāgārjuna, *Stages of Meditation*, v. 56, (Toh. 3908), Dg. T., dBu ma, vol. Ki, p. 7, l. 2. In the source, the last line reads: "does not occur in any real sense."
180. See Nāgārjuna, *Commentary on Bodhicitta*, (Toh. 1800), Dg. T., rGyud 'grel, vol. Ngi, p. 76, lines 1–2:

    Thus, bodhisattvas who engage in conduct through the avenue of the secret mantra approach do so by virtue of having aroused bodhicitta as aspiration by nature, using a relative framework, so that the ultimate aspect of bodhicitta will be aroused on the strength of their meditation; therefore, I will explain the nature of this. . . .

181. Source not identified.
182. That is, the Buddha Śākyamuni.
183. See Maitreya, *Highest Continuum*, chap. 5, v. 20, (Toh. 4024), Dg. T., Sems tsam, vol. Phi, p. 144, lines 6–7:

    Because there is no one whomsoever in this world wiser than the Victorious One,
    the Omniscient One knows the sublime state of suchness in its entirety, while others do not.
    Therefore, do not misinterpret the sūtras that were set forth by the Seer himself.

> Since this would destroy the way of the Sage, it would also bring harm to the sacred Buddhadharma.

184. That is, the Buddha Śākyamuni.
185. *Reunion of Father and Son*, (Toh. 60), Dg. K., dKon brtsegs (No. 16), vol. Nga, p. 122, lines 4–5. The verse in the source reads quite differently from the version cited by Kongtrul:

> For you, O Wise One of the World, there are two levels of truth;
> you did not hear of these from others, but saw them for yourself.
> They are the relative truth and the ultimate;
> there is not in any sense a third level of truth.

186. Nāgārjuna, *Source Verses on Sublime Intelligence*, chap. 24, v. 8, (Toh. 3824), Dg. T., dBu ma, vol. Tsa, p. 28, l. 7 to p. 29, l. 1.
187. The source text reads: "is the very nature of things."
188. Candrakīrti, *Entrance to the Middle Way*, chap. 6, v. 23, (Toh. 3861), Dg. T., dBu ma, vol. 'A, p. 409, lines 5–6.
189. The Tibetan term *ngo bo* (here rendered as "individual makeup") has different connotations in different contexts. The verse from Candrakīrti's *Entrance to the Middle Way* states that any and all things have "two essences" (*ngo bo gnyis*), but these do not have equal status ontologically. In the relative context, the "essence" of fire is to be hot and to burn, while from the ultimate perspective all phenomena have the same "essence," that of emptiness.
190. The Tibetan term *kun rdzob* (Skt. *saṃvṛti*), translated here as "relative," literally means "everything (*kun*) covered up (*rdzob*)," in the sense that the true nature of things remains inaccessible to one's perceptions on this level. Despite its ultimately deceptive quality, however, this level of our experience does exhibit a kind of internal validity and integrity that allows us to speak in terms of relative "truth."
191. The source text reads: "bewilderment . . ."
192. Ibid., chap. 6, v. 28, (Toh. 3861), Dg. T., dBu ma, vol. 'A, p. 410, lines 1–2.
193. The Tibetan term *don dam (pa)* (Skt. *paramārtha*), translated here as "ultimate," literally means "that which is sublimely (*dam pa*) meaningful (*don*)."
194. The source text reads: "Because bewilderment . . ."
195. Ibid., chap. 6, v. 28a, (Toh. 3861), Dg. T., dBu ma, vol. 'A, p. 410, l. 1.
196. This is synonymous with the term "conditioned," that is, ensured only by the coming together of certain causes and conditions.
197. That is, frameworks of dualistic consciousness. Candrakīrti, *Clear Words*, (Toh. 3860), Dg. T., dBu ma, vol. 'A, p. 325, l. 6.
198. Bhāvaviveka, *Blazing Logic*, (Toh. 3856), Dg. T., dBu ma, vol. Dza, p. 112, lines 3–4. The text in the source reads slightly differently:

> The "relative" is so termed due to its function of thoroughly differentiating all things—forms and so forth.

199. Haribhadra, *Illumination of the "Ornament of Manifest Realization": An Explanation of the Exalted Treatise on the Transcendent Perfection of Sublime Intelligence in Eight Thousand Verses*, (Toh. 3791), Dg. T., Śes phyin, vol. Cha, p. 474, l. 1.

200. This aspect of ultimate truth is an "approximation" of what is actually ultimate, which is termed the "unquantifiable" aspect.

201. In his *Source Verses on Differentiating the Two Levels of Truth*, v. 9ab, (Toh. 3881), Dg. T., dBu ma, vol. Sa, p. 3, l. 2, Jñānagarbha uses the term "parallel":

> The refutation of origination and so forth
> is held to be authentic [that is, ultimate] because of being parallel to it.

202. That is, the "unquantifiable aspect" of ultimate truth. Concerning these two aspects of ultimate truth, Longchen Rabjam (*The Precious Treasury of Philosophical Systems*, 103–4) makes the following statement:

> As for what is ultimate, this also has two aspects. There is a quantifiable aspect of the ultimate; this aspect entails the simple negation of production and so forth in any true sense, but other than that, it does not entail freedom from the conceptual elaboration of nonproduction. The unquantifiable aspect of the ultimate is a freedom from absolutely all elaboration such as production and nonproduction.

This distinction concerning ultimate truth dates back to the early development of Madhyamaka thought in Buddhist India, with the master Bhāvaviveka (also known as Bhavya):

> Bhāvaviveka (*Legs ldan 'byed pa*) (sixth century) was the Mādhyamika master retrospectively considered to be the originator of the Svātantrika-Madhyamaka school, said to have been the abbot of fifty monasteries in the region of Dhānyakaṭa, in South India. He excelled in debate and was the first to use the dialectical methods developed by Dignāga in a Madhyamaka context, which are found in his *Lamp of Wisdom*. He is also considered the first to make the distinction between a "nominal ultimate" (*paryāyaparamārtha, rnam grangs pa'i don dam*) and "non-nominal ultimate" (*aparyāyaparamārtha, rnam grangs ma yin pa'i don dam*), as found in his *Summary of the Meaning of the Middle Way* (*Madhyamakārthasaṃgraha, dBu ma'i don bsdus pa*). (Kongtrul, *The Treasury of Knowledge: Book Six, Part Three: Frameworks of Buddhist Philosophy*, 380, n. 694)

> The primary source for the twofold presentation of the ultimate seems to be Bhāvaviveka's *Summary of the Meaning of Madhyamaka* (*Madhyamakārthasaṃgraha, dBu ma'i don bsdus pa*) and the third chapter of his *Blaze of Reasoning*, in which texts he uses the terms "nominal ultimate" (*paryāyaparamārtha, rnam grangs pa'i don dam*) and "non-nominal ultimate" (*aparyāyaparamārtha, rnam grangs ma yin pa'i don dam*). (Kongtrul, *The Treasury of Knowledge: Book Six, Part Three: Frameworks of Buddhist Philosophy*, 383, n. 714)

Bhāvaviveka's treatment of ultimate truth was as follows:

> Bhavya considered the important objection that since the ultimate truth transcends the discursive intellect, it follows that no verbal formulation can possibly express it. How therefore is it possible even to talk about the two truths, distinguishing ultimate truth in opposition to the relative? If the ultimate cannot be talked about, how can it be distinguished from anything at all? In

> response, Bhavya draws a distinction between two kinds of ultimate truth. On the one hand, he says, there is the ultimate that is "world-transcending" (*'jig rten las 'das pa*). This is the ultimate truth in itself, the completely ineffable state beyond conceptual elaboration, which can only be experienced but never expressed. On the other hand, there is an ultimate that Bhavya describes as "pure worldly wisdom" (*dag pa 'jig rten pa'i ye shes*), which, in the context of the division of the two truths, is the counterpart of the relative and is the object of thought and word. It is "the ultimate that can be talked about." These expressions run parallel to another, better-known distinction, which first appears in another text also attributed to Bhavya, between the "ultimate truth in itself" (*rnam grangs ma yin pa'i don dam*) and the "approximate ultimate" (*rnam grangs pa'i don dam*) or "concordant ultimate" (*mthun pa'i don dam*). (Padmakara Translation Group, *The Adornment of the Middle Way*, 11–12)

Rather than being an invention by Bhāvaviveka and his followers, this distinction would seem to have been presaged in the sūtras of the Buddha himself:

> In his commentary on *The Ornament of the Middle Way* (a Svātantrika-oriented treatise by the Indian master Shantarakshita), Mipam Rinpoche notes, "The sūtras sometimes teach the inconceivable and inexpressible uncategorized ultimate [i.e., *rnam grangs ma yin pa'i don dam*], free from all extremes of existence, nonexistence, and so forth. At other times, their teaching is 'no form, no consciousness', the categorized ultimate's [i.e., *rnam grangs pa'i don dam*] mere existential negation." (Doctor, *Speech of Delight*, 151)

203. Concerning this distinction between two aspects of ultimate truth, Longchen Rabjam notes in *The Precious Treasury of Philosophical Systems*, 104–5:

> Proponents of the Madhyamaka approach give the following analysis: Using the negation of one part of a conceptual elaboration as their rationale, they apply the term "quantifiable ultimate truth" to what is, in fact, ultimate truth as a particular aspect of relative truth—that is, nonproduction [i.e., the negation of production].
>
> They apply the term "unquantifiable ultimate truth" to the simple transcendence, in the ultimate sphere, of all such elaborations, since these cannot in any way be established in light of their fundamentally unconditioned nature. Nevertheless, the Madhyamikas say that given this "freedom from all conceptual elaborations," nothing can possibly be defined as some ultimate thing in its own right.

204. The awareness referred to here is the timeless awareness experienced in formal meditation by spiritually advanced beings.

205. Regarding Patsap Lotsawa Nyima Drakpa (Pa tshab Lo tsa ba Nyi ma grags pa, b. 1055), see Ringu Tulku, *The Ri-me Philosophy of Jamgön Kongtrul the Great*, 71:

> The view of Prasangika Madhyamaka is the main view of all the schools of Tibetan Buddhism. It was firmly established in Tibet through the teaching of Patsap Lotsawa Nyima Dragpa, who lived in the eleventh century. Patsap went to Kashmir and studied with the two sons of Sajjana for twenty-three

years. While there, he translated Wisdom, a Root Text on the Middle Way [i.e., Nāgārjuna's *Source Verses on Sublime Intelligence*], the *Entrance to the Middle Way* [of Candrakīrti], the *Four Hundred Verses* [of Āryadeva], Chandrakirti's commentaries, and other Prasangika texts into Tibetan.

Patsap had four main students: Gangpa Sheu, who was learned in the words; Tsangpa Dregur, who was learned in the meaning; Mabja Jangtsön [i.e., Mabja Jangchub Tsöndrü, d. 1185], who was learned in both the words and the meaning; and Shangthang Sagpa Yeshe Jungne, who was not learned in either. They and their students opened the great way of teaching, debating, and writing based on the texts of Chandrakirti and other masters of Prasangika philosophy. It is important to recognize that all the study of Prasangika Madhyamaka in Tibet started with Patsap and his students.

The writings of Mabja Jangchub Tsöndrü were held in high regard by many Kagyü masters, including the eighth Karmapa, Mikyö Dorjé. His commentary on Nāgārjuna's *Source Verses on Sublime Intelligence* (Tib. *dBu ma rtsa ba shes rab kyi 'grel pa 'thad pa'i rgyan*) has been translated into English; see Dharmachakra Translation Committee, *Ornament of Reason*.

206. Source not identified.
207. That is, unlike many other commentators, Mabja Jangchub Tsöndrü does not consider inferential knowledge based on reasoning to be a state of consciousness based on confusion, even though it pertains to the state of an ordinary mortal individual.
208. Both the woodblock and computerized editions of *The Treasury of Knowledge* read, in error, "another name" (*gzhan ming*); the source reads "nothing other" (*gzhan min*).
209. Maitreya, *Distinguishing Center and Limit*, chap. 1, vv. 14–15a, (Toh. 4021), Dg. T., Sems tsam, vol. Phi, p. 81, l. 2. In his commentary on this source, Sthiramati makes reference to an earlier commentary by Vasubandhu in discussing verses 15 and 16 as follows (Sthiramati, *Explanatory Commentary on "Distinguishing Center and Limit,"* (Toh. 4032), Dg. T., Sems tsam, vol. Bi, p. 426, l. 1 to p. 427, l. 5):

The source text describes the synonyms as follows:

> As for emptiness, in brief
> suchness, the final authentic state,
> the absence of subtle traits, the ultimate,
> and the basic space of phenomena are its synonyms.

The term "synonym" refers to different words having the same meaning. . . . These expressions are used in other contexts in the sūtras to mean "emptiness." Since these five synonyms are the most important, I will not discuss any other synonyms, but confine myself to those spoken of in the foregoing verse. Nevertheless, in order for one to be fully conversant with the Buddha's excellent speech, other synonyms are as follows: the nondual state, nonconceptual basic space, the true nature of phenomena, ineffability, the unceasing state, the unconditioned, the transcendence of sorrow, and so forth.

If one wonders how the meanings of these synonyms are to be understood, that can be demonstrated; for these terms are not arbitrary, but are "imbued with meaning." As the source states:

Because it is nothing other, is unerring,
is cessation, is the domain of spiritually advanced beings,
and is the cause of the qualities of the spiritually advanced,
these are the respective meanings of the synonyms.

In this regard:

(1) [Vasubandhu's commentary says] "because it is nothing other, it is 'suchness itself,'" which is equivalent to saying, "The meaning is that it is unchanging." In order to demonstrate that, [Vasubandhu's commentary says] "because it is always just as it is"; since it is always and under all circumstances unconditioned, this is equivalent to saying "it is unchanging."

(2) [Vasubandhu's commentary says] "because it is unerring, it is 'the final authentic state.'" To say "authentic" is the equivalent of saying "true" or "unmistaken." The word "final" here means "without any limiting alternative"; because there is nothing else to be known beyond this, it is "the final authentic state," which is to say "the final limit of reality." One might ask, "How is it that what is termed 'suchness' could be called a 'limit'? Because it is the domain of timeless awareness, which is purified of the cognitive obscurations. [Vasubandhu's commentary says] "because it is unerring"; this means "because it involves neither naïve affirmation nor denial." In speaking of it being a cause, [Vasubandhu's commentary says] "because it is not the basis for anything erroneous." What is erroneous is ordinary conceptual thought; and since this is not the framework for ordinary conceptual thought, it is unerring.

(3) [Vasubandhu's commentary says] "because subtle traits have ceased, it is 'the absence of subtle traits.'" Here the absence of subtle traits means the cessation of subtle traits. In order to present this point emphatically, [Vasubandhu's commentary] here says "because *all* subtle traits are absent." Since the emptiness of all subtle traits of being conditioned or unconditioned is empty, it is said to be "the absence of subtle traits." Because all subtle traits are absent, there is the absence of subtle traits; the very fact that there are no subtle traits constitutes the absence of subtle traits.

(4) [Vasubandhu's commentary says] "because it is the domain of the timeless awareness of spiritually advanced beings, it is 'the ultimate.'" The term "ultimate" in this case means timeless awareness that transcends the mundane sphere; the significance of that awareness is what is ultimate.

(5) [Vasubandhu's commentary says] "since it is the cause of the qualities of spiritually advanced beings, it is 'the basic space of phenomena.'" In this context the word "phenomena" means the qualities of the spiritually advanced. It refers to authentic view and so forth, to authentic and complete freedom, and to all that pertains to timeless awareness. Since it is the cause of these, it is basic space. In order to demonstrate that point, [Vasubandhu's commentary says] "because the qualities of the spiritually advanced come about with this as their frame of reference." The term "realm" [as a synonym for "basic space"] is used also here, meaning that it upholds its own characteristics and its function of serving as a causal factor. Therefore, here [Vasubandhu's commentary says] "the meaning of basic space is that of a causal factor."

210. "[Vasubandhu] had four students who were more learned than himself: Sthiramati, who was more learned in Abhidharma; Dignāga, who was more learned in Pramāṇa; Guṇaprabha, who was more learned in the Vinaya; and Arya Vimuktisena, who was more learned in Prajñāpāramitā." Rigpa Shedra Wiki, http://www.rigpawiki.org/index.php?title=Vasubandhu. Vimuktisena composed two commentaries on Maitreya's *Ornament of Manifest Realization* (itself a synthetic commentary on the Prajñāpāramitā sūtras).
211. See, for example, Candrakīrti, *Entrance to the Middle Way*, chap. 6, vv. 222–3, (Toh. 3861), Dg. T., dBu ma, vol. 'A, p. 429, lines 1–2:

> Whether buddhas appear
> or whether they do not, in actuality
> there is the emptiness of all things,
> renowned as "alternate reality."
>
> "Furthest limit of authenticity" and "suchness itself"—
> such is the emptiness of things.
> In the tradition of the transcendent perfection of sublime intelligence,
> these are the terms that are renowned.

212. Source not identified.
213. Nāgārjuna, *Source Verses on Sublime Intelligence*, chap. 24, v. 8cd, (Toh. 3824), Dg. T., dBu ma, vol. Tsa, p. 28, l. 7 to p. 29, l. 1.
214. That is, one cannot experience it from the perspective of what is ultimately true.
215. That is, earth, water, fire, and air, of which the material world is composed.
216. Ordinarily, things that are impermanent are productive of suffering and thus are part of a state of confusion.
217. Tib. *gzugs sku*; Skt. *rūpakāya*. That is, sambhogakāya and nirmāṇakāya.
218. The Autonomists divide what is relative into two kinds, valid and invalid, the former being things that can be established to perform functions due to their specific characteristics. The Consequentialists make no distinction on the relative level; for them, whatever is relative is of necessity a state of confusion. See Kongtrul, *The Treasury of Knowledge: Book Six, Part Three: Frameworks of Buddhist Philosophy*, 212 and 215:

> Both Prāsaṅgikas and Svātantrikas discuss the two truths. They do not disagree in the slightest way about ultimate reality (as was just mentioned), because if they were to, it would follow that one of them would not be Mādhyamikas, since the abiding nature of things is not multiple. . . .
>
> . . . In the context of the ground, some points of difference are that Prāsaṅgikas do not assert that conventional [reality] is classified as either correct or mistaken, true or false, whereas Svātantrikas do. Prāsaṅgikas assert that all objects are false and all states of minds (*blo*) are deluded, whereas Svātantrikas do not.

See also *The Precious Treasury of Philosophical Systems*, 103 and 427, n. 274:

> That is, what is valid on the relative level comprises phenomena such as forms and so forth that are endowed with four characteristics: they are capable of performing functions according to the way they manifest, they come about from causes, they cannot bear up under mental examination, and they mani-

fest according to their respective types. They "exist" in that they have the ability to perform a function. What is erroneous on the relative level comprises those sensory appearances that manifest but are incapable of performing a function, such as the optical illusion of a hair falling across one's field of vision or the appearance of a double moon. The Svatantrikas hold that these erroneous sensory appearances can be distinguished from valid phenomena on the basis of their inability to perform a function. . . .

Valid relative phenomena do not "bear up under mental examination" in the sense that if they are examined as to their true nature, they prove to be empty and thus without any independent nature; if they are not so examined, they appear to manifest in a straightforward way. An example of something manifesting according to its type is a barley plant growing from a barley seed.

219. Śāntideva, *Engaging in the Conduct of a Bodhisattva*, chap. 9 . v. 8a, (Toh. 3871), Dg. T., dBu ma, vol. La, p. 61, l. 4.
220. Candrakīrti, *Entrance to the Middle Way*, chap. 6, v. 160ab, (Toh. 3861), Dg. T., dBu ma, vol. 'A, p. 423, lines 3–4. The lines are referring to the famous example of a chariot which, when subjected to a seven-step analysis, is found not to exist as such. The seven steps are summarized earlier in verse 151:

Similarly, a chariot cannot be held to be something other than its
components,
nor something not "other" [that is, the same], nor something that possesses
them,
nor something that depends on them, nor something on which they depend,
nor their mere concatenation, nor their shape.

221. The path of no more training is the fifth of five consecutive phases that make up the entire spiritual path according to the various Buddhist models; in the śrāvaka approach this corresponds to the level of an arhat. The spiritually advanced levels of the Mahāyāna approach of the bodhisattva are those that fall within the third and fourth paths, those of seeing and meditation. Kongtrul discusses these paths in Book 9, Part 1 of *The Treasury of Knowledge*; see *The Treasury of Knowledge: Books Nine and Ten: Journey and Goal*, pp. 63–105.
222. The term "knowledge based on reasoning" (Tib. *rigs shes*) can refer either to the situation of an ordinary mortal individual or to that of a spiritually advanced being. In the former case, it is a form of correct inferential knowledge, while in the latter case, it is knowledge based on direct experience but informed by reasoning.
223. Source not identified. The *Amassing of the Rare and Sublime* is an entire section of the Kangyur collection, comprising forty-nine separate sūtras in six volumes.
224. This is almost certainly a reference to Bhāvaviveka's *Summary of the Meaning of the Middle Way*, (Toh. 3857), Dg. T., dBu ma, vol. 'A, p. 658, l. 4 to p. 659, l. 3. This treatise is an extremely short work on the two levels of truth in forty-nine lines of verse. Lines 10 to 15 (p. 658, l. 6) read as follows:

Truth is subsumed in two levels:
ultimate and relative.
The meaning of what is ultimate is that of a freedom from
conceptual elaboration.

> That, moreover, can be considered to have two aspects—
> the quantifiable aspect of the ultimate
> and the unquantifiable aspect of the ultimate.

225. Here Kongtrul, consciously or otherwise, is paraphrasing Longchen Rabjam; see n. 204.
226. That is, the term "what is ultimate" refers to the fact that what is relative cannot stand up under investigation as being something that exists inherently. Other than this fact, there does not exist some "thing" that is the ultimate, or ultimate truth.
227. Both the computerized and woodblock editions of *The Treasury of Knowledge* read, in error, "fixation on truth" (*bden 'dzin*), which should read "two levels of truth" (*bden gnyis*).
228. Specifically the Consequentialist, or Prāsaṅgika, branch of the Middle Way school.
229. *Chapter Entitled "Heart Essence of the Speech of All Buddhas" from the Exalted and Precious Discourse on the Journey to Śrī Laṅka*, (Toh. 108), Dg. K., mDo sde, vol. Ca, p. 475, l. 4. This sūtra is actually a separate text from the *Journey to Śrī Laṅka*; in the source text, the last two lines read somewhat differently from the version cited by Kongtrul:

    > Imputations are explained as being the relative;
    > the stoppage of that is the domain of the spiritually advanced.

230. *Reunion of Father and Son*, (Toh. 60), Dg. K., dKon brtsegs (No. 16), vol. Nga, p. 120, l. 4. The source reads: "—the relative and the ultimate."
231. Source not identified.
232. Tib. *'du byed*; Skt. *saṃskāra*. These are literally "formative factors," here meaning modes of ordinary perception and thinking that "form" our impression of the relative level of experience.
233. *Definitive Commentary on Enlightened Intent*, (Toh. 106), Dg. K., mDo sde, vol. Ca, p. 18, lines 1–2.
234. In this context, those of the Particularist (Skt. *Vaibhāṣika*) school of Buddhist philosophy.
235. Vasubandhu, *Treasury of Abhidharma*, chap. 6, v. 4, (Toh. 4089), Dg. T., mNgon pa, vol. Ku, p. 36, lines 6–7. In his autocommentary to the verse cited, Vasubandhu gives the following explanation (Vasubandhu, *Explanation of the "Treasury of Abhidharma,"* chap. 6, (Toh. 4090), Dg. T., mNgon pa, vol. Khu, p. 13, l. 7 to p. 14, l. 5):

    > The transcendent and accomplished conqueror spoke of the "four truths;" he also spoke of the "two levels" of relative truth and ultimate truth. If one asks what the characteristics of these two are, [the source verse states]:
    >
    > > Whatever can be dismantled or mentally dissected
    > > such that the mind no longer entertains a concept—
    > > such as a vase or water—exists on the relative level;
    > > Anything else exists on the ultimate level.
    >
    > Whatever can be dismantled down to its components, such that the mind no longer entertains a concept of it, exists on the relative level. An example is that of something like a vase; if it is shattered into pieces, the mind no longer entertains the idea of "vase." Whatever can be mentally dissected, eliminating

extraneous factors, such that the mind no longer entertains a concept of it, that too is something that exists on the relative level. One must gain a thorough understanding of this. An example is that of water; that is to say, if the mind eliminates such factors as its form, the mind no longer entertains the idea of "water." These are entirely cases of things that are assigned labels on the relative level, but due to the circumstances of that relative level it is also entirely valid to say "Vases and water exist." Given that these are not false statements, this is relative truth.

Other than that, is what is ultimately true: anything that, even if one attempts to dismantle it, remains entirely something with which the mind still can engage; or anything that, once extraneous factors have been eliminated, remains something with which the mind still can engage. These things exist on the ultimate level. An example is something like a material form; that is to say, whether it is dismantled down to minute particles, or the mind has eliminated extraneous factors such as its taste, there remains the nature of "form" with which the mind still can engage. One should regard sensations and the rest [of the mind-body aggregates] in a similar way. Because these exist on the ultimate level, they constitute "ultimate truth."

Masters in the past stated, "Whatever is constitutes a transcendent state of consciousness, or whatever is perceived by a mundane state in the wake of such a consciousness, that is ultimately true. Whatever is perceived other than that is relatively true."

236. "What [the Vaibhāṣikas] say actually exists, are partless things. So in terms of matter, it is the fundamental particle of matter that cannot be divided any further and in terms of mind, it is the tiniest moment of mind that is indivisible. These two things, since they are indivisible, truly exist, according to the Particularist school. They argue that you have to have these things existing because they are the building blocks of everything else." Gyamtso, *The Two Truths*, 7.

237. Dharmakīrti, *Detailed Commentary on Valid Cognition*, chap. 3, v. 3, (Toh. 4210), Dg. T., Tshad ma, vol. Ce, p. 236, lines 4–5.

238. "The Sutra school divides apparent relative reality from genuine ultimate reality, by distinguishing between what is a mere abstraction; what has only general characteristics, and what is a specifically characterized thing; something that has its own unique characteristics. So a thing having unique characteristics, genuine reality, and genuinely real; these are all synonyms from their perspective. Whereas something that is mere conceptual abstraction, something that has only general characteristics, something that is only apparently real or relatively real, are all synonyms as well. If we define these; what is genuinely real means that it has its own unique characteristics independent of our concepts about whether those characteristics exist or not, the characteristics exist in the thing independent of what we think about it." Gyamtso, *The Two Truths*, 11.

"For example, if we think about a fire, then the actual thing that is there to which we give the name 'fire', is doing something; it has its own unique characteristics, unlike anything else. It is a unique object and it is performing the function of being hot and burning. . . . What actually does something is the fire that's there, that is beyond our names and concepts because whether we think it burns us or not, it's going to burn us.

For example, animals don't have any notion of the name 'fire', but the fire still burns them. We think, 'Oh, we know the name and we can conceive of this thing', but it doesn't matter one way or another in terms of its effect on us or the animal." Gyamtso, *The Two Truths*, 15.

239. See Guenther, *Buddhist Philosophy in Theory and Practice*, 79:

> The objectively given can be listed under six pairs: (1) the two truths [empirically real and ultimately real], . . .
>
> 1) That which irrespective of designation and conceptualization withstands the solvent influence of critical reflection by its very presence has the mark of the ultimately real. Hence, 'particular existent', 'ultimately real', 'being absolutely specific', 'transitory', 'concrete' and 'veridical' are synonymous.
>
> That which exists only conceptually has the mark of the relatively real. Hence, 'subsistent', 'relatively real', 'being general', 'permanent', 'absolute' and 'delusive' are synonymous.

240. This refers to things on the obvious, or coarse, level of perceptual experience, which are compounded of the particles mentioned in the second line. Such coarse things do not exist in ultimate truth, nor do the more subtle particles.

241. The line in the source text reads simply: "minute material particles do not exist."

242. The lines in the source text read:

> perceptions of individual things are like dream images,
> and are experienced . . .

243. Āryadeva, *Anthology on the Heart Essence of Timeless Awareness*, vv. 24–25, (Toh. 3851), Dg. T., dBu ma, vol. Tsha, p. 54, lines 2–3. In the source text, the last two lines read somewhat differently:

> In the approach of the transcendent perfections, for those with oceanic minds,
> this is expounded in the sources for Yogic Practitioners.

244. These three principles are general tenets of the Cittamātra school. Concerning the first principle, that of imputation, Longchen Rabjam states the following:

> Imputation is here defined as the mind assigning and describing things in terms of categories. If we analyze this, we find that there is "purely theoretical imputation," which concerns things that may be perceived clearly but are nonexistent (like the image of two moons, which is nonexistent in actuality yet can be described in conventional terms), as well as things such as "identity."
>
> In addition, there is "imputation involving categories," which includes all manner of systematic and detailed analyses, and all that can be labeled in terms of letters, words, and phrases. These ways of analyzing things—beginning with categories such as words and their underlying meaning, or the expressions of meaning and the meaning thus expressed, up to and including categories such as the mind-body aggregates, the components of perception, and so forth—are conceptual elaborations imposed by the ordinary mind. They are thus imputed, in that they serve as means to bring about understand-

ing, without there necessarily being any connection between them and the objects being analyzed. Longchen Rabjam, *The Precious Treasury of Philosophical Systems*, 83.

For the Chittamatrins, imputation is a purely adventitious process. Something that they say is "imputed" does not exist before a conceptual label is applied to it; in fact, it does not exist at all, even on the level of conventional designations, let alone on the ultimate level. Ibid., 418, n. 163.

245. According to Longchen Rabjam:

> Dependence has two aspects. First, "impure dependence" pertains to the myriad specific manifestations that constitute the animate and inanimate universe, arising because of mind's myriad habit patterns; these manifestations include sense objects, perception, and one's physical embodiment. Here the term "sense objects" refers to the five kinds of objects (visual forms and so forth). "Perception" refers to the eight avenues of consciousness—that is, consciousness that is established as fields for sensory experience as a result of other conditions. "Physical embodiment" refers to the mind-body aggregates that perpetuate saṃsāra. These manifestations are classified as dependent by virtue of the fact that they are dependent on other conditions, namely, karma and habit patterns.
>
> Second, "pure dependence" pertains to utterly pure realms of experience, aspects of timeless awareness, and so forth. These are considered dependent in that they rely on circumstances that are conditioned by the power of obscurations being purified. Ibid., 83–84.

Dependence pertains to things that are empirically verifiable. Such things are substantially existent and are brought about through causes and conditions other than the things under discussion; they then serve as bases for imputation and are aspects of the basis of all ordinary experience. Ibid., 418, n. 165.

246. Concerning the absolute in the Cittamātra system, Longchen Rabjam notes the following:

> The absolute also has two aspects. First, there is "the unchanging absolute"—that is, the way of abiding, the ultimate ground of all experience, the basic space of phenomena that is utterly lucid by its very nature, "buddha nature." . . . Second, "the unerring absolute" is the incorruptible spiritual path, together with its fruition, because one proceeds authentically and does not regress once the destination has been reached. Ibid., 84 and 86.

The absolute is the true nature of phenomena as it can be confirmed by correct reasoning. It is ultimately real, uncompounded, not imputed, and a pure state of nonconceptual consciousness devoid of dualistic perceptions of object and subject. Ibid., 418, n. 169.

The unchanging absolute corresponds to the basic space of phenomena; the unerring absolute, to timeless awareness. The unerring absolute as "the incorruptible spiritual path" refers to the timeless awareness experienced in meditative equipoise by spiritually advanced beings; some commentators also include the timeless awareness these beings experience in the postmeditation phase. Ibid., 420, n. 182.

247. Source not identified. *Middle Way Overcoming Confusion* is a treatise by Āryadeva, (Toh. 385), Dg. T., dBu ma, vol. Tsha, pp. 24a–26b. The lines cited are not, however, found in this or any other source in the dBu ma section of the Tengyur.
248. See Kongtrul, *The Treasury of Knowledge: Book Six, Part Three: Frameworks of Buddhist Philosophy*, 220–21.
249. This is not a blanket acceptance of any opinions or beliefs held by ordinary mundane people. The term "common sense in the world" (Tib. *'jig rten grags pa*) refers to what is accepted universally by all, without their minds having been influenced by any particular set of cultural values, religious dogma, or other indoctrination such as the identification of objects by name, the observance of processes in the natural world, and so forth.
250. Source not identified.
251. *Discourse Requested by Druma* (chap. 12 of *Reunion of Father and Son*), (Toh. 60), Dg. K., dKon brtsegs (No. 16), vol. Nga, p. 100, l. 1. The lines in the source sūtra read somewhat differently:

    Just as reflections appear
    in an utterly pure mirror
    without having any independent nature,
    O Druma, know phenomena to be just like that.

252. That is, solid objects such as walls or rock faces.
253. That is, without one's entertaining any opinion about sensory appearances, such as whether they exist or not per se.
254. That is, pure sambhogakāya realms that are expressions of the nature of mind that manifest in one's perception as one gains realization.
255. Ratnakīrti, *In Praise of the Deity of Fourfold Union*, lines 127–30, (Toh. 1170), Dg. T., bsTod tshogs, vol. Ka, p. 494, lines 5–6. This is one of the most well-known and often-cited verses in the Tibetan Buddhist tradition. It is almost always referred to as *In Praise of the Mother* and attributed to a "Rāhula" or "Rāhulabhadra," some even identifying the author as the Buddha Śākyamuni's son Rāhulabhadra. In the source text, the last line reads: "I pay homage to and praise the mother of victorious ones of the three times."
256. That is, even the moon that is the source of the reflection does not have true existence; the metaphor is often misunderstood to indicate that while the *reflection* of the moon is a mere manifestation on the relative level, the moon itself somehow represents some absolute "thing" that is ultimate truth.
257. Both the woodblock and computerized editions of the *Treasury of Knowledge* contain errors, reading: "these levels of truth are inseparable—the ultimate state of primordial unity. A mind that has not realized this . . . " The translation here follows the correct version of the text found in the Adzom Chögar woodblock edition of Longchen Rabjam's commentary (see following note).
258. Longchen Rabjam, *Great Chariot: A Commentary on the Great Perfection Treatise "Finding Ease in the Nature of Mind Itself,"* chap. 8 (ADz), p. 698, l. 4 to p. 700, l. 4.

259. Dolpopa Sherab Gyaltsen was the major figure in the development and transmission of the *zhentong* system of teachings in Tibet. For an account of his life and teachings, see Stearns, *The Buddha From Dölpo*.

260. The Sakya master Serdok Paṇchen Shakya Chokden (gSer mdog paṇ chen Śākya mchog ldan, 1428–1507), whose writings are valued by many, particularly in Kagyü circles, as explanations of the perspective of qualified emptiness. The eighth Karmapa, Mikyö Dorjé, used Serdok Panchen's writings as a basis for his commentary on the Prajñāpāramitā teachings (although he criticized both Serdok Panchen's interpretation and that of the Jonang school in his commentary on Candrakīrti's *Entrance to the Middle Way*, which Mikyö Dorjé wrote more from the standpoint of unqualified emptiness).

261. That is, the imputed and the dependent; see the discussion above concerning the Mind Only interpretation of the two levels of truth.

262. That is, the third Karmapa, Rangjung Dorjé.

263. That is, Tāranātha (1575–1634). The Jonang school was noted for its presentation and defense of the interpretation of qualified emptiness.

264. Jñānapāda (also known as Buddhajñāna) was an Indian master whose writings established a system of Vajrayāna teachings, focusing on the *Guhyasamājatantra*, that became widely studied in Tibet as the "tradition of the venerable Jñāna" (Tib. *Ye shes zhabs kyi lugs*). For an account of the life of Buddhajñāna, see Roerich, *The Blue Annals*, 367–72.

265. See, for example, Buddhajñāna, *Sphere of Freedom*, vv. 9–10, (Toh. 1859), Dg. T., rGyud 'grel, vol. Di, p. 93, lines 6–7:

> The process of refinement includes the path of accumulation,
> the path of linkage, the path of seeing,
> the path of meditation, and the paths
> of nonobstruction and the supreme state of total freedom.
>
> The nature of all of these
> is that of a freedom from all forms of elaboration,
> of total purity like that of the realm of space—
> timeless awareness as a profound and lucid nonduality.

And in Buddhajñāna, *Meditation on Suchness in the Two Stages*, (Toh. 1853), Dg. T., rGyud 'grel, vol. Di, p. 5, lines 3–4:

> The nature of phenomena, from forms and so forth
> up to and including the state of omniscience,
> is that of total purity like that of the vault of space—
> timeless awareness as a profound and lucid nonduality.

266. The point of the metaphor, of course, is not to suggest that the ultimate nature of mind is some "thing" with ordinary characteristics, like rope. Longchen Rabjam makes the following remarks concerning the use of metaphor and analogy in the teachings:

> A metaphor illustrates in only a partial way; it is not suitable for illustrating everything. Were it so suited, it would be the underlying meaning and not a metaphor. *The Precious Treasury of the Way of Abiding*, 252.

> Mind itself—naturally occurring timeless awareness—has no substance or characteristics. Since it is empty yet lucid and free of elaboration, it cannot be conceived of as "this" or "that." Although it can be illustrated by a metaphor—"It is like space"—if one reflects on space as the metaphor, it proves to have no color, or shape, or anything about it that is identifiable. Therefore, if the metaphor being used does not refer to some "thing," then the underlying meaning that it illustrates—mind itself, pure by nature—is not something that has ever existed in the slightest. At a certain point, this comes down to understanding space to be a convenient metaphor for what simply cannot be illustrated within a conceptual framework. *A Treasure Trove of Scriptural Transmission*, 54.

> Though awareness is illustrated by this metaphor of space, do not take it literally to mean that awareness is reduced to some state of voidness, because metaphors illustrate things partially, but not entirely. Ibid., 186.

267. "Support" refers to the immeasurable mansion and pure realm of the maṇḍala, corresponding to the inanimate universe; "what is supported" refers to the deities within the maṇḍala, corresponding to the animate universe.
268. This is a citation from Rangjung Dorjé's autocommentary to his *Profound Inner Meaning*.
269. The source tantra reads: "the unstable . . ."
270. *Compendium of the Vajra of Timeless Awareness*, (Toh. 447), Dg. K., rGyud 'bum, vol. Ca, p. 570, lines 6–7. The final line of the passage refers to ultimate truth as a "finality" (*mtha'*, as in "final authentic state," *yang dag pa'i mtha'*) that "abides" in the sense of being a fact that is ever-present, not as "something" abiding "somewhere." See also n. 212.
271. That is, the Buddha Śākyamuni.
272. That is, the approaches of the śrāvaka, pratyekabuddha, and bodhisattva.
273. Jñānagarbha, *Source Verses on Differentiating the Two Levels of Truth*, v. 2, (Toh. 3881), Dg. T., dBu ma, vol. Sa, p. 2, lines 2–3.
274. Nāgārjuna, *Source Verses on Sublime Intelligence*, chap. 24, v. 18, (Toh. 3824), Dg. T., dBu ma, vol. Tsa, p. 29, l. 6.
275. That is, with ultimate reality according to the interpretation of qualified emptiness, as well as the teachings of the Vajrayāna approach and the Mahāmudrā and Dzogchen teachings.
276. That is, that which transcends the domain of the relative level of conventional designations.
277. That is, the ultimate manifesting as the nature of the relative; although what is ultimate cannot by definition be something that manifests, under the circumstances it is said to be manifestly the true nature of what is relative.
278. That is, the light and warmth of the sun.
279. That is, this is not a case of the "thing" that is the seed somehow "becoming" the "thing" that is the seedling.
280. The seed of the banyan, or Indian fig, is extremely tiny; a fully-grown tree can span a number of acres.
281. That is, the twelve links in the process of interdependent connection that constitute the internal aspect of the process by which beings remain bound within the cycle of

saṃsāra. They are: 1) ignorance, 2) formative karmic patterning, 3) consciousness, 4) formation of the mind-body complex, 5) the six sense fields, 6) contact between mind and its objects, 7) sensation, 8) compulsion , 9) perpetuation, 10) the process of becoming involved in conditioned existence, 11) rebirth, and 12) aging and death. The first three links are the factors that propel the mind of a given being toward saṃsāra. The fourth, fifth, sixth, and seventh links are those that constitute the state of the mind having been thus propelled, due to ignorance as the motivating factor, formative patterning as the factors that reinforce karmic tendencies, and ordinary consciousness as the factor that is encumbered with habitual patterns. The eighth, ninth, and tenth links are those that ensure that the process of physical rebirth occurs. The eleventh and twelfth links are those that constitute the actual physical states of rebirth experienced by individual beings. These twelve links are defined and discussed in the following paragraphs.

282. That is, the earth element provides the body's mass and solidity; water, its liquid components; fire, its biological warmth; air, the respiration and circulation; and space the various bodily cavities and orifices.

283. That is, with each component depending on and being depended on by the others.

284. That is, the five sense consciousnesses (visual, auditory, olfactory, gustatory, and tactile) and the coordinating mental function that organizes the sense impressions of the other five avenues and also imagines and creates ideas and concepts.

285. That is, an ordinary being, or a life force, or a life form, or a member of the human race, or a human being (as listed previously).

286. "Sense field" is used here to render the Sanskrit term *āyatana*, which connotes an "abode," or "support." The equivalent Tibetan term (*skye mched*) emphasizes the sense that these are avenues through which experience arises (*skye*) and develops (*mched*).

287. That is, contact between the mind and its objects through the sense faculties.

288. This is a reference to a traditional "list" of synonyms, such as "ordinary being," "life force," "person," "member of the human race," "human being," "agent of actions," "experiencer of feelings." and so forth.

289. Tib. *dri za*; Skt. *gandharva*. That is, the consciousness in the intermediate state after death and prior to rebirth.

290. This is the distance mentioned in the Abhidharma teachings. A *yojana* is a measure of distance, ranging (depending on the source) from about 4 to 10 miles.

291. For example, a human being is not necessarily reborn as a human being.

292. *Journey to Śrī Laṅka*, (Toh. 107), Dg. K., mDo sde, vol. Ca, p. 175, lines 4–5.

293. The source reads: "formative patterning . . ."

294. Nāgārjuna, *Letter to a Friend*, vv. 109–111c, (Toh. 4182), Dg. T., sPriṅ yig, vol. Nge, p. 90, lines 5–7.

295. Ibid., v. 111d, (Toh. 4182), Dg. T., sPriṅ yig, vol. Nge, p. 90, l. 7.

296. Source not identified.

297. Nāgārjuna, *Source Verses on Sublime Intelligence*, chap. 24, v. 40, (Toh. 3824), Dg. T., dBu ma, vol. Tsa, p. 31, lines 4–5.

298. *Verdant Rice Seedling*, (Toh. 210), Dg. K., mDo sde, vol. Tsha. See especially p. 233, l. 7 to p. 245, l. 2; much of Kongtrul's discussion consists of verbatim extracts from this sūtra.

299. Nāgārjuna, *Letter to a Friend*, v. 47c–d, (Toh. 4182), Dg. T., sPriṅ yig, vol. Nge, p. 85, l. 1.

300. "Naïve affirmation" is the belief that things truly exist as they seem; "nihilistic denial" is the belief that nothing exists in any sense, and that there is no process of causality operating on the relative level, which removes the moral underpinnings of one's actions having any consequences.
301. From the perspective of the Madhyamaka school, even followers of lower Buddhist schools of thought (Vaibhāṣika, Sautrāntika, and Cittamātra) are philosophical materialists, in that they accept that certain things have ultimate existence.
302. Nāgārjuna and Asaṅga, who respectively transmitted the lineages known as "the lineage of profound view" (Tib. *zab mo lta brgyud*) and "the lineage of extensive conduct" (Tib. *rgya chen spyod brgyud*).
303. That is, the idea of a "self" or "I" based on the clear impression of the mind-body aggregates. The belief in this self as something with identity that is truly existent is a distorted and counterproductive form of "intelligence" (Tib. *shes rab log pa*).
304. That is, ignorance and the belief in a "self" or "I" that has more than merely nominal validity.
305. That is to say, initially there is ignorance, which is the lack of recognition of the true nature of things. This gives rise to belief in the reality of the "I," which in turn reinforces the ignorance that gave rise to it. This is not, however, a case of the belief *producing* ignorance (like fire producing smoke), for once the false belief in the "I" has been eliminated, there still remains some residual degree of fundamental ignorance.
306. That is, although the belief obscures direct experience of the true nature of things, it does not under the circumstances exert any influence at all on the mind, whether positive or negative.
307. Tib. *bdag*.
308. These are the four truths for spiritually advanced beings—the truth of suffering, of the origin of suffering, of the cessation of suffering, and of the spiritual path leading to that cessation.
309. The reverse, however, is not true, as Kongtrul noted above. Even after the false perception of a self or "I" has been eliminated, a degree of ignorance remains to be eliminated.
310. That is, ignorance is a primary state of mind, of which the belief in identity is an attendant mental event.
311. "Conditioned" (Tib. *'dus byas*; Skt. *saṃskṛta*) implies that something is brought about by, or compounded from, causes and conditions, and hence not some unitary "thing" with an independent status of its own.
312. That is, whether anything in the world external to the individual (the "outer level") or any aspect of the individual's own personal experience (the "inner level").
313. That is, subject to change and degeneration, rather than existing as something with independent status.
314. That is, the act of killing contributes to oneself as the perpetrator being reborn in a hell and undergoing the suffering of that state.
315. These are equivalent terms for saṃsāra and nirvāṇa, respectively. The deeply ingrained afflictive states of mind constitute the first two of the Four Truths (suffering and the all-pervasive origin of suffering); the totally refined state of enlightenment constitutes the latter two truths (the cessation of suffering and the spiritual path to that cessation).
316. According to Buddhist logic, if one accepts that there is a creator of all things, there

is a fundamental incongruity, in that the creator (as the perfect cause) produces both pleasure and pain (as imperfect results). Under all circumstances, there must be congruency between like cause and like result; otherwise the phenomenal world would behave in a completely random manner. In *Entrance to the Middle Way*, chap. 6, v. 14, (Toh. 3861), Dg. T., dBu ma, vol. 'A, p. 408, lines 4–5, Candrakīrti states:

> If it were the case that anything could occur in dependence on anything else,
> well, then, murky darkness could come about from flames,
> and everything could be produced by everything! Why is this so?
> Because even those things that do not produce something would all,
> without exception, be alike in being "other" than it.

317. These three properties are the traditional definition of the identity that non-Buddhists ascribe to the "self," or "soul," and other things, and that Buddhist philosophers argue is not tenable.
318. That is, the approaches of the śrāvaka, pratyekabuddha, and bodhisattva.
319. This is the last of the ten books of *The Treasury of Knowledge*. See Kongtrul, *The Treasury of Knowledge: Books Nine and Ten: Journey and Goal*, 253–451.
320. That is, the Buddha Śākyamuni.
321. In this context, the śrāvaka schools of the Vaibhāṣika and Sautrāntika.
322. The term "endowed with the potential for all manifestation" implies that all positive qualities that pertain to the completely enlightened state of buddhahood are present as naturally occurring attributes.
323. That is, being impermanent, things that act as causes cease in the very moment before the results that are in accordance with those causes come about; for example, the cessation of the seed is immediately followed by the outset of the seedling, for otherwise causes and results would be simultaneously present.
324. There are numerous differing interpretations that fall within the general category of Cittamātra thought. As Kongtrul notes here, some Cittamātra thinkers held that what is dependent (Tib. *gzhan dbang*; Skt. *paratantra*) is truly existent, but the same principle would apply to those who felt that both what is imputed and what is dependent (according to their definitions of these terms) are not truly existent but that the absolute is. In either case, the extremes of naïve affirmation and nihilistic denial would be avoided from the point of view of the respective Cittamātra proponents.
325. Here Kongtrul is referring to those who profess unqualified emptiness (Tib. *rang stong pa*).
326. That is, the "buddha nature" innate in all beings (Tib. *bde bar gshegs pa'i snying po*; Skt. *sugatagarbha*).
327. The issue here hinges on the distinction between phenomena that come about due to causes and conditions that are other than themselves (Tib. *gzhan byung*) and that which is "naturally occurring" (Tib. *rang byung*; Skt. *svayambhū*). The term for qualified emptiness (Tib. *gzhan stong*, literally "empty of other") emphasizes this distinction; since it does not depend on other causes and conditions, buddha nature is naturally occurring, as are its innate qualities, present as natural attributes. Buddha nature is "empty of other" in the sense that it is *empty of* phenomena that come about due to *other* causes and conditions but not empty of what is naturally occurring.
328. "True" (Tib. *bden pa*) in this context means "in accord with what is ultimately true."
329. Mañjughoṣa Narendrakīrti, *Brief Presentation of the Tenets of Buddhist Views*, bsTan

'gyur dpe bsdur ma, vol. 42. This text is not found in the Dergé edition of the Tengyur; it is, however, included in both the Peking (P 4610) and sNar thang editions.

330. That is, all phenomena subsumed within saṃsāra and nirvāṇa.

331. The phrase "what is commonly accepted in the ordinary mundane sphere" (Tib. *'jig rten grags pa*) refers to what "makes sense" in the light of conventional common sense, taking phenomena as they present themselves without examining or investigating them any further. Given that this discussion hinges on the principle of one's conduct in the world, the perspective is that of the relative level of experience.

332. That is, of denying the nominal validity of these phenomena.

333. There are many phenomena associated with the totally refined state of enlightenment that are nevertheless "tainted by causes of confusion," such as various kinds of meditative experiences and visions undergone on the spiritual path.

334. That is, of investing these phenomena with an independent nature, or true existence in and of themselves. This is not the same status as that of the qualities of enlightenment that indwell innately as natural attributes of the true nature of mind.

335. That is, generosity, ethical discipline, patience, enthusiastic diligence, meditative stability, and sublime intelligence.

336. This is one of the five major lines of reasoning employed in the Middle Way school to undermine the naïve tendency of the mind to regard phenomena as truly existing and bring one to an understanding of the way in which things truly abide according to their ultimate nature. For Kongtrul's discussion of these five lines of reasoning, see *The Treasury of Knowledge: Book Six, Part Three: Frameworks of Buddhist Philosophy*, 235–40 (including p. 235 for the line of reasoning in question here). In *The Precious Treasury of Philosophical Systems*, 108–11, Longchen Rabjam (who was one of Kongtrul's major sources in composing *The Treasury of Knowledge*) provides a Nyingma interpretation of these five arguments, including a detailed breakdown of the reasoning that things are free of being either unitary or manifold (109–11). This line of reasoning investigates phenomena from the point of view of what they constitute in essence and demonstrates their emptiness as an avenue of experience that leads one to total liberation.

337. That is, if one concludes that things are empty *because* they are proven to be through reasoning, emptiness then becomes the philosophical equivalent of a hammer that is used to smash a vase into shards, thus "proving" that the vase is empty of any independent nature as "vase." Here the consequence is being mistaken for the underlying reason: the smashing of the vase did not "make" it empty; rather, it could be smashed only because no "thing" called "vase" ever existed as such in the first place.

338. The Tibetan term *yul* is usually used in the sense of the "object" in a dualistic object-subject situation, with the "subject" being termed *yul can* (literally, "possessor of the object"). In the present context of a nondualistic view, for the purposes of discussion, the language used to describe the situation nevertheless refers provisionally to sublime intelligence as a "quasi-subject" (Tib. *yul can*) experiencing emptiness as its "quasi-object," or scope. In actual fact, however, the experience is not one of some "thing" being aware of some other "thing."

339. That is, emptiness as "what is the case" with respect to all things, not some other "thing" that is separate from them.

340. The term translated here as "objects in the phenomenal world" (Tib. *chos can*; Skt. *dharmin*)—rather than the more usual term "phenomena" (Tib. *chos*; Skt. *dharma*)—

is used in context to confine the discussion of the various aspects of emptiness to the perspective of specific situations and aspects within the relative level of truth, rather than that of what is ultimately true. Objects in the phenomenal world include everything that pertains to either the all-consuming afflictive state of saṃsāra or the totally refined state of nirvāṇa.

341. In Buddhist logic, there do exist separate terms for the factor that is to be negated (Tib. *dgag bya*) and that which provides the basis for such negation (Tib. *dgag gzhi*). Certain trends within the Tibetan tradition of Buddhism place great emphasis on distinguishing between these two. They would frame the issue as follows: "A thing like a vase is not empty of being a vase (that is, the basis for the negation); it is empty of any true existence (that is, what is being negated)."

For Kongtrul, however, and those whose writings he takes as his primary sources, there is no need to make such a distinction—in fact, to do so holds no real meaning. The eighth Karmapa, Mikyö Dorjé, whom Kongtrul acknowledges as one of his principal sources in writing *The Treasury of Knowledge* (see Kongtrul, *The Treasury of Knowledge: Books Nine and Ten: Journey and Goal*, 463), used the analogy of gold ore being smelted; what is to be eliminated (the ordinary rock) is eliminated, while what is not to be eliminated (the gold) is what remains. Mikyö Dorjé's stance on unqualified emptiness would be: "The vase is empty of being a vase" (that is, the basis for the negation is also that which is being negated).

342. Traditional examples of such things are the horns of a hare, the child of a barren woman, or a flower growing in the sky. While such things can be imagined, they do not constitute possibilities that are "suitable to be objects of ordinary consciousness."

343. That is, emptiness.

344. Candrakīrti, *Entrance to the Middle Way*, chap. 6, v. 181, (Toh. 3861), Dg. T., dBu ma, vol. 'A, p. 425, l. 7 to p. 426, l. 1.

345. While no analysis is tenable from the point of view of the true nature of phenomena (Tib. *chos nyid*; Skt. *dharmatā*), this analysis is from the perspective of specific aspects of the phenomenal world (Tib. *chos can*; Skt. *dharmin*). The point of such a thoroughgoing analysis is to focus on fundamental components of our total experience in order to eliminate any lingering trace in the mind that there is some "thing" whose true nature is *not* that of emptiness.

346. That is, the true and ultimate nature of phenomena, which can be realized only by nonconceptual timeless awareness. The term "alternate reality' (Tib. *gzhan gyi dngos po*) is specific to the teachings in the Prajñāpāramitā sūtras and the commentaries on these, such as Maitreya's *Ornament of Higher Realization*.

347. Subhūti was one of the ten main students of the Buddha Śākyamuni who were exemplars of the śrāvaka approach; he was considered the most excellent teacher of emptiness, and so figures in the sūtras as a principal interlocutor who requests and receives teachings on emptiness from the Buddha.

348. In the source sūtra, there are two further aspects of emptiness (which are the two components of the final aspect, treated as separate aspects) listed here: "emptiness of what has no substantiality, emptiness of the very essence of things." This brings the number of aspects to eighteen, which is a very common theme developed in the Prajñāpāramitā sūtras.

349. *Transcendent Perfection of Sublime Intelligence in Twenty-Five Thousand Verses*, chap. 15, (Toh. 9), Dg. K., Śes phyin (Nyi khri), vol. Ka, p. 441, l. 7 to p. 442, l. 3.

350. "Internal" refers to the sense faculties (visual, auditory, olfactory, gustatory, tactile, and imaginational) and the physical body that serves as their basis—that is, components of our experience that are imbued with subjective consciousness. The emptiness of these refers to the fact that in none of them is there an iota of anything that exists as a permanent thing, or self, or something with identity that stands on its own.

351. "External" refers to the six kinds of sense objects (forms, sounds, odors, tastes, tactile and kinesthetic sensations, and objects of the imagination), which are inanimate components in our experience, not imbued with consciousness. Again, the emptiness of what is external refers to the fact that in none of them is there anything that truly exists in and of itself.

352. "What is external and internal" refers to the sense faculties and their respective objects. While the mind has the impression that "something exists" within the general situation of a given faculty encountering its object, this is nothing more than a case of one of the six avenues of ordinary consciousness functioning, without there being any substantial "thing." In excluding the physical bases for the senses, Kongtrul is choosing to follow the interpretation found in the writings of the eighth and ninth Karmapas; see Wangchuk Dorje, *The Karmapa's Middle Way*, 462:

> The tradition of the master Haribhadra asserts "outer and inner" as the faculties and their [physical] supports. The explanation found here, however, follows the sūtras.

353. See ibid., 466:

> Other texts, such as *Distinguishing the Middle from the Extremes*, teach that the meaning of that quotation about the emptiness of the great refers to the environment of the world. Here, however, Chandrakīrti teaches in accordance with the *Mother* sūtras.
>
> Beyond the ten directions—all of space—there are no worlds consisting of environments and inhabitants. . . . Therefore, the ten directions are indeed "great."

354. That is, nirvāṇa is the most sublime goal sought by spiritual practitioners and, in fact, that can be sought by any and all beings.

355. These are goal states that pertain particularly to the śrāvaka and pratyekabuddha approaches. See Kongtrul, *The Treasury of Knowledge: Books Nine and Ten: Journey and Goal*, 106–7 and 109. In *The Precious Treasury of Philosophical Systems*, 140–2, Longchen Rabjam discusses these two alternatives in more detail, including the following remarks:

> For arhats who experience residual traces, there remains a slight residue of the truth of suffering (since they have not yet eliminated the mind-body aggregates that perpetuate samsara). . . . As for arhats who experience no such residual traces, it is held that like a fire once its fuel is exhausted, they no longer have physical bodies when they attain nirvana, but their minds enter a realm of cessation, a state of pristine cognition in which ordinary mind has ceased.

356. See Kongtrul, *The Treasury of Knowledge: Books Nine and Ten: Journey and Goal*, 286: "[Nirvāṇa as the natural state is] the suchness of phenomena . . . a state of complete purity by its very nature."

357. See ibid.: "Nonlimited nirvāṇa . . . does not fall into either extreme of conditioned existence or personal salvation."
358. Emptiness of what is conditioned refers to emptiness as the true nature of any and all phenomena within the three realms of saṃsāra. Phenomena that come about due to causes and conditions, and therefore are produced by these, endure as long as they are in place and cease once those causes and conditions no longer pertain. Emptiness of what is unconditioned refers to the fact that, even if one conceives of some unconditioned phenomena—not dependent on causes and conditions and therefore free of being produced, enduring, or ceasing—as being some "thing," no such thing exists.
359. An additional explanation of "what is not to be discarded" is that this refers to the fact that there does not exist, in any ultimate sense, some finite essence of any phenomenon that must not be discarded or eliminated. See Wangchuk Dorje, *The Karmapa's Middle Way*, 470:

> What should not be discarded is not an object of relinquishment and should in no way be abandoned. It is, rather, what should be adopted: the virtue of the two accumulations, such as generosity. Those very things that are not to be discarded are empty of what is not to be discarded. Therefore, this emptiness is called the emptiness of what is not to be discarded.

360. That is, any and every phenomenon of saṃsāra and nirvāṇa, without a single exception.
361. Candrakīrti, *Entrance to the Middle Way*, chap. 6, v. 216ab, (Toh. 3861), Dg. T., dBu ma, vol. 'A, p. 428, l. 5.
362. That is, one (unacceptable) sense of "no frame of reference" could be to say, "There is no elephant on top of this table"; there can be no frame of reference when there is no context to begin with.
363. These are, respectively, the *Transcendent Perfection of Sublime Intelligence in One Hundred Thousand Verses* and the *Transcendent Perfection of Sublime Intelligence in Twenty-Five Thousand Verses*.
364. See, for example, *Transcendent Perfection of Sublime Intelligence in Twenty-Five Thousand Verses*, chap. 15, (Toh. 9), Dg. K., Śes phyin (Nyi khri), vol. Ka, p. 441, l. 7 to p. 442, l. 3.
365. "Substantial" is defined as "capable of performing a function"; this may be either something material and inanimate, or an aspect of consciousness. "Nonsubstantial" means something incapable of performing a function, such as space.
366. Candrakīrti, *Explanation of "Entrance to the Middle Way,"* (Toh. 3862), Dg. T., dBu ma, vol. 'A, p. 648, lines 2–5 (commenting on chap. 6, vv. 221–222b in his own source verses):

> Whether buddhas appear,
> or whether they do not, in actuality
> there is emptiness of all things,
> renowned as "alternate reality."
>
> It is also called the "furthest limit of authenticity" and "suchness itself";
> such is the emptiness of all things.

> As for alternate reality, this is thatness itself as the most sublime state; and its very sublimity is that which is constantly present. In another sense, alternate

reality is the reality that is to be realized by consummate timeless awareness; and that awareness is empty of itself. Furthermore, that which is present in a transcendent context is alternate reality; because this is beyond saṃsāra, it is known as "alternate reality," that is, the furthest limit of authenticity. Since this is not subject to change in any way, it is suchness itself, characterized as emptiness, and emptiness is emptiness as alternate reality.

367. See n. 41.
368. The interpretation of qualified emptiness for the most part employs the Cittamātra model of the three principles—the imputed, the dependent, and the absolute. It is for this reason that the proponents of qualified emptiness can be, and often are, referred to as "Yogic Practitioners" (Yogācāra), but the name needs to be understood in context; it can refer to the Cittamātra school, to the Yogācāra-Svātantrika, or (as Kongtrul uses it here) to the proponents of qualified emptiness, since they all share this model of the three principles in their explanations.
369. Tib. *gzhan gyis stong pa*. This is the etymology for the term *gzhan stong* (pron. *zhentong*; literally, "empty of other"), which I have translated as "qualified emptiness." The idiom "empty of" does not imply total absence or denial, only that while imputed and dependent phenomena can and do arise in one's experience, they do not truly exist as such in the very essence of the absolute. To say here that the basis for negation is empty of the factors to be negated is not like saying that the table is empty of there being an elephant standing on it—that is, that something simply "is not." Rather, it is a case of saying that while things can and do manifest, in doing so they do not therefore exist as such. To claim otherwise would be to invalidate the primordial unity of manifest phenomena and their emptiness ("Form is emptiness, emptiness is form; other than form there is no emptiness, other than emptiness there is no form," as the *Heart Sūtra* puts it). Similarly, to state that the true nature of mind is "empty of" adventitious distortions does not mean that these distortions do not occur, but that even as they occur the nature of mind is unaffected by them.
370. See n. 261.
371. That is, in the case of the individual personality, the perceived object is a seemingly existent "I" or self that is imputed on the basis of the five mind-body aggregates; the perceiving subject is the mind's fixation on that object as though it were something truly existent. In the case of phenomena, the perceived objects are any and all seemingly existent phenomena that are included within the mind-body aggregates; the perceiving subject is the mind's fixation on those as though they were truly existent things.
372. Source not identified. Here Serdok Paṇchen, whose writings were much admired within the Kagyü school to which Kongtrul belonged, is in accord with that school's view that objects in the phenomenal world are "empty in and of themselves" (that is, unqualified emptiness), while the true nature of phenomena is "empty of other" (that is, qualified emptiness). The alternate view is the opposite: that objects in the phenomenal world are "empty of other" ("A vase is not empty of a vase, rather a vase is empty of being anything established to have true existence"), while the true nature of phenomena is empty in and of itself.
373. Although the basic space of phenomena is not subject to differentiation in its very essence, it can be provisionally analyzed with respect to specific situations.
374. These seem to be verses composed (perhaps by Kongtrul himself?) as a mnemonic device.

375. Maitreya, *Distinguishing Center and Limit*, chap. 1, v. 17, (Toh. 4021), Dg. T., Sems tsam, vol. Phi, p. 81, lines 3–4. The Indian commentary by Vasubandhu (student of Asaṅga, who received the source text from Maitreya) on Maitreya's source text gives the following explanation (*Commentary on "Distinguishing Center and Limit,"* (Toh. 4027), Dg. T., Sems tsam, vol. Bi, p. 9, lines 1–5):

> In this regard, the passage begins with the emptiness of that which experiences, that is, the internal components of the sense fields. As for the emptiness of *what it experiences*, this refers to the outer components. As for *their body*, this refers to the physical body, which is the context for both that which experiences and what it experiences; the emptiness of that is what is termed "emptiness of what is external and internal." The *basis for existence* refers to the inanimate universe; because this is vast in extent, the emptiness of it is what is termed "emptiness of what is great." If you wonder about *how there is also such perception of* the internal components of the sense fields, it is through understanding emptiness; the emptiness of that is "emptiness of emptiness." As for the emptiness of *what* is perceived—that which is ultimate—this is "emptiness of what is ultimate." As for why, this ensures the accomplishment of a bodhisattva, that is *also emptiness*.

The verse thus references the first six of the fourteen aspects of emptiness.

376. That is, the fifth and sixth aspects in the list of fourteen given previously—emptiness of emptiness and emptiness of what is ultimate.

377. That is, emptiness of what is conditioned, of what is unconditioned, of what is beyond limitations, of what is without beginning or end, of what is not to be discarded, of nature, of characteristics, and of phenomena.

378. See Sthiramati, *Explanatory Commentary on "Distinguishing Center and Limit,"* (Toh. 4032), Dg. T., Sems tsam, vol. Bi, p. 431, lines 1–3:

> Virtue is conditioned and unconditioned—that is to say, the spiritual path and nirvāṇa. These two apply, respectively, to emptiness of what is conditioned and emptiness of what is unconditioned.

379. Ibid., l. 3:

> *Because there is constant benefit for beings* refers to the intention, "Under any and all circumstances, I will ensure benefit for beings"; the emptiness of that is emptiness of what is beyond limitations.

380. Ibid., lines 3–5:

> *Because saṃsāra is not to be relinquished* means that one resolves, "For the sake of beings, I will not completely relinquish saṃsāra"; for if one were to completely relinquish saṃsāra, one would not find enlightenment, but be confined to the level of a śrāvaka. The emptiness associated with that is the emptiness of what is without beginning or end. Why is the emptiness of that explained? [Vasubandhu states] "if one does not see that saṃsāra is emptiness, without beginning or end, one becomes disheartened and completely relinquishes saṃsāra."

Both the woodblock and computerized editions of *The Treasury of Knowledge* read, in error, "due to saṃsāra not being emptied, . . ."

381. Ibid., lines 5–7:

> *Because virtue becomes inexhaustible* refers to the intention, "Even though I pass into nirvāṇa without any residual trace of the mind-body aggregates remaining, I will not exhaust the fundamental qualities of virtue." . . . One might wonder, "If such is the case, what would the situation be in the basic space of nirvāṇa in which no residual trace of the mind-body aggregates remains?" Although there would be no body due to the consequences of corruptible phenomena, the dharmakāya of the incorruptible reality of buddhas, transcendent and accomplished conquerors, would be uninterrupted in the basic space of nirvāṇa in which no residual trace of the mind-body aggregates remains. This is attested to in philosophical works. Therefore, the emptiness of this is what is termed "emptiness of what is not to be discarded."

382. The Tibetan term *rigs* (here rendered "spiritual potential") is a synonym for *tathāgatagarbha*, or "buddha nature." According to Sthiramati, ibid., p. 431, l. 7 to p. 432, lines 1 and 3:

> As for the line *because, moreover, their spiritual potential becomes evident in its total purity*, the emptiness of this is the emptiness of nature. For that very reason, "spiritual potential" is explained as being "nature." . . . In this context, the term "spiritual potential" is taken to mean "suchness."

383. That is, the thirty-two major and eighty minor marks that adorn the form of one who has awakened to perfect buddhahood and manifested as a "sublime nirmāṇakāya." According to Sthiramati, ibid., l. 3:

> The emptiness of the major marks of a great spiritual being's perfect form, as well as the minor marks, is what is known as "the emptiness of characteristics."

384. Ibid., lines 5–6:

> If one wonders what the attributes of buddhahood are, [Vasubandhu states that they are] the powers, states of fearlessness, unique qualities, and so forth. In brief, one undertakes to accomplish these with the intention, "I will strive in order to gain all the attributes of buddhahood!" . . . the emptiness of these is what is known as "the emptiness of all phenomena."

The ten strengths, four states of fearlessness, and eighteen unique qualities—known collectively as the "thirty-two qualities due to divestment"—are discussed by Kongtrul in Book 10 of *The Treasury of Knowledge*; see *The Treasury of Knowledge: Books Nine and Ten: Journey and Goal*, 313–18. See also Longchen Rabjam, *The Precious Treasury of Philosophical Systems*, 237–38.

385. Maitreya, *Distinguishing Center and Limit*, chap. 1, vv. 18–19, (Toh. 4021), Dg. T., Sems tsam, vol. Phi, p. 81, lines 4–5. See Vasubandhu, *Commentary on "Distinguishing Center and Limit,"* (Toh. 4027), Dg. T., Sems tsam, vol. Bi, p. 9, lines 5–7:

> If you wonder why this spiritual practice is pursued, it is *because the two kinds of virtue are to be gained*, these two kinds of virtue being that which is conditioned and that which is unconditioned. It is *because there is constant benefit for beings*, because benefit is being ensured in perpetuity for ordinary beings. The line *because saṃsāra is not to be relinquished* means that if one does not see

that saṃsāra is emptiness, without beginning or end, one becomes disheartened and completely relinquishes saṃsāra. *Because virtue becomes inexhaustible* refers to that which is not relinquished or discarded, even though one passes into nirvāṇa without any residual trace of the mind-body aggregates remaining. As for the line *because, moreover, their spiritual potential becomes evident in its total purity*, this is because one's spiritual potential—which is to say, one's true nature, is such in its very essence. The line *because the major and minor marks of perfect form are gained* means that the major marks of a great spiritual being, as well as the minor ones, are to be gained. *Because the attributes of buddhahood are revealed in their purity, bodhisattvas pursue spiritual accomplishment* refers to the powers, states of fearlessness, unique qualities, and so forth.

386. That is, no traces of the mind-body aggregates. Concerning the corresponding situation according to the śrāvaka approach, Longchen Rabjam, *The Precious Treasury of Philosophical Systems*, 142, gives the following account:

> As for arhats who experience no such residual traces, it is held that like a fire once its fuel is exhausted, they no longer have physical bodies when they attain nirvāṇa, but their minds enter a realm of cessation, a state of pristine cognition in which ordinary mind has ceased.

The term *nirvāṇa* here refers to the śrāvaka interpretation of the term as personal salvation from suffering. With the arrest of mind in the attainment of the state without residual traces, there is no longer any virtue (or nonvirtue) functioning. In the Mahāyāna context, the efforts a bodhisattva makes in spiritual practice ensure the continuity of virtuous factors beyond the attainment of the state without residual traces.

387. In the śrāvaka and pratyekabuddha approaches, an act is virtuous because of what motivates it; in the Mahāyāna approach, there are actions that are virtuous by their very nature.
388. That is, it is not the case that the potential is purified but rather that purely adventitious factors that obscure one's direct experience of it are removed, so that it becomes fully evident as ever-present.
389. Kongtrul discusses these marks in Book 10 of *The Treasury of Knowledge*. See *The Treasury of Knowledge: Books Nine and Ten: Journey and Goal*, 323–28; see also Longchen Rabjam, *The Precious Treasury of Philosophical Systems*, 216–18.
390. That is, emptiness (1) of the conditioned and (2) of the unconditioned (with the two kinds of virtue as the specific context), (3) of what is beyond limitations (with benefit for beings as the specific context), and (4) of what is without beginning or end (with engagement in saṃsāra as the specific context).
391. That is, emptiness (5) of what is not to be discarded, (6) of nature, (7) of characteristics, and (8) of phenomena.
392. See the preceding citation from *Distinguishing Center and Limit*. According to Sthiramati, *Explanatory Commentary on "Distinguishing Center and Limit,"* (Toh. 4032), Dg. T., Sems tsam, vol. Bi, p. 432, lines 4–5:

> "Pursue spiritual accomplishment" is stated after the final line, but it applies to all of them, as in:

> Because the two kinds of virtue are to be gained,
> bodhisattvas pursue spiritual accomplishment.
> Because there is constant benefit for beings,
> bodhisattvas pursue spiritual accomplishment.

and so forth.

393. That is, the twelfth aspect of emptiness for the interpretation of qualified emptiness is distinct from the equivalent twelfth aspect for the interpretation of unqualified emptiness; the thirteenth aspect, from the equivalent fourteenth aspect; and the fourteenth aspect, from the equivalent thirteenth aspect.
394. That is, the way in which the interpretation of qualified emptiness understands emptiness as the true nature of things.
395. That is, phenomena that come about due to causes and conditions other than themselves (Tib. *gzhan byung*), as distinct from what is naturally occurring (Tib. *rang byung*).
396. See, by way of comparison, the citation from Serdok Paṇchen above, at the beginning of the section on qualified emptiness.
397. That is, the sixteenth and seventeenth aspects of the eighteen aspects of emptiness as set forth in the Prajñāpāramitā sūtras.
398. That is, a distinction is made between the imputation of the individual and the relatively true phenomenon that is the basis for that imputation. The "factors of the true nature of reality" refer to the qualities of enlightenment that are innately present as natural attributes of the true nature of mind.
399. These are ways in which the mind digresses from an authentic perception of the true nature of things, by thinking in terms of (1) nonexistence, (2) existence, (3) overstatement, (4) understatement, (5) single entities, (6) manifold entities, (7) finite essences, (8) particular features, (9) names being the things they refer to, and (10) things being the names that refer to them. Kongtrul lists these in Part 2 of Book 6 of *The Treasury of Knowledge*, vol. 2, p. 417 (Tibetan text). See also *The Treasury of Knowledge: Book Six, Parts One and Two: Indo-Tibetan Classical Learning and Buddhist Phenomenology*.
400. Dignāga, *Summary of the Meaning of the Eight Thousand Verses*, lines 73–76, (Toh. 4032), Dg. T., Śes phyin, vol. Pha, p. 585, l. 7.
401. Candrakīrti, *Extensive Commentary on the "Four Hundred Verses for Engaging in a Bodhisattva's Conduct,"* (Toh. 3865), Dg. T., dBu ma, vol. Ya, p. 265, lines 6–7. In the lines preceding this citation, Candrakīrti (in commenting on chapter 8, verse 178 of Āryadeva's source text) states the following:

    > Thus, at any point at which the object of attention cannot be found to exist, this demonstrates that such reactions as desire [for that object] cannot be found to exist. For if the cause cannot be found to exist, neither can such reactions as desire be found to exist. It is therefore [that Āryadeva] stated:
    >
    > > In the absence of concepts, desire
    > > and so forth are not things that exist.
    > > And who endowed with intelligence would presume,
    > > "Authentic reality is a concept"? [chap. 8, v. 178]

For as it is said:

> Desire, aversion, and ignorance are explained as occurring
> due to the all-consuming conceptual process.

The causes of thoroughly afflictive mental states—afflictive states such as desire—lie in fallacious concepts about sense objects. Therefore, anytime there is [a case in which something exists . . .]

402. That is, the specific identities imputed to all phenomena.
403. Between the source verse and Kongtrul's prose commentary, the computerized edition of *The Treasury of Knowledge* contains, in error, an interpolated sentence that combines the first part of the commentary with the last part of the source verse. It has been disregarded in the translation.
404. Nāgārjuna, *Precious Garland*, chap. 1, v. 35, (Toh. 4158), Dg. T., sPriṅ yig, vol. Ge, p. 215, lines 5–6.
405. That is, subject, object, and the action that takes place (or relationship that exists) between them, all conceived of as separate, truly existent entities.
406. Maitreya, *Highest Continuum*, chap. 5, v. 14, (Toh. 4024), Dg. T, Sems tsam, vol. Phi, p. 144, lines 2–3.
407. Specifically, the afflictive obscuration acts as a hindrance to the attainment of liberation from saṃsāra, while the cognitive obscuration acts as a hindrance to the attainment of the omniscience of buddhahood.
408. Āryadeva, *Four Hundred Verses*, chap. 14. v. 350c–d, (Toh. 3846), Dg. T., dBu ma, vol. Tsha, p. 31, l. 5.
409. Dharmakīrti, *Detailed Commentary on Valid Cognition*, chap. 2, v. 221c–d, (Toh. 4210), Dg. T., Tshad ma, vol. Ce, p. 231, l. 3.
410. Śāntarakṣita, *Ornament of the Middle Way*, (Toh. 3884), Dg. T., dBu ma, vol. Sa, ff. 53a–56b.
411. That is, the lack of identity in mind itself (not the imputed individual).
412. That is, a factor that, while temporary, nevertheless contributes (even if indirectly) to the elimination of obscurations and the attainment of liberation from suffering, rather than simply reinforcing the habitual patterns that perpetuate saṃsāra.
413. See Kongtrul, *The Treasury of Knowledge: Book Six, Part Three: Frameworks of Buddhist Philosophy*, 385, n. 723:

> Sāṃkhyas (Calculators or Enumerators) (*Grangs can pa*) are followers of the oldest of the "orthodox" philosophical schools, that is, schools that take the Vedas as authoritative. The Vedic sage Kapila is traditionally said to be the founder of the Sāṃkhya school (though this is not verified), which also serves as the philosophical system for Patañjali's system of Yoga.

In the Sāṃkhya system, all things are subsumed within two categories, soul and primal matter. Primal matter, in turn, gives rise to ordinary consciousness or mind, leading to the conceit of self-identity, which then accounts for the manifestation of all that constitutes the material world. See Longchen Rabjam, *The Precious Treasury of Philosophical Systems*, 55–60. Here Kongtrul offers only the Sāṃkhya interpretation as an example of non-Buddhist schools that accept the most obvious aspect of the lack of identity in phenomena; Tibetan accounts of non-Buddhist philosophy tended to be limited to treatments of other ancient Indian schools as critiqued (often rather cursorily) in the writings of Indian Buddhist teachers.

414. For the Sautrāntika school, the material (Tib. *rdzas*; Skt. *dravya*) is defined as what is capable of performing a function or being of use to a person on the ultimate level, and not simply something ascribed by language or imputed by conceptual thought—things such as forms, sounds, and so forth. By contrast, mental determinants (Tib. *ldog pa*; Skt. *apoha*) are concepts that are based on the exclusion of everything that is not the thing itself—for example, a form that is perceived in the mind, such as the isolated form of a vase that simply excludes everything "not-a-vase."
415. That is, a tenet held in common by both the Particularists and Followers of the Sūtras.
416. Vasubandhu, *Treasury of Abhidharma*, chap. 6, v. 4a–c, (Toh. 4089), Dg. T., mNgon pa, vol. Ku, p. 36, lines 6–7. See n. 236.
417. Dharmakīrti, *Detailed Commentary on Valid Cognition*, chap. 1, v. 70c–d, (Toh. 4210), Dg. T., Tshad ma, vol. Ce, p. 194, l. 1.
418. Mental determinants are merely concepts that exclude everything that is not the thing that is the object of the concept.
419. These are Cittamātrin thinkers "who assert that external referents do not exist as real entities and yet, owing to the habitual tendencies for conceiving [of appearances] as objects, cognition itself arises as the image of a referent, as in the analogy of a crystal with a color. Thus, everything that appears as forms is simply the mind itself, which is the agent for appearances (*snang mkhan*) manifesting as distant cut-off objects (*rgyangs chad kyi don*) owing to the power of the deluded habitual tendencies. Moreover, [appearances,] in fact, are real in being the mind, which is the perceived object. Therefore, the aggregates, constituents, sense spheres, and even true cessation (which is considered to be mind free from the factors to be abandoned), all of which are taught in the sūtras, are real in being mental phenomena, which is to say, they are [only] the mind itself." Kongtrul, *The Treasury of Knowledge: Book Six, Part Three: Frameworks of Buddhist Philosophy*, 186–87.
420. That is to say, these Mind Only proponents accept the nonexistence of what is imputed but not that of what is dependent.
421. That is, Vasubandhu.
422. See Kongtrul, *The Treasury of Knowledge: Book Six, Part Three: Frameworks of Buddhist Philosophy*, 209–11, where Kongtrul outlines these lines of reasoning, which are used in both branches of the Middle Way school—Svātantrika and Prāsaṅgika:

    In Madhyamaka reasonings, generally speaking, the evidence (*liṅga*, *rtags*) is presented in two ways:
    (1) by setting up negations (*pratiṣheda*, *dgag pa*), or
    (2) by setting up affirmations (*viddhi*, *sgrub pa*).
    First: Negations
    (1) Negation through the analysis of causes is called the "vajra sliver [reasoning]."
    (2) Negation by means of analyzing results refutes the arising of [a result] existent [at the time of its cause] and the arising of [a result that is] nonexistent [at the time of its cause].
    (3) Negation that employs the analysis of both causes and their results refutes arising from the four possibilities.

> (4) Negation that analyzes a nature [demonstrates that a phenomenon] is neither a single unit nor a plurality.
>
> The first type of negation is taught in the *Rice Seedling Sūtra* and the last kind is presented in the *Descent into Laṅkā Sūtra*. The two middle ones appear in certain sūtras. These four eliminate the Realists' inflated ascription of inherent existence to things, thereby removing [their belief in] the extreme of existence. . . .
>
> [Second: Affirmations]
>
> Affirmations are set up as evidence in the following way. The reasoning of dependent origination is an analysis of mere appearances, and it is found in the *Questions of the Nāga King Anavatapta Sūtra*.

In Longchen Rabjam, *The Precious Treasury of Philosophical Systems*, 108, Longchen Rabjam presents these five in a slightly different order:

> These five can be understood to conform to four models. The argument known as "vajra shards" is a refutation that examines the causes of any object to be refuted. The argument called "the refutation of the production and cessation of what is existent or nonexistent" is a refutation that examines the results. The argument called "the refutation of production in any of four ways" is a refutation that examines both the causes and results. As for refutations that examine something in its essence, the argument known as "the supreme principle of interdependent connection" is one of establishing a line of reasoning that involves a qualified negation, and that called "freedom from being unitary or manifold entities" is one of establishing a line of reasoning that involves an unqualified negation.

He goes on (ibid., 109–10) to present each in more detail, and later (ibid., 120–23) examines the particular way in which they are used in the Prāsaṅgika approach.

423. Candrakīrti, *Entrance to the Middle Way*, chap. 6, v. 96c–d, (Toh. 3861), Dg. T., dBu ma, vol. 'A, p. 416, l. 7.
424. Āryadeva, *Four Hundred Verses*, chap. 8, v. 191a–b, (Toh. 3846), Dg. T., dBu ma, vol. Tsha, p. 18, l. 6; the lines in the source text read slightly differently:

> That which is the seeing of a single thing
> is explained to be the seeing of everything.

These lines are cited by Candrakīrti in *Clear Words*, (Toh. 3860), Dg. T., dBu ma, vol. 'A, p. 85, l. 6. The second half of Āryadeva's verse continues:

> Whatever is the emptiness of the one
> is the emptiness of everything.

425. As Kongtrul notes, even followers of lower Buddhist schools of thought have self-imposed limitations on their ability to investigate the true nature of things. It is only by evolving beyond those limitations of reasoning and inquiry that a given individual can truly embrace the Middle Way perspective.
426. That is, identity in the individual is a particular subset of the greater issue of identity in phenomena; for the latter to be completely realized, the former must also be.
427. Candrakīrti, *Extensive Commentary on the "Four Hundred Verses for Engaging in a*

Bodhisattva's Conduct," (Toh. 3865), Dg. T., dBu ma, vol. Ya, p. 380, lines 3–4. The source text reads: "on the basis of the five mind-body aggregates."

428. That is, were there some identity in any given phenomenon, it would necessarily be something that could stand on its own as an autonomous entity. Ibid., lines 2–3.

429. The computerized edition of *The Treasury of Knowledge* contains an error in reading: "such thoughts as 'I am following the path to liberation', or 'my path to liberation', . . ."

430. That is, a merely conventional sense of self that is not invested with any sense of its truly existing is useful in ordinary mundane contexts.

431. The source text reads: "all things . . ."

432. Candrakīrti, *Entrance to the Middle Way*, chap. 6, v. 44, (Toh. 3861), Dg. T., dBu ma, vol. 'A, p. 411, lines 6–7.

433. Dharmakīrti, *Detailed Commentary on Valid Cognition*, chap. 2, v. 219, (Toh. 4210), Dg. T., Tshad ma, vol. Ce, p. 231, lines 1–2.

434. Candrakīrti, *Entrance to the Middle Way*, chap. 1, v. 3a–b, (Toh. 3861), Dg. T., dBu ma, vol. 'A, p. 402, l. 3.

435. Ibid., chap. 6, v. 120 (p. 419, l. 4).

436. Because the Followers of the Sūtras (Sautrāntika) school is generally considered to be a more advanced system than that of the Particularist (Vaibhāṣika) school.

437. That is, one on a more obvious level (which they establish on the basis of external objects) and the other on a more subtle level (which they establish on the basis of the internal mind).

438. That is, the mind and the internal aspects of the sense fields; the "agent" being negated is the concept of a permanent, unitary, autonomous self as posited by non-Buddhist schools of thought.

439. That is, irreducible particles of matter and irreducible moments of consciousness, without which (according to the systems of the Particularists and the Followers of the Sūtras) the universe as we experience could not be the case, and on the basis of which they establish the lack of identity in the individual and the nonexistence of phenomena on the coarse, obvious level. The Mahāyāna schools (Cittamātra and Madhyamaka) reject the notions of these irreducible particles and moments existing ultimately.

440. Both material and mental "things" pertain to the internal level, which includes not only the mind's experience of the external world but the body and its sense organs as the supports for that experience. Only material "things" are required to account for the external inanimate world.

441. That is, with respect to realizing the lack of identity in the individual, the Middle Way and Mind Only schools are identical.

442. That is, at any given point the sense of "I" may be associated with the physical body (the aggregate of forms)—"I am hungry"—a sensation, a perception, a volitional state, or some aspect of consciousness. The mistaken assumption is that the "I" is the same entity in all situations, rather than a misperception that fixates on any given factor among the aggregates as its object depending on the circumstances.

443. This is a reference to a way of analyzing the relative level of truth from the Autonomist (Svātantrika) perspective; see Kongtrul, *The Treasury of Knowledge: Book Six, Part Three: Frameworks of Buddhist Philosophy*, 221:

> Svātantrikas classify conventionalities as being either correct conventionalities (*yang dag kun rdzob*) or mistaken conventionalities (*log pa'i kun rdzob*):

> (1) a correct conventionality is whatever is capable of performing a function that is consistent with the way it appears [to its corresponding cognizer]; and (2) a mistaken conventionality is whatever cannot perform a function consistent with its appearance.

See also Longchen Rabjam, *The Precious Treasury of Philosophical Systems*, 103:

> If we analyze relative truth, we find that it also has two aspects. There is what is erroneous on the relative level (what is apparent yet incapable of performing a function) and what is valid on the relative level (what is apparent and capable of performing a function).

444. That is, the Buddha.
445. That is, the beliefs that the "I" or "self" is identical with one or another of the five mind-body aggregates.
446. Nāgārjuna, *Letter to a Friend*, v. 49, (Toh. 4182), Dg. T., sPriṅ yig, vol. Nge, p. 85, l. 2.
447. See Kongtrul, *The Treasury of Knowledge: Book Six, Part Three: Frameworks of Buddhist Philosophy*, 240:

> The sevenfold reasoning [that uses the analogy of] a chariot proves the absence of a self of persons. The *Entrance* [*to the Middle Way*] states:
>
> > A chariot is not considered to be other than its parts.
> > It is not identical [with them,] nor does it possess them.
> > It is not in its parts, nor are the parts within it.
> > It is not the mere assembly nor the overall shape.
>
> In addition to the fivefold [analysis that begins with seeing that] a chariot is not something other than its parts (such as the nails), [Chandrakīrti] examines the collection [of parts] and the overall shape [of the chariot]. If we investigate [a chariot] using this sevenfold analysis, we will not find that it is the parts themselves nor will we find that it is something other than those [parts]. Similarly, if we look for a self using this sevenfold analysis, we will not find that it is something other than the aggregates nor will we find that it is the aggregates themselves. In this [analysis of the chariot], the overall shape and the collection are refuted implicitly, since they cannot be found apart from that which has the shape (*dbyibs can*) or that which is the collection (*tshogs pa can*).

This reasoning is also found in the Theravada tradition of Buddhism; see Rhys Davids, *The Questions of King Milinda*:

> And the venerable Nagasena said to Milinda the king: "How then did you come, on foot, or in a chariot?"
> "I did not come, Sir, on foot . I came in a carriage."
> "Then if you came, Sire, in a carriage, explain to me what that is. Is it the pole that is the chariot?"
> "I did not say that."
> "Is it the axle that is the chariot?"
> "Certainly not."
> "Is it the wheels, or the framework, or the ropes, or the yoke, or the spokes of the wheels, or the goad, that are the chariot?"

And to all these he still answered no.
"Then is it all these parts of it that are the chariot?"
"No, Sir."
"But is there anything outside them that is the chariot?"
And still he answered no.
"Then thus, ask as I may, I can discover no chariot. Chariot is a mere empty sound. What then is the chariot you say you came in ? It is a falsehood that your Majesty has spoken, an untruth! There is no such thing as a chariot! You are king over all India, a mighty monarch. Of whom then are you afraid that you speak untruth?" And he called upon the Yonakas and the brethren to witness, saying: "Milinda the king here has said that he came by carriage. But when asked in that case to explain what the carriage was, he is unable to establish what he averred. Is it, forsooth, possible to approve him in that?"
When he had thus spoken the five hundred Yonakas shouted their applause, and said to the king: "Now let your Majesty get out of that if you can?"
And Milinda the king replied to Nagasena, and said: "I have spoken no untruth, reverend Sir. It is on account of its having all these things—the pole, and the axle, the wheels, and the framework, the ropes, the yoke, the spokes, and the goad—that it comes under the generally understood term, the designation in common use, of 'chariot'."
"Very good! Your Majesty has rightly grasped the meaning of 'chariot'. And just even so it is on account of all those things you questioned me about—the thirty-two kinds of organic matter in a human body, and the five constituent elements of being—that I come under the generally understood term, the designation in common use, of 'Nâgasena'. For it was said, Sire, by our Sister Vagirâ in the presence of the Blessed One: 'Just as it is by the condition precedent of the co-existence of its various parts that the word "chariot" is used, just so is it that when the Skandhas are there we talk of a "being."'"
"Most wonderful, Nâgasena, and most strange. Well has the puzzle put to you, most difficult though it was, been solved. Were the Buddha himself here he would approve your answer. Well done, well done, Nâgasena!"

448. One early school of Buddhism in India, the Vātsīputrīya, accepted the existence of an "indescribable self"; see Longchen Rabjam, *The Precious Treasury of Philosophical Systems*, 68–69:

> As to the system of the Vatsiputriyas (Followers of Vatsiputra), . . . Vatsiputra then asked the Buddha whether the individual self is the same as the mind-body aggregates, or distinct from them, or both, or neither. The Buddha's answer was to say nothing at all, which Vatsiputra interpreted to mean that the self does exist but is indescribable. Although he had embraced the dharma, he accepted the existence of an indescribable self, for his view was tainted by a form of extremism.
>
> The source texts of this system maintain that the entity of the self is the agent that carries out all positive and negative actions, experiences the results (whether desired or not), which are its own creations, and casts off the mind-body aggregates of one life and takes up those of the next. They hold that this self is not eternal, because former lives are left behind and later ones are taken up. However, they also maintain that it is not impermanent, because

the self that has committed actions in this life has already experienced doing so, and the self in a future life will still experience the results of those actions, which it did not commit. These two selves in fact constitute a single self. It is this self that experiences the playing out of karmic results, which are thereby "exhausted," but will continue to experience those that are "not yet exhausted." The Vatsiputriyas hold that since the agent receiving, or undergoing, the experience is the same as the self, it cannot be impermanent. Therefore, they say that "self" is what exists as one's sense of identity, not describable in any way whatsoever, as eternal or impermanent.

Their position is not a sound one. In fact, it is untenable, because their refutation of this "self" being some permanent thing does not constitute proof that it is some impermanent thing; their refutation of its being some impermanent thing depends on the proof of its being some permanent thing. And how is it possible for something to be neither eternal nor impermanent?

449. The citation has been translated as in the source text; both the woodblock and computerized editions of *The Treasury of Knowledge* have an error of omission, reading: "what is called 'the world' and 'mine' . . ."

450. Kamalaśīla, *Stages of Meditation*, (Toh. 3916), Dg. T., dBu ma, vol. Ki, p. 96, lines 2–4. Kamalaśīla wrote three texts all entitled *Stages of Meditation*; these are generally referred to as the "first," "intermediate," and "final (or third)" versions. While Kongtrul cites this passage as being from the first version of *Stages of Meditation*, it is actually from the intermediate version.

451. The definition of a "substantial thing" (Tib. *dngos po*) is something that is capable of performing a function. Nonsubstantial phenomena (such as space) cannot perform functions.

452. Nāgārjuna, *Source Verses on Sublime Intelligence*, chap. 18, v. 1, (Toh. 3824), Dg. T., dBu ma, vol. Tsa, p. 20, l. 6.

453. That is, the function of consciousness that is aware of perception taking place. For example, when visual consciousness (which is nonconceptual) sees a flower, it is the reflexive function of consciousness that is aware that seeing is taking place, making a connection between nonconceptual visual consciousness and conceptual consciousness, which knows, "I am seeing a flower."

454. Valid inference is the process of arriving at some conclusion upon seeing some kind of evidence that leads one inevitably to that conclusion, thus revealing some conclusion that was formerly hidden. Examples are those of seeing smoke and inferring that there is a fire, or seeing waterfowl and inferring that there is a body of water nearby. Kongtrul is maintaining that no truly valid process of inference could definitively prove the existence of a self, or an identity in the individual.

455. In Buddhist epistemology, for a state of cognition to be a valid one (Tib. *tshad ma*; Skt. *pramāṇa*), it must meet criteria of being either a valid form of direct experience, or a valid state of deductive inference, or based upon scriptural authority from some authentic source. Inference is valid only when it meets very specific criteria; the fact that the self "feels like it exists" due to deeply entrenched patterns of habituation does not constitute a valid inference, or intuition, that such is the case.

456. In the sūtras, the terms "brahmin" and "spiritual practitioner" are used to refer to individuals who espouse spiritual values, but whose understanding is still immature. In Part 1 of Book 7, Kongtrul defines a brahmin as someone "who believes in the reality

of the perishable mind-body aggregates" and a spiritual practitioner as someone "who believes that personal rules of discipline and deportment are absolute principles in their own right."

457. Source not identified.
458. Source not identified.
459. Nāgārjuna, *Source Verses on Sublime Intelligence*, chap. 18, v. 2a–b, (Toh. 3824), Dg. T., dBu ma, vol. Tsa, p. 20, l. 6.
460. Candrakīrti, *Entrance to the Middle Way*, chap. 6, v. 165, (Toh. 3861), Dg. T., dBu ma, vol. 'A, p. 423, l. 7.
461. See n. 316.
462. For the source verses from which Kongtrul derives this discussion, see Maitreya, *Distinguishing Center and Limit*, chap. 3, vv. 15–16b, (Toh. 4021), Dg. T., Sems tsam, vol. Phi, p. 84, l. 4:

    As unitary, as a cause, as an agent of experience,
    as a creator, as a controller
    and owner, as something permanent,
    as the basis for afflictive states or purity,

    as a spiritual practitioner, or as what is not free and then free—
    these are ways of believing in terms of self-identity.

463. Ibid., vv. 16c–22 (p. 84, l. 4 to p. 85, l. 2).
464. There are eighteen such components. Six are external components—visual forms, sounds, odors, tastes, tactile sensations, and mental phenomena (this category includes the three aggregates of sensations, perceptions, and formative factors; indiscernible forms; and all unconditioned phenomena). Six are internal components—the faculties of vision, hearing, smell, taste, touch, and the mental faculty that coordinates sense data and creates ideas concerning what is perceived. Six are components that are based on consciousness—visual, auditory, olfactory, gustatory, and tactile consciousness, and the coordinating function of mind.
465. In any given perceptual or cognitive act, some external component functions as the support, the corresponding internal component provides the frame of reference, and the corresponding components based on consciousness are the supported factor; for example, when a visual form is seen, the form (external) is the support, the visual faculty provides the frame of reference, and the visual consciousness is what is supported in the situation. It is, therefore, these components that function as the causes of our ordinary experience, not some "self."
466. Of these twelve constituents, six are internal (the faculties of vision, hearing, smell, taste, touch, and mental coordination and imagination), and six are external (the sense objects of forms, sounds, odors, tastes, tactile sensations, and mental phenomena). The term translated here as "sense field" (Tib. *skye mched*; Skt. *āyatana*) is defined as that which functions like a cause, or avenue, for the arising (*skye*) and augmentation (*mched*) of some avenue of consciousness, such as visual consciousness. Again, no existent "self" is required to account for the sum total of ordinary experience, only the interaction between these twelve constituents.
467. What is or is not in accord with the nature of things (Tib. *gnas dang gnas ma yin pa*; Skt. *sthānāsthāna*) refers to the usual process by which events take place in our

experience and what it is appropriate to expect under the circumstances; for example, that planting rice will yield a harvest of rice not wheat. One of the ten powers of a buddha is that of "knowing what is or is not in accord with the nature of things," such as knowledge of the fact that karma and afflictive states are the causes of an ordinary being, not a self or creator god; or knowledge of the fact that virtuous actions lead to higher states of rebirth, not lower ones. The fact that such situations are the case proves that no self exists as something that could control an outcome.

468. A governing condition (Tib. *bdag po'i rkyen*; Skt. *adhipatipratyaya*) is one that exerts a primary controlling influence over some result coming about; for example, the sensory faculties act as governing conditions that contribute to the occurrence of their respective kinds of consciousness.

469. The "faculties" referred to here are twenty-two in number. Seven serve as bases for consciousness (the five physical sense faculties, the coordinating mental faculty, and the faculty of life force); two serve as further determinants of experience (the male and female sexual organs); five serve as vehicles for sensation (the two physical sensations of pleasure and pain, the two mental sensations of well-being and suffering, and the neutral state of experience); five are faculties that contribute to the totally refined state of enlightenment (faith, enthusiastic diligence, mindfulness, meditative absorption, and sublime intelligence); and three are faculties that are found in the makeup of those who are spiritually advanced beings (the faculty that brings all-knowing awareness, the faculty of all-knowing awareness, and the faculty endowed with all-knowing awareness). Concerning the latter three faculties, see Kongtrul, *The Treasury of Knowledge: Books Nine and Ten: Journey and Goal*, 104–5 and 577, notes 230–32.

470. Knowledge of the various spiritual approaches to enlightenment brings an awareness that the qualities associated with these approaches manifest as a result of the processes themselves, not due to one's "making them happen." This undermines the tendency toward the spiritual pride of identifying oneself as a practitioner, a tendency that undermines the effectiveness of one's chosen path to negate the mistaken belief in one's individual identity as something real and absolute and to allow the innate qualities of one's true nature to manifest.

471. That is, the belief that some self exists, which previously was not free but that "becomes" free at a later point in time.

472. For a commentary on these verses by Mipam Rinpoché of the Nyingma school, see Dharmachakra Translation Committee, *Middle Beyond Extremes*, 84–101. Mipam Rinpoché (1846–1912) structured one of his most famous works (Tib. *mKhas pa la 'jug pa'i sgo*) entirely on the theme of these ten ways of becoming learned; see Mipham Rinpoche, *Gateway to Knowledge*, vols. 1–3.

473. An idiomatic way of referring to all phenomena that could possibly manifest in any way that could be experienced.

474. That is, the Buddha Śākyamuni.

475. In the sense that it is the first genuine step in one's recognition of what is ultimately true, prior to the direct experience of that truth.

476. That is, the wording of the example makes it seem like a statement of affirmation, but in fact the point of the statement is to prove that X is devoid of true existence; hence, it is actually a statement of negation.

477. See Kongtrul, *The Treasury of Knowledge: Book Six, Part Three: Frameworks of Buddhist Philosophy*, 388, n. 734:

> Reasons of the imperception of something connected [to the predicate of the negandum] (*saṃbhandhānupalabdhihetu, 'brel zla ma dmigs pa'i gtan tshigs*): Something connected to the predicate of the negandum (*dgag bya'i chos*) may be (1) its nature (*rang bzhin*), (2) any of its results (*'bras bu*), (3) any of its causes (*rgyu*), or (4) a larger category to which it belongs (*khyab byed*).
>
> An example of a reason of the imperception of a result connected to the predicate is: "In this smoke-free room, there is no fire, because no smoke is perceived through any form of valid cognition." The predicate of the negandum is "there is a fire." The fact that a result (smoke) connected to the phenomenon in question (fire) is not perceived in this room serves as the reason that negates the existence of this phenomenon (fire).

478. Ibid., 388–89, n. 735:

> Reasons of the perception of something contradictory [to the predicate of the negandum] (*viruddhopalabdhihetu, 'gal zla dmigs pa'i gtan tshigs*): Something that is contradictory to the predicate of the negandum may be (1) its nature (*rang bzhin*), (2) its result (*'bras bu*), or (3) a subset of it (*khyab bya*).
>
> An example of using a reason of the perception of something whose nature is contradictory to the predicate is: "Right next to a hot fire, there is no lasting sensation of coldness, because a hot fire is perceived there." The predicate of the negandum is "a lasting feeling of coldness." The fact that something whose nature is contradictory (a hot fire) to the phenomenon in question (an ongoing sensation of cold) is perceived serves as the reason that negates the existence of this phenomenon (an ongoing sensation of cold).
>
> Or to use the reasoning of dependent origination: "Outer and inner phenomena do not come into being, because they are dependently originated." The predicate is "come into being." The perception of something contradictory (phenomena being dependently originated) to the predicate serves as the reason to negate it.

479. Ibid., 234–35:

> There are two types of negating reasons (*dgag rtags*):
> (1) reasons of the imperception of something connected [to the predicate of the negandum], and
> (2) reasons of the perception of something contradictory [to the predicate of the negandum].
>
> The reason of dependent origination is the second kind of reason, and the other [four reasons] are the first type.

That is, of the five major lines of reasoning employed in both the Svātantrika and Prāsaṅgika systems, the line of reasoning known as "the supreme principle of interdependent connection" (Tib. *rten 'brel chen po*) is a proof of negation due to an observation of something contradictory. The remaining four lines of reasoning, which are all proofs of negation due to a failure to observe something supportive are:
(1) the "vajra shards" (Tib. *rdo rje gzegs ma*), a proof of negation that examines the causes of what is to be negated (the term "vajra shards"uses the analogy of a powerful weapon that can destroy a rock face, which is comparable to this line of reasoning

destroying the erroneous arguments of materialist thinkers);
(2) the "negation of the production of what is existent or nonexistent" (Tib. *yod med skye 'gog*), a proof of negation that examines what is to negated as result;
(3) the "negation of production in any of four ways" (Tib. *mu bzhi skye 'gog*), a proof of negation that examines both the causes and results; and
(4) the "freedom from being unitary or manifold entities" (Tib. *gcig du bral*), a proof of negation that examines the nature of what is to be negated.

See also n. 423.

480. That is, a given phenomenon as the starting point for one's inquiry, something that has attributes that are "based" on it.
481. While the term used here (Tib. *ngo bo*; Skt., *svabhāva*) can refer in other contexts to the true and ultimate nature of reality (as in "all phenomena are, in essence, emptiness"), here it refers to that which makes a given phenomenon what it is, as distinct from all other phenomena; for example, the "essential quality" of fire is to be hot and burning, that of water to be wet and moistening.
482. This is one of the many traditional descriptions of things used in teaching logic and debate in Tibetan monastic institutions.
483. See Longchen Rabjam, *The Precious Treasury of Philosophical Systems*, 109–10:

> [This] argument, that of freedom from anything being a unitary or manifold entity, can be understood through a threefold process: establishing a line of reasoning, proving the properties of the subject under discussion, and examining the validity of the argument by ascertaining what is entailed. The first step in the process is described as follows: Something that is of necessity free of being a unitary or manifold entity is necessarily devoid of any attribute of true existence, as is the case, for example, with a generic idea, which is not a real entity. Specifically, although things manifest as they do, this necessarily entails their freedom from being unitary or manifold entities in the ultimate sense.

484. Ibid., 109:

> [This] argument is as follows: Something that is devoid of the status of being a single result from a single cause, a multiple result from a single cause, a single result from multiple causes, or a multiple result from multiple causes is utterly devoid of the status of being a real entity that is actually produced, as is the case, for example, with a generic idea, which is not a real entity. Specifically, although things manifest as they do, they are devoid of the status of being produced in any of four alternative ways: whether of one thing being produced from another thing, of many things being produced from one thing, of many things being produced from many things, or of one thing being produced from many things.

485. Nāgārjuna, *Source Verses on Sublime Intelligence*, introduction, v. 1–2b, (Toh. 3824), Dg. T., dBu ma, vol. Tsa, p. 2, l. 2–3.
486. That is, any deliberate attempt to prove that the true nature of things is a freedom from elaboration would of necessity involve the very elaborations that one was trying to disprove.
487. That is, in Book 6, Part 3 of *The Treasury of Knowledge*; see Kongtrul, *The Treasury of Knowledge: Book Six, Part Three: Frameworks of Buddhist Philosophy*, 204–47.

488. This ordinarily refers to a branch of the Autonomist school of the Middle Way, which on the relative level accepts consciousness as a mere convention but does not accept external objects. In this context, however, Kongtrul is using the term to refer to the consummate view of qualified emptiness (*zhentong*).
489. That is, Maitreya, who, as the next buddha to appear after Śākyamuni, is known as the Buddha's "regent."
490. Maitreya, *Ornament of the Mahāyāna Sūtras*, chap. 7, v. 8, (Toh. 4020), Dg. T., Sems tsam, vol. Phi, p. 12, l. 5–6.
491. These are buddha, dharma, sangha, buddha nature, enlightenment, qualities, and enlightened activity. They are innately present as natural attributes of the basic space of phenomena, the true nature of reality. These seven properties also constitute the "table of contents" of Maitreya's *Highest Continuum*.
492. Tib. *bde bar gshegs pa'i snying po*; Skt. *sugatagarbha*. That is, the "buddha nature."
493. That is, the true nature of everything—ordinary beings, buddhas, and all phenomena—is not some substantial thing that is subject to change. Different terms (such as "tathāgatagarbha" and "buddhahood") are used purely as conventions to refer to different contexts.
494. The three phases are the impure phase (the state of an ordinary being, in which karma, afflictive mental states, and other adventitious factors temporarily obscure the ever-present buddha nature), the partially pure phase (the state of bodhisattvas, who have removed these obscurations to some degree and have thus gained partial access to the experience of this ultimate nature), and the utterly pure phase (the state of buddhas, in which all obscurations have been removed and the buddha nature is expressed in full evidence).
495. Tib. *de bzhin gshegs pa'i snying po*; Skt. *tathāgatagarbha*. Another term for the "buddha nature."
496. Source not identified.
497. The passage as cited by Kongtrul reads: "those who take overt delight in . . ."
498. Asaṅga, *Detailed Explanation of the "Highest Continuum,"* (Toh. 4025), Dg. T., Sems tsam, vol. Phi, p. 224, lines 2–4.
499. The first of five consecutive paths leading to buddhahood; see Kongtrul, *The Treasury of Knowledge: Books Nine and Ten: Journey and Goal*, 66–72.
500. That is, the Buddha Śākyamuni and the future buddha Maitreya.
501. That is to say, the fact that the buddha nature is present and has the qualities it does is not enough to allow one to experience it directly simply by intellectually appreciating that presence and those qualities.
502. That is, bodhisattvas on either the path of seeing (which corresponds to the first of the ten levels of realization) or the path of meditation (the second through the tenth levels); see ibid., 81–100 and 107–27.
503. This is due to the truly inconceivable quality of the buddha nature, which cannot be fully fathomed or embraced by ordinary rational consciousness. Even though ever-present in ordinary beings, under ordinary circumstances buddha nature does not carry out its "function"—that is, is not experienced as enlightenment—and even though it is innately endowed with, for example, the ten strengths of buddhahood, it has no power in and of itself to dispel the distortions that obscure its presence.
504. The Tibetan idiom *phur khung thug pa* conveys the image of a tent peg being blocked by a stone when one tries to drive it into the ground.

505. That is, the tradition of Nāgārjuna—who is regarded as the consummate interpreter of the unqualified interpretation of emptiness (*rang stong*) in the Consequentialist branch of the Middle Way school—is more short-term (that is, applicable to the spiritual path), more obvious, and oriented toward investigating externals and putting an end to concepts regarding them. The tradition of Asaṅga—who is regarded as the consummate interpreter of the qualified interpretation of emptiness (*gzhan stong*) in the school of Middle Way Yogic Practitioners—is more far-reaching (that is, applicable to the fruition state), more subtle, and oriented toward internal investigation and the ultimate point of meditation.
506. Gargyi Wangpo Chökyi Wangchuk (Gar gyi dbang po chos kyi dbang phyug, 1584–1630) was the sixth Zhamar incarnation of the Karma Kagyü lineage, student of the ninth Karmapa Wangchuk Dorjé (dBang phyug rdo rje, 1556–1603?), and tutor of the tenth Karmapa Chöying Dorjé (Chos dbyings rdo rje, 1604–1674). Noted for his erudition, he authored works that are still important sources, especially on the "six yogic practices of Nāropa" (Tib. *Nā ro chos drug*).
507. That is, India.
508. That is, in the secret mantra approach of Vajrayāna (the "esoteric" branch of the Mahāyāna approach) as compared to the equivalent aspect in the Pāramitāyāna (the "exoteric" branch). While the terms "subjective aspect" (Tib. *yul can*) and "objective aspect" (Tib. *yul*) are employed, in this context these are pure conventions to facilitate understanding on the level of ordinary language and concepts. The consummate view of both branches of the Mahāyāna is that of nondual timeless awareness; nevertheless, one can provisionally speak of the subjective aspect (timeless awareness) being "aware of" the objective aspect (emptiness).
509. That is, the Pāramitāyāna.
510. This is a reference to a traditional method of divination, in which the diviner beholds visions arising on the surface of a mirror, without the usual process of causes and conditions to account for these manifestations, which are termed "expressions of emptiness" (Tib. *stong gzugs*).
511. Sakya Paṇḍita Kunga Gyaltsen (Sa skya paṇḍi ta Kun dga' rgyal mtshan, 1182–1251) was perhaps the most learned master of the Sakya school of Tibetan Buddhism, whose writings have served as a basis for the school's view, termed "the inseparability of saṃsāra and nirvāṇa" (Tib. *'khor 'das dbyer med*).
512. Kongtrul is obliquely implying that Sakya Paṇḍita accepted the latter point, in that he did not specifically or explicitly refute it in his writings.
513. That is, (1) the elimination of origination, (2) the elimination of cessation, (3) profundity, and (4) lucidity.
514. The Tibetan term for Middle Way is *dbu ma*, which some translators render as "Centrist"; the same term is used in Vajrayāna contexts to refer to the central subtle channel. Thus, the central channel is a particular expression in Vajrayāna contexts of the "central principle" of the greater Mahāyāna.
515. The Sanskrit term *avadhūti*, used untranslated by Tibetans, is another term for the central subtle channel:

> The term *avadhūti* can be translated as deriving from *avadhūnoti*, which means "banishing the harmful effects of actions." It can also be translated as "eliminating duality," or "shaking everything off." Kongtrul, *The Treasury of Knowledge: Books Nine and Ten: Journey and Goal*, 181.

516. These are techniques in the practice of the stage of development according to the Kālacakra cycle. Once one has visualized a deity and the attendant features, such as the mandala and mansion, and maintained the visualization during a session of meditation, the entire visualization is mentally dissolved into a formless state of meditation, either all at once (instantaneous dissolution) or step by step (gradual dissolution). This dissolution technique is a powerful means of directing the mind toward a realization of the emptiness of all phenomena.
517. A reference to a model found in Vajrayāna teachings, which involves four factors:
 (1) the ground for the refinement process (Tib. *sbyang gzhi*), which is a way of referring to the buddha nature that is primordially present as a natural attribute in all beings, comparable to a flawless wish-granting gem with many facets (representing the manifold qualities innately present in the buddha nature as natural attributes);
 (2) the factors that are to be refined away (Tib. *sbyang bya*), which are all the adventitious distortions, both subtle and more obvious, that obscure the ground of being, which are comparable to a layer of mud that covers the gem without in any way affecting or diminishing it;
 (3) the factors that effect the refinement process (Tib. *sbyong byed*), which are the techniques employed in the two stages of Vajrayāna practice (the stage of development and the stage of completion), which are comparable to the water and cleansing substance used to remove the superficial layer of mud; and
 (4) the result of the refinement process (Tib. *sbyangs 'bras*), which is the context in which the qualities of enlightenment, innately present in the ground of being, have become fully evident once the adventitious distortions have been refined away, comparable to the revealing of the gem once the mud has been removed, so that it can function as the answer to all one's wishes.
518. Jamyang Chökyi Nangwa ('Jam dbyangs chos kyi snang ba) is another name for the sixth Zhamar Gargyi Wangpo Chökyi Wangchuk (1584–1630). The title "vajra of enlightened speech" refers to the successive Zhamar incarnations being considered emanations of the buddha Amitābha, associated with the padma, or lotus, family and the principle of enlightened speech. The "crown marked with light" is a reference to the formal red crown of the Zhamarpas. The reference to "the north" is to Tibet, which lies to the north of India, the historical home of Buddhism.
519. That is, as white as a conch shell.
520. That is, sublime intelligence that derives from hearing, contemplating, and meditating on teachings.
521. The source verses of *The Treasury of Knowledge* read "one trains with precision" (*zhib mor sbyong*), but the verses as cited by Kongtrul in the commentary, as well as the prose commentary itself, read "one conducts oneself with precision" (*zhib mor spyod*).
522. Implicit in this statement is Kongtrul's deeply held belief that indulging in intolerant sectarian biases constitutes nothing less than a rejection of the Buddha's teachings.
523. The tradition of pith instructions is the approach that presents the Buddhist teachings in a concise way so that one can incorporate them into one's spiritual practice immediately, without having to go through a more lengthy process of study beforehand.
524. These four divisions are those of monks, nuns, laymen, and laywomen.
525. This would have been particularly true in traditional societies that lacked modern technology and training to aid those with such challenges to receiving spiritual instruction.

526. Nāgārjuna, *Letter to a Friend*, v. 64a, (Toh. 4182), Dg. T., sPriṅ yig, vol. Nge, p. 86, l. 4: "to be reborn among any of the long-lived gods, . . ." The explanation is actually from Mahāmati, *Clear Words: An Extensive Explanation of "Letter to a Friend,"* (Toh. 4190), Dg. T., sPriṅ yig, vol. Nge, p. 192, l. 4:

> The text "to be reborn among any of the long-lived gods" is a reference to those in the state devoid of perception and the realm of formlessness.

527. The realm of form in saṃsāra is divided into four major levels of meditative stability, further divided into seventeen states (three each in the first three levels of meditative stability and eight in the fourth level). The state of the Mahāphala gods is the third of the eight states in the fourth level of meditative stability.
528. A metaphor for their special state of mental isolation.
529. The realm of formlessness comprises four states, those of infinite space, infinite consciousness, nothingness, and "neither nothingness nor not nothingness" (also referred to as the pinnacle state of conditioned existence). Those reborn in these states are, as the text notes, ordinary mortal beings still within the cycle of saṃsāra, not spiritually advanced beings who have gained liberation from that cycle.
530. See Aśvaghoṣa, *Account of the Eight States Devoid of Opportunity*, (Toh. 4167), Dg. T., sPriṅ yig, vol. Ge, p. 353, l. 7.
531. Source not identified; see, by way of comparison, sGam.po.pa, *The Jewel Ornament of Liberation*, 24, n. 11: "In the 'rDzogs chen kun.bzaṅ bla.ma', fol. 13b, this verse is attributed to Nāgārjuna."
532. There are five such acts: parricide, matricide, killing an arhat, causing a schism in the Buddhist spiritual community, or causing physical injury to a buddha. So severe are the karmic consequences of these acts that the perpetrator's mind is immediately reborn in a hell realm upon death, without passing through the usual intermediate state after death and before rebirth.
533. The Three Repositories of the Buddhist teachings are those of the ethical codes (Vinaya), the discourses (Sūtra), and the further teachings (Abhidharma).
534. Source not identified.
535. On this note, it is traditionally said in the Hīnayāna teachings that the Buddha's teachings would endure in this world for five thousand years following his passing, this period being divided into ten periods of five hundred years each, during which the fruition that beings could hope to attain would steadily decline. The first three periods of five hundred years, known collectively as the "time of mastery of pristine awareness," are periods during which beings could attain the state of arhats, nonreturners, or "stream-winners," respectively. The fourth through sixth periods, known as the "time of accomplishment," are marked by emphasis on the attainment of profound insight, meditative absorption, and ethical discipline, respectively. The seventh through ninth periods, known as the "time of scriptural transmission," are marked by emphasis on the abhidharma, sūtra, and vinaya teachings, respectively. The tenth and final period of five hundred years is known as the "time of mere outer signs," during which people will continue to wear the robes of Buddhist monastics without there being any genuine view or conduct.
536. Candragomin, *Letter to Students*, v. 64, (Toh. 4183), Dg. T., sPriṅ yig, vol. Nge, p. 99, lines 2–3. All of these are nonhuman beings in traditional Buddhist cosmology. The term *vidyādhara* ("master of awareness") in this context refers to non-Buddhist

saints and renunciates. Kiṃnaras were beings who adopted human form in order to attend and listen to the Buddha's teachings, but were unable to put those teachings into practice effectively because they were, in fact, not human.

537. The three realms of desire, form, and formlessness that comprise saṃsāra, the cycle of conditioned existence.

538. See *Foundation of Scriptural Transmission*, (Toh. 1), Dg. K., 'Dul ba, vol. Ka, p. 173, l. 7 to p. 174, l. 4:

> Then the transcendent and accomplished conqueror took some motes of dust on his fingernail and addressed the monks in the following manner:
>
> "O monks, what do you think of this? Between whatever motes of dust I have taken on my fingernail and whatever motes of dust there are on the surface of the earth, which are more numerous?"
>
> The venerable ones replied, "However many motes of dust the transcendent and accomplished conqueror has taken on his fingernail, these are few, they are very few, they are extremely few, they are the least amount. If they are compared to the motes of dust on the surface of the earth, the former do not come close to being one hundredth of the latter. They do not come close to one thousandth, they do not come close to one hundred thousandth, they do not come close to any fraction, or portion, or enumeration of the latter, nor even to any sample or rudimentary part thereof."
>
> The transcendent and accomplished conqueror addressed them in the following manner:
>
> "O monks, as many motes of dust as there are on the surface of the earth, these represent as many beings there are that pass from their lives as beings in hell realms and are reborn again as beings in hell realms. As many motes of dust as there are on my fingernail, these represent as many beings there are that pass from their lives as beings in hell realms and are reborn as human beings."

539. Śāntideva, *Engaging in the Conduct of a Bodhisattva*, chap. 4, v. 20b–d, (Toh. 3871), Dg. T., dBu ma, vol. La, p. 16, lines 6–7.

540. The legendary udumbara flower is said to bloom only when a fully awakened buddha appears in the world, and hence is a traditional symbol of something very rare.

541. That is, the personification of one's inevitable mortality.

542. In the traditional cosmology of the Buddhist Abhidharma teachings, human beings occupy four "continents" in our (and every other) world system. Of these four, our human world (that is, the equivalent of the Earth in Western experience) is the southern continent of Jambudvīpa, in which the life spans of human beings are highly individual and unpredictable; the life spans of the human beings on the other three "continents" are by and large fixed at a set number of years, due to the relatively greater merit of beings reborn in those realms. These humans, however, do not have any significant advantage with respect to spiritual practice, since it is the very unpredictability of our life span that motivates us to use the opportunity for spiritual practice while it still exists, rather than procrastinate, knowing that we will live a specific number of years.

543. Source not identified.

544. Nāgārjuna, *Letter to a Friend*, v. 84, (Toh. 4182), Dg. T., sPriṅ yig, vol. Nge, p. 88, lines 3–4.

545. Ibid, v. 86, p. 88, lines 4–5.
546. Ibid, v. 91, p. 89, l. 1.
547. Ibid, v. 89, p. 88, lines 6–7.
548. The transition from the state of an ordinary mortal individual to that of a spiritually advanced being is the attainment of the path of seeing; see n. 120 above.
549. Arhats of a certain kind are subject to a small degree of suffering, such as headaches. See Longchen Rabjam, *The Precious Treasury of Philosophical Systems*, 140:

> For arhats who experience residual traces, there remains a slight residue of the truth of suffering (since they have not yet eliminated the mind-body aggregates that perpetuate saṃsāra), and so they must guard their senses closely with respect to sense objects.

550. Nāgārjuna, *Precious Garland*, chap. 1, v. 21, (Toh. 4158), Dg. T., sPriṅ yig, vol. Ge, p. 214, lines 5–6.
551. See Longchen Rabjam, *The Precious Treasury of Philosophical Systems*, 56:

> The Samkhya system, the progenitor of the main systems of Indian philosophy, posits that all objects of knowledge are subsumed within the two categories of soul and primal matter.

The Sāṃkhyas held that the soul (Tib. *skyes bu*; Skt. *puruṣa*) is the passive subjective perceiver, with primal matter (Tib. *gtso bo*; Skt. *prakṛti*) being its object as the creative force that is responsible for the evolution of all other objects of knowledge, including the mental and physical components of ordinary experience in the world. As a nontheistic system, Buddhism does not posit either a creative force like primal matter or a creator god to account for the way things manifest in our experience.

552. Where, for example, a single seed leads to a single plant and not multiple ones.
553. The source text reads "very destructive" (Tib. *'jig chen*); *The Treasury of Knowledge* reads "very frightening" (Tib. *'jigs chen*).
554. Dharmatrāta, *Didactic Aphorisms*, chap. 28, (Toh. 4099), Dg. T., mNgon pa, vol. Tu, p. 57, lines 4–5.
555. That is, the Buddha Śākyamuni.
556. That is, the magnification factor of small causes producing much greater results brings about enormous results, far beyond a "one-to-one" connection between actions as causes and experiences as results. Those causes, however, must be present for the results to ensue.
557. *Foundation of Ethical Codes* (that is, *Foundation of Scriptural Transmission*), chap. 4, (Toh. 1), Dg. K., 'Dul ba, vol. Ka, p. 81, l. 2.
558. That is, through physical, verbal, and mental actions.
559. That is, the Buddha Śākyamuni.
560. The ten kinds of nonvirtuous, harmful action are three of body (killing, stealing, and sexual misconduct, with the latter differing depending on lay or monastic status), four of speech (lying, divisive speech, abusive language, and idle gossip), and three of mind (covetousness, malicious intent, and dogmatic belief systems). The ten kinds of virtuous, positive action, as Kongtrul notes, do not lie simply in the avoidance of the ten negative kinds of action, but in the active pursuit of their opposites (preserving life, being generous, observing sexual ethics, being truthful, resolving conflicts, speaking kindly, speaking with purpose, cultivating contentment, fostering benevolent

attitudes, and seriously investigating spiritual truths). See sGam.po.pa, *The Jewel Ornament of Liberation*, 74–90.

561. Vasubandhu, *Treasury of Abhidharma*, chap. 4, v. 66b–d, (Toh. 4089), Dg. T., mNgon pa, vol. Ku, p. 25, l. 7 to p. 26, l. 1.

562. That is, by the Buddha. *Detailed Analysis of Ethical Codes* (that is, *Detailed Analysis of Scriptural Transmission*), chap. 83, (Toh. 3), Dg. K., 'Dul ba, vol. Nya, p. 536, l. 7 to p. 537, l. 1. This verse also appears in *Discourse on Individual Liberation for Fully Ordained Nuns*, (Toh. 4), Dg. K., 'Dul ba, vol. Ta, p. 49, lines 1–2; and in *Detailed Analysis of Ethical Codes for Fully Ordained Nuns*, chap. 28, (Toh. 5), Dg. K., 'Dul ba, vol. Ta, p. 654, l. 7 to p. 655, l. 1.

563. See Kongtrul, *The Treasury of Knowledge: Book Five: Buddhist Ethics*.

564. See Asaṅga, *Levels of Yogic Practitioners*, (Toh. 4035), Sems tsam, vol. Tshi, p. 166, l. 4 to p. 167, l. 2:

> If one wonders how one should understand what characterizes afflictive mental states as being powerful, what characterizes them as being intense, what characterizes them as being weighty, in brief this is due to six factors: failing, origination, psychological makeup, focus, deeply ingrained motivation, and consummation. Of these, "failing" refers to all moral failings without exception occurring due to deeply ingrained afflictive mental states. "Origination" refers to that which leads to experience in the realm of desire, or to lower states of rebirth. "Psychological makeup" refers to any conduct due to desire and attachment and so forth, or any states that are not associated with complete nirvāṇa, that occur when one is in the prime of life, with all one's faculties fully developed. "Focus" refers to someone who serves as a guru being the point of reference, or someone or something imbued with positive qualities being the point of reference, or any situation in which one should not be involved being the point of reference. "Deeply ingrained motivation" refers to deeply ingrained patterns of afflictive mental states overwhelming and completely controlling one's mind, such that one's physical and verbal actions are completely influenced. "Consummation" refers to whatever by its very nature constitutes one's predominant pattern; in its initial stages, this can be eliminated by a relatively small antidote.

In the discussion that follows of the factors that give weight to a specific action, Kongtrul employs somewhat different terminology and explanations.

565. The three emotional poisons are those of attachment, aversion, or ignorance. See Nāgārjuna, *Precious Garland*, chap. 1, v. 19, (Toh. 4158), Dg. T., sPriṅ yig, vol. Ge, p. 214, l. 5:

> That which is produced by attachment, aversion,
> or delusion is nonvirtuous;
> that which is produced by nonattachment, the absence of aversion,
> and the absence of delusion is virtuous.

566. That is, of the three kinds of nonvirtuous or virtuous physical actions, killing (or preserving life) has more karmic impact than stealing (or being generous), which has more impact than sexual misconduct (or ethical sexual behavior). Of the four kinds of verbal actions, lying (or speaking the truth) has more impact than divisive speech (or resolving conflicts with speech), which has more impact than abusive speech (or

speaking kindly), which has more impact than idle gossip (or speaking with purpose). Of the three kinds of mental actions, covetousness (or cultivating contentment) has less impact than malicious intent (or fostering benevolent attitudes), which has less impact than dogmatic belief systems (or the investigation of spiritual truths).

567. Nāgārjuna, *Letter to a Friend*, v. 42, (Toh. 4182), Dg. T., sPriṅ yig, vol. Nge, p. 84, lines 4–5.
568. *Mound of Precious Gems*, (Toh. 88), Dg. K., dKon brtsegs (No. 44), vol. Cha, p. 303, l. 1 to p. 350, l. 2 is the forty-fourth of the forty-nine sections that comprise the five-volume sūtra collection entitled *Amassing of the Rare and Sublime*. Kongtrul seems here to be summarizing a passage rather than citing it verbatim; while many examples similar to the one to which Kongtrul refers are found throughout this collection, this particular passage has not been located as presented here.
569. Śāntideva, *Engaging in the Conduct of a Bodhisattva*, chap. 6 . v. 1, (Toh. 3871), Dg. T., dBu ma, vol. La, p. 28, l. 3.
570. This could mean either an ordained monastic or an arhat.
571. That is, someone who has sincerely given rise to bodhicitta (not necessarily a spiritually advanced being).
572. Asaṅga, *Levels of Yogic Practitioners*, (Toh. 4035), Sems tsam, vol. Tshi, p. 183, l. 6 to p. 184, l. 1:

    If one asks what the situations affecting karma are, briefly speaking they are to be understood as . . . the situation of a small degree, the situation of a middling degree, the situation of a greater degree. . . . Of these, a small degree of nonvirtuous action leads to rebirth in animal states; a middling degree leads to rebirth in preta states; and a greater degree leads to rebirth in hell states.

573. *Ten Levels of Realization*, (Toh. 44), Dg. K., Phal chen, vol. Kha, p. 378, l. 7 to p. 379, l. 1:

    Greater degrees of involvement in, cultivation of, and repeated commission of paths of nonvirtuous action become the causes for rebirth in hell states. Middling degrees become the causes for rebirth in animal states of existence. Smaller degrees become the causes for rebirth in the world of the lord of death [that is, preta states].

574. That is, the perpetrator who kills another being will experience a shortening of life (usually in a future lifetime) as a consequence. Each line refers to a specific action causing the mind stream of the perpetrator to experience the corresponding result.
575. Nāgārjuna, *Precious Garland*, chap. 1, v. 13–15c, (Toh. 4158), Dg. T., sPriṅ yig, vol. Ge, p. 214, lines 2–3.
576. Source not identified.
577. Asaṅga, *Levels of Yogic Practitioners*, (Toh. 4035), Sems tsam, vol. Tshi, p. 184, lines 1–2:

    A small degree of virtuous action leads to rebirth in human states; a middling degree leads to rebirth in states of gods who experience the realm of desire; and a greater degree leads to rebirth in states of gods who experience the realms of form and formlessness.

578. That is, actions that set karmic tendencies in motion or reinforce them versus those that are expressions of the result of such tendencies.

579. The most common traditional model for the states of ordinary beings in saṃsāra is of six kinds of beings—hell beings, pretas, animals, human being, demigods, and gods. An alternate model combines the states of demigods and gods as one higher state of rebirth, for a total of five states of ordinary being.
580. Maitreya, *Highest Continuum*, chap. 4, v. 53b–c, (Toh. 4024), Dg. T, Sems tsam, vol. Phi, p. 138, l. 5.
581. Since it entails eventual death.
582. In addition to the pain and discomfort of the illness itself, this also refers to the physical and mental distress that invasive cures might entail.
583. This refers to one's sense of physical threat at being separated from what one finds appealing.
584. That is, due to one's having taken rebirth.
585. Here Kongtrul is paraphrasing the content of Nāgārjuna's *Letter to a Friend* (vv. 66–76 in particular), rather than citing specific passages; see Kangyur Rinpoche, *Nagarjuna's "Letter to a Friend" with Commentary by Kangyur Rinpoche*, 123–28.
586. See, for example, an account concerning one of the Buddha's main disciples, Kātyāyana, in Patrul Rinpoche, *The Words of My Perfect Teacher*, 50–51:

> One day while the Arhat Kātyāyana was out on his alms-round he came across a man with a child on his lap. The man was eating a fish with great relish, and throwing stones at a bitch that was trying to get at the bones. What the master saw with his clairvoyance, however, was this. The fish had been the man's own father in that very lifetime, and the bitch had been his mother. An enemy he had killed in a past existence had been reborn as his son, as the karmic repayment for the life the man had taken. Kātyāyana cried out:
>
> > He eats his father's flesh, he beats his mother off,
> > He dandles on his lap the enemy that he killed;
> > The wife is gnawing at her husband's bones.
> > I laugh to see what happens in saṁsāra's show!

587. That is, pass from this life.
588. That is, pretas.
589. That is, the human state. Kongtrul actually cites the line as reading: "For humans, there is also . . ."
590. That is, a relentless process of suffering. Vasubandhu, *Advice for the Multitude*, vv. 17–18, (Toh. 4166), Dg. T., sPriṅ yig, vol. Ge, p. 347, lines 4–5.
591. Kongtrul cites the phrase "the two kinds of suffering" (Tib. *sdus bsngal **gnyis***) as "suffering itself" (Tib. *sdug bsngal **nyid***), possibly conflating the homophonous words.
592. Āryadeva, *Four Hundred Verses*, chap. 2, v. 33, (Toh. 3846), Dg. T., dBu ma, vol. Tsha, p. 5, lines 5–6. In his *Extensive Commentary on the "Four Hundred Verses for Engaging in a Bodhisattva's Conduct,"* (Toh. 3865), Dg. T., dBu ma, vol. Ya, p. 96, lines 2–6, Candrakīrti comments:

> Therefore, if one thinks that the body cannot thus be the epitome of suffering, [Āryadeva] has this to say:
>
> > For the highly placed there is mental suffering,
> > while for the lowly it is born of the body;

day by day, the two kinds of suffering
bring destruction in the world.

Suffering is of two kinds, that of body and that of mind. Of these, for those who are the highest placed—with vast wealth, of good family, possessed of enormous desires—it is difficult for them to attain the enormous things they obsess about. Therefore, they feel intense jealousy and cannot find what they desire, which causes them inescapable mental suffering. On the other hand, lowly ones—those of ignoble family, with the poorest of diets and beds and dwellings and clothing—are overwhelmed by suffering on the physical level.

Thus, how can there be any chance of real happiness for anyone? Therefore, for the foregoing reasons, these two kinds of suffering bring destruction to the entire world each and every day.

593. Although gods in the realm of desire experience great pleasure during their extremely long lifetimes, they experience intense and demoralizing suffering toward the end of their lives as they see indications of their impending demise and fall into lower states of great suffering; see Nāgārjuna, *Letter to a Friend*, vv. 99–100b, (Toh. 4182), Dg. T., sPriṅ yig, vol. Nge, p. 89, lines 6–7:

The complexions of their bodies becomes ugly,
they are no longer comfortable on their seats, their garlands of flowers wither,
their clothing begins to smell, and from their bodies
issues sweat (which has not happened previously)—such are the five indications
of impending death, signaling to those in higher states that they will die and fall,
which occur for gods who inhabit the celestial states.

594. That is, in their battle with the demigods. Although gods can be healed of their wounds with the nectar that is found in their world, they still undergo pain when those wounds are inflicted.
595. That is, the realms of form and formlessness.
596. That is, the higher trainings in ethical discipline, meditative stability, and sublime intelligence. The entire text of *The Treasury of Knowledge* began as a treatise on these three higher trainings.
597. For if they reverted to higher states of rebirth in saṃsāra, they would eventually fall again into lower ones.
598. *Cluster of Stems*, (Toh. 44), Dg. K., Phal chen, vol. A, p. 618, l. 1.
599. The distinction here is between the specific cause, also called the "direct cause" (Tib. *dngos rgyu*), of a specific result (such as the grain of barley for the barley seedling) and other contributing causes, also called "indirect causes" (Tib. *brgyud rgyu*), that are needed but not essential for the specific result to occur.
600. That is, enlightenment as defined in the śrāvaka, pratyekabuddha, and bodhisattva approaches; see Kongtrul, *The Treasury of Knowledge: Books Nine and Ten: Journey and Goal*, 285–87.
601. Maitreya, *Highest Continuum*, chap. 1, v. 34a–b, (Toh. 4024), Dg. T, Sems tsam, vol. Phi, p. 111, lines 6–7.

602. The point of the analogy is, of course, that bodhicitta is the specific cause of the enlightenment of buddhahood, while the realization of some degree of emptiness is the common cause of all corresponding degrees of enlightenment. While Kongtrul's analogy has been translated here as given in his original text, it is obviously a product of a patriarchal culture that, without the benefits of modern genetics, accepted the assumption (found in many ancient cultures, and in Aristotelian thought, for example) that the mother played a passive role in conception, being simply the receptacle for the father's sperm, which alone determined the sex (or even the life itself) of the child. A more accurate analogy might be that the father is responsible for the sex of the child, while the mother bears all children in common, regardless of gender.

603. Nāgārjuna, *In Praise of She Who Is the Transcendent Perfection of Sublime Intelligence*, v. 17, (Toh. 1127), Dg. T., bsTod tshogs, vol. Ka, p. 152, lines 3–4. In the source, the last two lines read slightly differently than as cited by Kongtrul:

> The path to liberation is one only—you;
> thus, it is certain that there is no other.

604. For example, the three longest versions of the Prajñāpāramitā sūtras are referred to by Tibetans as the "Extensive Mother" (Tib. *Yum rgyas pa*), the "Middle-Length Mother" (Tib. *Yum 'bring po*), and the "Concise Mother" (Tib. *Yum bsdus pa*).

605. That is, the Bengali master Atīśa Dipaṃkara Śrījñāna (982?–1054?), who was arguably the single most important figure in the introduction to Tibet of teachings on the cultivation of bodhicitta. His Tibetan students founded the famous Kadampa school of Tibetan Buddhism, whose teachings are found in all Tibetan schools surviving to modern times.

606. Atīśa's principal Tibetan student was the layman Dromtön Gyalwai Jungné ('Brom ston rGyal ba'i 'byung gnas, 1004/5–1064), who in turn had three main students—the "three spiritual brothers" Potowa Rinchen Sal (Po to ba Rin chen gsal, 1027–1105), Chen-ngawa Tsultrim Bar (sPyan snga ba Tshul khrims 'bar, 1033/38–1103), and Puchungwa Shönnu Gyaltsen (Phu chung ba gZhon nu rgyal mtshan, 1031–1106). Sharawa Yönten Drak (Sha ra ba Yon tan grags, 1070–1141) was a student of Potowa, and it was Sharawa's student Tumtön Lodrö Drak (gTum ston bLo gros grags, 1106–1166) who codified the five-stage method of arousing bodhicitta; he is also credited with founding the monastery of Narthang, which became the source of an important edition of the Kangyur and Tengyur collections. See Roerich, *The Blue Annals*, 282.

607. The Tibetan term for "mental training" (*blo sbyong*) refers specifically to these and other processes of arousing and cultivating bodhicitta, all based on the teachings of Atīśa, whose impact on the future development of the Tibetan Buddhist tradition was enormous.

608. Jayulwa Shönnu Ö (Bya yul ba gZhon nu 'od, 1075–1138) was a student of Chen-ngawa Tsultrim Bar. Jayulwa's principal student was Tsangpa Dorjé Mikyö (gTsang pa rDo rje mi bskyod, 1077–1161), who succeeded to the abbatial throne of Jayul monastery after his master's passing. See ibid., 292–97.

609. The Tibetan term *yid du 'ong ba* (literally meaning "appealing to one's mind") implies that bodhisattvas feel connected to others, can empathize with their suffering, and feel inspired to relieve it. Everyone can feel compassion to a limited extent, but the resulting sense of being emotionally overwhelmed or incapacitated in the face of that suffering hinders the development of the "supreme compassion" that leads to bodhi-

citta. It is a common misconception that in order to "be compassionate" one must become as upset as the one whom one sees is suffering.

610. See Kamalaśīla, *Stages of Meditation*, (Toh. 3916), Dg. T., dBu ma, vol. Ki, p. 85, l. 1.
611. See n. 612.
612. Nāgārjuna, *Precious Garland*, chap. 3, v. 85, (Toh. 4158), Dg. T., sPriṅ yig, vol. Ge, p. 234, lines 3–5.
613. The term "corruptible" (Tib. *zag bcas*; Skt. *āsrāvin*) refers to situations that are still based on conceptual consciousness, and thus susceptible to the onset of afflictive mental states.
614. That is, one confers virtue as the *cause* of happiness, rather than merely the happiness that is the result of virtue.
615. That is, sūtras such as the *Ten Levels of Realization* and the *Garland of Buddhas*, which emphasize the principle of sublime intelligence. Kamalaśīla develops this theme in the intermediate version of *Stages of Meditation*, (Toh. 3916), Dg. T., dBu ma, vol. Ki, (see especially p. 84, l. 5 to p. 87, l. 2).
616. Kamalaśīla, *Stages of Meditation*, (Toh. 3915), Dg. T., dBu ma, vol. Ki, p. 46, l. 7 to p. 47, l. 1.
617. The enlightenment attained by śrāvakas and pratyekabuddhas entails their personal liberation from the sufferings of saṃsāra but limited insight into the true nature of things and limited ability to benefit others. The supreme enlightenment of buddhahood, attainable only through the Mahāyāna approach, entails both liberation and omniscience, as well as an infinite capacity to benefit others.
618. There are two factors that obscure the true nature of one's being, preventing access to, and direct experience of, that nature. They are the afflictive obscurations (that is, thought patterns and emotional responses based on afflictive mental states, which hinder the attainment of liberation from suffering) and the cognitive obscurations (that is, thought patterns based on dualistic consciousness, which hinder the attainment of omniscience).
619. *Chapter of Kāśyapa*, (Toh. 87), Dg. K., dKon brtsegs (No. 43), vol. Cha, p. 265, l. 7 to p. 266, l. 1. The *Chapter of Kāśyapa* is the forty-third of the forty-nine sections that comprise the five-volume sūtra collection entitled *Amassing of the Rare and Sublime*.
620. Kongtrul's citation of this passage reads simply: "Whenever an advanced spiritual practitioner . . ."
621. The source text simply reads: "also will not lead . . ."
622. Kamalaśīla, *Stages of Meditation*, (Toh. 3916), Dg. T., dBu ma, vol. Ki, p. 98, lines 4–6. It is not clear whether Kamalaśīla is quoting the Buddha ("the transcendent and accomplished conqueror") directly or simply paraphrasing similar statements made by the Buddha.
623. Given that Kongtrul attributes these remarks to "holy masters of the past," it is likely that he is paraphrasing a number of such observations, rather than citing any one source in particular.
624. The Tibetan idiom *nyams su blang ba*, translated here as "to put into practice," could literally be rendered "to incorporate into one's experience."
625. Kongtrul has discussed the process of developing this intelligence throughout the previous book (Book 7) of *The Treasury of Knowledge*.
626. This chapter has been published as Kongtrul, *The Treasury of Knowledge: Book Eight, Part Three: The Elements of Tantric Practice*, translated by Elio Guarisco and Ingrid

McLeod.

627. This chapter has been published as Kongtrul, *The Treasury of Knowledge: Book Eight, Part Four: Esoteric Instructions*, translated by Sarah Harding.
628. That is, the Buddha.
629. *Definitive Commentary on Enlightened Intent*, (Toh. 106), Dg. K., mDo sde, vol. Ca, p. 68, l. 5. In the source sūtra, the text omits the phrase "within calm abiding and profound insight," but this is found in the line immediately following as part of Maitreya's further inquiry to the Buddha.
630. That is, whether they merely contribute temporarily to the improvement of one's circumstances in saṃsāra or to one's attainment of liberation and enlightenment.
631. Ibid., p. 68, l. 7 to p. 69, l. 1.
632. *Cloud of the Rare and Excellent*, (Toh. 231), Dg. K., mDo sde, vol. Wa, p. 184, l. 1. The source sūtra gives a fuller description of profound insight: "Profound insight is discernment of phenomena in an authentic manner, just as they are."
633. The source text reads: "settling intimately in mind . . ."
634. Vasubandhu, *Explanation of the "Ornament of the Mahāyāna Sūtras,"* (Toh. 4026), Dg. K., Sems tsam, vol. Phi, p. 457, lines 3–4.
635. See Kunga Tenpai Nyima, "A Lamp on the Path to Liberation":

> Through familiarization with such a one-pointed mind of the desire realm, your body and mind become attuned. This is termed "thorough pliancy." The mind, being mastered like a well-disciplined horse, can be placed at will in any positive state. Your mind experiences a sense of well-being, for it is completely freed of any potential for future negative states such as the unhappiness that comes from anxiety and other factors. By the power of this mental well-being, a finely attuned energy moves through your body. Your body is free of heaviness and other impediments to its functioning which contain some potential for future negative states. Your spinal column feels like a stack of golden coins, while your body feels light as a ball of cotton. You feel as though your body were flooded throughout by a warm flow of milk, as this sense of well-being brings pliancy of the body, which can function at will in positive activities. Such pliancy is coarse at first, growing progressively more subtle. From these initial coarse and subtle phases, eventually this pliancy clearly becomes total. While the coarse phase of pliancy distracts the mind, gradually the strength of this distraction weakens, and a subtle phase of pliancy sets in, light as a shadow, serving to complement unwavering meditative absorption. This is termed "calm abiding that is included within the stages of meditative stability." This process ensures that any meditative technique you employ—the stage of development, the stage of completion, or whatever—becomes authentic.

636. Kamalaśīla, *Stages of Meditation*, (Toh. 3916), Dg. T, dBu ma, vol. Ki, p. 92, l. 7 to p. 93, l. 2.
637. From the Sanskrit root *sthā* (to abide or remain or stay).
638. Kongtrul is here using a Sanskrit term that is cognate to the more usual *vipaśyanā*.
639. From the Sanskrit root *vi-śaṣ* (to cut up or dissect).
640. From the Sanskrit root *paś* (to see or look at).
641. Kongtrul discusses this topic in Book 7, Part 3.

642. Śāntideva, *Engaging in the Conduct of a Bodhisattva*, chap. 8, v. 4a–c, (Toh. 3871), Dg. T., dBu ma, vol. La, p. 46, l. 1–2.
643. Atīśa Dipaṃkara Śrījñāna, *Chapter on the Circumstances for Meditative Absorption*, (Toh. 2460), Dg. T. rGyud 'grel, vol. Zi, p. 268, l. 6 to p. 269, l. 6.
644. The line in the source text reads simply: "With respect to any focus whatsoever, . . ."
645. The computerized edition of *The Treasury of Knowledge* reads, in error, "nonvirtuous."
646. Atīśa Dipaṃkara Śrījñāna, *Lamp on the Path to Enlightenment*, vv. 39–41b, (Toh. 3947), Dg. T., dBu ma, vol. Khi, p. 478, l. 7 to p. 479, l. 2. The title "Lord" (Tib. *Jo bo*) is commonly used as an affectionate nickname for Atīśa.
647. Kamalaśīla, *Stages of Meditation*, (Toh. 3916), Dg. T., dBu ma, vol. Ki, p. 90, l. 2. The source text reads simply: "to completely avoid the concepts of desire and so forth."
648. Maitreya, *Ornament of the Mahāyāna Sūtras*, chap. 14, v. 7, (Toh. 4020), Dg. T., Sems tsam, vol. Phi, p. 34, l. 7 to p. 35, l. 1. In the source text, the last line reads: "and the qualities that delight . . ."
649. The Tibetan term *rten* refers to the particular physical embodiment of a given being, as the working basis for spiritual development in that lifetime.
650. These constitute what are collectively known as the "nine successive stages of meditative equipoise." The states of meditative stability are four in number and under ordinary circumstances are associated with taking rebirth in the realm of form, while the four states of meditative equipoise are associated with taking rebirth in the formless realm.

    > These eight states of equipoise are distinguished from the usual states of mundane meditation that lead to rebirth in the realms of form or formlessness; they involve mental focus and insight that free one of the attachments that are ordinarily part of such states of rebirth, and thus bring a degree of control over the mind in such states. Kongtrul, *The Treasury of Knowledge: Books Nine and Ten: Journey and Goal*, 630, n. 783.

    > The equipoise of cessation is a meditative state that brings about the cessation of more obvious perceptions and sensations—that is, the seven avenues of ordinary consciousness. The eighth avenue, that of consciousness as the basis of all ordinary experience, continues. Ibid., n. 784.

651. See Kongtrul, *The Treasury of Knowledge: Book One: Myriad Worlds* and *The Treasury of Knowledge: Books Nine and Ten: Journey and Goal.*
652. This description is found in the intermediate version; see Kamalaśīla, *Stages of Meditation*, (Toh. 3916), Dg. T., dBu ma, vol. Ki, p. 92, lines 5–7:

    > On a very soft and comfortable seat, one sits with legs crossed like the venerable Vairocana; alternatively, it is acceptable to sit with the legs half-crossed. The eyes are neither too open nor too closed, and are directed beyond the tip of one's nose. One sits with one's body neither leaning too far forward nor leaning too far backward, but held erect as one's mindfulness is directed inward. Then one's shoulders rest on an equal level with one another, neither hunched up nor slouching, but resting without moving on that one level. One's posture is in a straight vertical line from nose to navel. As well, the teeth and lips rest in their regular positions. The tongue is raised against the hard palate behind the upper teeth. One's breathing moves in and out without

> making noises, or panting, or breathing heavily; rather, one breathes so gently that one cannot, under the circumstances, really feel it happening, as one inhales and exhales in a spontaneous manner.

The identical description is given in the final version; see Kamalaśīla, *Stages of Meditation*, (Toh. 3917), Dg. T., dBu ma, vol. Ki, p. 113, lines 1–3.

653. That is, one's eyes gaze along the sides of one's nose out into the space beyond its tip.
654. That is, the Buddha Śākyamuni.
655. The general principle for a pervasive focus is that of focusing in some way (conceptual or otherwise) on the true nature that pervades all phenomena.
656. The focus on the limit of things in their multiplicity involves the understanding that all that is knowable is subsumed within, for example, the model of the four truths of spiritually advanced beings (the truths of suffering, the origins of suffering, the cessation of suffering, and the path to that cessation), the model of the mind-body aggregates, and so forth; the "limit" is the realization one has that nothing knowable lies outside the limits of these models. The focus on the limit of things from the perspective of their true nature just as it is involves the understanding that all phenomena are emptiness by their very nature, and that nothing lies beyond the limit of this fact.
657. That is, having first analyzed things on the relative level, one then investigates the significance of their being empty, lacking identity, and so forth.
658. That is, from the perspective of the fruition of calm abiding, one's mind has relied on all the frameworks of calm abiding, become familiar with them, and carried them out over and over. This effects a transformation that eliminates the tendencies in one that perpetuate ignoble states of existence.
659. In each case, the point is one of counterbalancing the existing pattern by applying an antidote, not of veering to the other extreme. To meditate on what is unattractive is simply a means to undermine one's obsessive desires, not to make one, for example, a misogynist or a misandrist.
660. That is, knowledge that accords with the nature of things—for example, the fact that ordinary beings are born as a result of karma and afflictive mental states, and not as a result of a soul, or creator god, and so forth; or that virtuous action leads to higher states of rebirth, while nonvirtuous action leads to lower states.
661. That is, calm abiding associated with any of the levels of the realm of form; by comparison with one another, each succeeding level is more subtle ("higher") than the last, while each previous level is more coarse ("lower") than the next.
662. See Longchen Rabjam, *The Precious Treasury of Philosophical Systems*, 131–32:

> What are these sixteen topics? Four concern the truth of suffering: impermanence, suffering, emptiness, and the lack of identity. Four concern the universal origin of suffering: the fact that all things in essence have causes, that these causes are the universal origin of suffering, that they are produced relentlessly, and that they are perpetuated by conditions. Four concern the cessation of suffering: cessation, peace, the ideal situation, and disengagement. Four concern the path: the path itself, the logic of this process, the proven attainment to which it leads, and the certainty of release.

Concerning the "four truths," see Longchen Rabjam, *The Precious Treasury of Philosophical Systems*, 392, n. 27:

> A term more accurate than "the four noble truths" might be "the four truths of spiritually advanced beings." They are not truths that are evident to ordinary beings, but are seen to be so by those who are spiritually advanced, i.e., who have attained the path of seeing in any of the three approaches of śrāvakas, pratyekabuddhas, or bodhisattvas.

663. That is, the context in which all sense of some object and the subjective perceiver thereof falls away; this ushers in the experience of profound insight, although it does not constitute such insight.
664. These are emblems such as vajras, lotuses, and so forth, which also figure prominently in Vajrayāna methods of deity meditation.
665. For example, a tiny sphere of white light at one's midbrow point.
666. An example is the remedial techniques of counteracting mental laxity by imagining a sphere of white light that rises from one's heart center up through the crown of one's head, and counteracting mental agitation by imagining a sphere of black light sinking from one's heart center down into the earth.
667. See Bodhibhadra, *Essay on Meditative Absorption*, (Toh. 3924), Dg. T., dBu ma, vol. Ki, p. 179, lines 3–7.
668. That is, the fundamental level of consciousness in which all sense of object and perceiving subject has fallen away. See Kongtrul, *The Treasury of Knowledge: Books Nine and Ten: Journey and Goal*, 615–16, n. 716:

> In the model of ordinary mind that involves eight avenues of consciousness (used particularly by the Cittamātra school of Buddhist philosophy), this term refers to that aspect of ordinary mind that is unaffected by obscuration and karmically "neutral" and that serves as the basis for the formation of habitual patterns. It thus provides a support for all aspects of the karmic process—both the complete maturation of its natural consequences and the potentials—and is aware of the essential qualities of the objects of one's experience (that is, the aspect of any given phenomenon that serves as a basis for its specific characteristics).

669. The term translated here as "mainstream sources" (Tib. *gzhung*) refers primarily to the texts found in the *śāstra* tradition of Indian Buddhism; the explanations in these sources can be extensive, often exhaustive. More streamlined presentations are found in texts called "personal advice" (Tib. *gdams ngag*), in which learned masters have synthesized and condensed the material found in the mainstream sources into a more accessible and practical format. This streamlining approach finds its culmination in the "pith instructions" (Tib. *man ngag*), which are extremely concise statements that in few words sum up the main principles of the subject matter. Such instructions, however, are often most useful only once one has some familiarity with the more extensive background material; otherwise, too concise a presentation can lead to one coming to flawed conclusions and making "snap judgments."
670. Maitreya, *Distinguishing Center and Limit*, chap. 4, vv. 3–5, (Toh. 4021), Dg. T., Sems tsam, vol. Phi, p. 85, lines 3–5.
671. This term is glossed as referring to the four "bases of supernormal powers"—intention, diligence, attention, and mental analysis. These four factors are called "bases" because they serve as causes for one's attainment of such powers as clairvoyance, clairaudience,

telepathy, and so forth. They focus on the elimination of factors in one's makeup that obscure the true nature of mind and its innate qualities, so that these powers are not so much gained as they are revealed. In the Buddhist tradition, such powers are seen as natural by-products of one's growing realization, not as ends in themselves; one must guard against them becoming distractions or means of self-aggrandizement.

672. The Tibetan term *le lo*, usually translated as "laziness," is here rendered as "faint-heartedness" in an attempt to include all three aspects of *le lo*, only one of which corresponds to the English word "lazy." Faintheartedness in general is defined as a secondary afflictive state that undermines one's enthusiasm for what is virtuous and spiritually productive. "Lethargy" refers to the inability to exert oneself diligently due to an addiction to pleasure. "Obsession with ignoble activities" is obviously an impediment to virtuous endeavor, and equally obviously not laziness, in that one could be extremely busy with such activities and thus fainthearted at pursuing virtue. "Diffidence" is faintheartedness in the sense that one feels inadequate and unable to make progress in spiritual practice.

673. That is, the failure to apply a remedial technique when appropriate.

674. This enumeration is found in the first version of the text; see Kamalaśīla, *Stages of Meditation*, (Toh. 3915), Dg. T., dBu ma, vol. Ki, p. 63, l. 4:

> In brief, there are six flaws that affect all states of meditative absorption: faintheartedness, forgetting the focus, mental laxity, mental agitation, lack of effort, and [too much] effort.

The identical passage is found in the final version of the text; see Kamalaśīla, *Stages of Meditation*, (Toh. 3917), Dg. T., dBu ma, vol. Ki, p. 118, l. 5.

675. In the foregoing citation from *Distinguishing Center and Limit, the context* refers to intention; *remaining within that*, to effort; *cause*, to confidence; and *effect*, to pliancy. See Kunga Tenpai Nyima, "A Lamp on the Path to Liberation":

> These are the *intention* to seek meditative absorption purposefully, the *effort* to persevere in that absorption, the *confidence* that comes from seeing the positive qualities of that absorption, and the *pliancy* that results from that perseverance. Of these, the intention is the context for meditative absorption, perseverance is remaining within that context, confidence is the cause of the intention, and pliancy is the result of perseverance. Among these, the principal factor is perseverance.

676. See, for example, ibid.:

> Among these flaws, you should recognize the two extremes of laxity and agitation to be the principal faults to be avoided. In the case of laxity, reduce the quantity of food you eat before a session of meditation, sit on an elevated seat with a thin cushion, recite prayers of refuge and supplication in a loud voice, and meditate with your body held erect. In the case of agitation, the opposite methods will eliminate the problem. Once laxity and agitation have been pacified, meditate in a relaxed state.

677. See Maitreya, *Ornament of the Mahāyāna Sūtras*, chap. 15, vv. 11–14, (Toh. 4020), Dg. T., Sems tsam, vol. Phi, p. 37, lines 5–7:

Directing the mind toward its focus,
one does not become distracted from that ongoing attention.
Swiftly realizing when there is distraction,
one returns repeatedly to that object.

The intelligent progress more and more,
directing the mind inward.
Then, because they perceive its qualities,
they guide the mind in meditative absorption.

Because they perceive the flaws in being distracted,
they pacify resistance to that absorption.
Similarly, they pacify covetous attitudes, unhappy states of mind,
and other states that rise up.

Then, those with commitment and diligence
deliberately use application on the mind,
gaining what this brings as a matter of course.
Once familiar with that, they no longer use application.

678. The terminology used in this source is slightly different from that employed by Kongtrul; see Asaṅga, *Levels of the Śrāvaka*, (Toh. 4036), Dg. T., Sems tsam, vol. Dzi, p. 266, l. 1 to p. 267, l. 1:

> The nine steps of settling the mind are ensured through six powers. These are as follows: the power of listening to teachings, the power of contemplation, the power of mindfulness, the power of alertness, the power of diligence, and the power of thorough familiarization.
>
> Of these, due to the powers of listening to and contemplating teachings, at a certain point the influence of whatever listening and contemplating one has done causes the mind first and foremost to settle on its focus, and then to settle authentically by a process of being directed to that. In the same way, the power of mindfulness with respect to the directing of the mind ensures that it concentrates effectively and does not indulge in distraction, and so causes it to settle in a concentrated manner and to settle more intimately. Then, the power of alertness ensures that the mind is not stirred toward the traces of concepts or afflictive mental states, and so causes it to be guided and pacified. The power of diligence ensures that the occurrence of either of these is not encouraged, and causes one's ongoing experience to be one-pointed. The power of thorough familiarization brings about the state of meditative absorption.
>
> One should understand that these nine steps of settling the mind involve four attitudes—those of involvement with tension, involvement with occasional interruption, involvement without occasional interruption, and effortless involvement.
>
> That is to say, in the mind's settling and settling authentically, there is the attendant attitude of involvement with tension. In the mind's settling in a concentrated manner, settling more intimately, being guided, being pacified, and being thoroughly pacified, there is the attendant attitude of

involvement with occasional interruption. In the state of one's ongoing experience's becoming one-pointed, there is the attendant attitude of involvement without occasional interruption. And with the bringing about of a state of meditative absorption, there is the attendant attitude of effortless involvement.

Thus, these attendant attitudes are factors in calm abiding as it relates to the ongoing experience of the nine steps in settling the mind.

679. *Definitive Commentary on Enlightened Intent*, (Toh. 106), Dg. K., mDo sde, vol. Ca, p. 52, lines 5–7.

680. Maitreya, *Ornament of the Mahāyāna Sūtras*, chap. 15, vv. 14d–15c, (Toh. 4020), Dg. T., Sems tsam, vol. Phi, p. 37, l. 7.

681. That is, calm abiding requires that the mind rest one-pointedly on its focus, but there is still some function for the mind to perform; it's not an inert unconscious state.

682. Asaṅga, *Compendium of Abhidharma*, chap. 1, (Toh. 4049), Dg. T., Sems tsam, vol. Ri, p. 97, l. 2.

683. Asaṅga, *Levels of the Śrāvaka*, (Toh. 4036), Dg. T., Sems tsam, vol. Dzi, p. 325, lines 3–6:

> As premonitory indications that thorough flexibility of mind and body will develop before long, the solidity of these is felt as a heaviness. This is not, however, something that could be characterized as harmful, for as soon as it has occurred any mental tendencies that perpetuate ignoble states (that is, all that pertains to afflictive mental states, which interfere with one's enjoyment of the process of refinement) are eliminated, as their antidotes—mental flexibility and thorough mental pliancy—develop.
>
> Due to the development of these, subtle energies of the major elements, promoting the development of thorough physical pliancy, move through one's body. With their movement as the cause, any physical tendencies that perpetuate ignoble states (that is, all that pertains to afflictive mental states, which interfere with one's enjoyment of the process of refinement) are eliminated, as their antidote—thorough physical pliancy—is felt to be spreading throughout and filling one's entire body.

684. Ibid., p. 325, lines 3–6:

> Following that, whatever the initial force of thorough pliancy is becomes slowly but surely very subtle, so that the body is imbued with a thorough pliancy as light as a shadow.

685. Kunga Tenpai Nyima, "A Lamp on the Path to Liberation":

> While the coarse phase of pliancy distracts the mind, gradually the strength of this distraction weakens, and a subtle phase of pliancy sets in, light as a shadow, serving to complement unwavering meditative absorption. This is termed "calm abiding that falls within the stages of meditative stability" [as distinct from calm abiding that still falls within the realm of desire].

686. That is, mastery over the states of meditative stability associated with the realm of form.

687. See, for example, the previous reference to one alternative of the focus that purifies afflictive mental states, that of focusing on the sixteen topics pertaining to the four truths.
688. These five obscurations are: mental agitation and worry, attitudes of ill will, mental torpor and sleepiness, fascination with objects of desires, and indecisiveness.
689. Asaṅga, *Levels of the Śrāvaka*, (Toh. 4036), Dg. T., Sems tsam, vol. Dzi, p. 326, l. 5 to p. 327, l. 1:

> If one directs one's mind, settling authentically by turning inward, swiftly, rapidly, the mind and body become thoroughly pliable, so that physical tendencies that perpetuate ignoble states no longer cause any great harm; so that obscurations do not stir in the mind to any great extent; and so that ideas associated with desire or ebullience or deeply felt sadness do not stir in the mind to any great extent. As well, when one arises from meditation, one's mind and body are sometimes endowed with thorough pliancy. Things that are in accord with the foregoing should be understood to be indications that one is imbued with this state of mental engagement [that is, a stable degree of calm abiding].

690. The Tibetan term *yid byed* ("[state of] mental engagement") here refers specifically to the state of stable calm abiding. In the current context, as long as one is an ordinary mortal (that is, one who has not yet attained the path of seeing), calm abiding and profound insight are "mental events," which is to say, attendant functions of the ordinary mind. Once one has attained the path of seeing (and thus has become a spiritually advanced being), these both become one's primary state of mind.
691. Kamalaśīla, *Stages of Meditation*, (Toh. 3915), Dg. T., dBu ma, vol. Ki, p. 60, l. 7.
692. Kamalaśīla, *Stages of Meditation*, (Toh. 3916), Dg. T., dBu ma, vol. Ki, p. 91, lines 3–4.
693. See Book 7, Part 1 (this volume).
694. A reference to Nāgārjuna and Asaṅga, who founded the two major lineages of teachings in the Indian tradition of Mahāyāna Buddhism. Nāgārjuna is held to have transmitted the "lineage of profound view" (Tib. *zab mo lta brgyud*), which originated with Mañjuśrī, the bodhisattva of wisdom, while Asaṅga is held to have transmitted the "lineage of extensive conduct" (Tib. *rgya chen spyod brgyud*), which originated with Maitreya, the bodhisattva of loving-kindness.
695. Each of the four states of meditative stability associated with the realm of form and the four states associated with the formless realm has a preparatory phase of meditative absorption that precedes the attainment of the actual state itself; for the purposes of this discussion, the eighth preparatory phase is not counted.
696. Kongtrul discusses the mundane path in the third and final section of Part 1 in Book 6 of *The Treasury of Knowledge: Book Six, Parts One and Two: Indo-Tibetan Classical Learning and Buddhist Phenomenology*.
697. That is, from the path of seeing (the first level of realization) onward.
698. *Definitive Commentary on Enlightened Intent*, (Toh. 106), Dg. K., mDo sde, vol. Ca, p. 52, lines 4–5:

> Thus, with respect to the mental images that are the sphere of meditative absorption, concerning the significance of these objects of knowledge, there is discernment, thorough discernment, thoroughgoing examination,

thoroughgoing investigation, forbearance, intention, distinction, view, and conceptualization—any of which constitutes what is called "profound insight." Thus does a bodhisattva become proficient in profound insight.

699. That is, the true nature of all phenomena, as distinct from distinct phenomena in all their multiplicity.
700. The passage as cited by Kongtrul is not found in the *Definitive Commentary on Enlightened Intent*, although it contains many similar passages.
701. That is, each of the two aspects of analytical insight and thoroughly analytical insight is further divided into two modes—thoroughgoing examination and thoroughgoing investigation, making a total of four aspects. Each of these is further divided according to the four ways in which insight is realized—thorough examination, certain examination, thorough evaluation, and intimate evaluation—making for a total of sixteen degrees.
702. Asaṅga, *Compendium of Abhidharma*, chap. 4, (Toh. 4049), Dg. T., Sems tsam, vol. Ri, p. 197, lines 5–6.
703. *Definitive Commentary on Enlightened Intent*, (Toh. 106), Dg. K., mDo sde, vol. Ca, p. 54, l. 6. The source continues (p. 54, l. 6 to p. 55, l. 2):

> "What is that which derives from the ordinary distinctions one makes?" you ask. "It is whatever insight constitutes mental engagement solely with images that involve conceptual thought as the sphere of one's meditative absorption."
>
> "What is that which derives from a thoroughgoing search?" you ask. "It is whatever insight constitutes mental engagement in order to gain an excellent understanding of phenomena that have not yet been well understood in their distinctness through sublime intelligence."
>
> "What is that which derives from discernment?" you ask. "It is whatever insight constitutes mental engagement in order to experience bliss in a completely excellent manner, due to one's gaining a total freedom concerning phenomena that have been well understood in their distinctness through sublime intelligence."

704. These are the three methods used in Buddhism to ascertain what constitutes valid cognition.
705. That is, the fact that the true nature of reality cannot be fathomed by ordinary rational consciousness, and the fact that this nature is innately present as a natural attribute of being itself.
706. That is, without looking for any further reason of "why" things are the way they are.
707. That is, the exploration of meaning.
708. That is, the explorations of influences, time, and lines of reasoning.
709. That is, profound insight involving four essential experiences.
710. That is, insight that derives from ordinary distinctions, insight that derives from a thoroughgoing search, and insight that derives from discernment.
711. Here Kongtrul is specifically referring to the Kagyü, Nyingma, and Sakya schools of Tibetan Buddhism.
712. Also known as the Gelukpa (Tib. dGe lugs pa), a school founded by Tsongkhapa Lobsang Drakpa (Tsong kha pa bLo bzang grags pa, 1357–1419).
713. The Gelukpa approach to meditation has historically emphasized the need for the

meditator to maintain a strong sense of apprehending emptiness (Tib. *stong 'dzin dam spring nge ba*). In the Kagyü, Nyingma, and Sakya schools, generally speaking this is regarded as an error, in that any and all deliberate focus must be allowed to subside for the authentic experience of the true nature of things to ensue. See, for example, the famous line in *Parting from Four Fixations* (Tib. *Zhen pa bzhi bral*), a teaching imparted by the bodhisattva Mañjuśrī to Sachen Kunga Nyingpo (Sa chen Kun dga' snying po, 1092–1158), the founder of the Sakya school: "If there is deliberate apprehension, this is not the view." (Tib. *'dzin pa yod na lta ba min*).

714. Forms that arise in the mind may be those that are based on sense perceptions of external objects (that is, that "accord with external circumstances"), or those that are entirely products of the imagination. Both kinds of forms can be objects of one's discerning intelligence, although investigation of forms based on externals is not to be undertaken deliberately in meditation that is to develop profound insight.
715. The preliminary phase is one of coming to a definitive conclusion, through the exercise of sublime intelligence, that the object in question has no independent nature; this leads to the main point of meditation—the direct experience of that lack of independent nature.
716. This passage is repeated four times over in Asaṅga, *Compendium of Abhidharma*, chap. 4, (Toh. 4049), Dg. T., Sems tsam, vol. Ri, p. 184, l. 6 to p. 185, l. 1.
717. These are: ignorance, desire and attachment, anger, pride, indecision, and opinionatedness (which primarily refers to the belief that the perishable mind-body aggregates constitute a permanent self or soul).
718. That is, even in the case of positive thoughts.
719. That is, there is nothing to be found when the mind of the present moment is examined.
720. That is, tangible or intangible. The source text reads: "Mind cannot be found to exist in essence in either of two ways . . ."
721. That is, the function of mind that realizes that mind does not exist in its own right.
722. The source omits the phrase "free of all conceptual elaborations."
723. The source reads: "a flaw . . ."
724. The source text reads: "should abide . . ."
725. The source text reads: "—thoughts concerning ordinary distinctions— . . ."
726. Atīśa Dipaṃkara Śrījñāna, *Pith Instructions on the Middle Way*, chap. ?, v. ?, (Toh. 3929), Dg. T., dBu ma, vol. Ki, p. 190, l. 5 to p. 191, l. 2.
727. *Definitive Commentary on Enlightened Intent*, (Toh. 106), Dg. K., mDo sde, vol. Ca, p. 52, l. 7 to p. 53, l. 1:

> "O transcendent and accomplished conqueror! As long as a bodhisattva has not gained thorough pliancy of body and mind, but during that time is mentally engaged internally with the images that are within the scope of meditative absorption, contemplating them precisely in some way, what does one call that mental engagement?"
>
> "O Maitreya! That is not profound insight. That is what would be referred to as a state that is in accord with an intent that is a valid approximation of profound insight."

728. See Ratnākaraśānti, *Pith Instructions on the Transcendent Perfection of Sublime Intelligence*, (Toh. 4079), Dg. T., Sems tsam, vol. Hi, p. 316, l. 6:

> Thus, with one's analyzing things in detail, for as long as it takes for body and mind to become thoroughly pliant, for that long one examines and investigates precisely, and so perfects profound insight.

729. Bhāvaviveka, *Blazing Logic*, (Toh. 3856), Dg. T., dBu ma, vol. Dza, p. 115, lines 3–4:

> For those who are sullied by the distortions that soil them—of intense attachment for objects of desire, or aversion, or anger, or ignorance—conceptual elaborations have not completely subsided, and they are not in control. They should completely refine themselves by cleansing themselves with the pure water of [meditating on] what is unattractive, of loving-kindness, and of interdependent origination.

730. See Śāntideva, *Engaging in the Conduct of a Bodhisattva*, (Toh. 3871), chap. 8, v. 4, Dg. T., dBu ma, vol. La, p. 46, lines 1–2:

> Knowing that one completely overcomes afflictive mental states
> through profound insight imbued with calm abiding,
> one first seeks calm abiding....

731. That is, the Buddha Śākyamuni.
732. See Kamalaśīla, *Stages of Meditation*, (Toh. 3916), Dg. T., dBu ma, vol. Ki, p. 94, lines 4–5 and p. 95, lines 3–4:

> The mind is to rest on an image of the Buddha. As is stated in the *Most Majestic State of Meditative Absorption*:
>
> > The lord protector of the world is utterly lovely
> > with a form of a color like that of gold.
> > Those who focus their attention on that frame of reference
> > practice what is called "the meditative equipoise of bodhisattvas."
>
> Thus, having rested one's mind within whatever frame of reference one wishes, one continues to use that same framework, resting one's mind in an ongoing way. Having rested the mind thoroughly, one then engages in investigation as follows... then, having attained calm abiding, one cultivates profound insight, thinking as follows...

733. That is, Candrakīrti.
734. That is, using some object or visualization, as distinct from a formless approach in meditation.
735. Kongtrul is distinguishing two senses of "integration" with respect to calm abiding and profound insight. In the first case, involving some construct as the object of meditation, the aspect of calm abiding is nonconceptual while that of profound insight is still conceptual; they can nevertheless be said to be "integrated." In the second case (the "present discussion"), the still-conceptual aspect of sublime intelligence involved in profound insight has become the nonconceptual component of timeless awareness with the attainment of the first level of realization (also termed the "path of seeing"); the two aspects of abiding and insight have thus merged in the nondual state.
736. Kamalaśīla, *Stages of Meditation*, (Toh. 3915), Dg. T, dBu ma, vol. Ki, p. 74, l. 4.
737. Source not identified. There is a text attributed to Sahajavajra entitled *Extensive Commentary on the "Ten Topics of Suchness,"* (Toh. 2254), Dg. T, rGyud 'grel, vol. Wi, p. 320, l. 7 to p. 353, l. 7. The passage cited, however, is not found in this source.

738. Source not identified, although it is presumably the same as the one just cited.
739. That is, the extremes of saṃsāra and the limited nirvāṇa of mere personal liberation from suffering without regard for others' welfare.
740. *Definitive Commentary on Enlightened Intent*, (Toh. 106), Dg. K., mDo sde, vol. Ca, p. 18, l. 2.
741. That is, the sūtra tradition of Hīnayāna and Mahāyāna.
742. See Longchen Rabjam, *The Precious Treasury of Philosophical Systems*, 190:

> As for the nine perceptions of impurity, one meditates as if perceiving corpses decomposing, ridden with maggots, mottled with dark blotches, rotting, putrefying, devoured by wild animals, scattered in pieces, being cremated, and disintegrating.

743. This would include the Mahāyāna system of "mind training" (Tib. *blo sbyong*).
744. Tib. *stong rva*. A reference to the "structure" of the subtle channels that is visualized in any given system of advanced Vajrayāna meditation, but which is not conceived of as solid or corporeal.
745. Tib. *zhu bde*. A reference to the process of higher yogic practices such as the "inner warmth" (Tib. *gtum mo*) that involves visualizations of heat rising as fire from the region below the navel to the crown of the head, causing the bindu there to melt and flow down, producing a blissful sensation that gradually permeates the entire body.
746. Tib. *tshad ma*; Skt. *pramāṇa*. This is one of the five major sciences of the Buddhist tradition; Kongtrul discusses this in Part 1 of Book 6 in *The Treasury of Knowledge: Book Six, Parts One and Two: Indo-Tibetan Classical Learning and Buddhist Phenomenology*.
747. The usual progression (Tib. *lugs 'byung*) of the "twelve links" of interdependent connection accounts for the way in which saṃsāra is perpetuated; the reversal of this process (Tib. *lugs ldog*) is the key to liberation. These links are a particular topic of contemplation in the pratyekabuddha approach. See Longchen Rabjam, *The Precious Treasury of Philosophical Systems*, 144–45:

> The twelve links of interdependent connection are as follows:
>
> > Ignorance, karmic patterning, consciousness, the mind-body complex,
> > the six fields of experience, contact, sensation,
> > compulsion, perpetuation, becoming, birth,
> > and aging and death: these are the twelve links of interdependent connection.
>
> Here ignorance means a fundamental lack of understanding. Because of it, beings continually fall into samsara, whereby karmic patterning occurs. This leads to consciousness, in that overt consciousness emerges from the basis of each being's ordinary experience. From consciousness arises the mind-body complex, consisting of the five mind-body aggregates—that is, the four aggregates of mind (which include each individual being's aggregates of sensation, perception, and formative factors) and the physical form on which these depend. On that basis, the six fields of experience—visual, auditory, olfactory, gustatory, tactile, and conceptual—develop. This leads to contact, which is the coming together of three factors: objects, faculties, and mental focus. This leads to sensation, in that it produces sensations that are pleasant,

painful, or neutral. This leads to compulsion, in that the mind takes objects to be its own, rejecting or accepting them according to various responses of attraction, aversion, and so forth. This leads to perpetuation, in that yearning arises for what is desired and one takes this as a goal. This leads to becoming, with conception taking place in a womb in the next lifetime. This leads to birth—the birth of the physical body. This leads to aging as youth fades, and then to death as one's life force comes to an end. As a result of karma, ordinary beings continually cycle thus in samsara.

748. See n. 423.
749. These ten indications are quasi-visual experiences one undergoes as one's realization of emptiness and the utterly lucid nature of mind develops. According to Dorje and Kapstein, *The Nyingma School of Tibetan Buddhism*, vol. 2, 167:

> These are enumerated in Longcenpa, *Dispelling Darkness in the Ten Directions*, p. 344, as smoke (*du-ba*), mirage (*smig-rgyu*), clouds (*sprin*), fire-flies (*me-khyer*), sunlight (*nyi-ma*), moonlight (*zla-ba*), the blazing of gemstones (*rin-po-che 'bar-ba*), eclipse (*sgra-gcan*), starlight (*skar-ma*), and rays of light (*'od-zer*).

750. The term "identical taste" (Tib. *ro gcig*) used here is synonymous with "equal taste" (Tib. *ro mnyam*) used in the preceding source verses and immediately following in the commentary. Both idioms refer to the way in which one experiences ("tastes") phenomena from the perspective of their ultimate nature.
751. That is, sublime intelligence that derives from hearing spiritual teachings, contemplating them, and meditating on them.
752. The source verses of *The Treasury of Knowledge*, as well as those verses as cited in the commentary, both read "existence" (Tib. *srid pa*), but the prose commentary itself reads "isolation" (Tib. *sring ba*), which accords with Vasubandhu, *Explanation of the "Treasury of Abhidharma,"* (Toh. 4090), Dg. T., mNgon pa, vol. Khu, p. 15, lines 5–6:

> If one wonders, "How does someone who strives intently at meditation perfect that meditation," the source text states:
>
> > With twofold isolation . . .
>
> If one isolates oneself physically and mentally in order to distance oneself from busyness and nonvirtuous thoughts, meditation will become perfected.

753. These are the seeking of gain, fame, praise, and pleasure, and the attempts to avoid loss, notoriety, blame, and pain.
754. Of these seven kinds of ordination, two pertain to the householder situation (the ordination of a male or female lay practitioner), while five pertain to a monastic situation (those of a fully ordained monk or nun, a novice monk or nun, or a female aspirant). The vows of a female aspirant are an intermediate step between the ordination of a novice nun and full ordination; there is no corresponding ordination for men. See Kongtrul, *The Treasury of Knowledge: Book Five: Buddhist Ethics*, 89.
755. See Vasubandhu, *Explanation of the "Treasury of Abhidharma,"* (Toh. 4090), Dg. T., mNgon pa, vol. Khu, p. 15, lines 1–5 (commenting on chap. 6, v. 5c–d of his source text):

If one wonders what characterizes these aspects of sublime intelligence, the source verses state:

> The minds that derive from hearing and so forth
> take words, both, and meaning as their respective objects.

According to the Particularists, sublime intelligence that derives from hearing focuses on the words, while that which derives from contemplation focuses on words and meaning, with the words occasionally eliciting the meaning. That which derives from meditation focuses entirely on the meaning; it engages the meaning without relying on the letter. They give the analogy of someone who has not learned to swim well having to be pulled along in the water without swimming at all, while someone who has learned to a small degree can occasionally swim while occasionally having to be pulled along. Someone who has learned thoroughly can cross the water without having to be pulled along. They are known for stating that this is the analogy.

Others say, concerning this understanding, that whatever focuses on the words is that which derives from hearing, while whatever focuses on the meaning is that which derives from meditation, so that sublime intelligence that derives from contemplation cannot be established [as focusing on both words and meaning]. They say, rather, that sublime intelligence that derives from hearing constitutes the certainty that develops from authoritative and reliable scriptural sources; that which derives from contemplation constitutes that which develops from convincing examinations through reasoning; and that which develops from meditation constitutes that which develops from meditative absorption. It is my opinion that these characterizations are not without merit.

756. Nāgārjuna, *Letter to a Friend*, v. 29, (Toh. 4182), Dg. T., sPriṅ yig, vol. Nge, p. 83, l. 3. The remarks are addressed to a king of ancient India—the one "wise in the ways of the world"—who is the "friend" to whom Nāgārjuna wrote his letter.
757. Source not identified.
758. Agriculture because of the loss of animal and insect life it entails; trading because of the fact that one's own profit and gain is at another's expense; and the selling of religious objects because it makes a common commodity of what should be held sacred.
759. That is, the paths of accumulation, linkage, seeing, and meditation; the fifth of the five paths is that of no more learning, which corresponds to the fruition state of an arhat in the śrāvaka approach.
760. Vasubandhu, *Treasury of Abhidharma*, chap. 6, v. 70, (Toh. 4089), Dg. T., mNgon pa, vol. Ku, p. 41, lines 6–7.
761. The foregoing are collectively known as the "thirty-seven factors that contribute to enlightenment."
762. These are discussed in the extensive explanation immediately following.
763. Ibid., chap. 6, v. 9d, (Toh. 4089), Dg. T., Sems tsam, vol. Ku, p. 37, lines 2–3.
764. These eight mental images (which may be purely imaginary or may arise from the actual observation of corpses during a meditation exercise) are of a decomposing corpse, a swollen corpse, a maggot-ridden corpse, a corpse in an advanced stage of putrefaction, a corpse scattered in pieces, a corpse being cremated, a corpse devoured by wild animals, and a disintegrating corpse.

765. For the Particularist school of the śrāvaka approach, what is ultimately real are irreducible particles of matter and indivisible moments of consciousness. This view is not accepted by other, higher schools of Buddhist thought.

766. That is, sensations, mind, and mental states as the focus for the application of mindfulness.

767. These formative factors, which are posited by proponents of the schools of the Particularists and the Followers of the Sūtras in the śrāvaka approach, are considered distinct from the other three "bases of the knowable": forms, mind, and mental states. See Longchen Rabjam, *The Precious Treasury of Philosophical Schools*, 408, n. 90:

> These are factors that have no congruence (of time, etc.) with mind or mental states, yet are evident in certain situations. The Vaibhashikas accept that these patterns are substantial entities. In *The Treasury of Abhidharma*, . . . Vasubandhu's fourteen factors are acquisition, nonacquisition, equality, the meditative stability of cessation, the meditative stability of a trance state, the trance state itself, the faculty of life force, production, deterioration, duration, impermanence, groups of words, groups of phrases, and groups of letters. Asanga's list of twenty-four [in his *Compendium of Abhidharma*] adds the following factors: the ordinary state of being, continuity, differentiation, connectedness, speed, sequence, time, location, number, and grouping.

768. Such forms are considered by the śrāvaka schools to be of two kinds. "Forms associated with the sense field of subjective consciousness" are forms that exist within the realm of ideas, such as atomic particles (as hypothetical conceptual models) or dream images. "Indiscernible material forms" are experienced only subjectively by one's own consciousness and are indiscernible by others; they include various kinds of vows and ordination, which are held to contribute a subtle material component to the makeup of one taking and upholding them.

769. Unconditioned (or uncompounded) phenomena are things within one's ordinary experience that are not brought about through causes and conditions and thus are not subject to origination, location, and cessation. See Longchen Rabjam, *The Precious Treasury of Philosophical Schools*, 73, 77, and 95:

> There are three uncompounded phenomena: space (that is, the absence of any tactile sensation), the cessation of consciousness owing to discernment (an absence that comes about through the application of an antidote), and the cessation of consciousness independent of discernment (in which something does not happen, because its necessary conditions are incomplete). For the Vaibhashikas, what is incorruptible are these three uncompounded phenomena, plus consciousness as the coordinating mental faculty when it is focused on the truth of the path, as well as all that is associated with that consciousness. Everything else is corruptible. . . .
>
> For the Sautrantikas, the three types of uncompounded phenomena do not exist as substantial entities, for they are as utterly nonexistent as the son of a barren woman. . . .
>
> With respect to the group of uncompounded phenomena, the Chittamatrins are in agreement with the Sautrantikas. However, to the three phenomena listed previously, they add suchness and the basic space of phenomena, as well as others.

770. That is, the application of mindfulness with respect to the body.
771. That is, the application of mindfulness with respect to sensations.
772. This refers specifically to the relentless drive to avoid any and all painful experiences and seek pleasurable ones.
773. That is, the application of mindfulness with respect to the mind.
774. That is, the application of mindfulness with respect to phenomena.
775. Maitreya, *Distinguishing Center and Limit*, chap. 4, v. 1a–c, (Toh. 4021), Dg. T., Sems tsam, vol. Phi, p. 85, l. 2. The verses as cited by Kongtrul differ somewhat:

> Because of the perpetuation of ignoble states—the causes of craving,
> because of the ground of being, and because of the absence of delusion,
> and because one comes to terms with the four truths, . . .

776. That is, the five points—the scope, the content, the essence, the result, and the context—as these apply to the remaining stages for beginning practitioners, as well as those for meditation in the four anticipatory phases, on the path of seeing, and on the path of meditation.
777. Ibid., chap. 4, v. 3c–d, (Toh. 4021), Dg. T., Sems tsam, vol. Phi, p. 85, lines 3–4.
778. These flaws and remedial techniques were discussed in detail in Part 1 of Book 8.
779. That is, the decisive breakthrough that comes with the attainment of the path of seeing, with the direct experience of the true nature of reality that it entails. What one experiences on the paths of accumulation and linkage is a conceptually based approximation of that true nature; it is only with the attainment of the path of seeing that this is experienced in a nondual state free of any conceptual factor.
780. See n. 665.
781. See Longchenpa, *Kindly Bent to Ease Us*, vol. 1, 243: "As 'powers', these five initiate processes of refinement . . . as 'strengths' [they] overcome all that impedes the link-up with the Stage [i.e., path] of Seeing."
782. That is, the paths of seeing, meditation, and no more learning. The path of seeing marks one's transition from the status of an ordinary mortal being (Tib. *so so skye bo*) to that of a spiritually advanced one (Tib. *'phags pa*).
783. That is, the *content* (as in the preceding treatments).
784. Maitreya, *Distinguishing Center and Limit*, chap. 4, v. 7c–d, (Toh. 4021), Dg. T., Sems tsam, vol. Phi, p. 85, l. 6.
785. That is, the *content* (as in the preceding treatments).
786. That is, what they constitute in their *essence* (as in the preceding treatments).
787. Ibid. v. 8, (Toh. 4021), Dg. T., Sems tsam, vol. Phi, p. 85, lines 6–7.
788. These are the three branches of the path that are referred to in Kongtrul's commentary as "aids that bring conviction." See Sthiramati, *Explanatory Commentary on "Distinguishing Center and Limit,"* (Toh. 4032), Dg. T., Sems tsam, vol. Bi, p. 556, lines 3–4:

> There are three branches that inspire conviction in others—those of authentic speech and action and livelihood. How is this so? As the source text states, referring to them successively:
>
> > It is held that others are made aware
> > of view, discipline, and few material needs.
>
> This is a reference, respectively, to authentic speech, action, and livelihood.

789. Maitreya, *Distinguishing Center and Limit*, chap. 4, v. 9c–11b, (Toh. 4021), Dg. T., Sems tsam, vol. Phi, p. 85, l. 7 to p. 86, l. 1. The last two lines refers to the roles (referred to in Kongtrul's commentary) that authentic effort, mindfulness, and meditative absorption play, respectively, in counteracting the primary *afflictive states* (which are factors to be eliminated on the path of seeing), counteracting *secondary afflictive states* (which contribute to mental laxity and agitation), and in bringing *mastery* over what is counterproductive to the attainment of special spiritual qualities. See Sthiramati, *Explanatory Commentary on "Distinguishing Center and Limit,"* (Toh. 4032), Dg. T., Sems tsam, vol. Bi, p. 557, l. 4 to p. 558, l. 7:

> How is it that these are remedies to counterproductive influences? It is because, according to the source text, they are successively:
>
> > remedies to counterproductive influences
> > that involve afflictive states, secondary afflictive states, and mastery.
>
> Of these, the remedy in the first case is what is termed "authentic effort." The first kind of counterproductive influence is that of afflictive states that are to be eliminated through meditation; their remedy is authentic effort. How is this the case? [When Vasubandhu says,] "By that," he means that this is due to one meditating on the path with authentic effort. Diligence that is in the context of meditative absorption free of mental laxity or agitation and that is subsumed within authentic view is authentic effort. Because meditation using that brings about the elimination of afflictive states (which are to be eliminated), one meditates with that remedy on the path. Therefore, given that one is practicing to accomplish authentic meditative absorption, authentic effort is termed the "remedy in the first case."
>
> For one who is meditating on the path, the second case is that of secondary afflictive states—characterized as mental laxity and agitation—to which what is termed "authentic mindfulness" is applied as what is termed the "remedy." How it this so? [Vasubandhu says,] "Because the causes of calm abiding and so forth are due to an extremely intimate association with mindfulness, since mental laxity and agitation are absent therein." (The phrase "and so forth" should be understood to mean that this is also the cause of total attentiveness and the cause of impartiality.)
>
> In this regard, since this ensures that the causes of distraction are thoroughly pacified, there is calm abiding. The "causes of calm abiding" refer to the efficient causes that bring about calm abiding and so forth. In this regard, should one's mind become agitated, or threaten to become agitated, to focus one's mind on something that arouses a feeling of disenchantment is a cause of calm abiding. Should one's mind become lax, or threaten to become lax, to focus one's mind on something that inspires joy is a cause of total attentiveness. Whether a case of one's focusing uniquely on calm abiding, or focusing uniquely on profound insight, or engaging in their integration, these two secondary afflictive states constitute the "secondary afflictive states," and so to focus one's mind on a sense of being spontaneously present is the cause of impartiality.
>
> As to what constitutes a counterproductive influence (with respect to one's

gaining mastery of such things as powers of deeper discernment, which are by nature qualities of enlightenment), it is a state of ignorance that is not an overt afflictive state, but which by its nature constitutes an obscuration that interferes with meditative equipoise. This is the third case, to which authentic meditative absorption is applied as what is termed its "remedy." How is this the case? Because [as Vasubandhu says,] "it ensures that, when one is abiding in meditative stability, such qualities of enlightenment as deeper levels of discernment become fully evident." Meditative stability is the context that ensures that all special qualities become fully evident. That being the case, in becoming a supportive influence for the actual accomplishment of such qualities as deeper levels of discernment, this constitutes the remedy for obscurations that interfere with meditative equipoise.

The foregoing being the case, authentic effort thus demonstrates a freedom from the obscuring influence of afflictive states; authentic mindfulness ensures that meditative absorption is completely pure; and authentic meditative absorption ensures that there is freedom from obscurations that interfere with meditative equipoise.

790. See Vasubandhu, *Treasury of Abhidharma*, chap. 6, v. 54a–b (Toh. 4089), Dg. T., mNgon pa, vol. Ku, p. 40, lines 5–6:

> The wheel of dharma is the path of seeing,
> with its spokes and so forth that permit it to move swiftly, . . .

And Vasubandhu, *Explanation of the "Treasury of Abhidharma,"* (Toh. 4090), Dg. T., mNgon pa, vol. Khu, p. 59, l. 7 to p. 60, l. 2:

> The venerable Ghoṣaka states that, because the eight branches of the path of spiritually advanced beings are analogous to spokes and so forth, they are termed a "wheel." Authentic view, thought, effort, and mindfulness are comparable to the spokes; authentic speech, action, and livelihood are comparable to the hub; and meditative absorption is comparable to the rim.

Concerning the reference to Ghoṣaka, see Kongtrul, *The Treasury of Knowledge: Book Six, Part Three: Frameworks of Buddhist Philosophy*, 332, n. 334:

> The four great venerable ones (*mahābhadanta, btsun pa chen po*) are Dharmatrāta (*Chos skyob*), Vasumitra (*dByig bshes*), Ghoṣhaka (*dByig sgrog*), and Buddhadeva (*Sangs rgyas lha*), all of whom lived around the first century CE. The views of these four masters are often cited by Vasubandhu in his *Explanation of the "Treasury of Abhidharma,"* and they are said to be particularly important within the Vaibhāṣhika abhidharma tradition in that they represent four different interpretations of how phenomena exist in the three time periods. Of the four, only Vasumitra's works are found in the Tengyur.

791. That is, the fifth of the five successive paths of accumulation, linkage, seeing, meditation, and no more training (or consummation). See Kongtrul, *The Treasury of Knowledge: Books Nine and Ten: Journey and Goal*, 64–105.

792. That is, unlike the four preceding paths, the path of no more training does not involve any specific scope for one's focus or content.

793. Tib. *dngos po drug*. These are: the mind-body aggregates, the components of ordinary perception, the sense fields, interdependent connection, what is or is not in accord with the nature of things, and the Truths.
794. The rhinoceros's solitary habits make it a traditional metaphor for those pratyekabuddhas who live alone.
795. Kongtrul discusses the pratyekabuddha approach elsewhere in the *Treasury of Knowledge*; see *The Treasury of Knowledge: Book Six, Part Three: Frameworks of Buddhist Philosophy*, 151–58 and (in a less cohesive treatment) *The Treasury of Knowledge: Books Nine and Ten: Journey and Goal* (Part 1 of Book 9), 63–127. For a discussion by the Nyingma master Longchen Rabjam, see *The Precious Treasury of Philosophical Systems*, 142–49.
796. See nn. 39 and 126. The foregoing two paragraphs are identical to the discussions found in Longchen Rabjam's *The Precious Treasury of Philosophical Systems*, 143 and 145. It should be noted that Kongtrul was as much a compiler as he was an original author; in traditional Tibetan literature, the use of a previous author's words without overt attribution was not considered a flaw in one's own writing but a case of "plagiarism being the highest form of praise." In acknowledging Longchen Rabjam's writings as one of his sources in writing *The Treasury of Knowledge* (see *The Treasury of Knowledge: Books Nine and Ten: Journey and Goal*, 463), Kongtrul was alerting his readership to the fact that some of the text was not his original work.
797. *Discourse of Queen Śrīmālā*, (Toh. 92), Dg. K., dKon brtsegs, vol. Cha, p. 509, l. 1 to p. 554, l. 7 is the forty-eighth of the forty-nine sections in the sūtra collection entitled *Amassing of the Rare and Sublime*. The line cited by Kongtrul, although very well known and often quoted in the Tibetan tradition, is not found in the sūtra, although Longchen Rabjam (*The Precious Treasury of Philosophical Systems*, 155) also cites this same line as being from the *Discourse of Queen Śrīmālā*; Kongtrul may simply have been copying Longchen Rabjam's attribution. In *The Jewel Ornament of Liberation*, 2, Gampopa cites the line as occurring in the sūtra entitled *Most Majestic State of Meditative Absorption*, but the line as cited is not found in that source either.
798. Maitreya, *Highest Continuum*, chap. 1, v. 27, (Toh. 4024), Dg. T., Sems tsam, vol. Phi, p. 111, lines 2–3.
799. Gampopa Sönam Rinchen (sGam po pa bSod nams rin chen, 1079–1153), *Dam chos yid bzhin gyi nor bu thar pa rin po che'i rgyan*, p. 199, lines 1–3. See also *The Jewel Ornament of Liberation*, 6. Gampopa is echoing the description found in Asaṅga, *Levels of the Bodhisattva*, (Toh. 4037), Dg. T., Sems tsam, vol. Wi, p. 4, lines 3–5:

> What is this spiritual affinity? In brief, there are two aspects—that which is naturally abiding and that which is perfectly developed.
>
> Of these, the naturally abiding aspect of this affinity is that which is exceptional within the six sense fields of bodhisattvas. It is, as it were, that which continues from one lifetime to another, for it partakes of a timeless quality and is obtained by the true nature of reality.
>
> As for the perfectly developed aspect of this affinity, it is that which is gained due to previous familiarization with fundamentally positive qualities.
>
> In this context, then, it is held that there are these two aspects.

800. Gampopa Sönam Rinchen, *Dam chos yid bzhin gyi nor bu thar pa rin po che'i rgyan*, p. 199, l. 5: "That affinity is also termed 'potential'; 'fundamental being' is also termed 'natural state.'"

801. See especially Maitreya, *Ornament of the Mahāyāna Sūtras*, chap. 4 (Toh. 4020), Dg. T., Sems tsam, vol. Phi, p. 6, l. 7 to p. 8, l. 2.
802. See sGam.po.pa, *The Jewel Ornament of Liberation*, 4:

> The 'Dubious-family' are those whose future way of life depends on certain conditions. Those who rely on a spiritual friend who is a Śrāvaka, or who are friends and acquaintances of one and believe in the Śrāvaka way of life after they have perused the Śrāvaka-sūtras, will become members of that family and disclose themselves as such. Similarly when they meet a Pratyekabuddha or a follower of the Mahāyāna way of life they will become respectively either Pratyekabuddhas or followers of the Mahāyāna way of life.

803. See ibid., 12, n. 21:

> sGam.po.pa was mindful of the humane idea . . . that the foundation of all that is good and wholesome, which may temporarily have broken down, can again be restored so that no one is lost forever.

804. That is, both the afflictive obscurations (which obstruct the attainment of personal liberation from the sufferings of saṃsāra) and the cognitive obscurations (which obstruct the attainment of omniscience). Only with the removal of both kinds of obscuration does one attain the completely awakened state of buddhahood.
805. *Discourse on the Ten Attributes*, (Toh. 53), Dg. K., dKon brtsegs, vol. Kha, p. 134, l. 7. In the source, the text is slightly different and the line order is reversed:

> Just as one can know fire from the presence of smoke
> or know water from that of water fowl,
> so the affinity of bodhisattvas, who are intelligent,
> can be known from indications.

806. Ibid., p. 334, l. 7 to p. 335, l. 1.
807. Maitreya, *Ornament of the Mahāyāna Sūtras*, chap. 4, v. 5, (Toh. 4020), Dg. T., Sems tsam, vol. Phi, p. 7, l. 3. In the source text, the last line cited reads as follows: "are explained as definitely being the indications of spiritual affinity."
808. Maitreya, *Highest Continuum*, chap. 1, v. 40, (Toh. 4024), Dg. T., Sems tsam, vol. Phi, p. 112, l. 3.
809. These are traditionally described as being eight in number: to be reborn as a hell being, as an animal form of life, as a tormented spirit (*preta*), as a long-lived god, in a barbaric culture, as someone whose faculties are impaired, as someone with incorrect opinions concerning the nature of things, or as someone in a world in which no buddha has appeared. See sGam.po.pa, *The Jewel Ornament of Liberation*, 14–15.
810. This is defined as a state of mind in which one takes no account of whether one's actions are appropriate or not, or of their consequences.
811. Although the passage as cited by Kongtrul is highly suggestive of the idiom found through the Prajñāpāramitā sūtras, the exact passage is not found in the source text. *Intermediate Length "Mother,"* (Toh. 9), Dg. K., Śes phyin (Nyi khri), vols. Ka–Ga.
812. The passage as cited by Kongtrul does not appear in the source text. Ratnākaraśānti, *Sublime Heart Essence: Commentary on the Difficult Points in the "Exalted Transcendent Perfection of Sublime Intelligence in Eight Thousand Verses,"* (Toh. 3803), Dg. T., Śes phyin, vol. Tha, pp. 2–459.
813. That is, when loving-kindness and the other attitudes are not motivated by bodhi-

citta, they are called "pure states" and only contribute to the very best possibilities within saṃsāra. It is only when they are motivated by bodhicitta that they are termed "immeasurable"; this is due to their objects (that is, all beings) and their ultimate result (that is, buddhahood) being correspondingly immeasurable.

814. Source not identified. The collective title *Categories of the Spiritual Levels* refers to five works by Asaṅga:
(1) *Levels of Yogic Practitioners* (Toh. 4035), Dg. T., Sems tsam, vol. Tshi. This includes two auxiliary texts: *Levels of the Śrāvaka*, (Toh. 4036), Dg. T., Sems tsam, vol. Dzi and *Levels of the Bodhisattva*, (Toh. 4037), Dg. T., Sems tsam, vol. Wi;
(2) *Synopsis of the Definitive Conclusion concerning the Levels of Yogic Practitioners*, (Toh. 4038), Dg. T., Sems tsam, vol. Zhi (p. 2)–vol. Zi (p. 253);
(3) *Synopsis of Bases in the Levels of Yogic Practitioners* (Toh. 4039), Dg. T., Sems tsam, vol. Zi (pp. 253–669);
(4) *Synopsis of Enumerations in the Levels of Yogic Practitioners* (Toh. 4041), Dg. T., Sems tsam, vol. 'I (pp. 44–94); and
(5) *Synopsis of Explanations in the Levels of Yogic Practitioners* (Toh. 4042), Dg. T., Sems tsam, vol. 'I (pp. 95–136).

815. That is, nonreferential loving-kindness and so forth.

816. For example, the scope of immeasurable loving-kindness is the intention that all beings have happiness and the causes of happiness.

817. That is, those who have realized the lack of identity in the individual personality and realized partially ("50 percent") the lack of identity in phenomena, in that they have realized the lack of identity in external objects in the phenomenal world but not that lack in the internal subjective consciousness.

818. Asaṅga, *Levels of the Bodhisattva*, (Toh. 4037), Dg. T., Sems tsam, vol. Wi, p. 257, l. 6 to p, 258, l. 1. The passage in the source text reads as follows:

> [For a bodhisattva, with respect to immeasurable loving-kindness and the rest,] those contexts that involve having beings as the frame of reference are processes held in common with others—that is, with non-Buddhist proponents of extreme views. Those contexts that involve having phenomena as the frame of reference should be understood to be processes that are held in common with śrāvakas and pratyekabuddhas, but not held in common with proponents of extreme views. To have no fixed frame of reference should be understood to be a process that has nothing in common with any of the foregoing, whether proponents of extreme views, śrāvakas, or pratyekabuddhas.

819. Feeling regret at having committed a positive action undermines the merit such an act generates.

820. Source not identified.

821. Maitreya, *Distinguishing Center and Limit*, chap. 5, vv. 9–10b, (Toh. 4021), Dg. T., Sems tsam, vol. Phi, p. 87, lines 4–5. In the source text, the final line reads: "the merit of which is immeasurable."

822. Chökyi Gyaltsen (Chos kyi rgyal mtshan, 1586?–1657?) was the fifth Tai Situ incarnation of the Karma Kagyü school.

823. That is, one dedicates the virtue of the practice to the enlightenment of all beings. All practice in the Mahāyāna approach is meant to be framed in the "three sacred principles": the arousal of bodhicitta as the preparation, the maintaining of (ideally)

a nonreferential state during the main period of meditation (or, failing that, at least an undistracted focus on the object of meditation), and dedication of the virtue as the conclusion.

824. These may be perceptions of an actual corpse (viewed in a cemetery as a meditation exercise) or images brought to mind as the focus of attention. See n. 745.
825. That is, immersing oneself in the experience of ultimate truth at the expense of engaging with relative truth and acting to benefit beings.
826. The source text reads: "their perceptual faculties . . ."
827. Maitreya, *Ornament of the Mahāyāna Sūtras* chap. 6, v. 9, (Toh. 4020), Dg. T., Sems tsam, vol. Phi, p. 11, l. 4–5.
828. In traditional Tibetan culture, clothing for both sexes (whether lay or monastic) consisted of robes that were tied at the waist with a sash.
829. That is, the seat upon which the Buddha Śākyamuni attained buddhahood.
830. The foregoing discussions of the nine perceptions of impurity, the eight thoughts of a superior spiritual practitioner, and the thorough purification of one's sphere of activity are taken virtually verbatim from Longchen Rabjam, *The Precious Treasury of Philosophical Systems*, fol. 103b, l. 4 to fol. 104b, l. 2.
831. Tib. *zung 'jug*. In this context, the primordial union of the phases of formal practice and postmeditation. For the Autonomists, these are distinct contexts that must be dealt with in distinct ways.
832. That is, the three focal points of subject, object, and their interaction; none of these is conceived of as existing autonomously, separate from the others.
833. The teachings of the Buddhadharma in general, and those of the Mahāyāna approach in particular, are characterized as being both vast and profound.
834. See n. 48.
835. This summary presents a concise discussion of the eight major topics discussed in the Prajñāpāramitā sūtras: (1) knowledge of the ground, (2) knowledge of the path, and (3) omniscience (that is, the fruition state of buddhahood), collectively termed the "three aspects of knowledge"; (4)–(7) the four applications; and (8) the dharmakāya of buddhahood. For an excellent discussion of these topics, see Karl Brunnhölzl, *Gone Beyond: Volume One: The Prajñāpāramitā Sūtras, "The Ornament of Clear Realization," and Its Commentaries in the Tibetan Kagyü Tradition.*

Bibliography of Works Cited by the Author

Scriptures

Amassing of the Rare and Sublime
Ārya mahāratna kūṭa dharma paryāya śata sāhasrika granthe tri saṃvara nirdeśa parivarta nāma mahāyāna sūtra
'Phags pa dKon mchog brtsegs pa chen po'i chos kyi rnam grangs stong phrag brgya pa las sdom pa gsum bstan pa'u le'u zhes bya ba theg pa chen po'i mdo
Toh. 45 (Dg. K., dKon brtsegs, vol. Ka, ff. 1b–45a)

Chapter Entitled "Heart Essence of the Speech of All Buddhas" from the Exalted and Precious Discourse on the Journey to Śrī Laṅka
'Phags pa Lang kar gshegs pa rin po che'i mdo las sangs rgyas thams cad kyi gsung gi snying po zhes bya ba'i le'u
Toh. 108 (Dg. K., mDo sde, vol. Ca, ff. 192a–284b)

Chapter of Kāśyapa
Ārya kāśyapa parivarta nāma mahāyāna sūtra
'Phags pa 'od srung gi le'u zhes bya ba theg pa chen po'i mdo
Toh. 87 (Dg. K., dKon brtsegs (No. 43), vol. Cha, ff. 119b–151b)

Cloud of the Rare and Excellent
Ārya ratna megha nāma mahāyāna sūtra
'Phags pa dKon mchog sprin zhes bya ba theg pa chen po'i mdo
Toh. 231 (Dg. K., mDo sde, vol. Wa, ff. 1b–112b)

Cluster of Stems
Gaṇḍa vyūha sūtra
sDong po bkod pa'i mdo
(last chapter of *Garland of Buddhas*, q.v.)

Compendium of the Vajra of Timeless Awareness
Vajra jñāna samuccaya nāma tantra
Ye shes rdo rje kun las btus pa zhes bya ba'i rgyud
Toh. 447 (Dg. K., rGyud 'bum, vol. Ca, ff. 282a–286a)

Definitive Commentary on Enlightened Intent
Ārya saṃdhinirmocana nāma mahāyāna sūtra
'Phags pa dgongs pa nges par 'grel pa zhes bya ba theg pa chen po'i mdo
Toh. 106 (Dg. K., mDo sde, vol. Ca, ff. 1b–55b)

Detailed Analysis of Ethical Codes
Vinaya vibhaṅga
'Dul ba rnam par 'byed pa
Toh. 3 (Dg. K. 'Dul ba, vol. Ca 21a–vol. Nya 269a)

Discourse of Queen Śrīmālā
Ārya śrīmālādevī siṃha nāda nāma mahāyāna sūtra
'Phags pa lha mo dpal phreng gi seng ge'i sgra zhes bya ba theg pa chen po'i mdo
Toh. 92 (Dg. K., dKon brtsegs, vol. Cha, ff. 255a–277b)

Discourse of the Great Drum
Ārya mahābherīhāraka parivarta nāma mahāyāna sūtra
'Phags pa rnga bo che chen po'i le'u zhes bya ba theg pa chen po'i mdo
Toh. 222 (Dg. K., mDo sde, vol. Dza, ff. 84b–126b)

Discourse on the Supreme Passing Beyond Sorrow
Ārya mahāparinirvāṇa sūtra
'Phags pa yongs su mya ngan las 'das pa chen po'i mdo
Toh. 119 (Dg. K., mDo sde, vols. Ña and Ta)

Discourse on the Ten Attributes
Ārya daśa dharmaka nāma mahāyāna sūtra
'Phags pa chos bcu pa zhes bya ba theg pa chen po'i mdo
Toh. 53 (Dg. K., dKon brtsegs, vol. Kha, ff. 164a–184b)

Discourse Requested by Dhāraṇīśvararāja
(a chapter within the *Discourse That Definitively Presents the Supreme Compassion of the Tathāgata*, q.v.)

Discourse Taught by Akṣayamati
Ārya akṣayamati nirdeśa nāma mahāyāna sūtra
'Phags pa blo gros mi zad pas bstan pa zhes bya ba theg pa chen po'i mdo
Toh. 175 (Dg. K., mDo sde, vol. Ma, ff. 79a–174b)

Discourse That Definitively Presents the Supreme Compassion of the Tathāgata
Ārya tathāgata mahākaruṇā nirdeśa nāma mahāyāna sūtra
'Phags pa de bzhin gshegs pa'i snying rje chen po nges par bstan pa zhes bya ba theg pa chen po'i mdo
Toh. 147 (Dg. K., mDo sde, vol. Pa, ff. 142a–242b)

Discourse to Benefit Aṅgulimālā
Ārya aṅgulimālīya nāma mahāyāna sūtra
'Phags pa sor mo'i phreng ba la phan pa zhes bya ba theg pa chen po'i mdo
Toh. 213 (Dg. K., mDo sde, vol. Tsha, ff. 126a–206b)

Expansive Gem
Ārya mahāmaṇi vipula vimāna viśva supratiṣṭhita guhya parama rahasya kalpa rāja nāma dhāraṇī
'Phags pa nor bu chen po rgyas pa'i gzhal med khang shin tu rab tu gnas pa gsang ba dam pa'i gsang ba'i cho ga zhib mo'i rgyal po zhes bya ba'i gzungs
Toh. 506 (Dg. K., rGyud, vol. Da, ff. 286b–309a)

Foundation of Ethical Codes
see *Foundation of Scriptural Transmission*

Foundation of Scriptural Transmission
Vinaya vastu
'Dul ba gzhi/Lung gzhi
Toh. 1 (Dg. K., 'Dul ba, vols. Ka–Nga)

Garland of Buddhas
Buddhāvataṃsaka nāma mahāvaipulya sūtra
Sangs rgyas phal po che zhes bya ba shin tu rgyas pa chen po'i mdo
Toh. 44 (Dg. K., Phal chen, vols. Ka–A)

Heart Essence of Secrets
Śrī guhya garbha tattva viniścaya
dPal gsang ba'i snying po de kho na nyid rnam par nges pa
Toh. 832 (Dg. K., rÑiṅ rgyud, vol. Kha, ff. 110b–132a)

Hevajra Tantra
This tantra consists of two texts:
(A) Hevajra tantra rāja nāma
Kye'i rdo rje zhes bya ba rgyud kyi rgyal po
Toh. 417 (Dg. K., rGyud 'bum, vol. Nga, ff. 1b–13b)
(B) Hevajra ḍākinī jvāla sambara tantra rāja nāma
Kye'i rdo rje mkha' 'gro ma drva ba'i sdom pa'i rgyud kyi rgyal po
Toh. 418 (Dg. K., rGyud 'bum, vol. Nga, ff. 13b–30a)

Journey to Śrī Laṅka
Ārya laṅkāvatāra mahāyāna sūtra
'Phags pa lang kar gshegs pa'i theg pa chen po'i mdo
Toh. 107 (Dg. K., mDo sde, vol. Ca, ff. 56a–191b)

Manifest Adornment of Timeless Awareness
Ārya sarva buddha viṣayāvatāra jñānālokālaṃkāra nāma mahāyāna sūtra
'Phags pa sangs rgyas thams cad kyi yul la 'jug pa'i ye shes snang ba'i rgyan ces bya ba theg pa chen po'i mdo
Toh. 100 (Dg. K. mDo sde, vol. Ga, ff. 276a–305a)

Most Majestic State of Meditative Absorption
Ārya sarva dharma svabhāva samatā vipañcita samādhi rāja nāma mahāyāna sūtra
'Phags pa chos thams cad kyi rang bzhin mnyam pa nyid rnam par spros pa ting nge 'dzin gyi rgyal po zhes bya ba theg pa chen po'i mdo
Toh. 127 (Dg. K., mDo sde, vol. Da, ff. 1b–170b)

"Mother" (can refer to any of the following:)

Transcendent Perfection of Sublime Intelligence in Eight Thousand Verses
Ārya aṣṭa sāhasrikā prajñāpāramitā
'Phags pa shes rab kyi pha rol tu phyin pa brgyad stong pa
Toh. 12 (Dg. K., Śes phyin, vol. Ka, ff. 1b–286a)

Transcendent Perfection of Sublime Intelligence in One Hundred Thousand Verses
Śata sāhasrikā prajñāpāramitā
Shes rab kyi pha rol tu phyin pa stong phrag brgya pa
Toh. 8 (Dg. K., Śes phyin, vols. Ka–A)

Transcendent Perfection of Sublime Intelligence in Twenty-Five Thousand Verses
Pañca viṃśati sāhasrikā prajñāpāramitā
Shes rab kyi pha rol tu phyin pa stong phrag nyi shu lnga pa
Toh. 9 (Dg. K., Śes phyin, vols. Ka–Ga)

Mound of Precious Gems
Ārya ratna rāśi nāma mahāyāna sūtra
'Phags pa rin po che'i phung po zhes bya ba theg pa chen po'i mdo
Toh. 88 (Dg. K., dKon brtsegs (No. 44), vol. Cha, ff. 152a–175b)

Reunion of Father and Son
Ārya pitā putra samāgama nāma mahāyāna sūtra
'Phags pa yab dang sras mjal ba zhes bya ba theg pa chen po'i mdo
Toh. 60 (Dg. K., dKon brtsegs (No. 16), vol. Nga, ff. 1b–168a)

Supreme Illusion
Mahāmāyā tantra nāma
sGyu 'phrul chen po'i rgyud ces bya ba
Toh. 425 (Dg. K. , rGyud, vol. Ṅa, ff. 167a–171a)

Ten Levels of Realization (Chapter 26 of *Garland of Buddhas*)
Daśa bhūmika sūtra
Sa bcu pa'i mdo

Verdant Rice Seedling
Ārya śālistamba nāma mahāyāna sūtra
'Phags pa sā lu'i ljang ba zhes bya ba theg pa chen po'i mdo
Toh. 210 (Dg. K., mDo sde, vol. Tsha, ff. 116b–123b)

Treatises

Āryadeva
Anthology on the Heart Essence of Timeless Awareness
Jñāna sāra samuccaya nāma
Ye shes snying po kun las btus pa zhes bya ba
Toh. 3851 (Dg. T., dBu ma, vol. Tsha, ff. 26b–28a)

Four Hundred Verses
Catuḥśataka śāstra kārikā nāma
bsTan bcos bzhi brgya pa zhes bya ba'i tshig le'ur byas pa
Toh. 3849 (Dg. T., dBu ma, vol. Tsha, ff. 1b–18a)

Asaṅga
Compendium of Abhidharma
Abhidharma samuccaya
Chos mgnon pa kun las btus pa
Toh. 4049 (Dg. T., Sems tsam, vol. Ri, ff. 44b–120a)

Detailed Explanation of the "Highest Continuum"
Mahāyānottara tantra śāstra vyākhyā
Theg pa chen po'i rgyud bla ma'i bstan bcos kyi rnam par bshad pa
Toh. 4025 (Dg. T., Sems tsam, vol. Phi, ff. 74b–129a)

Levels of the Bodhisattva
Yogacaryā bhūmau bodhisattva bhūmi
rNal 'byor spyod pa'i sa las byang chub sems dpa'i sa
Toh. 4037 (Dg. T., Sems tsam, vol. Wi, ff. 1b–213a)

Levels of the Śrāvaka
Yogacaryā bhūmau śrāvaka bhūmi
rNal 'byor spyod pa'i sa las nyan thos kyi sa
Toh. 4036 (Dg. T., Sems tsam, vol. Dzi, ff. 1a–195a)

Levels of Yogic Practitioners
Yogacaryā bhūmi
rNal 'byor spyod pa'i sa
Toh. 4035 (Dg. T, Sems tsam, vol. Tshi, ff. 1a–283a)

Asvabhāva
Explanatory Essays Commenting on the "Compendium of the Supreme Spiritual Approach"
Mahāyāna saṁgrahopanibandhana
Theg pa chen po bsdus pa'i bshad sbyar
Toh. 4051 (Dg. T., Sems tsam, vol. Ri, ff. 190b–296a)

Aśvaghoṣa
Account of the Eight States Devoid of Opportunity
Aṣṭākṣaṇakathā
Mi khom pa brgyad kyi gtam
Toh. 4167 (Dg. T., sPriṅ yig, vol. Ge, ff. 175a–178a)

Atīśa Dipaṃkara Śrījñāna
Chapter on the Circumstances for Meditative Absorption
Samādhi sambhāra parivarta
Ting nge 'dzin gyi tshogs kyi le'u
Toh. 2460 (Dg. T. rGyud 'grel, vol. Zi, 134b–135a)

Lamp on the Path to Enlightenment
Bodhi patha pradīpa
Byang chub lam gyi sgron ma
Toh. 3947 (Dg. T., dBu ma, vol. Khi, ff. 238a–241a)

Pith Instructions on the Middle Way
Madhyamakopadeśa nāma
dBu ma'i man ngag ces bya ba
Toh. 3929 (Dg. T., dBu ma, vol. Ki, ff. 95b–96a)

Bhāvaviveka
Blazing Logic
Madhyamaka hṛdaya vṛtti tarka jvālā
dBu ma'i snying po'i 'grel pa rtog ge 'bar ba
Toh. 3856 (Dg. T., dBu ma, vol. Dza, ff. 40b–329b)

Bodhibhadra
Essay on Meditative Absorption
Samādhi sambhāra parivarta nāma
Ting nge 'dzin gyi tshogs kyi le'u zhes bya ba
Toh. 3924 (Dg. T., dBu ma, vol. Ki, ff. 79b–91a)

Candragomin
Letter to Students
Śiṣyalekha
sLob ma la springs pa'i spring yig
Toh. 4183 (Dg. T., sPriṅ yig, vol. Nge, ff. 46b–53a)

Candrakīrti
Clear Words
Mūla madhyamaka vṛtti prasanna pāda nāma
dBu ma rtsa ba'i 'grel pa tshig gsal ba zhes bya ba
Toh. 3860 (Dg. T., dBu ma, vol. 'A, ff. 1b–200a)

Entrance to the Middle Way
Madhyamakāvatāra nāma
dBu ma la 'jug pa zhes bya ba
Toh. 3861 (Dg. T., dBu ma, vol. 'A, ff. 201b–219a)

Explanation of "Entrance to the Middle Way"
Madhyamakāvatāra bhāṣya nāma
dBu ma la 'jug pa'i bshad pa zhes bya ba
Toh. 3862 (Dg. T., dBu ma, vol. 'A, ff. 220b–348a)

Extensive Commentary on the "Four Hundred Verses for Engaging in a Bodhisattva's Conduct"
Bodhisattva yogacaryā catuḥ śataka ṭīkā
Byang chub sems dpa'i rnal 'byor spyod pa bzhi brgya pa'i rgya cher 'grel pa
Toh. 3865 (Dg. T., dBu ma, vol. Ya, ff. 30b239a)

Dharmakīrti
Detailed Commentary on Valid Cognition
Pramāṇa vārttika kārikā
Tshad ma rnam 'grel gyi tshig le'ure byas pa
Toh. 4210 (Dg. T., Tshad ma, vol. Ce, ff. 94b–151a)

Dharmapāla
Decision concerning Conscious Awareness
Vijñapti siddhi [?]
rNam par rig par grub pa
(source not located)

Dharmatrāta
Didactic Aphorisms
Udānavarga
Ched du brjod pa'i tshoms
Toh. 326 (Dg. K., mDo sde, vol. Sa, ff. 209a–253a) and
Toh. 4099 (Dg. T., mNgon pa, vol. Tu, ff. 1b–45a)

Dignāga
Summary of the Meaning of the Eight Thousand Verses
Ārya prajñā pāramitā saṃgraha kārikā
'Phags pa shes rab kyi pha rol tu phyin ma bsdus pa'i tshig le'ur byas pa
Toh. 3809 (Dg. T., Śes phyin, vol. Pha, ff. 292b–294b)

Haribhadra
Illumination of the "Ornament of Manifest Realization": An Explanation of the Exalted Treatise on the Transcendent Perfection of Sublime Intelligence in Eight Thousand Verses
Ārya aṣṭa sāhasrikā prajñā pāramitā vyākhyābhisamayālaṃkārāloka nāma
'Phags pa shes rab kyi pha rol tu phyin pa brgyad stong pa'i bshad pa mngon par rtogs pa'i rgyan gyi snang ba
Toh. 3791 (Dg. T., Śes phyin, vol. Cha, ff. 1b–341a)

Jñānagarbha
Source Verses on Differentiating the Two Levels of Truth
Satya dvaya vibhaṅga vṛtti
bDen pa gnyis rnam par 'byed pa'i tshig le'ur byas pa
Toh. 3881 (Dg. T., dBu ma, vol. Sa, ff. 1b–3b)

Kamalaśīla
Stages of Meditation
Bhāvanā krama
sGom pa'i rim pa
Toh. 3916 (Dg. T., dBu ma, vol. Ki, ff. 42a–55b)

Longchen Rabjam
Great Chariot: A Commentary on the Great Perfection Treatise "Finding Ease in the Nature of Mind Itself"
rDzogs pa chen po sems nyi ngal gso'i 'grel pa shing rta chen po
A 'dzom chos sgar edition. Edited and published by Do Drupchen Rinpoche. Gangtok, Sikkim: n.d.

Maitreya
Distinguishing Center and Limit
Madhyānta vibhaṅga kārikā
dBus dang mtha rnam par 'byed pa'i tshig le'ur byas pa
Toh. 4021 (Dg. T., Sems tsam, vol. Phi, ff. 40b–45a)

Highest Continuum
Mahāyānottara tantra śāstra
Theg pa chen po rgyud bla ma'i bstan bcos

Toh. 4024 (Dg. T., Sems tsam, vol. Phi, ff. 54b–73a)

Ornament of the Mahāyāna Sūtras
Mahāyāna sūtrālaṃkāra nāma kārikā
Theg pa chen po mdo sde'i rgyan zhes bya ba'i tshigs le'ur byas pa
Toh. 4020 (Dg. T., Sems tsam, vol. Phi, ff. 1b–39a)

Mañjughoṣa Narendrakīrti
Brief Presentation of the Tenets of Buddhist Views
Pradarśanānumatoddeśa parīkṣā nāma
Rang gi lta ba'i 'dod pa mdor bstan pa yongs su brtag pa zhes bya ba / lTa 'dod mdor bstan
P 4610 (Peking bsTan 'gyur, rGyud 'grel, vol. Pu, ff. 21a–50b)
(sNar thang bsTan 'gyur, rGyud 'grel, vol. Pu, ff. 22a–52ab)

Nāgārjuna
Commentary on Bodhicitta
Bodhicitta vivaraṇa nāma
Byang chub sems kyi 'grel pa zhes bya ba
Toh. 1800 (Dg. T., rGyud 'grel, vol. Ngi, ff. 38a–42b)

In Praise of She Who Is the Transcendent Perfection of Sublime Intelligence
Prajñā pāramitā stotra
Shes rab kyi pha rol tu phyin ma'i bstod pa
Toh. 1127 (Dg. T., bsTod tshogs, vol. Ka, ff. 76a–76b)

In Praise of the Inconceivable Middle Way
Acintya stava
bSam gyis mi khyab par bstod pa
Toh. 1128 (Dg. T., bsTod tshogs, vol. Ka, ff. 76b–79a)

Letter to a Friend
Suhṛllekha
bShes pa'i phrin yig
Toh. 4182 (Dg. T., sPriṅ yig, vol. Nge, ff. 40b–46b)

Precious Garland: Conversation with a King
Rāja parikathā ratna mālā
rGyal po la gtam bya ba rin po che'i phreng ba
Toh. 4158 (Dg. T., sPriṅ yig, vol. Ge, ff. 107a–126a)

Sixty Verses on Reasoning
Yukti ṣaṣṭikā kārikā nāma
Rigs pa drug cu pa'i tshig le'ur byas pa zhes bya ba
Toh. 3825 (Dg. T., dBu ma, vol. Tsa, ff. 20b–22a)

Source Verses on Sublime Intelligence
Prajñā nāma mūla madhyamaka kārikā
dBu ma rtsa ba'i tshig le'ur byas pa shes rab ces bya ba
Toh. 3824 (Dg. T., dBu ma, vol. Tsa, ff. 1b–19a)

Stages of Meditation
Bhāvanā krama

sGom pa'i rim pa
Toh. 3908 (Dg. T., dBu ma, vol. Ki, ff. 1a–4a)

Puṇḍarīka
Stainless Light
Vimala prabhā nāma mūla tantrānusāriṇī dvādaśa sāhasrikā laghu kālacakra tantra rāja ṭīkā
bsDus pa'i rgyud kyi rgyal po dus kyi 'khor lo'i 'grel bshad rtsa ba'i rgyud kyi rjes su 'jug pa stong phrag bcu gnyis pa dri ma med pa'i 'od ces bya ba
Toh. 845 (Dg. K., Dus 'khor 'grel bshad, vol. Śrī, ff. 1b–469a)
Toh. 1347 (Dg. T., rGyud, vol. Tha, ff. 107b–277a and vol. Da, ff. 1b–297a)

Ratnākaraśānti
Pith Instructions on the Transcendent Perfection of Sublime Intelligence
Prajñā pāramitopadeśa
Shes rab kyi pha rol tu phyin pa'i man ngag
Toh. 4079 (Dg. T., Sems tsam, vol. Hi, ff. 133b–162b)

Sublime Heart Essence: Commentary on the Difficult Points in the "Exalted Transcendent Perfection of Sublime Intelligence in Eight Thousand Verses"
Ārya aṣṭa sāhasrikā prajñā pāramitā pañjikā sārottama nāma
'Phags pa shes rab kyi pha rol tu phyin pa brgyad stong pa'i dka' 'grel snying po mchog ces bya ba
Toh. 3803 (Dg. T., Śes phyin, vol. Tha, ff. 1b–230a)

Ratnakīrti
In Praise of the Deity of Fourfold Union
Yoga catur deva stotra nāma
sByor ba bzhi'i lha la bstod pa zhes bya ba
Toh. 1170 (Dg. T., bsTod tshogs, vol. Ka, ff. 246b–249a)

Śāntarakṣita
Ornament of the Middle Way
Madhyamakālaṃkāra kārikā
dBu ma'i rgyan gyi tshig le'ur byas pa
Toh. 3884 (Dg. T., dBu ma, vol. Sa, ff. 53a–56b)

Śāntideva
Engaging in the Conduct of a Bodhisattva
Bodhisattva caryāvatāra
Byang chub sems dpa'i spyod pa la 'jug pa
Toh. 3871 (Dg. T., dBu ma, vol. La, ff. 1b–40a)

Vajrapāṇi
Detailed Explanation of the Summary of the Concise Tantra Extracted from the One Hundred Thousand Verses of the Definitive Expression
Lakṣābhidhānāduddhṛta laghu tantra piṇḍārtha vivaraṇa nāma

mNgon par brjod pa 'bum pa las phyung ba nyung ngu'i rgyud kyi bsdus pa'i don rnam par bshad pa zhes bya ba
Toh. 1402 (Dg. T., rGyud, vol. Ba, ff. 78b–141a)

Vasubandhu

Advice for the Multitude
Sambhāra parikathā
Tshogs kyi gtam
Toh. 4166 (Dg. T., sPrin yig, vol. Ge, ff. 173b–175a)

Explanation of the "Treasury of Abhidharma"
Abhidharma koṣa bhāṣya
Chos mngon pa mdzod kyi bshad pa
Toh. 4090 (Dg. T., mNgon pa, vol. Ku, f. 26b–vol. Khu, f. 95a)

Reasoning for a Detailed Explanation
Vyākhyā yukti
rNam par bshad pa'i rigs pa
Toh. 4061 (Dg. T., Sems tsam, vol. Shi, ff. 29a–134b)

Treasury of Abhidharma
Abhidharma koṣa kārikā
Chos mngon pa'i mdzod kyi tshig le'ur byas pa
Toh. 4089 (Dg. T., mNgon pa, vol. Ku, ff. 1b–25a)

Reference Bibliography

Tibetan Works and Sanskrit Works Consulted in Tibetan Translation

Dezhung Rinpoché, Kunga Tenpai Nyima (sDe gzhung rin po che Kun dga' bstan pa'i nyi ma)
Nges don phyas rdzogs dbu gsum gyi lta sgom gyi gnas mdor bsdus 'khrul bral legs bshad mkhas pa'i zhal lung
sDe gzhung lung rigs sprul sku Kun dga' bstan pa'i nyi ma'i gsung 'bum, pp. 1–118
Zhi lhag gi ting 'dzin sgom tshul thar lam sgron me
sDe gzhung lung rigs sprul sku Kun dga' bstan pa'i nyi ma'i gsung 'bum, pp. 119–50
n.p., n.d.

Gampopa Sönam Rinchen (sGam po pa bSod nams rin chen)
Dvags po'i thar rgyan/ Dam chos yid bzhin gyi nor bu thar pa rin po che'i rgyan
Khams gsym chos kyi rgyal po dpal mnyam med sGam po pa 'gro mgon bsod nams rin chen mchog gi gsung 'bum yid bzhin nor bu, vol. 4, pp. 185–662
Kathmandu: Khenpo S. Tendzin and Lama T. Namgyal, 2000

Jamgön Kongtrul Lodrö Tayé ('Jam mgon kong sprul blo gros mtha' yas)
Shes bya mdzod composed of:
Theg pa'i sgo kun las btus pa gsung rab rin po che'i mdzod bslab pa gsum legs par ston pa'i bstan bcos Shes bya kun khyab
(source verses)
Shes bya kun la khyab pa'i gzhung lugs nyung ngu'i tshig gis rnam par 'grol ba legs bshad yongs 'du Shes bya mtha' yas pa'i rgya mtsho
(commentary)
1 vol. Beijing: Mi rigs dpe skrun khang, 2002
4 vols. Delhi: Shechen Publications, 1997

Longchen Rabjam (kLong chen rab 'byams)
Grub pa'i mtha' rin po che'i mdzod/ Theg pa mtha' dag gi don gsal bar byed pa grub pa'i mtha' rin po che'i mdzod
Published by Do Drupchen Rinpoche, Deorali, Sikkim, n.d.

Theg pa'i mchog rin po che'i mdzod
Published by Do Drupchen Rinpoche, Deorali, Sikkim: n.d.

Mipham Gyamtso, Ju ('Ju mi pham rgya mtsho)
mKhas pa la 'jug pa'i sgo
Xining, China: mTsho sngon mi rigs dpe skrun khang, 1988

Sherab Puntsok, Khenpo (mKhan po Shes rab phun tshogs)
dBu ma gzhan ston gla 'jug pa'i sgo gong ma'i gsung gi bdud rtsi
Varanasi, India: Vajra Vidya Institute Library, 2007

Vasubandhu
Commentary on "Distinguishing Center and Limit"
Madhyānta vibhāṅga ṭīka
dBus dang mtha' rnam par 'byed pa'i 'grel pa
Toh. 4027 (Dg. T., Sems tsam, vol. Bi, ff. 1a–29b)

Explanation of the "Ornament of the Mahāyāna Sūtras"
Sūtrālaṃkāra vyākhyā
mDo sde rgyan gyi bshad pa
Toh. 4026 (Dg. T., Sems tsam, vol. Phi, ff. 129b–260a)

Yaktön Sang-gyé Pal (gYag ston Sangs rgyas dpal)
mNgon rtogs rgyan dang 'grel pa don gsal rtsa 'grel gyi dgos don stsol ba rin chen bsam 'phel dbang gi rgyal po

Zhang, Yisun et al., ed.
Bod rgya tshig mdzod chen mo
3 vols. Beijing: Mi rigs dpe skrun khang, 1985

Western Works and Translations

Amos, Flora Ross. *Early Theories of Translation*. New York: Octagon Books, 1973.

Āryadeva, and Gyel-tsap. *Āryadeva's Four Hundred Stanzas on the Middle Way with Commentary by Gyel-tsap*. Translated by Geshe Sonam Rinchen and Ruth Sonam. Ithaca, N.Y.: Snow Lion Publications, 2008.

Batchelor, Stephen, trans. *A Guide to the Bodhisattva's Way of Life*. Repr., Dharamsala, India: Library of Tibetan Works and Archives, 1997.

Bhikkhu Bodhi, trans. *The Connected Discourses of the Buddha: A New Translation of the Saṃyutta Nikāya*. 2 vols. Boston: Wisdom Publications, 2000.

Biguenet, John, and Rainer Schulte, ed. *The Craft of Translation*. Chicago: University of Chicago Press, 1989.

Blumenthal, James. 2004. *The Ornament of the Middle Way: A Study of the Madhyamaka Thought of Śāntarakṣita*. Ithaca, N.Y.: Snow Lion Publications, 2004.

Bly, Robert. *Eight Stages of Translation*. 2nd ed. Boston: Rowan Tree Press, 1986.

Boin-Webb, Sara, trans. *Abhidharmasamuccaya: The Compendium of the Higher Teaching (Philosophy)*. Fremont, Calif.: Asian Humanities Press, 2001.

Broido, Michael M. "Intention and Suggestion in the Abhidharmakośa: Sandhābhāṣā Revisited." *Journal of Indian Philosophy* 13, no. 4 (1985): 327–81.

Brown, Brian Edward. *The Buddha Nature: A Study of the Tathāgatagarbha and Ālayavijñāna*. Repr., Delhi: Motilal Banarsidass, 1994.

Brunnhölzl, Karl. *The Center of the Sunlit Sky: Madhyamaka in the Kagyü Tradition*. Ithaca, N.Y.: Snow Lion Publications, 2004.

———. *Gone Beyond, Volume One: The Prajñāpāramitā Sūtras, The "Ornament of Clear Realization," and Its Commentaries in the Tibetan Kagyü Tradition*. Ithaca, N.Y.: Snow Lion Publications, 2011.

———, trans. *In Praise of Dharmadhātu: Nāgārjuna and the Third Karmapa, Rangjung Dorje*. Ithaca, N.Y.: Snow Lion Publications, 2007.

———. *Luminous Heart: The Third Karmapa on Consciousness, Wisdom, and Buddha Nature*. Ithaca, N.Y.: Snow Lion Publications, 2009.

Buddhaghosa, Bhadantācariya. *The Path of Purification (Visuddhimagga)*. Translated by Bhikkhu Ñyāṇamoli. 2 vols. Berkeley: Shambhala, 1976.

Cabezón, José I., and Roger Jackson, eds. *Tibetan Literature: Studies in Genre, Essays in Honor of Geshe Lhundrup Sopa*. Ithaca, N.Y.: Snow Lion Publications, 1996.

Campbell, Gordon. *Bible: The Story of the King James Version 1611–2011*. New York: Oxford University Press, 2010.

Candragomin. *Difficult Beginnings: Three Works on the Bodhisattva Path*. Translated by Mark Tatz. Boston: Shambhala, 2001.

Catalogue-Index of the Tibetan Buddhist Canons (Bkaḥ-ḥgyur and Bstan-ḥgyur). Delhi: Sri Satguru Publications, 1983.

Chandra, Lokesh. *Tibetan-Sanskrit Dictionary*. Kyoto: Rinsen Book Co., 1982.

Chenique, François, trans. *Le Message du Futur Bouddha, ou La Lignée Spirituelle des Trois Joyaux*. Paris: Éditions DERVY, 2001.

A Comparative Analytical Catalogue of the Kanjur Division of the Tibetan Tripitaka: Edited in Peking during the K'ang hsi Era, and At Present Kept in the Library of the Otani Daigaku Kyoto. 3 vols. The Otani Daigaku Library, Kyoto, 1930–1932. Otani University Shin Buddhist Comprehensive Research Institute: Tibetan Works Research Project, 2005. http://web.otani.ac.jp/cri/twrp/tibdate/Peking_online_search.html.

Cleary, Thomas, trans. *The Flower Ornament Scripture: A Translation of the "Avatamsaka Sutra."* Boston: Shambhala, 1993.

Conze, E. *The Large Sūtra on the Perfection of Wisdom*. Berkeley: University of California Press, 1975.

———. *The Perfection of Wisdom in Eight Thousand Lines and Its Verse Summary*. Bolinas, Calif.: Four Seasons Foundation, 1973.

Dayal, Har. *The Bodhisattva Doctrine in Buddhist Sanskrit Literature*. Repr., Delhi: Motilal Banarsidass, 1975.

Dharmachakra Translation Committee, trans. *Middle Beyond Extremes: Maitreya's "Madhyāntavibhāga" with Commentaries by Khenpo Shenga and Ju Mipham*. Ithaca, N.Y.: Snow Lion Publications, 2007.

———. *Ornament of Reason: The Great Commentary to Nāgārjuna's "Root of the Middle Way."* Ithaca, N.Y.: Snow Lion Publications, 2011.

Doboom Tulku, ed. *Buddhist Translation: Problems and Perspectives*. New Delhi: Manohar Publishers and Distributors, 1995.

Doctor, Thomas H., trans. *Speech of Delight: Mipham's Commentary on Śāntarakṣita's "Ornament of the Middle Way."* Ithaca, N.Y.: Snow Lion Publications, 2004.

Dudjom Rinpoche, *The Nyingma School of Tibetan Buddhism: Its Fundamentals and History*. Translated and edited by Gyurme Dorje and Matthew Kapstein. 2nd ed. Boston: Wisdom Publications, 2002.

Duerlinger, James. *Indian Buddhist Theories of Persons: Vasubandhu's "Refutation of the Theory of a Self."* Critical Studies in Buddhism. New York: RoutledgeCurzon, 2003.

Eckel, Malcolm David, trans. *Jñānagarbha's Commentary on the Distinction between the Two Truths*. Albany: State University of New York Press, 1987.

Frauwallner, Erich. *Studies in Abhidharma Literature and the Origins of Buddhist Philosophical Systems*. Translated by Sophie Francis Kidd. Albany: State University of New York Press, 1995.

Fuchs, Rosemarie, trans. *Buddha Nature: The Mahāyāna Uttaratantra Shastra*. Ithaca, N.Y.: Snow Lion Publications, 2000.

sGam.po.pa. *The Jewel Ornament of Liberation*. Translated by Herbert V. Guenther. Repr., Boulder: Shambhala, 1971.

Garfield, Jay L., trans. *The Fundamental Wisdom of the Middle Way: Nāgārjuna's "Mūlamadhyamakakārikā."* New York: Oxford University Press, 1995.

Goldfield, Ari, Jules Levinson, Jim Scott, and Birgit Scott, trans. *The Moon of Wisdom: Chapter Six of Chandrakirti's "Entering the Middle Way."* Ithaca, N.Y.: Snow Lion Publications, 2005.

Goodman, Steven D. *Frogs in the Custard: An Exploration of the View and Practice of Abhidharma*. Lerab Ling, France: Rigpa, 2002.

Grossman, Edith. *Why Translation Matters*. New Haven: Yale University Press, 2010.

Guenther, Herbert V. *Buddhist Philosophy in Theory and Practice*. Baltimore: Penguin, 1972.

———. *Philosophy and Psychology in the Abhidharma*. Berkeley: Shambhala, 1976.

———. *Treasures on the Tibetan Middle Way*. Berkeley: Shambhala, 1971.

Guenther, Herbert V., and Leslie S. Kawamura, trans. *Mind in Buddhist Psychology*. Emeryville, Calif.: Dharma Publishing, 1975.

Guenther, Herbert V., and Chögyam Trungpa. *The Dawn of Tantra*. Boston: Shambhala, 2001.

Gupta, Rita. "Apoha and the Nominalist/Conceptualist Controversy." *Journal of Indian Philosophy* 13, no. 4 (1985): 383–98.

Gyamtso, Khenpo Tsultrim, Rinpoche. *Ascertaining Certainty about the View: Chapter Seven, Section Three from "The Treasury of Knowledge" by Jamgon Longtrul Lodro Thaye, commentary by Khenpo Tsultrim Gyamtso Rinpoche*. Translated by Michele Martin. Auckland: Zhyisil Chokyi Ghatsal Publications (Prajna Editions), 2001.

———. *Progressive Stages of Meditation on Emptiness*. Translated by Shenpen Hookham. Oxford: Longchen Foundation, 1986.

———. *Stars of Wisdom: Analytical Meditation, Songs of Yogic Joy, and Prayers of Aspiration*. Translated by Ari Goldfield and Rose Taylor. Boston: Shambhala, 2010.

———. *The Sun of Wisdom: Teachings on the Noble Nāgārjuna's "Fundamental Wisdom of the Middle Way."* Translated by Ari Goldfield. Boston: Shambhala, 2003.

———. *The Two Truths*. Translated by Ari Goldfield. Auckland: Zhyisil Chokyi Ghatsal Publications (Prajna Editions), 2001.

Gyatrul Rinpoche. *The Generation Stage in Buddhist Tantra*. Translated by Sangye Khandro. 2nd ed. Ithaca, N.Y.: Snow Lion Publications, 2005.

Hampden-Turner, Charles. *Maps of the Mind*. New York: Collier Books, 1982.

Holmes, Ken, and Katia Holmes, trans. *The Changeless Nature*. Eskdalemuir, Scotland: Karma Drubgyud Darjay Ling, 1985.

———, trans. *Gems of Dharma, Jewels of Freedom*. Forres, Scotland: Altea Publishing, 1995.

Hookham, S. K. *The Buddha Within: Tathagatagarbha Doctrine according to the Shentong Interpretation of the Ratnagotravibhaga*. Albany: State University of New York Press, 1991.

Hopkins, Jeffrey, trans. *Buddhist Advice for Living and Liberation: Nāgārjuna's "Precious Garland."* Ithaca, N.Y.: Snow Lion Publications, 1998.

———. *Compassion in Tibetan Buddhism*. Ithaca, N.Y.: Snow Lion Publications, 1980.

———. *Meditation on Emptiness*. London: Wisdom Publications, 1983.

Hopkins, Jeffrey, and Geshe Lhundrup Sopa. *Cutting through Appearances: Practice and Theory of Tibetan Buddhism*. Ithaca, N.Y.: Snow Lion Publications, 1989.

Inada, Kenneth. *Nāgārjuna: A Translation of His "Mūlamadhyamakakārikā" with an Introductory Essay*. Bibliotheca Indo-Buddhica Series 127. Delhi: Sri Satguru Publications, 1993.

Jamspal, L., R. Clark, J. Wilson, L. Zwilling, M. Sweet, and R. Thurman, trans. *The Universal Vehicle Discourse Literature (Mahāyānasūtrālaṃkāra) by Maitreyanātha/ Āryāsaṅga together with Its Commentary (Bhāṣya) by Vasubandhu*. Treasury of the Buddhist Sciences. New York: American Institute of Buddhist Studies, 2004.

Jamspal, L., Ngawang Samten Chophel, and Peter Della Santina, trans. *Nāgārjuna's Letter to King Gautamīputra*. Delhi: Motilal Banarsidass Publishers, 1996.

Jiang, Tao. *Contexts and Dialogue: Yogacara Buddhism and Modern Psychology on the Subliminal Mind*. Monograph 21, Society for Asian and Comparative Philosophy. Honolulu: University of Hawai'i Press, 2006.

Jinpa, Thubten, trans. *The Book of Kadam: The Core Texts*. Library of Tibetan Classics. Somerville, Mass.: Wisdom Publications, 2008.

———. *Mind Training: The Great Collection*. Library of Tibetan Classics. Somerville, Mass.: Wisdom Publications, 2006.

Kalupahana, David J. *Nāgārjuna: The Philosophy of the Middle Way*. Albany: State University of New York Press, 1986.

Kanakura, Yensho. *Hindu-Buddhist Thought in India*. Translated by Shotaro Iida and Neal Donner. Yokohama: Hokke Journal, Inc., 1980.

Kangyur Rinpoche, Kyabje. *Nagarjuna's "Letter to a Friend" with Commentary by Kangyur Rinpoche*. Translated by the Padmakara Translation Group. Ithaca, N.Y.: Snow Lion Publications, 2005.

Katsura, Shōryū, trans. *The Summary of the Great Vehicle*. BDK English Tripiṭaka 46 III. Berkeley: Numata Center for Buddhist Translation and Research, 1992.

Katz, Nathan. *Buddhist Images of Human Perfection: The Arahant of the Sutta Piṭaka Compared with the Bodhisattva and the Mahāsiddha*. 2nd ed. Delhi: Motilal Banarsidass, 2004.

Komito, David. *Nāgārjuna's "Seventy Stanzas": A Buddhist Psychology of Emptiness*. Ithaca, N.Y.: Snow Lion Publications, 1987.

Kongtrul, Jamgön. *The Autobiography of Jamgön Kongtrul: A Gem of Many Colors*. Translated by Richard Barron. Ithaca, N.Y.: Snow Lion Publications, 2003.

———. *Creation and Completion*. Translated by Sarah Harding. 2nd ed. Somerville, Mass.: Wisdom Publications, 2002.

———. *The Treasury of Knowledge: Book Eight, Part Four: Esoteric Instructions*. Translated by Sarah Harding. Ithaca, N.Y.: Snow Lion Publications, 2007.

———. *The Treasury of Knowledge: Book Eight, Part Three: The Elements of Tantric Practice*. Translated by Elio Guarisco and Ingrid Loken McLeod. Ithaca, N.Y.: Snow Lion Publications, 2008.

———. *The Treasury of Knowledge: Book Five: Buddhist Ethics*. Translated by the International Translation Committee of Kalu Rinpoché. Ithaca, N.Y.: Snow Lion Publications, 2003.

———. *The Treasury of Knowledge: Book One: Myriad Worlds.* Translated by the International Translation Committee of Kalu Rinpoché. Ithaca, N.Y.: Snow Lion Publications, 1995.

———. *The Treasury of Knowledge: Book Six, Part Four: Systems of Buddhist Tantra.* Translated by Elio Guarisco and Ingrid McLeod. Ithaca, N.Y.: Snow Lion Publications, 2005.

———. *The Treasury of Knowledge: Book Six, Part Three: Frameworks of Buddhist Philosophy.* Translated by Elizabeth Callahan. Ithaca, N.Y.: Snow Lion Publications, 2007.

———. *The Treasury of Knowledge: Book Six, Parts One and Two: Indo-Tibetan Classical Learning and Buddhist Phenomenology.* Translated by Gyurme Dorje. Ithaca, N.Y.: Snow Lion Publications, forthcoming.

———. *The Treasury of Knowledge: Books Nine and Ten: Journey and Goal.* Translated by Richard Barron (Chökyi Nyima). Ithaca, N.Y.: Snow Lion Publications, 2011.

———. *The Treasury of Knowledge: Books Two, Three, and Four: Buddhism's Journey to Tibet.* Translated by Ngawang Zangpo. Ithaca, N.Y.: Snow Lion Publications, 2010.

Kuhn, Thomas S. *The Structure of Scientific Revolutions.* 2nd ed. Chicago: University of Chicago Press, 1970.

Kunga Tenpai Nyima, Dezhung Lungrik Tulku III. "A Lamp on the Path to Liberation: A Way to Cultivate the Meditative Absorption of Calm Abiding and Profound Insight." Translated by Richard Barron. Unpublished translation.

Lati Rinpoche. *Mind in Tibetan Buddhism.* Translated by Elizabeth Napper. 3rd ed. Ithaca, N.Y.: Snow Lion Publications, 1986.

Lati Rinpoche, and Denma Lochö Rinpoche. *Meditative States in Tibetan Buddhism: The Concentrations and Formless Absorptions.* Leah Zahler and Jeffrey Hopkins, trans. London: Wisdom Publications, 1983.

Levinson, Jules Brooks. "The Metaphors of Liberation: A Study of Grounds and Paths according to the Middle Way Schools." PhD diss., University of Virginia, 1994.

Lindtner, Christian. *Master of Wisdom: Writings of the Buddhist Master Nāgārjuna.* Berkeley: Dharma Publishing, 1986.

———. *Nagarjuniana: Studies in the Writings and Philosophy of Nāgārjuna.* Repr., Delhi: Motilal Banarsidass, 1987.

Long, Lynne, ed. *Translation and Religion: Holy Untranslatable?* Topics in Translation 28. Buffalo: Multilingual Matters, 2005.

Longchen Rabjam. *The Precious Treasury of Philosophical Systems.* Translated by Richard Barron. Junction City, Calif.: Padma Publishing, 2007.

———. *The Precious Treasury of the Way of Abiding.* Translated by Richard Barron. Junction City, Calif.: Padma Publishing, 1998.

———. *A Treasure Trove of Scriptural Transmission: A Commentary on "The Precious Treasury of the Basic Space of Phenomena."* Translated by Richard Barron. Junction City, Calif.: Padma Publishing, 2001.

———. *See also* Longchenpa.

Longchenpa. *Kindly Bent to Ease Us.* Translated and annotated by Herbert V. Guenther. 3 vols. Emeryville, Calif.: Dharma Publishing, 1975–77.

———. *See also* Longchen Rabjam.

Lopez, Donald S., Jr. *Elaborations on Emptiness: Uses of the Heart Sutra.* Princeton: Princeton University Press, 1996.

———. *The Madman's Middle Way: Reflections on Reality of the Tibetan Monk Gendun Chopel.* Chicago: University of Chicago Press, 2006.

Loy, David. *Nonduality: A Study in Comparative Philosophy*. Amherst, N.Y.: Humanity Books, 1998.

Mabja Jangchub Tsöndrü. *Ornament of Reason*. Dharmachakra Translation Committee, trans. Ithaca, N.Y.: Snow Lion Publications, 2011.

McGrath, Alister. *In the Beginning: The Story of the King James Bible and How It Changed a Nation, a Language, and a Culture*. New York: Doubleday, 2001.

Mipham Rinpoche. *Gateway to Knowledge*. Translated by Erik Hein Schmidt. 3 vols. Hong Kong: Rangjung Yeshe Publications, 1997–2002.

———. *Ways of Enlightenment: Buddhist Studies at Nyingma Institute*. Berkeley: Dharma Publishing, 1993.

Monier-Williams, Sir Monier. *A Sanskrit-English Dictionary*. New York: Oxford University Press, 2000.

Nāgārjuna. *Nāgārjuna's "Reason Sixty" with Chandrakīrti's Reason Sixty Commentary*. Translated by Joseph John Loizzo and the AIBS Translation Team. Treasury of the Buddhist Sciences. New York: American Institute of Buddhist Studies, 2007.

Nicolson, Adam. *God's Secretaries: The Making of the King James Bible*. New York: HarperCollins, 2003.

Norman, K. R. *A Philological Approach to Buddhism*. Oxford: Pāli Text Society, 2008.

Padmakara Translation Group, trans. *The Adornment of the Middle Way: Shantarakshita's "Madhyamakalankara" with Commentary by Jamgön Mipham*. Boston: Shambhala, 2005.

———, trans. *Introduction to the Middle Way: Chandrakīrti's "Madhyamakāvatāra" with Commentary by Jamgön Mipham*. Boston: Shambhala, 2002.

Patrul Rinpoche. *The Words of My Perfect Teacher*. Rev. ed. Boston: Shambhala, 1998.

Powers, John. *Two Commentaries on the Samdhinirmocana-Sutra by Asanga and Jnanagarbha*. Studies in Asian Thought and Religion 13. Lewiston, N.Y.: Edward Mellen Press, 1992.

———, trans. *Wisdom of Buddha: The Saṃdhinirmocana Sūtra*. Berkeley: Dharma Publishing, 1995.

Prebish, Charles S., ed. *Buddhism: A Modern Perspective*. University Park: The Pennsylvania State University Press, 1975.

Pruden, Leo M., trans. *Abhidharmakośabhaṣyaṃ*. 4 vols. Berkeley: Asian Humanities Press, 1988–1990.

Reat, Noble Ross. "A Buddhist Proof for the Existence of God." *Journal of Indian Philosophy* 13, no. 4 (1985): 265–72.

Rhys Davids, T. W., trans. *The Questions of King Milinda Part I: The Sacred Books of the East Part Thirty-Five*. Repr., Whitefish, Mont.: Kessinger Publishing, 2004.

Rigzin, Tsepak. *Tibetan-English Dictionary of Buddhist Terminology*. 2nd ed. Dharamsala, India: Library of Tibetan Works and Archives, 1993.

Ringu Tulku. *The Ri-me Philosophy of Jamgön Kongtrul the Great: A Study of the Buddhist Lineages of Tibet*. Boston: Shambhala, 2006.

Roerich, George N., trans. *The Blue Annals*. Repr., Delhi: Motilal Banarsidass, 1979.

Ruegg, David Seyfort. "Purport, Implicature, and Presupposition: Sanskrit *Abhiprāya* and Tibetan *Dgoṅs pa/dgoṅs Gži* as Hermeneutical Concepts." *Journal of Indian Philosophy* 13, no. 4 (1985): 309–25.

———. "Some Reflections on Translating Buddhist Philosophical Texts from Sanskrit and Tibetan." *Asiatische Studien* 46, no. 1 (1992): 367–91.

———. *Le Traité du Tathāgatagarbha de Bu Ston Rin Chen Grub*. Paris: École Française d'Extrême-Orient, 1973.

Sakya Pandita. *Illuminations: A Guide to Essential Buddhist Practices.* Translated by Geshe Wangyal and Brian Cutillo. Novata, Calif.: Lotsawa, 1988.

Schulte, Rainer, and John Biguenet, ed. *Theories of Translation: An Anthology of Essays from Dryden to Derrida.* Chicago: University of Chicago Press, 1992.

Sherburne, Richard, S. J. *The Complete Works of Atīśa Śrī Dīpaṃkara Jñāna, Jo bo rje: The "Lamp for the Path" and Commentary, together with the Newly Translated "Twenty-Five Key Texts."* Repr., Delhi: Aditya Prakashan, 2003.

Smith, E. Gene. *Among Tibetan Texts: History and Literature of the Himalayan Plateau.* Boston: Wisdom Publications, 2001.

Snellgrove, David. *Indo-Tibetan Buddhism.* Boston: Shambhala, 1987.

Sopa, Geshe Lhundrup. *Steps on the Path to Enlightenment.* Vol. 1, *A Commentary on the Lamrim Chenmo, The Foundational Practices.* Boston: Wisdom Publications, 2004.

———. *Steps on the Path to Enlightenment.* Vol. 2, *Karma: A Commentary on the Lamrim Chenmo.* Boston: Wisdom Publications, 2004.

———. *Steps on the Path to Enlightenment.* Vol. 3, *The Way of the Bodhisattva.* Boston: Wisdom Publications, 2007.

Sparham, Gareth, trans. *The Tibetan Dhammapada.* Boston: Wisdom Publications, 1995.

Spence, Jonathan D. *The Memory Palace of Matteo Ricci.* New York: Penguin Books, 1985.

Stcherbatsky, F. Th. *The Central Conception of Buddhism and the Meaning of the Word "Dharma."* Repr., Delhi: Motilal Banarsidass, 1974.

Stearns, Cyrus. *The Buddha from Dölpo: A Study of the Life and Thought of the Tibetan Master Dölpopa Sherab Gyaltsen.* Rev. and enlarged ed. Tsadra Foundation Series. Ithaca, N.Y.: Snow Lion Publications, 2010.

Steiner, George. *After Babel: Aspects of Language and Translation.* 3rd ed. Oxford: Oxford University Press, 1998.

Steiner, T. R. *English Translation Theory 1650–1800.* Approaches to Translation Studies 2. Assen, The Netherlands: Koninklijke Van Gorcum and Comp. B. V., 1975.

Suzuki, D. T., trans. *The Laṅkāvatāra Sūtra: A Mahāyāna Text.* Repr., Delhi: Motilal Banarsidass, 1999.

———. *Studies in the Laṅkāvatāra Sūtra.* Repr., Delhi: Motilal Banarsidass, 1999.

Thera, Nyānaponika. *The Heart of Buddhist Meditation.* New York: Citadel Press, 1969.

Thera, Soma, trans. *Kalama Sutta: The Buddha's Charter of Free Inquiry.* Kandy: Buddhist Publication Society, 1981.

Thondup, Tulku. *Buddhist Civilization in Tibet.* New York: Routledge and Kegan Paul, 1987.

Thrangu Rinpoche, Khenchen. *Essential Practice: Lectures of Kamalashila's Stages of Meditation in the Middle Way School.* Translated by Jules B. Levinson. Ithaca, N.Y.: Snow Lion Publications, 2002.

———. *King of Samadhi: Commentaries on the Samadhi Raja Sutra and The Song of Lodrö Thaye.* Hong Kong: Rangjung Yeshe Publications, 1994.

———. *The Uttaratantra, A Treatise on Buddha-Essence: A Commentary on the Uttaratantra Shastra of Maitreya.* Translated by Ken and Katia Holmes. Auckland: Zhyisil Chokyi Ghatsal Charitable Trust Publications, 2003.

———. *See also* Thrangu Rinpoche, Venerable Khabje.

Thrangu Rinpoche, Venerable Khabje. *The Uttaratantra: A Treatise on Buddha-Essence.* Translated by Ken Holmes and Katia Holmes. Auckland: Zhyisil Chokyi Gatsal Charitable Trust Publications, 2003.

———. *See also* Thrangu Rinpoche, Khenchen.

Tsang Nyön Heruka. *The Life of Marpa the Translator: Seeing Accomplishes All.* Nālandā Translation Committee, trans. under the direction of Chögyam Trungpa. Boulder: Shambhala, 1995.

Tsong-ka-pa. *The Great Treatise on the Stages of the Path to Enlightenment.* Translated by the Lamrim Chenmo Translation Committee. 3 vols. Ithaca, N.Y.: Snow Lion Publications, 2000–2004.

Tytler, Alexander Fraser (Lord Woodhouslee). *Essay on the Principles of Translation.* New York: E. P. Dutton and Co., 1907.

Ui, Hakuju, Munetada Suzuki, Yensho Kanakura, and Tokan Tada, eds. *A Complete Catalogue of the Tibetan Buddhist Canons (Bkaḥ ḥgyur and Bstan ḥgyur).* Sendai, Japan: Tohoku Imperial University, 1934.

Venuti, Lawrence, ed. *The Translation Studies Reader.* New York: Routledge, 2000.

Wangchuk Dorje, the Ninth Karmapa. *The Karmapa's Middle Way: Feast for the Fortunate.* Translated by Tyler Dewar. Ithaca, N.Y.: Snow Lion Publications, 2008.

Wechsler, Robert. *Performing Without A Stage: The Art of Literary Translation.* North Haven, Conn.: Catbird Press, 1998.

Williams, Paul. "A Note on Some Aspects of Mi bskyod rdo rje's Critque of dGe lugs pa Madhyamaka." *Journal of Indian Philosophy* 11, no. 2 (1983): 125–45.

———. "Rma bya pa Byang chub brtson 'grus on Madhyamaka Method." *Journal of Indian Philosophy* 13 (1985): 205–25.

Willis, Janice Dean. *On Knowing Reality: The Tattvārtha Chapter of Asaṅga's "Bodhisattvabhūmi."* Repr., Delhi: Motilal Banarsidass, 2002.

Yates, Frances A. *The Art of Memory.* Chicago: University of Chicago Press, 1974.

Zahler, Leah. *Study and Practice of Meditation: Tibetan Interpretations of the Concentrations and Formless Absorptions.* Ithaca, N.Y.: Snow Lion Publications, 2009.

Index